ECONOMIC ANALYSIS AND POLICY

Background Readings for Current Issues

4th Edition

ECONOMIC ANALYSIS AND POLICY

Background Readings for Current Issues

MYRON L. JOSEPH

Professor of Economics
Carnegie-Mellon University

NORTON C. SEEBER

Dean of School of
Economics and Management
Oakland University

GEORGE LELAND BACH

Frank E. Buck Professor
Economics and Public Policy
Stanford University

PRENTICE-HALL, INC., Englewood Cliffs, New Jersey

55051

Library of Congress Cataloging in Publication Data

JOSEPH, MYRON L., comp.
  Economic analysis and policy.

  Includes bibliographical references.
  1. Economic history—Addresses,
essays, lectures.   2. Economic policy—Addresses,
essays, lectures.   I. Seeber, Norton C., joint comp.
II. Bach, George Leland, joint comp.
III. Title.
HC59.J6 1974   330.9'04   74-4047
ISBN   0-13-222950-1

10 9 8 7 6 5 4 3 2

Printed in the United States of America

PRENTICE-HALL INTERNATIONAL, INC., *London*
PRENTICE-HALL OF AUSTRALIA, PTY. LTD., *Sydney*
PRENTICE-HALL OF CANADA, LTD., *Toronto*
PRENTICE-HALL OF INDIA PRIVATE LTD., *New Delhi*
PRENTICE-HALL OF JAPAN, INC., *Tokyo*

CONTENTS

PART THREE
MARKET SYSTEMS

PART SEVEN
ECONOMIC GROWTH

PART EIGHT
COMPARATIVE SYSTEMS

PREFACE

This volume of readings is designed for students who want to apply economic history to the big public policy issues of the day. It selects a relatively small number of major economic problem areas (inflation, growth, unemployment, poverty, government spending, gold and international payments, and the like) and provides *in depth* readings as materials to which students may *apply the relevant micro and macro theory* taken from the text *to reach their own conclusions.*

We believe that economics can be a lively science to students when they can see its relevance to important issues of concern. The selections provide a rich source of material on the crucial economic problems of our time and will give students vital problem-solving experience. If students become involved and interested in using their economics to analyze important problems, it is likely that they will remember and use their economics five or ten years later—after the threat of the final examination is long past.

The readings are not brief paragraphs or excerpts. Each is long enough to convey the "substance and feel" of the position being stated by the author, and can be understood and analyzed by students. Thus, students can achieve a thorough and deep understanding without having to purchase a paperback for each problem area studied.

The volume accomplishes its objectives in the following ways:

1. The selections are especially chosen to provide materials for independent student problem-solving on prominent, relatively unstructured economic problems such as economic decisions in the public sector, inflation, unemployment and poverty, and the special problems of the ghetto. Many of the selections in this fourth edition are included for the first time. This new material has been provided to focus on the more important contemporary developing economic issues. There are new, or substantially revised sections in the areas of monetary and fiscal policy (including reactions to the wage-price control mechanisms of the

Nixon administration "phase" approach to stabilization policies), unemployment and manpower problems, the question of whether economic growth is really desirable, government policy in the marketplace, environmental and energy problems, labor markets and poverty, the public sector, "radical" economic approaches to major economic themes, discrimination *vis-à-vis* women and minorities, and the nagging problem of long-term inflation. In general, we have increased the emphasis on pressing current economic problems and have provided substantially enriched backgrounds for the analysis of major policy alternatives (for example, in the area of public sector economics, environment and energy problems, and long-term inflation).

2. To illuminate and clarify the outstanding public policy issues of today we have included directly conflicting statements by economists, political leaders, and other observers. These are intended not only to sharpen the economic issues, but to help students understand the deep cross currents often involved in economics, how economic analysis is used by different people, and the interactions of economic and non-economic forces in the policy-making process. Some examples are:

(a) The widely divergent views of Leonard Woodcock, Arthur Okun, and George Schultze on economic stabilization and the impact of controls of varying kinds on the economy.

(b) The contrasting views of the inevitabilities and desirabilities of economic growth as expressed by E. J. Mishan and Robert Solow.   . . . .

(c) The views of James Tobin and Representative Curtis on the effects of income guarantees.

3. There are several selections concerning political, sociological, and organizational aspects of the environment within which solutions to economic problems must be reached. For example:

(a) Selections on the plight of the unemployed, and the world of poverty and the ghetto.

(b) The potential effects of the unionization of public sector employees.

(c) Selections relating to the "radical" approach to the question of consumer sovereignty in a market economy.

(d) The long-term prospects for inflation and its distributional effects in the American economic system of the 1970s and 1980s.

4. Several selections provide concrete historical background for current economic problems, enabling students to consider current issues against the events and the attitudes that have produced them. For example:

(a) The unemployment and desperation of the great depression of the 1930s which were crucial in shaping modern attitudes toward economic stabilization and social security policies.

(b) The financial panic and bank holiday of the depression days which provide a vivid backdrop for current monetary and financial problems.

(c) The lessons of history for developing.

We have included historical readings on all of these subjects, covering both the economic and noneconomic forces at work.

This volume should be a significant aid to teachers who want to supplement a solid, analytically-oriented text with readings that offer a wealth of materials for a sample of major policy problems. These readings should help to crystallize the issues with which students must grapple. By applying economic analysis, they are to reach their own solutions to complex, real-world issues.

We are greatly indebted to the marvelously cooperative librarians at our respective institutions.

M.L.J.
N.C.S.
G.L.B.

ECONOMIC ANALYSIS AND POLICY

Background Readings for Current Issues

FOUNDATIONS

PART ONE

1

ECONOMIC GENERALIZATIONS OR LAWS

Alfred Marshall

What is economics about? How should it be studied? Is it a science in the same sense of the natural sciences? The famous English economist Alfred Marshall presents the classical view that "economics is a study of mankind in the ordinary business of life" and discusses its relation to other scientific fields.

Alfred Marshall was perhaps the most influential economist in the world during the last part of the nineteenth and early part of the twentieth century. He was Professor of Economics at Cambridge University.

From *Principles of Economics*, 8th ed. (New York: The Macmillan Company, Inc., 1920), pp. 1–2, 15, 31–33, 36–37. Reprinted by permission.

Political Economy or Economics is a study of mankind in the ordinary business of life; it examines that part of individual and social action which is most closely connected with the attainment and with the use of the material requisites of well-being.

Thus it is on the one side a study of wealth; and on the other, and more important side, a part of the study of man. For man's character has been moulded by his everyday work, and the material resources which he thereby procures, more than by any other influence unless it be that of his religious ideals; and the two great forming agencies of the world's history have been the religious and the economic. Here and

1

there the ardour of the military or the artistic spirit has been for a while predominant: but religious and economic influences have nowhere been displaced from the front rank even for a time; and they have nearly always been more important than all others put together. Religious motives are more intense than economic, but their direct action seldom extends over so large a part of life. For the business by which a person earns his livelihood generally fills his thoughts during by far the greater part of those hours in which his mind is at its best; during them his character is being formed by the way in which he uses his faculties in his work, by the thoughts and the feelings which it suggests, and by his relations to his associates in work, his employers or his employees.

. . .

The advantage which economics has over other branches of social science appears then to arise from the fact that its special field of work gives rather larger opportunities for exact methods than any other branch. It concerns itself chiefly with those desires, aspirations and other affections of human nature, the outward manifestations of which appear as incentives to action in such a form that the force or quantity of the incentives can be estimated and measured with some approach to accuracy; and which therefore are in some degree amenable to treatment by scientific machinery. An opening is made for the methods and the tests of science as soon as the force of a person's motives—not the motives themselves—can be approximately measured by the sum of money, which he will just give up in order to secure a desired satisfaction, or again by the sum which is just required to induce him to undergo a certain fatigue.

It is essential to note that the economist does not claim to measure any affection of the mind in itself, or directly, but only indirectly through its effect. No one can compare and measure accurately against one another even his own mental states at different times; and no one can measure the mental states of another at all except indirectly and conjecturally by their effects.

. . .

It is the business of economics, as of almost every other science, to collect facts, to arrange and interpret them, and to draw inferences from them. "Observation and description, definition and classification are the preparatory activities. But what we desire to reach thereby is a knowledge of the interdependence of economic phenomena. . . . Induction and deduction are both needed for scientific thought as the right and left foot are both needed for walking." The methods required for this twofold work are not peculiar to economics; they are the common property of all sciences.

. . .

Let us then consider more closely the nature of economic laws, and their limitations. Every cause has a tendency to produce some definite result if nothing occurs to hinder it. Thus gravitation tends to make things fall to the ground: but when a balloon is full of gas lighter than air, the pressure of the air will make it rise in spite of the tendency of gravitation to make it fall. The law of gravitation states how any two things attract one another; how they tend to move towards one another and will move towards one another if nothing interferes to prevent them. The law of gravitation is therefore a statement of tendencies.

It is a very exact statement—so exact that mathematicians can calculate a Nautical Almanac, which will show the moments at which each satellite of Jupiter will hide itself behind Jupiter. They make this calculation for many years beforehand; and navigators take it to sea and use it in finding out where they are. Now there are no economic tendencies which act as steadily and can be measured as exactly as gravitation can; and consequently there are no laws of economics which can be compared for precision with the law of gravitation.

But let us look at a science less exact than astronomy. The science of the tides explains how the tide rises and falls twice a day under the action of the sun and the moon; how there are strong tides at new and full moon, and weak tides at the moon's first and third quarter; and how the tide running up into a closed channel, like that of the Severn, will be very high; and so on. Thus, having studied the lie of the land and the water all round the British isles, people can calculate beforehand when the tide will *probably* be at its highest on any day at London Bridge or at Gloucester; and how high it will be there. They have to use the word *probably*, which the astronomers do not need to use when talking about the eclipses of Jupiter's satellites. For, though many forces act upon Jupiter and his satellites, each one of them acts in a definite manner which can be predicted beforehand: but no one knows enough about the weather to be able to say beforehand how it will act. A heavy downpour of rain in the upper Thames valley, or a strong northeast wind in the German Ocean, may make the tides at London Bridge differ a good deal from what had been expected.

The laws of economics are to be compared with the laws of the tides, rather than with the simple and exact law of gravitation. For the actions of men are so various and uncertain, that the best statement of tendencies, which we can make in a science of human conduct, must needs be inexact and faulty. This might be urged as a reason against making any statements at all on the subject; but that would be almost to abandon life. Life is human conduct, and the thoughts and emotions that grow up around it. By the fundamental impulses

of our nature we all—high and low, learned and unlearned—are in our several degrees constantly striving to understand the courses of human action and to shape them for our purposes, whether selfish or unselfish, whether noble or ignoble. And since we *must* form to ourselves some notions of the tendencies of human action, our choice is between forming those notions carelessly and forming them carefully. The harder the task, the greater the need for steady patient inquiry; for turning to account the experience, that has been reaped by the more advanced physical sciences; and for framing as best we can well thought-out estimates, or provisional laws, of the tendencies of human action.

. . .

Economic laws, or statements of economic tendencies, are those social laws which relate to branches of conduct in which the strength of the motives chiefly concerned can be measured by a money price.

There is thus no hard and sharp line of division between those social laws which are, and those which are not, to be regarded also as economic laws. For there is a continuous gradation from social laws concerned almost exclusively with motives that can be measured by price, to social laws in which such motives have little place, and which are therefore generally as much less precise and exact than economic laws, as those are than the laws of the more exact physical sciences.

. . .

It is sometimes said that the laws of economics are "hypothetical." Of course, like every other science, it undertakes to study the effects which will be produced by certain causes, not absolutely, but subject to the condition that *other things are equal,* and that the causes are able to work out their effects undisturbed. Almost every scientific doctrine, when carefully and formally stated, will be found to contain some proviso to the effect that other things are equal: the action of the causes in question is supposed to be isolated; certain effects are attributed to them, but only on *the hypothesis* that no cause is permitted to enter except those distinctly allowed for. It is true however that the condition that time must be allowed for causes to produce their effects is a source of great difficulty in economics. For meanwhile the material on which they work, and perhaps even the causes themselves, may have changed; and the tendencies which are being described will not have a sufficiently "long run" in which to work themselves out fully.

. . .

Though economic analysis and general reasoning are of wide application, yet every age and every country has its own problems; and every change in social conditions is likely to require a new development of economic doctrines.

2

THE THREE SOLUTIONS TO THE ECONOMIC PROBLEM

What to produce and how to divide up the goods and services produced—these are the key economic questions faced by all societies. Professor Heilbroner describes three broad approaches to the allocation of resources and the distribution of products.

Robert L. Heilbroner

Robert L. Heilbroner is Chairman of the Department of Economics at the New School for Social Research and a well-known free-lance writer.

From Robert L. Heilbroner, *The Making of Economic Society*, 2nd ed., copyright 1968 by R. L. Heilbroner, pp. 9–16. Reprinted by permission of Prentice-Hall, Inc., publisher.

THE THREE SOLUTIONS TO THE ECONOMIC PROBLEM

Thus to the economist, society presents itself in an unaccustomed aspect. He sees it essentially as an elaborate mechanism for survival, a mechanism for accomplishing the complicated tasks of production and distribution necessary for social continuity.

But the economist sees something else as well, something which at first seems quite astonishing. Looking not only over the diversity of contemporary societies but back over the sweep of all history, he sees that man has succeeded in solving the production and distribution problems in but three ways. That is, within the enormous diversity of the actual social institutions which guide and shape the economic process, the economist divines but three overarching *types* of systems which separately or in combination enable humankind to solve its economic challenge. These great systemic types can be called economies run by Tradition, economies run by Command, and economies run by the Market. Let us briefly see what is characteristic of each.

Tradition

Perhaps the oldest and, until a very few years [ago], by far the most generally prevalent way of solving the economic challenge has been tradition. It has been a mode of social organization in which both production and distribution were based on procedures devised in the distant past and rigidified as the outcome of a long process of historic trial and error.

Societies based on tradition solve the economic problems very manageably. First, they deal with the production problem—the problem of assuring that the needful tasks will be done—by assigning the jobs of fathers to their sons. Thus a hereditary chain assures that skills will be passed along and that the ongoing jobs will be staffed from generation to generation. In ancient Egypt, wrote Adam Smith, the first great economist, "every man was bound by a principle of religion to follow the occupation of his father and was supposed to commit the most horrible sacrilege if he changed it for another."[1] And it was not merely in antiquity that tradition preserved a productive orderliness within society. In our own Western culture, until the fifteenth or sixteenth centuries, the hereditary allocation of tasks was also the main stabilizing force within society. Although there was some movement from country to town and from occupation to occupation, birth usually determined one's role in life. One was born to the soil or to a trade; and on the soil or within the trade, one followed in the footsteps of one's forebears.

Thus tradition has been the stabilizing and impelling force behind a great repetitive cycle of society, assuring that society's work would be done each day very much as it had been done in the past. Even today, among the less industrialized nations of the world, tradition continues to play this immense organizing role. In India, until very recently at least, one was born to a caste which had its own occupation. "Better thine own work is, though done with fault," preached the Bhagavad-Gita, the great philosophic moral poem of India, "than doing other's work, even excellently."

Tradition not only provides a solution to the production problem of society, but it also regulates the distribution problem. Take, for example, the Bushmen of the Kalahari Desert in South Africa who depend for their livelihood on hunting prowess. Elizabeth Marshall Thomas, a sensitive observer of these peoples, reports on the manner in which tradition solves the problem of distributing their kill.

> The gemsbok has vanished . . . Gai owned two hind legs and a front leg, Tsetchwe had meat from the back, Ukwane had the other front leg, his wife had one of the feet and the stomach, the young boys had lengths of intestine. Twikwe had received the head and Dasina the udder.

It seems very unequal when you watch Bushmen divide the kill, yet it is their system, and in the end no person eats more than any other. That day Ukwane gave Gai still another piece because Gai was his relation, Gai gave meat to Dasina because she was his wife's mother. . . . No one, of course, contested Gai's large share, because he had been the hunter and by their law that much belonged to him. No one doubted that he would share his large amount with others, and they were not wrong, of course; he did.[2]

[1] *The Wealth of Nations* (New York: Modern Library, Inc., 1937), p. 62.

[2] *The Harmless People* (New York: Alfred A. Knopf, Inc., 1959), pp. 49–50.

The manner in which tradition can divide a social product may be, as the illustration shows, very subtle and ingenious. It may also be very crude and, by our standards, harsh. Tradition has often allocated to women, in nonindustrial societies, the most meager portion of the social product. But however much tradition may accord with or depart from our accustomed moral views, we must see that it is a workable method of dividing society's production.

Traditional solutions to the economic problems of production and distribution are most commonly encountered in primitive agrarian or nonindustrial societies, where in addition to serving an economic function, the unquestioning acceptance of the past provides the necessary perseverance and endurance to confront harsh destinies. Yet even in our own society, tradition continues to play a role in solving the economic problem. It plays its smallest role in determining the distribution of our own social output, although the persistence of such traditional payments as tips to waiters, allowances to minors, or bonuses based on length of service are all vestiges of old traditional ways of distributing goods, as is the differential between men's and women's pay for equal work.

More important is the place which tradition continues to hold, even in America, as a means of solving the production problem—that is, in allocating the performance of tasks. Much of the actual process of selecting an employment in our society is heavily influenced by tradition. We are all familiar with families in which sons follow their fathers into a profession or a business. On a somewhat broader scale, tradition also dissuades us from certain employments. Sons of American middle-class families, for example, do not usually seek factory work, even though factory jobs may pay better than office jobs, because "blue-collar employment" is not in the middle-class tradition.

Even in our society, which is clearly not a "traditional" one, custom provides an important mechanism for solving the economic problem. But now we must note one very important consequence of the mechanism of tradition. *Its solution to production and distribution is a static one.* A society which follows the path of tradition in its regulation of economic affairs does so at the expense of large-scale rapid social and economic change.

Thus the economy of a Bedouin tribe or a Burmese village is in few essential respects changed today from what it was a hundred or even a thousand years ago. The bulk of the peoples living in tradition-bound societies repeat, in the daily patterns of their economic life, much of the routines which characterized them in the distant past. Such societies may rise and fall, wax and wane, but external events—war, climate, political adventures and misadventures—are mainly responsible for their changing fortunes. Internal, self-generated economic change is but a small factor in the history of most tradition-bound states. Tradition solves the economic problem, but it does so at the cost of economic progress.

Command

A second manner of solving the problem of economic continuity also displays an ancient lineage. This is the method of imposed authority, of economic command. It is a solution based not so much on the perpetuation of a viable system by the changeless reproduction of its ways, as on the organization of a system according to the orders of an economic commander-in-chief.

Not infrequently we find this authoritarian method of economic control superimposed upon a traditional social base. Thus the Pharaohs of Egypt exerted their economic dictates above the timeless cycle of traditional agricultural practice on which the Egyptian economy was based. By their orders, the supreme rulers of Egypt brought into being the enormous economic effort which built the pyramids, the temples, the roads. Herodotus, the Greek historian, tells us how the Pharaoh Cheops organized the task.

> [He] ordered all Egyptions to work for himself. Some, accordingly, were appointed to draw stones from the quarries in the Arabian mountains down to the Nile, others he ordered to receive the stones when transported in vessels across the river. . . . And they worked to the number of a hundred thousand men at a time, each party during three months. The time during which the people were thus harassed by toil lasted ten years on the road which they constructed, and along which they drew the stones; a work, in my opinion, not much less than the Pyramid.[3]

The mode of authoritarian economic organization was by no means confined to ancient Egypt. We encounter it in the despotisms of medieval and classical China which produced, among other things, the colossal Great Wall or in the slave labor by which many of the great public works of ancient Rome were built. Of course, we find it today in the dictates of the communist economic authorities. In less drastic form, we find it also in our own society, for example, in the form of *taxes*—that is, in the preemption of part of our income by the public authorities for public purposes.

Economic command, like tradition, offers solutions to the twin problems of production and distribution. In times of crises, such as war or famine, it may be the only way in which a society can organize its manpower or distribute its goods effectively. Even in America, we commonly declare martial law when an area has been devastated by a great natural disaster. On such occasions we may press people into service, requisition homes, impose curbs on

[3] *Histories*, trans. Cary (London: 1901), Book II, p. 124.

the use of private property such as cars, or even limit the amount of food a family may consume.

Quite aside from its obvious utility in meeting emergencies, command has a further usefulness in solving the economic problem. Unlike tradition, the exercise of command has no inherent effect of slowing down economic change. Indeed, the exercise of authority is the most powerful instrument society has for *enforcing economic change*. One example is, of course, the radical alterations in the systems of production and distribution which authority has effected in modern China or Russia. But again, even in our own society, it is sometimes necessary for economic authority to intervene into the normal flow of economic life to speed up or bring about change. The government may, for instance, utilize its tax receipts to lay down a network of roads which brings a backwater community into the flux of active economic life. It may undertake an irrigation system which will dramatically change the economic life of a vast region. It may very considerably affect the distribution of income among social classes.

To be sure, economic command which is exercised within the framework of a democratic political process is very different from that which is exercised by strongarm methods: there is an immense social distance between a tax system controlled by Congress and outright expropriation or labor impressment by a supreme and unchallengeable ruler. Yet whilst the means may be much milder, the *mechanism* is the same. In both cases, command diverts economic effort toward goals chosen by a higher authority. In both cases it interferes with the existing order of production and distribution, to create a new order ordained from "above."

This does not in itself serve to commend or condemn the exercise of command. The new order imposed by the authorities may offend or please our sense of social justice, just as it may improve or lessen the economic efficiency of society. Clearly, command can be an instrument of a democratic as well as of a totalitarian will. There is no implicit moral judgment to be passed on this second of the great mechanisms of economic control. Rather, it is important to note that no society—certainly no modern society—is without its elements of command, just as none is devoid of the influence of tradition. If tradition is the great brake on social and economic change, so economic command can be the great spur to change. As mechanisms for assuring the successful solution to the economic problem, both serve their purposes, both have their uses and their drawbacks. Between them, tradition and command have accounted for most of the long history of man's economic efforts to cope with his environment and with himself. The fact that human society *has* survived is testimony to their effectiveness.

The Market

There is also a third solution to the economic problem—that is, a third solution to the problem of maintaining socially viable patterns of production and distribution. This is the *market organization of society,* an organization which, in truly remarkable fashion, allows society to insure its own provisioning with a minimum of recourse either to tradition or command.

Because we live in a market-run society, we are apt to take for granted the puzzling —indeed, almost paradoxical—nature of the market solution to the economic problem. But assume for a moment that we could act as economic advisers to a society which had not yet decided on its mode of economic organization. Suppose, for instance, that we were called on to act as consultants to one of the new nations emerging from the continent of Africa.

We could imagine the leaders of such a nation saying, "We have always experienced a highly tradition-bound way of life. Our men hunt and cultivate the fields and perform their tasks as they are brought up to do by the force of example and the instruction of their elders. We know, too, something of what can be done by economic command. We are prepared, if necessary, to sign an edict making it compulsory for many of our men to work on community projects for our national development. Tell us, is there any other way we can organize our society so that it will function successfully—or better yet, more successfully?"

Suppose we answered, "Yes, there is another way. Organize your society along the lines of a market economy."

"Very well, " say the leaders. "What do we then tell people to do? How do we assign them to their various tasks?"

"That's the very point," we would answer. "In a market economy no one is assigned to any task. The very idea of a market society is that each person is allowed to decide for himself what to do."

There is consternation among the leaders. "You mean there is *no* assignment of some men to mining and others to cattle raising? No manner of selecting some for transportation and others for cloth weaving? You leave this to people to decide for themselves? But what happens if they do not decide correctly? What happens if no one volunteers to go into the mines, or if no one offers himself as a railway engineer?"

"You may rest assured," we tell the leaders, "none of that will happen. In a market society, all the jobs will be filled because it will be to people's advantage to fill them."

Our respondents accept this with uncertain expressions. "Now look," one of them finally says, "let us suppose that we take your advice and let our people do as they please. Now let's talk about something important, like cloth production. Just how do we fix the right level of cloth output in this 'market society' of yours?"

"But you don't," we reply.

"We don't! Then how do we know there will be enough cloth produced?"

"There will be," we tell him. "The market will see to that."

"Then how do we know there won't be *too much* cloth produced?" he asks triumphantly.

"Ah, but the market will see to that too!"

"But what *is* this market that will do all these wonderful things? Who runs it?"

"Oh, nobody runs the market," we answer. "It runs itself. In fact there really isn't any such *thing* as 'the market.' It's just a word we use to describe the way people behave."

"But I thought people behaved the way they wanted to!"

"And so they do," we say. "But never fear. They will want to behave the way you want them to behave."

"I am afraid," says the chief of the delegation, "that we are wasting our time. We thought you had in mind a serious proposal. But what you suggest is madness. It is inconceivable. Good day, sir." And with great dignity the delegation takes its leave.

Could we seriously suggest to such an emergent nation that it entrust itself to a market solution of the economic problem? . . . But the very perplexity which the market idea would rouse in the mind of someone unacquainted with it may serve to increase our own wonderment at this most sophisticated and interesting of all economic mechanisms. How *does* the market system assure us that our mines will find miners, our factories workers? How does it take care of cloth production? How does it

happen that in a market-run nation each person can indeed do as he wishes and, withal, fulfill the needs which society as a whole presents?

Economics and the Market System

Economics, as we commonly conceive it . . ., is primarily concerned with these very problems. Societies which rely primarily on tradition to solve their economic problems are of less interest to the professional economist than to the cultural anthropologist or the sociologist. Societies which solve their economic problems primarily by the exercise of command present interesting economic questions, but here the study of economics is necessarily subservient to the study of politics and the exercise of power.

It is a society which solves its economic problems by the market process that presents an aspect especially interesting to the economist. For here, as we shall see, economics truly plays a unique role. Unlike the case with tradition and command, where we quickly grasp the nature of the economic mechanism of society, when we turn to a market society we are lost without a knowledge of economics. For in a market society it is not at all clear that the problems of production and distribution will be solved by the free interplay of individuals without guidance from tradition or command.

. . . But . . . there is a problem which has surely occurred to the reader. As our hypothetical interview with the leaders of an emergent nation must have suggested, the market solution appears very strange to someone brought up in the ways of tradition or command. Hence the question arises: how did the market solution itself evolve? Was it imposed, full-blown, on our society at some earlier date? Or did it arise spontaneously and without forethought? These are the questions to which we must first turn, as we retrace the evolution of our own market system out of the tradition- and authority-dominated societies of the past.

ECONOMIC STABILIZATION: PROBLEMS AND POLICIES

PART TWO

3

THE GERMAN NIGHTMARE

The German experience following World War I provides a vivid picture of what happens when a great inflation breaks loose and runs wild. This account emphasizes the close ties of most such inflations to major wars and their aftermath. How does this description of inflation relate to the American inflationary experiences of the late 1960s and early 1970s?

Donald B. Woodward and Marc A. Rose

Donald B. Woodward is an economist with wide experience in government and business. Marc A. Rose was a newspaper and magazine editor and served as a senior editor of Reader's Digest.

Wildest of all the inflations the world ever has seen, the German orgy after the war is the horrible example held up in solemn warning before the eyes of anyone who ventures to suggest that money might be managed to avert, or at least to soften, the impact of violent price upheavals.

Indeed, it was a nightmare. Large classes of the population paid bitterly for it. But the candid historian must record that there were some compensations to the nation at large. At least it wiped out internal debt, albeit by the brutality of complete repudiation.

Before the war, the German mark was firmly based on gold, with a parity of 23 cents. Germany, in fact, was the nation which broke up bimetallism in Europe. Demanding a $1,000,000,000 gold indemnity from France at the close of the Franco-

Prussian war, she seized the opportunity to use the gold as a base for a single-standard currency.

The war put a severe strain on the German economy, but the depreciation of the mark was not beyond recovery; after the armistice, the mark was quoted at about 12 cents.

Then came the peace negotiations. When the full weight of the terms imposed under the Treaty of Versailles became apparent, the Germans felt their situation hopeless—and so did financiers in other countries. The new government's financial difficulties kept increasing. The nation's debt was heavy, and much of it was not funded. It was necessary to resort to the expedient of printing marks, mere fiat money, to pay the government's expenses. By early 1920, the mark was worth about one cent, gold. The decline was checked at that point, and there was even some improvement; but late in 1921, the mark began to sink again in terms of foreign exchange. Reparations had been fixed at 132,000,000,000 gold marks, or some $33,-000,000,000. More and more, Germany was completely discouraged at the outlook; financial recovery looked impossible, and the occupation of the Ruhr in January, 1923, seemed to show that the harder the Germans tried to beat their way upward the more the demands that would be made upon them.

The Treasury proceeded to issue bills to the Reichsbank at an accelerating rate, discounting them for paper money. The printing presses ran more and more rapidly; pieces of currency were issued in denominations of millions of marks. Prices, of course, kept rising, which steadily increased the government's expenses and made it necessary to print more currency. The spiral was started; nothing, it seemed, could break it. Under the conditions, there was little incentive to try.

The banks, which had participated very little at the outset, began to discount bills at the Reichsbank and to increase their loans and deposits. Ultimately, the municipalities began to issue money, also the railroads, and many other institutions. Metal coins previously used for small change disappeared into hoarding or were converted into paper, the bullion content being worth vastly more than the stamped value of the coins.

Before the war, the total money in circulation in Germany had averaged about 6,000,000,000 marks. At the end of 1923, the authorized circulation was 518,000,000,-000,000,000,000—518 billions of billions. No estimate ever has been attempted of the amount of other currencies in circulation. Conditions were utterly chaotic.

In November, 1923, the situation was taken in hand. A new currency unit, the rentenmark, was established, its value put at 1,000,000,000,000—a million million—of the marks it was to supersede. The new rentenmark was fixed at parity with the prewar mark—that is, at 23 cents. Incidentally, it was pure fiat money, but its value was successfully controlled in terms of gold.

The Dawes plan was made effective in 1924, fixing Germany's obligations to the outside world at a point more nearly within reason. With that encouragement, the reichsmark was established on a gold basis, also at 23 cents.

That was the end of inflation. Behind this bare story of the course of events are a million human comedies and tragedies. No one ever will record even a small part of them. But some of the most fantastic and absurd incidents are remembered.

As this one: the total German mortgage debt before the war was about 40,000,000,-000 marks. At the peak of the inflation, 40,000,000,000 marks were worth less than a cent. All the mortgages in Germany could have been paid off for one cent, American. A box of matches sold for more than 6,000,-

000,000 marks, which it will be remembered was the total amount of money in circulation in Germany in prewar years.

Things happened as in a fever-ridden dream. Prices changed by the hour. Before the summit was reached, a ham sandwich was quoted at 14,000 marks one day and 24,000 marks the next. An article in a retail store priced at 5,000,000,000 marks in the morning had increased to 12,000,000,000 by afternoon. A sheet of writing paper cost 120 marks—$30 at prewar exchange—while yet the inflation was young. Interest rates rose to 900 per cent, and even then lenders at times were not protected, because by the time they were paid—even tenfold—the sum they received was worth less than the sum they lent.

What this meant in terms of human hardship can easily be imagined. Savings patiently built up by a lifetime of thrift might buy as much as a package of cigarettes. Life insurance policies matured— and the proceeds would not buy a handkerchief. It might be cheaper to light a cigar with a bond than to buy a match. The thrifty were penalized; the only wise folk were the spendthrifts. The nation became a spendthrift one, of course; everyone who received money rushed madly to convert it into goods. Things would be worth more tomorrow, perhaps this very afternoon. Money would be worth less. Debts were wiped out; farm mortgages were paid off with a sack of potatoes.

Translated into economic jargon, the creditor class was ruined; debtors were freed. People who had lived on investments were paupers.

The government tried to protect its citizens but could not do much. Prices of necessities were fixed from time to time to assure people of food and a roof over their heads, but fixing prices at a reasonable level one day did not solve the problem the next. Wages were moved up frequently—in the early stages, every month, then every ten days, but they always lagged behind the cost of living. The principle of fixing wages on a sliding scale geared to the cost of living was adopted, but it never was very popular with labor, because most workingmen did not understand its complexities, and those who did protested that the scale was inadequate. Labor troubles were widespread.

While great classes were being pauperized, other skillful manipulators were becoming fabulously wealthy. The speculators' method was to borrow money, buy goods or real estate or factories, then pay off the debt in worthless money. Then they could either keep the tangibles or sell them and repeat the operation.

Business of course boomed, for everyone was buying goods. A great boom developed in the stock market, from the scramble to buy shares in tangible properties.

Toward the close of the era, many localities began to quote prices of foreign currencies, usually dollars. Various institutions issued scrip redeemable in goods—rye, barley, coal, wood, and even kilowatt hours.

It was impossible, obviously to plan ahead in terms of paper money. Construction and similar industries languished.

After monetary stabilization, there was a brief depression, but business did not for long stay inordinately dull, since there had been an accumulation of demands for goods and services that could not be supplied during the inflation—demands for new homes and improved factories, for example. So recovery progressed with reasonable rapidity.

But profound changes had been made in the social structure. There were new rich and new poor. The middle class, by and large, suffered most. The very poor had had little to lose; many of the wealthy had known how to protect themselves. Businesses emerged with most of their debts wiped out.

4

WHY INFLATION WILL CONTINUE

In recent years, the rate of inflation has increased markedly in the United States. Professor Bach argues that inflation will almost inevitably continue because of structural, political, and ideological characteristics of the American and world economies. At the same time, various factors combine to make runaway inflation unlikely.

G. L. Bach

G. L. Bach is Frank E. Buck Professor of Economics and Public Policy at Stanford University, and a frequent adviser to the Federal Reserve Board.

From *The New Inflation* (Providence, R.I.: Brown University Press, 1973), p. 40 ff. Reprinted by permission.

SIX REASONS WHY INFLATION WILL CONTINUE

What has happened to so increase the likelihood of persistent inflation in America, while still keeping price increases far short of real runaway inflation? What are the foundations of the new inflation? Surely not the failure of the vaunted American productivity that pours goods and services onto the market. There is every indication that the economy's post–World War II performance has improved on this score and no visible reason why the full-employment productive capacity of the economy will not continue to grow at something like the same rate that has prevailed over past decades—perhaps 4 per cent per year, as a rough approximation. This spectacular increase in potential real output is one of the main reasons why peacetime inflation will not increase beyond modest proportions.

But why should there be inflation at all in the face of this huge increase of goods and services available for purchase—an additional $50 billion or so per year on top of the already huge gross national product of over $1 trillion annually? Six major reasons, when combined, create a formidable presumption.

1. The sanctity of high employment. In the United States—indeed, in all of the Western world—maintenance of high employment has become not only a goal but probably the main goal of economic policy. Republican and Democrat, liberal and conservative, employer and employee—all are agreed that, above all, we must avoid another major depression like that of the 1930s, with its millions of desolate unemployed, its never-ending breadlines, its cold gray desperation, and its massive waste of men and machines. There is, of course, much argument over what is the practical minimum level of unemployment at which to aim. After World War II it was 5 percent. In prosperous times it slid down to 4, and even to 3, per cent. More recently, with stubborn unemployment in spite of easier money and other moves toward prosperity, 4 per cent or even more has again seemed a reasonable target. Our aspirations vary with recent experience.

Here and there a voice is raised that, indeed, a little more unemployment would be good, to discourage inflationary wage demands and to slow rising prices. But no one in a position of responsibility, governmental or otherwise, dares to urge this openly. Political responsibility burns deeply, and government leaders quickly develop a profound concern with keeping the specter of unemployment under tight control—and understandably so. It is true that a whole generation of young workers has never known the mass unemployment and the gripping fear of hunger and desolation of the 1930s. But their belief in the right to a job has supplanted their fathers' fear of unemployment, and the result is the same in both cases. Unemployment must not, and, in the minds of the younger generation at least, need not, be tolerated.

Is this picture of the sanctity of high employment exaggerated? The evidence of political and economic behavior clearly shows that it is not. No party in power or out can seriously contemplate inaction for long when unemployment mounts. Unemployment above moderate "frictional" levels has stirred both parties to vigorous action and to strong assurances of their willingness to do quickly what may be required to avoid mass layoffs. Even to fight a widely dreaded inflation President Nixon could tolerate unemployment above 5 per cent for only a few months before adopting expansionary policies.

2. *The apparent World War II demonstration that massive government spending can produce high employment.* World War II showed vividly the power of government spending—when it is big enough and when it is financed largely by deficits—to put millions of unemployed people back to work. What all the efforts of the New Deal could not manage in the 1930s, massive war spending accomplished in record time in the early 1940s. By late 1941, unemployment had vanished. It would be naïve to argue that government spending alone was responsible for this abrupt end to the long stagnation in the 1930s, and, indeed, the creation of billions of dollars of new money to finance the spending clearly deserves much of the credit. But it would be equally naïve not to recognize the central role played by such spending.

This lesson, following the Keynesian revolution in economic thought of the 1930s and the desperate struggle against mass unemployment during those years, was learned perhaps too well by economists, government officials, labor leaders and their followers, and even by many businessmen. In many cases the learning was almost subconscious and often had to overcome the bitter resistance of previous training in fiscal and financial orthodoxy. But consciously or subconsciously, the lesson was learned. By spending enough the government can put unemployed men back to work and keep them there—not just a few men but millions of them. The later consequences may be painful—inflation or even financial collapse —but government spending can put men back to work, if that is the first objective.

It was this realization that made it thinkable to give the goal of high employment first place in economic action. For a generation that suffered through the desolation of the 1930s there was now a chance to be rid of its greatest disaster, even if the bankers and the businessmen cried out against government spending. For generations maturing through the war and postwar years, history seemed to show clearly that unemployment need not be tolerated. Aspirations, like politics, are the art of the possible. Continuous high employment has become a reasonable goal.

3. *The increasing political and economic strength of major socioeconomic groups and the increasingly administered structure of prices.* Another force increasing the likelihood of inflation is the growing political and economic strength of major socioeconomic groups and the administered structure of many important wages and prices in the American economy. In all democratic countries trade unions have become stronger since the Great Depression. This means an increasingly powerful upward push on wages—the major component of costs in

the modern economy. Nor are most industrial prices in the American economy established impersonally in highly competitive markets. Instead, many are administered—set by leading firms and by bargains between leading buyers and sellers. Assertions by radical critics that big businesses are free to gouge consumers through higher prices at will, without concern for the constraints of demand, merely demonstrate the naïveté of such critics. Often both wage and price decisions are closely constrained by the competitive pressure of the market. But, nonetheless, the wages and prices are administered; and many services are also priced this way.

Most significant of all, important economic groups have discovered their power through the political process to achieve goals they cannot achieve satisfactorily through the market place. If farmers cannot get higher prices through the free market, they can through Congress. If workers cannot get livable wages through the market, they can exert great pressure on their governments, directly and by swaying public opinion, for protection against foreign competition, for higher minimum wages, and the like. If businessmen cannot get high enough prices through the market for coal or milk, they can get help from Washington or their state capital. If unemployment comes or retirement brings poverty, Congress's power to provide benefits and raise social security payments is vast.

The import of this discovery is far reaching. For with this recognition sellers need not be content with what the market gives them, even though individually they may be very small sellers indeed. A century or even a half century ago the decision of the market on prices and incomes was inexorable, except under the most exceptional circumstances. This is no longer true. Congress intervenes in the market in many ways, direct and devious. And the pressures on Congress

to act in these ways will be very strong indeed if the outcome of the market is not satisfactory to the major socioeconomic groups and individuals in the market.

4. *The trend to the left and increased government responsibility for the welfare of the masses.* The century of the common man is no time for deflation. Deflation is essentially undemocratic—it obviously takes something away from many people. On the contrary, modern democracy is established to maximize the responsiveness of the government to the common man and his wants. All of the Western democratic nations have seen during this century a persistent, if not steady, move to the left and toward increased government responsibility for the welfare of the masses.

It is noteworthy that in the United States neither the Eisenhower nor the Nixon administration showed much enthusiasm for a return to the pre–New Deal days—for abolition of the sweeping welfare policies of the liberal Democrats. Indeed, both Republican and Democratic Congresses have shown great enthusiasm for huge increases in social security benefits, and welfare payments have grown astronomically under the policies sponsored by both parties. The economic group in trouble, especially if it is a group of "little men," can turn to the government for help with a reasonable expectation that it will not go away empty-handed.

Significantly for the inflation problem, help costs money, through government expenditures or through higher prices to the consumer produced directly or indirectly by government policies. Democratic governments, as *The Economist* (London) has trenchantly pointed out, will always tend to spend more and tax less. They will always tend to underestimate the inflationary forces at work during an inflation and to accept the more optimistic of two estimates being put forward. If they do not, they will be replaced before long with governments that do.

5. *War hot and cold.* Another force pushing toward more inflation is war. War—hot or cold—is immensely expensive. History shows that all modern wars have brought inflation. This is even truer today than in the past because of the fantastic cost of preparing for, fighting, and cleaning up after modern war. Even small (not worldwide) wars like Korea and Vietnam cost billions. The Vietnam war alone caused about $125 billion of military spending. With only a nonshooting cold war, the "national defense" drain on the public purse is enormous, requiring a painful and ill-received mass of taxation to keep the federal budget balanced. Government spending of this magnitude for an "unproductive" purpose cannot avoid pushing upward on prices in a democratic society.

6. *The end of the gold standard.* The last factor underlying the prospect for inflation is the end of the gold standard. It is now four decades since the gold standard went to its generally unlamented death. Surely the gold standard had many failings, though the present international monetary system still accords a substantial role to gold. But with all its failings, the gold standard did provide a monetary "religion" that brought the government and the public up short when they felt the urge to spend more than they were taking in, both through the check it imposed on expansion of the money supply to finance new spending and through the international gold drain if inflation exceeded the rate in other countries. Today most of the gold standard, fair-weather friend that it was, is gone, and there is little to put in its place save our own resolution. With the dollar now the world's key currency, those gold standard watchdogs, the international bankers, have far less power than they once did to make the United States squirm when our prices rise. Individ-

ual nations are by no means free of the international constraints of monetary responsibility, but the ties are far looser than they were before the 1930s.

This concatenation of factors creates in the American democratic society a strong presumption of persistent inflationary pressure. Put together the six points. The government is committed to maintaining high employment. Economists, government officials, labor leaders, businessmen, and most important, ordinary citizens are convinced, or at least suspect strongly, that government spending or tax cuts can produce high employment—even though the spending program implied by this belief makes many of these same people extremely uncomfortable.

With many important wages and prices in the economy set on a bargaining or administered basis by large organizations and economic power groups, wage-price setting reflects the views and judgments of the wage and price makers. And these large organizations and power groups recognize the power they have through the political process to achieve what they may not be able to accomplish unaided in the market place. The end of monetary expansion imposed by the government or by gold could put a monetary ceiling on price increases, forcing employers to resist more vigorously the wage demands of their unions. But if the unions and businessmen can, instead, count on the government to add enough spending power to maintain sales and high employment even at higher prices, it is little wonder that they push wages and prices steadily upward in search of larger income shares for themselves. What have they to lose?

It is important to recognize that this process is by no means confined to wage bargains followed by price increases, nor is it limited solely to big unions and big businesses. As long as income groups feel confident that total demand will be continually expanded to bail out any substantial overpricing of goods or labor in the economy, they need not be powerful price setters or effective political pressure units themselves to be reasonably secure in pushing up wages and prices. The big, powerful, visible price setter, such as the United Auto Workers or General Electric, can feel secure that large-scale unemployment generated in its industry will be an immediate cause of widespread concern and reasonably prompt government remedial action. This is especially true since it is a wage-price leader for a much wider sector of the economy, and similar increases can be expected to follow there without undue delay. The little union or little firm must worry much more lest it simply price itself out of a market, and it dare not get far ahead of the parade. But for a groupistic economy, the pattern of wage and price behavior, though far from simple and orderly, is sufficiently clear to permit most sellers to judge reasonably well how far and how fast they can safely go in relation to the leaders.

The tendency of businesses to raise prices, often by a standard markup on rising wages and other costs, is further increased by their growing emphasis on obtaining funds for expansion through retained earnings rather than through the open market. When management refuses to dilute the ownership of its stockholders by raising funds through new ownership shares, the pressure to increase profits is intensified correspondingly. Profits must provide both adequate dividends and funds to expand in a rapidly growing economy. When costs rise, prices must keep pace to provide the funds needed for these parallel purposes.

To be sure, neither unions nor businesses will raise wages or prices rapidly in periods of depression and mass unemployment. Their excess income claims generate inflationary pressure only when the economy is at least fairly close to high employment and capacity output. The problem arises at 5 or 6 per cent unemployment, not 10 or 15 per cent. But if massive unemployment occurs, expansionary government monetary-fiscal policy can be counted on to move the economy upward, and unemployment is likely to remain nearer the 4–6 per cent range. It is the *combination* of union-business market power and confidence in government expansionary action against depression that generates the high probability of a strong upward push on costs and the price level in the important partially monopolized sectors of the economy. Cost-push and demand-pull interact with a dynamic momentum, with no sharp line between the two; each is a matter of degree, not an absolute condition.

Events since 1969 have underscored this problem. Wages and prices continued to rise rapidly with little, if any, slowing for two full years after excess aggregate demand had been eliminated—a situation ended only with the dramatic Nixon wage-price freeze of August 1971. One plausible explanation, which will be explored more thoroughly later, grows out of the preceding analysis—strong inflationary expectations, developed over the preceding years and partially built into long-term wage and other costs, persisted and led to widespread wage and price increases. The inflation had a dynamic momentum of its own. Other observers stress shifts in the composition of the labor force relative to the demand for labor. The post–World War II baby boom is now producing a flood of young entrants into the labor force, and advancing technology and shifting consumer demands have generated needs for experienced, skilled workers. The result has been tight labor markets for many types of skilled, mature workers when aggregate demand rose, long before all the young, unskilled workers have found jobs. In 1972, with overall unemployment near 6 per cent, the rate for mature, experienced, married males was 2.7 per cent, while that for inexperienced teen-agers reached over

20 per cent. Female unemployment rates
rose as unskilled women entered the labor
force in large numbers. Understandably,
wage rates rose in the tight labor markets
in spite of substantial unemployment elsewhere. Especially where unions restrict
membership (as in the construction trades),
widespread unemployment among young
nonmembers did little to restrain union demands for big wage increases as aggregate
demand rose.

To this general picture must be added
the pervasive attitude that the government
needs to take care of economic groups that
fall behind in the competitive struggle for
one reason or another—poor farmers, coal
miners, New England mill workers, children, the aged. If the government takes care
of these, is it unreasonable for workers to
expect and obtain substantial pay increases?
And can we object if businesses raise prices
when their costs creep steadily upward? Is
not live and let live the right attitude for a
democratic nation? On the one hand, benefits for the needy cost money, increasing
the persistent tendency toward an unbal-
anced budget. On the other hand, they
weaken the moral and operational position
of the government in fighting undue wage
and price increases by those who pay the
bills.

In the gold standard days there was a
ceiling on all this. When bank reserves were
used up and no more gold was available,
tight money laid its cold hand on the boom.
Even without the gold standard, the monetary and fiscal authorities today can play
this same role of limiting the inflationary
upsweep of wages and prices, if the government does not feel obliged to assure
high employment. But a government committed to high employment is no longer
the authority in the economy establishing
the level of income, employment, and prices.
Organized labor, business, and the other
major economic groups have power comparable to that of the government itself.

If they insist on claiming more income
through pushing up wages and prices, the
government has no real alternative but to
increase government spending and the
money supply to support employment at
the higher costs and prices.

In such a world, possibly the government
can guarantee high employment, but it cannot guarantee high employment without
inflation. On the contrary, in explicitly or
implicitly guaranteeing high employment it
comes dangerously close at the same time
to guaranteeing inflation. The price level
becomes indeterminate, governed by a kind
of trilateral bargaining among wage setters,
price setters, and the government. This
bargaining has a strong presumption of inflation, as money-income disputes are ad-
judicated upward at the expense of the non-
active, fixed incomes in society. And confusion over the real effects of inflation, coupled
with the present diffused economic responsibilities in government, provides an ideal
opportunity for powerful income groups to
advance their own interests without ever
exposing the real issues to the public gaze.

The crux of the matter is that in such a
world the central issue, income distribution,
is shifted from the impersonal market place
to the combined bargaining processes of the
market place and the halls of Washington—
an arena where the government monetary-
fiscal authorities are only one of the powerful authorities. As long as none of the major
nongovernmental groups believes that the
government will bail out unemployment and
falling sales by expansionary monetary-fiscal
policy, the fear of going too far and inducing unemployment and lower sales serves
as a major moderating force on the struggle
for income position and power. This has
clearly been an important restraint over
most of our history. But today this barrier
may be perilously close to disappearing. In
the modern democracy it would be a re-
markably insulated and politically insensitive government that would consistently

permit the development of widespread un-employment rather than expand purchasing power (and raise prices) to maintain total output and employment.

In recent years a group of eminent mone-tary economists, led by Professor Milton Friedman, have, from this same process, drawn a radically different conclusion, that a government committed to guaranteeing high employment will find that it succeeds mainly in guaranteeing inflation, with little or no long-run effect on the level of unem-ployment. Inflation anticipations play the key role. In a world of excess income claims and government insertion of new money to avoid (reduce) unemployment, everyone will come to understand the inflationary process or, at least, to anticipate continued inflation. Thus wage earners, businessmen, borrowers, lenders—all the participants in the economic process—will begin to build inflation anticipations into their bargains on wages, prices, and interest rates on loans. But once they do, the government's power to reduce unemployment by government spending of new money is undercut. The main way expansionary government mone-tary-fiscal policy creates more jobs is by ex-panding demand, which induces businesses to hire more workers. But if workers push up wage costs as fast as demand increases and prices rise, businesses have no incentive to expand output and hire more workers. The result is simply higher wages, costs, and prices all around, but no more jobs. And the more government spends to reduce unem-ployment, the more inflationary expectations will rise and the more inflation will occur, without more than temporarily reducing unemployment.

Whichever analysis is correct—whether expansionary government policy in a world of excess income claims produces high em-ployment with inflation or inflation without high employment—the logical result of the argument is alarming indeed. For what limit is there on the inflationary spiral? Will

not groups soon begin to anticipate the re-sponses of the other groups and of the gov-ernment itself, increasing their own income demands accordingly? In such a world the government may be in the unhappy pre-dicament of trying to keep up with the ever-rising income demands of unions, busi-nesses, and farmers or lagging just a little behind to slow the spiral, but never too far behind, lest unemployment pile up, nor too far ahead lest the inflationary spiral is further speeded.

FOUR REASONS WHY RUNAWAY INFLATION IS UNLIKELY

In spite of the logic of these arguments, a runaway inflationary spiral in the United States seems extremely unlikely for four main reasons.

1. People do not yet understand what they can get away with. While the preced-ing analysis would be far from novel to some union leaders and some businessmen, it is probably only dimly perceived by most of the American public that any major in-come group can safely demand a continu-ally rising income share and, to a limited extent, get it, as long as the government underwrites high employment and there are some relatively fixed-income groups left for inflation to squeeze out. (But this bar-rier to inflation may not last long; such ig-norance can hardly be expected to continue indefinitely, and in any event complete understanding by all the public is not necessary for the inflationary process to work reasonably well.)

2. A closely related reason is the pervasive force of competition. The individual busi-nessman always fears most the loss of cus-tomers to his competitors. Before he raises a price, he thinks long and hard unless he is sure his competitors will do likewise. And his competitors may not be in his own in-dustry. Alcoa must be concerned with the relationship of its prices to those of copper and steel as well as to the prices set by Reynolds and Kaiser for aluminum. Thus, although the businessman may understand the final responsibility of the government monetary-fiscal policy to provide adequate total monetary demand for high employment, his immediate concern is for his competitive position, and he will resist wage pressures long and hard if they would force him to raise his prices above those of his competitors.

3. *Another reason is the prodigious American productivity.* The American economy pours out ever more goods and services at a rate to match even a rapid rise in total spending—in other words, to offset even a rapid rise in the income claims of major economic groups. (But this alone would not be enough to stop runaway inflation, for there is nothing to keep income groups from raising their claims even faster as they learn how fast productivity grows.)

4. *The last reason is at once the most tenuous and most powerful.* It is the pervasiveness and persistence of strong stable money mores, even among many who suspect they may personally gain from a little inflation. There is little evidence that the American public is much worried about creeping inflation of 1 or 2 per cent a year. But as faster inflation continues for several years, as in 1965–72, public concern rises rapidly, and there is much evidence that the American people view as a major, though dimly understood, calamity galloping inflation like that in Central Europe after World War I. Every American schoolboy seems to hear that the German people needed a wheelbarrow full of marks to buy a loaf of bread. The American man in the street, that mythical individual, seems clearly in favor of a better standard of living, higher wages, and even profits for everybody except ne'er-do-wells and maybe a few of his special antagonists. But at the same time he is terribly afraid of runaway inflation, which he vaguely associates with economic disruption and collapse and with poverty for the working man.

Thus, if this picture is accurate, the man in the street is little inclined to support painful restraint against his neighbors, or even against the economist royalists, for their attempts to improve their economic lots within reason. But he will be strongly opposed to any group that blatantly and obviously brings on drastic inflation. And he will be very alarmed should a rapid spiral of wage-price increases get under way at a rate far short of 10 to 20 per cent a year—still a modest figure in comparison with the debacle he fears.

Widespread public support will thus develop for strong measures to stop any rapid peacetime inflation induced by spiraling income claims and supported by expansionary monetary-fiscal policy. In such a case the essence of the inflationary process would be widely seen, and the authority of the government to resist inflationary income claims would be strengthened by this public support. Such widespread anti-inflation support would not necessarily be economically rational for all groups concerned, but the support would come and it would drastically limit the possibility of rapid, pressure-group inflation. This judgment of the public temper may, of course, be wrong, or even if it is right today that temper may change tomorrow. If the latter is the case, the possibility of really drastic inflation becomes ever more real as awareness grows of the implications of a government high-employment guarantee.

Does historical evidence support this analysis? History offers many cases where inflation has spurted and then slowed or stopped without turning into a runaway spiral; a few cases (mainly associated with wars) where true hyperinflations developed; and some (notably in Latin America) where rapid but uneven rates of inflation have persisted over many years. But none of this evidence helps much, for the recognized government role as a high-employment guarantor, plus excess income claims, is essentially new since World War II.

Recent econometric studies have analyzed postwar experience in the United States to determine how much inflation anticipation can explain observed wage increases, a crucial issue in the argument above. If, for example, a 1 per cent rise in the price level generates a 1 per cent or larger wage increase, this would tend to generate a cumulative upward wage-price spiral. Most studies suggest a wage coeffi-

cient well under 1; that is, a 1 per cent increase in prices seems to produce wage increases of less than 1 per cent, so that an upward inflationary spiral would tend to die out unless reinforced by other factors. But the measurement and analytical problems are subjects of dispute by experts. And even if the results are right, they would fail to settle the issue because there has not yet been enough time for a real historical test of the cumulative inflation hypothesis under excess income claims and under a widely recognized government high-employment guarantee.

5

BLACK DEPRESSION

Words are inadequate to convey the human misery, the despair, the baffled uncertainty and hopelessness in the Great Depression of the 1930s. The long bread lines, the silent factories, the wandering "Okies," the "dust bowl," the evicted hungry families huddled in cardboard shacks —these were the desperate reality of the depression behind the statistics. These pages should convey a little of this reality to a generation for whom the Great Depression is increasingly far away and unreal.

Frederick Lewis Allen

Frederick Lewis Allen has been editor of Harper's Magazine and was a well-known journalist and writer on historical topics.

From pp. 57–65, 82–88, 199–203 in *Since Yesterday* by Frederick Lewis Allen. Copyright 1939, 1940 by Harper & Row, Publishers, Inc.

. . .

Statistics are bloodless things.

To say that during the year 1932, the cruelest year of the Depression, the average number of unemployed people in the country was 12¼ million by the estimates of the National Industrial Conference Board, a little over 13 million by the estimates of the American Federation of Labor, and by other estimates (differently arrived at, and defining unemployment in various ways)

anywhere from 8½ to 17 million—to say this is to give no living impression of the jobless men going from office to office or from factory gate to factory gate; of the disheartening inevitability of the phrase, "We'll let you know if anything shows up"; of men thumbing the want ads in cold tenements, spending fruitless hours, day after day and week after week, in the sidewalk crowds before the employment offices; using up the money in the savings bank, borrowing on their life insurance, selling whatever possessions could be sold, borrowing from relatives less and less able to lend, tasting the bitterness of inadequacy, and at last swallowing their pride and going to apply for relief—if there was any to be got. (Relief money was scarce, for charitable organizations were hard beset and cities and towns had either used up their available funds or were on the point of doing so.)

A few statistical facts and estimates are necessary, however, to an understanding of the scope and impact of the Depression. For example:—

Although the amount of money paid out in interest during the year 1932 was only 3.5 per cent less than in 1929, according to the computations of Dr. Simon Kuznets for the National Bureau of Economic Research, on the other hand the amount of money paid out in salaries had dropped 40 per cent, dividends had dropped 56.6 per cent, and wages had dropped 60 per cent. (Thus had the debt structure remained comparatively rigid while other elements in the economy were subjected to fierce deflation.)

Do not imagine, however, that the continuation of interest payments and the partial continuation of dividend payments meant that business as a whole was making money. Business as a whole lost between five and six billion dollars in 1932. (The government figure for all the corporations in the country—451,800 of them—was a net deficit of $5,640,000,000.) To be sure, most of the larger and better-managed companies did much better than that. E. D. Kennedy's figures for the 960 concerns whose earnings were tabulated by Standard Statistics—mostly big ones whose stock was active on the Stock Exchange—show that these 960 leaders had a collective profit of over a third of a billion. Yet one must add that "better managed" is here used in a special sense. Not only had labor-saving devices and speedups increased the output per man-hour in manufacturing industries by an estimated 18 per cent since 1929, but employees had been laid off in quantity. Every time one of the giants of industry, to keep its financial head above water, threw off a new group of workers, many little corporations roundabout sank further into the red.

While existing businesses shrank, new ones were not being undertaken. The total of domestic corporate issues—issues of securities floated to provide capital for American corporations—had dropped in 1932 to just about *one twenty-fourth* of the 1929 figure.

But these cold statistics give us little sense of the human realities of the economic paralysis of 1932. Let us try another approach.

Walking through an American city, you might find few signs of the Depression visible—or at least conspicuous—to the casual eye. You might notice that a great many shops were untenanted, with dusty plate-glass windows and signs indicating that they were ready to lease; that few factory chimneys were smoking; that the streets were not so crowded with trucks as in earlier years; that there was no uproar of riveters to assail the ear; that beggars and panhandlers were on the sidewalks in unprecedented numbers (in the Park Avenue district of New York a man might be asked for money four or five times in a ten-block walk). Traveling by railroad, you might notice that the trains were shorter, the Pullman cars fewer—and that fewer freight trains were on the line. Traveling overnight, you might find only two or three other passengers in your sleeping car. (By contrast, there were more filling stations by the motor highways than ever before, and of all the retail businesses in "Middletown" only the filling stations showed no large drop in business during the black years; for although few new automobiles were being bought, those which would still stand up were being used more than ever—to the dismay of the railroads.)

Otherwise things might seem to you to be going on much as usual. The major phenomena of the Depression were mostly negative and did not assail the eye.

But if you knew where to look, some of them would begin to appear. First, the breadlines in the poorer districts. Second, those bleak settlements ironically known as "Hoovervilles" in the outskirts of the cities and on vacant lots—groups of makeshift shacks constructed out of packing boxes, scrap iron, anything that could be picked up free in a diligent combing of the city dumps: shacks in which men and sometimes whole families of evicted people were sleeping on automobile seats carried from auto-graveyards, warming themselves before fires of rubbish in grease drums. Third, the homeless people sleeping in doorways or on park benches, and going the rounds of the restaurants for leftover half-eaten biscuits, piecrusts, anything to keep the fires of life burning. Fourth, the vastly increased number of thumbers on the highways, and particularly of freight-car transients on the railroads: a huge army of drifters ever on the move, searching half-aimlessly for a place where there might be a job. According to Jonathan Norton Leonard, the Missouri Pacific Railroad in 1929 had "taken official cognizance" of 13,745 migrants; by 1931 the figure had already jumped to 186,028. It was estimated that by the beginning of 1933, the country over, there were a million of these transients on the move. Forty-five thousand had passed through El Paso in the space of six months; 1,500 were passing through Kansas City every day. Among them were large numbers of young boys, and girls disguised as boys. According to the Children's Bureau, there were 200,000 children thus drifting

about the United States. So huge was the number of freight-car hoppers in the Southwest that in a number of places the railroad police simply had to give up trying to remove them from the trains: there were far too many of them.

Among the comparatively well-to-do people of the country (those, let us say, whose pre-Depression incomes had been over $5,000 a year) the great majority were living on a reduced scale, for salary cuts had been extensive, especially since 1931, and dividends were dwindling. These people were discharging servants, or cutting servants' wages to a minimum, or in some cases "letting" a servant stay on without other compensation than board and lodging. In many pretty houses, wives who had never before—in the revealing current phrase—"done their own work" were cooking and scrubbing. Husbands were wearing the old suit longer, resigning from the golf club, deciding, perhaps, that this year the family couldn't afford to go to the beach for the summer, paying seventy-five cents for lunch instead of a dollar at the restaurant or thirty-five instead of fifty at the lunch counter. When those who had flown high with the stock market in 1929 looked at the stock-market page of the newspapers nowadays their only consoling thought (if they still had any stock left) was that a judicious sale or two would result in such a capital loss that they need pay no income tax at all this year.

Alongside these men and women of the well-to-do classes whose fortunes had been merely reduced by the Depression were others whose fortunes had been shattered. The crowd of men waiting for the 8:14 train at the prosperous suburb included many who had lost their jobs and were going to town as usual not merely to look stubbornly and almost hopelessly for other work but also to keep up a bold front of activity. (In this latter effort they usually succeeded: one would never have guessed, seeing them chatting with their friends as train-time approached, how close to desperation some of them had come.) There were architects and engineers bound for offices to which no clients had come in weeks. There were doctors who thought themselves lucky when a patient paid a bill. Mrs. Jones, who went daily to her stenographic job, was now the economic mainstay of her family, for Mr. Jones was jobless and was doing the cooking and looking after the children (with singular distaste and inefficiency). Next door to the Joneses lived Mrs. Smith, the widow of a successful lawyer: she had always had a comfortable income, she prided herself on her "nice things," she was pathetically unfitted to earn a dollar even if jobs were to be had; her capital had been invested in South American bonds and United Founders stock and other similarly misnamed "securities," and now she was completely dependent upon handouts from her relatives and didn't even have carfare in her imported pocketbook.

The Browns had retreated to their "farmhouse" in the country and were trying to raise crops on its stony acres; they talked warmly about primal simplicities but couldn't help longing sometimes for electric light and running hot water, and couldn't cope with the potato bugs. (Large numbers of city dwellers thus moved to the country, but not enough of them engaged in real farming to do more than partially check the long-term movement from the farms of America to the cities and towns.) It was being whispered about the community that the Robinson family, though they lived in a $40,000 house and had always spent money, freely, were in desperate straits: Mr. Robinson had lost his job, the house could not be sold, they had realized on every asset at their command, and now they were actually going hungry—though their house still looked like the abode of affluence.

Further down in the economic scale,

particularly in those industrial communities in which the factories were running at 20 per cent of capacity or had closed down altogether, conditions were infinitely worse. Frederick E. Croxton's figures, taken in Buffalo, show what was happening in such communities: out of 14,909 persons of both sexes willing and able to work, his house-to-house canvassers found in November, 1932, that 46.3 per cent were fully employed, 22.5 per cent were working part time, and as many as 31.2 per cent were unable to find jobs. In every American city, quantities of families were being evicted from their inadequate apartments; moving in with other families till ten or twelve people would be sharing three or four rooms; or shivering through the winter in heatless houses because they could afford no coal, eating meat once a week or not at all. If employers sometimes found that former employees who had been discharged did not seem eager for reemployment ("They won't take a job if you offer them one!"), often the reason was panic: a dreadful fear of inadequacy which was one of the Depression's commonest psychopathological results. A woman clerk, offered piecework after being jobless for a year, confessed that she almost had not dared to come to the office, she had been in such terror lest she wouldn't know where to hang her coat, wouldn't know how to find the washroom, wouldn't understand the boss's directions for her job.

For perhaps the worst thing about this Depression was its inexorable continuance year after year. Men who have been sturdy and self-respecting workers can take unemployment without flinching for a few weeks, a few months, even if they have to see their families suffer; but it is different after a year . . . two years . . . three years. . . . Among the miserable creatures curled up on park benches or standing in dreary lines before the soup kitchens in 1932 were men who had been jobless since the end of 1929.

At the very bottom of the economic scale the conditions may perhaps best be suggested by two brief quotations. The first, from Jonathan Norton Leonard's *Three Years Down*, describes the plight of Pennsylvania miners who had been put out of company villages after a blind and hopeless strike in 1931: "Reporters from the more liberal metropolitan papers found thousands of them huddled on the mountainsides, crowded three or four families together in one-room shacks, living on dandelions and wild weed roots. Half of them were sick, but no local doctor would care for the evicted strikers. All of them were hungry and many were dying of those providential diseases which enable welfare authorities to claim that no one has starved." The other quotation is from Louis V. Armstrong's *We Too Are the People*, and the scene is Chicago in the late spring of 1932:—

"One vivid, gruesome moment of those dark days we shall never forget. We saw a crowd of some fifty men fighting over a barrel of garbage which had been set outside the back door of a restaurant. American citizens fighting for scraps of food like animals!"

Human behavior under unaccustomed conditions is always various. One thinks of the corporation executive to whom was delegated the job of discharging several hundred men: he insisted on seeing every one of them personally and taking an interest in each man's predicament, and at the end of a few months his hair had turned prematurely gray. . . . The Junior League girl who reported with pride a Depression economy: she had cut a piece out of an old fur coat in the attic and bound it to serve as a bathmat. . . . The banker who had been plunged deeply into debt by the collapse of his bank: he got a $30,000 job with another bank, lived on $3,000 a year, and honorably paid $27,000 a year to his creditors. . . . The wealthy family who lost most of their money but announced bravely that they had "solved their Depression problem" by discharging fifteen of their twenty servants, and showed no signs of curiosity as to what would happen to these fifteen. . . . The little knot of corporation officials in a magnificent skyscraper office doctoring the books of the company to dodge bankruptcy. . . . The crowd of Chicago Negroes standing tight-packed before a tenement-house door to prevent the landlord's agents from evicting a neighbor family: as they stood there, hour by hour, they sang hymns. . . . The one-time clerk carefully cutting out pieces of cardboard to put inside his shoes before setting out on his endless job-hunting round, and telling his wife the shoes were now better than ever. . . . The man in the little apartment next door who had given up hunting for jobs, given up all interest, all activity, and sat hour by hour in staring apathy. . . .

. . .

Not only were ideas boiling; the country was losing patience with adversity. That instinct of desperate men to rebel which was swelling the radical parties in a dozen Depression-hit countries and was gathering stormily behind Hitler in Germany was working in the United States also. It was anything but unified, it was as yet little organized, and only in scattered places did it assume the customary European shape of communism. It had been slow to develop—partly because Americans had been used to prosperity and had expected it to return automatically, partly because when jobs were vanishing those men who were still employed were too scared to be rebellious and simply hung on to what they had and waited and hoped. (It is not usually during a collapse that men rebel, but after it.) There had been riots and hunger-marches here and there but on the whole the orderliness of the country had been striking, all things considered. Yet men could not be expected to sit still forever in the expectation that an economic system which they did not understand would right itself. The ferment of dissatisfaction was working in many places and taking many forms, and here and there it was beginning to break sharply through the orderly surface of society.

In the summer of 1932 the city of Washington was to see an exciting example of this ferment—and a spectacular demonstration of how not to deal with it.

All through June thousands of war veterans had been streaming into Washington, coming from all over the country by boxcar and by truck. These veterans wanted the government to pay them now the "adjusted compensation" which Congress had already voted to pay them in 1945. They set up a camp—a shantytown, a sort of big-scale "Hooverville"—on the Anacostia flats near the city, and they occupied some vacant land with disused buildings on it on Pennsylvania Avenue just below the Capitol. More and more of them straggled to Washington until their number had reached fifteen or twenty thousand.

Among such a great crowd there were inevitably men of many sorts. The Hoover Administration later charged that many had had criminal records or were communists. But unquestionably the great majority of them were genuine veterans; though there was one small communist group, it was regarded with hostility by the rest; in the main this "Bonus Expeditionary Force" consisted of ordinary Americans out of luck. They were under at least a semblance of military discipline and were on the whole well-behaved. Many brought their wives and children along, and as time went on the Anacostia camp took on an air half military and half domestic, with the family wash hanging on the line outside the miserable shacks, and entertainers getting up impromptu vaudeville shows.

General Pelham D. Glassford, the Wash-

ington superintendent of police, sensibly regarded these invaders as citizens who had every right to petition the government for a redress of grievances. He helped them to get equipment for their camp and treated them with unfailing consideration. But to some Washingtonians their presence was ominous. A group of the veterans—under a leader who wore a steel neckbrace and a helmet with straps under the chin, to support a broken back—picketed the Capitol for days while the Bonus bill was being considered; and on the evening when the bill was to come to a vote, the great plaza before the Capitol was packed with veterans. The Senate voted No. What would the men do? There were people looking out the windows of the brightly lighted Senate wing who wondered breathlessly if those thousands of ragged men would try to rush the building. But when their leader announced the news, a band struck up "America" and the men dispersed quietly. So far, so good.

Some of them left Washington during the next few days, but several thousand stayed on, hopelessly, obstinately. (Where had they to go?) Officialdom became more and more uneasy. The White House was put under guard, its gates closed and chained, the streets about it cleared, as if the man there did not dare face the unrest among the least fortunate of the citizenry. It was decided to clear the veterans out of the disused buildings below the Capitol (to make way for the government's building program); and on the morning of July 28, 1932, General Glassford was told that the evacuation must be immediate. He set about his task.

It began peacefully, but at noon somebody threw a brick and there was a scuffle between the veterans and the police, which quickly subsided. Two hours later there was more serious trouble as a policeman at whom the veterans had thrown stones pulled his gun; two veterans were killed before Glassford could get the police to stop shooting. Even this battle subsided. All Glassford wanted was time to complete the evacuation peacefully and without needless affront. But he was not to get it.

Earlier in the day he had told the District Commissioners that if the evacuation was to be carried out speedily, troops would be required. This statement had been needlessly interpreted as a request for military aid, which Glassford did not want at all. President Hoover had ordered the United States Army to the rescue.

Down Pennsylvania Avenue, late that hot afternoon, came an impressive parade —four troops of cavalry, four companies of infantry, a machine-gun squadron, and several tanks. As they approached the disputed area they were met with cheers from the veterans sitting on the curb and from the large crowd which had assembled. Then suddenly there was chaos: cavalrymen were riding into the crowd, infantrymen were throwing tear-gas bombs, women and children were being trampled and were choking from the gas; a crowd of three thousand or more spectators who had gathered in a vacant lot across the way were being pursued by the cavalry and were running wildly, pell-mell across the uneven ground, screaming as they stumbled and fell.

The troops moved slowly on, scattering before them veterans and homegoing government clerks alike. When they reached the other end of the Anacostia bridge and met a crowd of spectators who booed them and were slow to "move on," they threw more gas bombs. They began burning the shacks of the Anacostia camp—a task which the veterans themselves helped them accomplish. That evening the Washington sky glowed with fire. Even after midnight the troops were still on their way with bayonets and tear-gas bombs, driving people ahead of them into the streets of Anacostia.

The Bonus Expeditionary Force had been dispersed, to merge itself with that greater army of homeless people who were drifting about the country in search of an ever-retreating fortune. The United States Army had completed its operation "successfully" without killing anybody—though the list of injured was long. The incident was over. But it had left a bitter taste in the mouth. Bayonets drawn in Washington to rout the dispossessed—was this the best that American statesmanship could offer hungry citizens?

The farmers were rebellious—and no wonder. For the gross income of American agriculture had declined from nearly 12 billion dollars in 1929—when it had already for years been suffering from a decline in export sales—to only 5¼ billions in 1932. While most manufacturing businesses dropped their prices only a little and met slackened demand with slackened production, the farmer could not do this, and the prices he got went right down to the cellar. Men who found themselves utterly unable to meet their costs of production could not all be expected to be philosophical about it.

Angry Iowans, organized by Milo Reno into a Farmers' Holiday Association, were refusing to bring food into Sioux City for thirty days or "until the cost of production had been obtained"; they blockaded the highway with spiked telegraph poles and logs, stopped milk trucks and emptied the milk into roadside ditches. Said an elderly Iowa farmer with a white mustache to Mary Heaton Vorse, "They say blockading the highway's illegal. I says, 'Seems to me there was a Tea Party in Boston that was illegal too.'"

Elsewhere farmers were taking the obvious direct means to stop the tidal wave of mortgage foreclosure sales. All through the prairie country there were quantities of farmers who not only had heavy mortgages on their property but had gone deeply into debt for the purchase of farm machinery or to meet the emergencies of years of falling prices; when their corn and wheat brought to even the most industrious of them not enough money to meet their obligations, they lost patience with the laws of bankruptcy. If a man sees a neighbor of his, a formerly successful farmer, a substantial, hard-working citizen with a family, coming out of the office of the referee in bankruptcy stripped of everything but an old team of horses, a wagon, a few dogs and hogs, and a few sticks of furniture, he is likely to see red. Marching to the scene of the next foreclosure sale, these farmers would drive off prospective bidders, gather densely about the auctioneer, bid in horses at 25 cents apiece, cows at 10 cents, fat hogs at a nickel—and the next morning would drive off prospective bidders, gather owner.

In a quiet county seat, handbills would appear: "Farmers and workers! Help protect your neighbors' from being driven off their property. Now is the time to act. For the past three and a half years we have waited for our masters, who are responsible for the situation, to find a way out. . . . On Friday the property of _____ is to be sold at a forced auction at the courthouse. . . . The Farmers Committee has called a mass protest meeting to stop the above-mentioned sale." And on Friday the trucks would drive up to the courthouse and men by the hundreds, quiet, grim-faced, would fill the corridors outside the sheriff's office while their leaders demanded that the sale be not held.

They threatened judges in bankruptcy cases; in one case a mob dragged a judge from his courtroom, beat him, hanged him by the neck till he fainted—and all because he was carrying out the law.

These farmers were not revolutionists. On the contrary, most of them were by habit conservative men. They were simply striking back in rage at the impersonal forces which had brought them to their present pass.

. . .

But it was during 1934 and 1935—the years when Roosevelt was pushing through his financial reforms, and Huey Long was a national portent, and the languishing NRA was put out of its misery by the Supreme Court—that the thermometer in Kansas stayed week after week at 108° or above and the black storms raged again and again. The drought continued acute during much of 1936. Oklahoma farms became great dunes of shifting sand (so like seashore dunes, said one observer, that one almost expected to smell the salt). Housewives in the drought belt kept oiled cloths on the window sills and between the upper and lower sashes of the windows, and some of them tried to seal up every aperture in their houses with the gummed paper strips used in wrapping parcels, yet still the choking dust filtered in and lay in ripples on the kitchen floor, while outside it blew blindingly across a No Man's Land; roads and farm buildings and once green thickets half-buried in the sand. It was in those days that a farmer, sitting at his window during a dust storm, remarked that he was counting the Kansas farms as they came by.

Retribution for the very human error of breaking the sod of the Plains had come in full measure. And, as often happens, it was visited upon the innocent as well as upon the guilty—if indeed one could single out any individuals as guilty of so pervasive an error as social shortsightedness.

Westward fled the refugees from this new Sahara, as if obedient to the old American tradition that westward lies the land of promise. In 1934 and 1935 Californians became aware of an increasing influx into their state of families and groups of families of "Okies," traveling in ancient family jalopies; but for years the streams of humanity continued to run. They came along U.S. Highway 30 through the Idaho hills, along Highway 66 across New Mexico and Arizona, along the Old Spanish Trail through El Paso, along all the other westward trails. They came in decrepit, square-shouldered 1925 Dodges and 1927 La Salles; in battered 1923 Model-T Fords that looked like relics of some antique culture; in trucks piled high with mattresses and cooking utensils and children, with suitcases, jugs, and sacks strapped to the running boards. "They roll westward like a parade," wrote Richard L. Neuberger. "In a single hour from a grassy meadow near an Idaho road I counted 34 automobiles with the license plates of states between Chicago and the mountains."

They left behind them a half-depopulated countryside. A survey of the farmhouses in seven counties of southeastern Colorado, made in 1936, showed 2,878 houses still occupied, 2,811 abandoned; and there were also, in that area, 1,522 abandoned homesites. The total number of drought refugees who took the westward trek over the mountains was variously estimated in 1939 at from 200,000 upwards—with more coming all the time.

As these wanderers moved along the highways they became a part of a vast and confused migratory movement. When they camped by the wayside, they might find themselves next to a family of evicted white Alabama sharecroppers who had been on the move for four years, snatching seasonal farm-labor jobs wherever they could through the Southwest; or next to tenant families from the Arkansas Delta who had been "tractored off" their land—expelled in order that the owner might consolidate two or three farms and operate them with tractors and day labor; or next to lone wanderers who had once held industrial jobs and had now for years been on relief or on the road—jumping freights, hitchhiking, panhandling, shunting back and forth across

the countryside in the faint hope of a durable job. And when these varied streams of migrants reached the Coast they found themselves in desperate competition for jobs with individuals or families who for years had been "fruit tramps," moving northward each year with the harvests from the Imperial Valley in southern California to the Sacramento Valley or even to the apple-picking in the Yakima Valley in Washington.

Here in the land of promise, agriculture had long been partly industrialized. Huge farms were in the control of absentee owners or banks or corporations and were accustomed to depend upon the labor of migratory "fruit tramps," who had formerly been mostly Mexicans, Japanese, and other foreigners but now were increasingly Americans. Those laborers who were lucky enough to get jobs picking cotton or peas or fruit would be sheltered temporarily in camps consisting typically of frame cabins in rows, with a water line between every two rows; they were very likely to find in their cabin no stove, no cots, no water pail. Even the best of the camps offered a way of life strikingly different from that of the ruggedly individualist farmer of the American tradition, who owned his farm or else was preparing, by working as a resident "hired man," or by renting a farm, for the chance of ultimate ownership. These pickers were homeless, voteless nomads, unwanted anywhere save at the harvest season.

When wave after wave of the new migrants reached California, the labor market became glutted, earnings were low, and jobs became so scarce that groups of poverty-stricken families would be found squatting in makeshift Hoovervilles or bunking miserably in their awkward old Fords by the roadside. Being Americans of native stock and accustomed to independence, they took the meager wages and the humiliation bitterly, sought to organize, talked of striking, sometimes struck. At every such threat, something like panic seized the growers. If this new proletariat were permitted to organize and were to strike at picking time, they might ruin the whole season's output of a perishable crop. There followed antipicketing ordinances; the spectacle of armed deputies dislodging the migrants from their pitiful camps; violence by bands of vigilantes, to whom these ragged families were not fellow-citizens who had suffered in a great American disaster but dirty, ignorant, superstitious outlanders, failures at life, easy dupes for "red" agitators. This engulfing tide of discontent must be kept moving.

Farther north the refugees were likely to be received with more sympathy, especially in regions where the farms were small and not industrialized; here and there one heard of instances of real hospitality, such as that of the Oregon town which held a canning festival for the benefit of the drought victims in the neighborhood. The well-managed camps set up by the Farm Security Administration were havens of human decency. But to the vast majority of the refugees the promised land proved to be a place of new and cruel tragedy.

. . .

6

JOB HUNTERS

What it means to look for a job when there aren't any jobs is the picture conveyed by this diary of a few weeks in the life of an unemployed job hunter in 1933. The creeping, deadening impact of week after week of such job hunting was the human side of unemployment for millions of men.

E. Wight Bakke

E. Wight Bakke is Sterling Professor of Economics, and Director of the Labor and Management Center, Yale University.

From "Job Hunters," in *The Unemployed Worker* by E. Wight Bakke. Copyright © 1940 by Yale University Press. Reprinted by permission of Yale University Press.

The foreman tapped Joseph Torrio on the shoulder as he pulled the switch on his machine. "Clapham wants to see you, Joe."

"You mean—I'm getting my time, Jim?"

"Just temporary, I hope, and you know what I think of your work, old man. It won't be long—unless—but why worry about it? Clapham will give you the dope."

With a slow step Joe headed for the front office where Clapham, the company's personnel department, was already telling some of his mates what Joe knew to be "the bad news." He sat down on a bench in the outer office. His turn had come! Here he was an eighteen-year man. Others had been laid off one by one, but he had thought his job was safe. Why, he had been a foreman in the night shift during the War, and now Clapham was going to tell him the bad news! It wouldn't be easy for Clapham, for in spite of the fact that the workers dubbed the personnel department, "the worse-n-hell department," Clapham was a good egg. He knew most of the men by sight if not by name.

"Torrio," called the office boy.

As he walked out the front gate he could hardly remember what Clapham had said. He had been thinking his own thoughts. A phrase or two penetrated his preoccupation. "Tough break . . . no new orders . . . maybe only a short time . . . but better look around, no telling when . . . call you if things pick up."

This was not the first time he had been laid off, but this time the ugly rumors that "the company was slipping," that "the whole damned country is on the rocks," had created a fear he had not felt before. He'd lay off a couple of weeks—he deserved a vacation after eight years of steady work. But if he didn't get called back in that time, he'd start hunting another job.

Joseph Torrio in 1933 had about 18,000 companions in the city who joined him in this search for work. What kind of job is looking for a job, and how did these workers who had been "told the bad news" go about that task? They came to unemployment with an economic equipment which we have attempted to describe in some detail. We have suggested that they are motivated in their economic activity by the desire: to play one or more socially respected roles, to obtain the measure of economic security deemed possible by their associates, to gain an increasing degree of control over their own affairs, to understand the casual forces in their problems of self-maintenance. We have surveyed the essential controlling conditions of their economic environment and the effect of these in furthering or frustrating their progress toward these goals. We have recorded the normal adjustments made in the face of these conditions, which adjustments provide them with a stock of habitual practices available as suggestive alternatives in meeting the problem of unemployment.

How did they use this equipment in effecting the new economic adjustments made necessary by the loss of their jobs? In the following chapters we shall try to share the experience of Torrio and his mates as they set about bridging the gap between jobs.

THE JOB OF JOB HUNTING

In a factory town the great majority of workers are accustomed to assume that factory employment is the major, if not the only, possibility of making a living. Joseph Torrio after his two weeks' vacation "pounded pavements" for an additional four weeks. We need not go with him to every gate, but a sample of his experiences taken from his diary kept for us during that time will help us to understand why he left off searching for that kind of job six weeks after his layoff.

April 19, 1934

Decided to have a go at the State Employment Office. Got there at eight. Fellow I knew sitting on steps. Big sign there "No loitering in the doorway." Janitor or someone came down and asked him to move.

"Are you going upstairs?" he asked. "If you are, go, but don't sit here." The fellow jumped; not looking at the janitor, he began a loud bluster about his father paying taxes to support the place and he could sit on the steps if he wanted to. When the janitor left, he returned to the steps for a moment. Meanwhile a group of people had gathered to see what was going on.

Asked the janitor when the manager would be in. He said, "Nine o'clock." Decided to come back. When I got back, a line had formed clear out into the street. I took my place. Officials and clerks kept coming and had a good cheery word for us as they passed. But after they had gone, many sarcastic remarks followed them like, "Gives you a nice smile, but that's all."

The manager himself drove up before

the office a little past nine—appeared sore that there was no parking space in front of the office. The fellows standing outside purposely raised their voices so he could hear and made remarks such as, "Not much use coming here, they never do anything but tell you to come back in sixty days"; "What'd they ever do for me?—Nothing"; "First it was April 1st, then it was the 15th, and now it will be God knows when."

One of the young fellows asked an official of the Bureau as he entered the building if there was anything in his line available—stated he was a soda jerker or plumber's helper—or he'd "take anything." The official smiled and wanted to know if the fellow was following the ads in the newspaper. The fellow returned to the group, swore a moment, and asked, "Who ever got a job from the ads in a paper?"

Fellow next to me was apparently an electrician. He was sore because he couldn't get a P.W.A. job. He said, "All these contractors have their own men and when this Employment Office tries to do the hiring for the P.W.A. jobs, it doesn't know where to get off. The P.W.A. provision reads that the contractor must take men from the State Employment Bureau where they are able to do the work. Well, the Bureau sends its men out. They work for a day, and then they are let go as not fit for the job; then the contractor has fulfilled the specifications and hires his own men."

I register, but they say not much chance today; maybe a week from today. I go out. Tony grabs my arm. He says, "Work?— there is no work. I go to the Employment Office. I stand and wait. Soon—my turn. I give the girl my card. She takes it, turns it over and over in her hand. Bluff—just to take up time. By and by, she gives it back. 'Sorry, nothing today.' I say, 'But I no work in three years, with seven children, what do I eat?' She reply, 'Come back again, maybe soon there will be something.' It is the big bluff."

Jim joins us at the foot of the stairs. He's mad too. "God, I'm disgusted with this place, and everybody else is that I know. Some fine day a mob's going to drop down on this place and tear it apart. I'm telling you, these fellows from down around Wooster Street aren't going to take this tomorrow business forever."

Looks as though I'd be better off to depend on the grapevine. Word gets around plenty fast if they're taking men on any place.

April 27

Up at seven, cup of coffee, and off to Sargent's. Like to be there when the gang comes to work, the lucky devils. Employment manager not in. Waited in his outer office fitted with six benches and about thirty nearly worn out chairs. Took a bench —looked more likely to stay up. Three others waiting, two reporting for compensation. Other one laid off two weeks ago and said he called at office every day. He inquired what I was doing and when I said "looking for work" he laughed. "You never work here? No? What chance you think you got when 400 like me who belong here out?" Employment manager showed up at 9:30. I had waited two hours. My time has no value. A pleasant fellow; told me in a kind but snappy way business was very bad. What about the future, would he take my name? Said he referred only to the present. Nothing more for me to say, so left. Two more had drifted into office. Suppose they got the same story. Must be a lot of men in New Haven that have heard it by now.

Down Chestnut Street to Peck Brothers. Thought something might be going there. Since beer bill they have been calling back old employees, might have use for another hand. No real employment office here. From street into a long hall with two offices both with clerks on each side of hall. Picked the wrong one. Smart flapper didn't even speak just tossed her head and thumb in the direction of across the hall. Went across and another girl at an information desk asked if I had ever worked there before. Told her "No." She said no immediate chance then, but I could file an application; but added, "It won't do you no good as there is plenty of our own men to fill the jobs for some time to come." Guess I won't get a job till they've skimmed the cream from their own men. That's proper of course and a good break for them. But if it's like this all over, what's the point in applying for jobs? Filled out application anyway—might as well, didn't have any better way to spend my time. No one else here looking for work.

No heart for any more so dropped into Jake's for a doughnut and a glass of milk and then went home.

April 28

To New Haven Clock Company. Met a company "dick" who said plant was shut down till Monday. Gave me an application blank and said, "You look all right, fill this out in ink. Do it neatly, and they may give you a break. Do you know anybody inside?" I said, "No." Then he shrugs his shoulders and says, "Well, I don't know if there is much use you sending this in then, but you might try."

In the afternoon went to the park and talked with men trying to find out what luck they had had. No good news.

May 2

Started out at seven for New Haven Clock Shop. No one in employment office. Lady at information desk asked, "What do you want?" I told her. She wanted to know if I had worked there before and when I said "No," she didn't even ask if I had any experience in clockmaking (which I have). And when I started to tell her so, she cut me off with, "No use—sorry." Suppose she gets tired too.

From Clock Shop to E. Cowells and Co. who make auto equipment. If they want to have old men, well, I worked here in 1916 and 1917. Didn't get to see anyone here, because just as you get to the hall there is a big sign "No Help Wanted." You can't miss it, and I find it kind of hard to disregard a sign of that type. I assume it means what it says or they wouldn't have gone to the trouble and expense to have it painted. I'll have to see a fellow I know who works there. He may know some way to get me on the call list, seeing how I once worked there.

Having heard Seamless Rubber was working quite steady I went down there. Regular employment office furnished with one bench. Another chap, a foreigner, waiting also. In about ten minutes a fellow asked us our business and told us very politely they had no jobs even for skilled men, let alone laborers. No use to tell him I wasn't always a laborer for I never had done the skilled jobs on rubber.

Saw a sign hanging out of one place in gilt letters, "No Help Wanted." In gilt, mind you, as if to make it more permanent.

Then to Bradley-Smith candymakers, where I had also worked before. The first few days I hadn't had the heart for more than a couple of tries a morning. I'm getting hardened to the word "No" now, though, and can stick it out most of the morning. Bradley-Smith has no employment office. The telephone switchboard operator is apparently instructed to switch off anyone looking for work, as she made quick work of my question. I notice no one seems to be instructed to find out if we know anything about the business or work. Firms might be passing up some good bets for their force. But apparently that isn't important now.

Walking away, met two friends out going the rounds too. They said it was useless and that they were only looking through force of habit. That's going to be me before long. Even if they hadn't said so. I'm thinking it is useless to run around like this; you just appear ridiculous, and that gets your goat—or would if you kept it up too long. Wish I had some drag with someone on the inside of one of those gates. I expect it's

that everyone knows they have to know someone that keeps me from having more company at the employment offices. This is what a former pal of mine who is up at Yale calls "competition in the labor market," I guess. Well, it's a funny competition and with guys you never see.

. . .

7

There has been a lively controversy among economists concerning the proper role of monetary policy in managing the economy. Professor Friedman, long a leading advocate of the importance of money as a determinant of aggregate spending and prices, points out what monetary policy can and cannot do in affecting economic activity. His conclusion is that money is so important, and its effects so unpredictable, that monetary policy should be used with great caution.

THE ROLE OF MONETARY POLICY

Milton Friedman

Milton Friedman is Professor of Economics at the University of Chicago.

From *American Economic Review* (March 1968), pp. 5–17.

I. WHAT MONETARY POLICY CANNOT DO

From the infinite world of negation, I have selected two limitations of monetary policy to discuss: (1) It cannot peg interest rates for more than very limited periods; (2) It cannot peg the rate of unemployment for more than very limited periods. I select these because the contrary has been or is widely believed, because they correspond to the two main unattainable tasks that are at all likely to be assigned to monetary policy and because essentially the same theoretical analysis covers both.

Pegging of Interest Rates

History has already persuaded many of you about the first limitation. As noted earlier, the failure of cheap money policies

was a major source of the reaction against simple-minded Keynesianism. In the United States, this reaction involved widespread recognition that the wartime and postwar pegging of bond prices was a mistake, that the abandonment of this policy was a desirable and inevitable step, and that it had none of the disturbing and disastrous consequences that were so freely predicted at the time.

The limitation derives from a much misunderstood feature of the relation between money and interest rates. Let the Fed set out to keep interest rates down. How will it try to do so? By buying securities. This raises their prices and lowers their yields. In the process, it also increases the quantity of reserves available to banks, hence the amount of bank credit, and, ultimately the total quantity of money. That is why central bankers in particular, and the financial community more broadly, generally believe that an increase in the quantity of money tends to lower interest rates. Academic economists accept the same conclusion, but for different reasons. They see, in their mind's eye, a negatively sloping liquidity preference schedule. How can people be induced to hold a larger quantity of money? Only by bidding down interest rates.

Both are right, up to a point. The *initial* impact of increasing the quantity of money at a faster rate than it has been increasing is to make interest rates lower for a time than they would otherwise have been. But this is only the beginning of the process not the end. The more rapid rate of monetary growth will stimulate spending, both through the impact on investment of lower market interest rates and through the impact on other spending and thereby relative prices of higher cash balances than are desired. But one man's spending is another man's income. Rising income will raise the liquidity preference schedule and the demand for loans; it may also raise prices, which would reduce the real quantity of money. These three effects will reverse the initial downward pressure on interest rates fairly promptly, say, in something less than a year. Together they will tend, after a somewhat longer interval, say, a year or two, to return interest rates to the level they would otherwise have had. Indeed, given the tendency for the economy to overreact, they are highly likely to raise interest rates temporarily beyond that level, setting in motion a cyclical adjustment process.

A fourth effect, when and if it becomes operative, will go even farther and definitely mean that a higher rate of monetary expansion will correspond to a higher, not lower, level of interest rates than would otherwise have prevailed. Let the higher rate of monetary growth produce rising prices, and let the public come to expect that prices will continue to rise. Borrowers will then be willing to pay and lenders will then demand higher interest rates—as Irving Fisher pointed out decades ago. This price expectation effect is slow to develop and also slow to disappear. Fisher estimated that it took several decades for a full adjustment, and more recent work is consistent with his estimates.

These subsequent effects explain why every attempt to keep interest rates at a low level has forced the monetary authority to engage in successively larger and larger open market purchases. They explain why, historically, high and rising nominal interest rates have been associated with rapid growth in the quantity of money, as in Brazil or Chile or in the United States in recent years, and why low and falling interest rates have been associated with slow growth in the quantity of money, as in Switzerland now or in the United States from 1929 to 1933. As an empirical matter, low interest rates are a sign that monetary policy *has been* tight—in the sense that the quantity of money has grown slowly; high interest rates are a sign that monetary policy *has been* easy—in the sense that the quantity of money has grown rapidly. The broadest facts of experience run in precisely the opposite direction from that which the financial community and academic economists have all generally taken for granted.

Paradoxically, the monetary authority could assure low nominal rates of interest —but to do so it would have to start out in what seems like the opposite direction, by engaging in a deflationary monetary policy. Similarly, it could assure high nominal interest rates by engaging in an inflationary policy and accepting a temporary movement in interest rates in the opposite direction.

These considerations not only explain

why monetary policy cannot peg interest rates; they also explain why interest rates are such a misleading indicator of whether monetary policy is "tight" or "easy." For that, it is far better to look at the rate of change of the quantity of money.[1]

Employment as a Criterion of Policy

The second limitation I wish to discuss goes more against the grain of current thinking. Monetary growth, it is widely held, will tend to stimulate employment; monetary contraction, to retard employment. Why, then, cannot the monetary authority adopt a target for employment or unemployment—say, 3 per cent unemployment; be tight when unemployment is less than the target; be easy when unemployment is higher than the target; and in this way peg unemployment at, say, 3 per cent? The reason it cannot is precisely the same as for interest rates—the difference between the immediate and the delayed consequences of such a policy.

Thanks to Wicksell, we are all acquainted with the concept of a "natural" rate of interest and the possibility of a discrepancy between the "natural" and the "market" rate. The preceding analysis of interest rates can be translated fairly directly into Wicksellian terms. The monetary authority can make the market rate less than the natural rate only by inflation. It can make the market rate higher than the natural rate only by deflation. We have added only one wrinkle to Wicksell—the Irving Fisher distinction between the nominal and the real rate of interest. Let the monetary authority keep the nominal market rate for a time below the natural rate

by inflation. That in turn will raise the nominal natural rate itself, once anticipations of inflation become widespread, thus requiring still more rapid inflation to hold down the market rate. Similarly, because of the Fisher effect, it will require not merely deflation but more and more rapid deflation to hold the market rate above the initial "natural" rate.

This analysis has its close counterpart in the employment market. At any moment of time, there is some level of unemployment which has the property that it is consistent with equilibrium in the structure of *real* wage rates. At that level of unemployment, real wage rates are tending on the average to rise at a "normal" secular rate, i.e., at a rate that can be indefinitely maintained so long as capital formation, technological improvements, etc., remain on their long-run trends. A lower level of unemployment is an indication that there is an excess demand for labor that will produce upward pressure on real wage rates. A higher level of unemployment is an indication that there is an excess supply of labor that will produce downward pressure on real wage rates. The "natural rate of unemployment," in other words, is the level that would be ground out by the Walrasian system of general equilibrium equations, provided there is imbedded in them the actual structural characteristics of the labor and commodity markets, including market imperfections, stochastic variability in demands and supplies, the cost of gathering information about job vacancies and labor availabilities, the costs of mobility, and so on.[2]

You will recognize the close similarity between this statement and the celebrated Phillips Curve. The similarity is not coinci-

---

[1] This is partly an empirical not theoretical judgment. In principle, "tightness" or "ease" depends on the rate of change of the quantity of money supplied compared to the rate of change of the quantity demanded excluding effects on demand from monetary policy itself. However, empirically demand is highly stable, if we exclude the effect of monetary policy, so it is generally sufficient to look at supply alone.

[2] It is perhaps worth noting that this "natural" rate need not correspond to equality between the number unemployed and the number of job vacancies. For any given structure of the labor market, there will be some equilibrium relation between these two magnitudes, but there is no reason why it should be one of equality.

dental. Phillips' analysis of the relation between unemployment and wage change is deservedly celebrated as an important and original contribution. But, unfortunately, it contains a basic defect—the failure to distinguish between *nominal* wages and *real* wages—just as Wicksell's analysis failed to distinguish between *nominal* interest rates and *real* interest rates. Implicitly, Phillips wrote his article for a world in which everyone anticipated that nominal prices would be stable and in which that anticipation remained unshaken and immutable whatever happened to actual prices and wages. Suppose, by contrast, that everyone anticipates that prices will rise at a rate of more than 75 per cent a year—as, for example, Brazilians did a few years ago. Then wages must rise at that rate simply to keep real wages unchanged. An excess supply of labor will be reflected in a less rapid rise in nominal wages than in anticipated prices,[3] not in an absolute decline in wages. When Brazil embarked on a policy to bring down the rate of price rise, and succeeded in bringing the price rise down to about 45 per cent a year, there was a sharp initial rise in unemployment because under the influence of earlier anticipations, wages kept rising at a pace that was higher than the new rate of price rise, though lower than earlier. This is the result experienced, and to be expected, of all attempts to reduce the rate of inflation below that widely anticipated.[4]

To avoid misunderstanding, let me emphasize that by using the term "natural" rate of unemployment, I do not mean to suggest that it is immutable and unchangeable. On the contrary, many of the market characteristics that determine its level are man-made and policy-made. In the United States, for example, legal minimum wage rates, the Walsh-Healy and Davis-Bacon Acts, and the strength of labor unions all make the natural rate of unemployment higher than it would otherwise be. Improvements in employment exchanges, in availability of information about job vacancies and labor supply, and so on, would tend to lower the natural rate of unemployment. I use the term "natural" for the same reason Wicksell did—to try to separate the real forces from monetary forces.

Let us assume that the monetary authority tries to peg the "market" rate of unemployment at a level below the "natural" rate. For definiteness, suppose that it takes 3 per cent as the target rate and that the "natural" rate is higher than 3 per cent. Suppose also that we start out at a time when prices have been stable and when unemployment is higher than 3 per cent. Accordingly, the authority increases the rate of monetary growth. This will be expansionary. By making nominal cash balances higher than people desire, it will tend initially to lower interest rates and in this and other ways to stimulate spending. Income and spending will start to rise.

[3] Strictly speaking, the rise in nominal wages will be less rapid than the rise in anticipated nominal wages to make allowance for any secular changes in real wages.

[4] Stated in terms of the rate of change of nominal wages, the Phillips Curve can be expected to be reasonably stable and well defined for any period for which the *average* rate of change of prices, and hence the anticipated rate, has been relatively stable. For such periods, nominal wages and "real" wages move together. Curves computed for different periods or different countries for each of which this condition has been satisfied will differ in level, the level of the curve depending on what the average rate of price change was. The higher the

average rate of price change, the higher will tend to be the level of the curve. For periods or countries for which the rate of change of prices varies considerably, the Phillips Curve will not be well defined. My impression is that these statements accord reasonably well with the experience of the economists who have explored empirical Phillips Curves.

Restate Phillips' analysis in terms of the rate of change of real wages—and even more precisely, anticipated real wages—and it all falls into place. That is why students of empirical Phillips Curves have found that it helps to include the rate of change of the price level as an independent variable.

To begin with, much or most of the rise in income will take the form of an increase in output and employment rather than in prices. People have been expecting prices to be stable, and prices and wages have been set for some time in the future on that basis. It takes time for people to adjust to a new state of demand. Producers will tend to react to the initial expansion in aggregate demand by increasing output, employees by working longer hours, and the unemployed, by taking jobs now offered at former nominal wages. This much is pretty standard doctrine.

But it describes only the initial effects. Because selling prices of products typically respond to an unanticipated rise in nominal demand faster than prices of factors of production, real wages received have gone down—though real wages anticipated by employees went up, since employees implicitly evaluated the wages offered at the earlier price level. Indeed, the simultaneous fall *ex post* in real wages to employers and rise *ex ante* in real wages to employees is what enabled employment to increase. But the decline *ex post* in real wages will soon come to affect anticipations. Employees will start to reckon on rising prices of the things they buy and to demand higher nominal wages for the future. "Market" unemployment is below the "natural" level. There is an excess demand for labor so real wages will tend to rise toward their initial level.

Even though the higher rate of monetary growth continues, the rise in real wages will reverse the decline in unemployment, and then lead to a rise, which will tend to return unemployment to its former level. In order to keep unemployment at its target level of 3 per cent, the monetary authority would have to raise monetary growth still more. As in the interest rate case, the "market" rate can be kept below the "natural" rate only by inflation. And, as in the interest rate case, too, only by accelerating infla-

tion. Conversely, let the monetary authority choose a target rate of unemployment that is above the natural rate, and they will be led to produce a deflation, and an accelerating deflation at that.

What if the monetary authority chooses the "natural" rate—either of interest or unemployment—as its target? One problem is that it cannot know what the "natural" rate is. Unfortunately, we have as yet devised no method to estimate accurately and readily the natural rate of either interest or unemployment. And the "natural" rate will itself change from time to time. But the basic problem is that even if the monetary authority knew the "natural" rate, and attempted to peg the market rate at that level, it would not be led to a determinate policy. The "market" rate will vary from the natural rate for all sorts of reasons other than monetary policy. If the monetary authority responds to these variations, it will set in train longer term effects that will make any monetary growth path it follows ultimately consistent with the rule of policy. The actual course of monetary growth will be analogous to a random walk, buffeted this way and that by the forces that produce temporary departures of the market rate from the natural rate.

To state this conclusion differently, there is always a temporary trade-off between inflation and unemployment; there is no permanent trade-off. The temporary trade-off comes not from inflation per se, but from unanticipated inflation, which generally means, from a rising rate of inflation. The widespread belief that there is a permanent trade-off is a sophisticated version of the confusion between "high" and "rising" that we all recognize in simpler forms. A rising rate of inflation may reduce unemployment, a high rate will not.

But how long, you will say, is "temporary"? For interest rates, we have some systematic evidence on how long each of the several effects takes to work itself out.

For unemployment, we do not. I can at most venture a personal judgment, based on some examination of the historical evidence, that the initial effects of a higher and unanticipated rate of inflation last for something like two to five years; that this initial effect then begins to be reversed; and that a full adjustment to the new rate of inflation takes about as long for employment as for interest rates, say, a couple of decades. For both interest rates and employment, let me add a qualification. These estimates are for changes in the rate of inflation of the order of magnitude that has been experienced in the United States. For much more sizable changes, such as those experienced in South American countries, the whole adjustment process is greatly speeded up.

To state the general conclusion still differently, the monetary authority controls nominal quantities—directly, the quantity of its own liabilities. In principle, it can use this control to peg a nominal quantity—an exchange rate, the price level, the nominal level of national income, the quantity of money by one or another definition—or to peg the rate of change in a nominal quantity—the rate of inflation or deflation, the rate of growth or decline in nominal national income, the rate of growth of the quantity of money. It cannot use its control over nominal quantities to peg a real quantity—the real rate of interest, the rate of unemployment, the level of real national income, the real quantity of money, the rate of growth of real national income, or the rate of growth of the real quantity of money.

II. WHAT MONETARY POLICY CAN DO

Monetary policy cannot peg these real magnitudes at predetermined levels. But monetary policy can and does have important effects on these real magnitudes. The one is in no way inconsistent with the other.

My own studies of monetary history have made me extremely sympathetic to the oft-quoted, much reviled, and as widely misunderstood, comment by John Stuart Mill. "There cannot . . . ," he wrote, "be intrinsically a more insignificant thing, in the economy of society, than money; except in the character of a contrivance for sparing time and labour. It is a machine for doing quickly and commodiously, what would be done, though less quickly and commodiously, without it: and like many other kinds of machinery, it only exerts a distinct and independent influence of its own when it gets out of order" [7, p. 488].

True, money is only a machine, but it is an extraordinarily efficient machine. Without it, we could not have begun to attain the astounding growth in output and level of living we have experienced in the past two centuries—any more than we could have done so without those other marvelous machines that dot our countryside and enable us, for the most part, simply to do more efficiently what could be done without them at much greater cost in labor.

But money has one feature that these other machines do not share. Because it is so pervasive, when it gets out of order, it throws a monkey wrench into the operation of all the other machines. The Great Contraction is the most dramatic example but not the only one. Every other major contraction in this country has been either produced by monetary disorder or greatly exacerbated by monetary disorder. Every major inflation has been produced by monetary expansion—mostly to meet the overriding demands of war which have forced the creation of money to supplement explicit taxation.

The first and most important lesson that history teaches about what monetary policy can do—and it is a lesson of the most profound importance—is that monetary policy can prevent money itself from being a major source of economic disturbance. This sounds like a negative proposition: avoid major mistakes. In part it is. The Great Contraction might not have occurred at all, and if it had, it would have been far less severe, if the monetary authority had avoided mistakes, or if the monetary arrangements had been those of an earlier time when there was no central authority with the power to make the kinds of mistakes that the Federal Reserve System made. The past few years, to come closer to home, would have been steadier and more productive of economic well-being if the Federal Reserve had avoided drastic and erratic changes of direction, first expanding the money supply at an unduly rapid pace, then, in early 1966, stepping on the brake too hard, then, at the end of 1966, reversing itself and resuming expansion until at least November, 1967, at a more rapid pace than can long be maintained without appreciable inflation.

Even if the proposition that monetary policy can prevent money itself from being a major source of economic disturbance were a wholly negative proposition, it would be none the less important for that. As it happens, however, it is not a wholly negative proposition. The monetary machine has gotten out of order even when there has been no central authority with anything like the power now possessed by the Fed. In the United States, the 1907 episode and earlier banking panics are examples of how the monetary machine can get out of order largely on its own. There is therefore a positive and important task for the monetary authority—to suggest improvements in the machine that will reduce the chances that it will get out of order, and to use its own powers so as to keep the machine in good working order.

A second thing monetary policy can do is provide a stable background for the economy—keep the machine well oiled, to

continue Mill's analogy. Accomplishing the first task will contribute to this objective, but there is more to it than that. Our economic system will work best when producers and consumers, employers and employees, can proceed with full confidence that the average level of prices will behave in a known way in the future—preferably that it will be highly stable. Under any conceivable institutional arrangements, and certainly under those that now prevail in the United States, there is only a limited amount of flexibility in prices and wages. We need to conserve this flexibility to achieve changes in relative prices and wages that are required to adjust to dynamic changes in tastes and technology. We should not dissipate it simply to achieve changes in the absolute level of prices that serve no economic function.

In an earlier era, the gold standard was relied on to provide confidence in future monetary stability. In its heyday it served that function reasonably well. It clearly no longer does, since there is scarcely a country in the world that is prepared to let the gold standard reign unchecked—and there are persuasive reasons why countries should not do so. The monetary authority could operate as a surrogate for the gold standard, if it pegged exchange rates and did so exclusively by altering the quantity of money in response to balance of payment flows without "sterilizing" surpluses or deficits and without resorting to open or concealed exchange control or to changes in tariffs and quotas. But again, though many central bankers talk this way, few are in fact willing to follow this course—and again there are persuasive reasons why they should not do so. Such a policy would submit each country to the vagaries not of an impersonal and automatic gold standard but of the policies—deliberate or accidental —of other monetary authorities.

In today's world, if monetary policy is to provide a stable background for the economy it must do so by deliberately employing its powers to that end. I shall come later to how it can do so.

Finally, monetary policy can contribute to offsetting major disturbances in the economic system arising from other sources. If there is an independent secular exhilaration —as the postwar expansion was described by the proponents of secular stagnation— monetary policy can in principle help to hold it in check by a slower rate of monetary growth than would otherwise be desirable. If, as now, an explosive federal budget threatens unprecedented deficits, monetary policy can hold any inflationary dangers in check by a slower rate of monetary growth than would otherwise be desirable. This will temporarily mean higher interest rates than would otherwise prevail —to enable the government to borrow the sums needed to finance the deficit—but by preventing the speeding up of inflation, it may well mean both lower prices and lower nominal interest rates for the long pull. If the end of a substantial war offers the country an opportunity to shift resources from wartime to peacetime production, monetary policy can ease the transition by a higher rate of monetary growth than would otherwise be desirable—though experience is not very encouraging that it can do so without going too far.

I have put this point last, and stated it in qualified terms—as referring to major disturbances—because I believe that the potentiality of monetary policy in offsetting other forces making for instability is far more limited than is commonly believed. We simply do not know enough to be able to recognize minor disturbances when they occur or to be able to predict either what their effects will be with any precision or what monetary policy is required to offset their effects. We do not know enough to be able to achieve stated objectives by delicate, or even fairly coarse, changes in the mix of monetary and fiscal policy. In this

area particularly the best is likely to be the enemy of the good. Experience suggests that the path of wisdom is to use monetary policy explicitly to offset other disturbances only when they offer a "clear and present danger."

III. HOW SHOULD MONETARY POLICY BE CONDUCTED?

How should monetary policy be conducted to make the contribution to our goals that it is capable of making? This is clearly not the occasion for presenting a detailed "Program for Monetary Stability"—to use the title of a book in which I tried to do so. I shall restrict myself here to two major requirements for monetary policy that follow fairly directly from the preceding discussion.

The first requirement is that the monetary authority should guide itself by magnitudes that it can control, not by ones that it cannot control. If, as the authority has often done, it takes interest rates or the current unemployment percentage as the immediate criterion of policy, it will be like a space vehicle that has taken a fix on the wrong star. No matter how sensitive and sophisticated its guiding apparatus, the space vehicle will go astray. And so will the monetary authority. Of the various alternative magnitudes that it can control, the most appealing guides for policy are exchange rates, the price level as defined by some index, and the quantity of a monetary total—currency plus adjusted demand deposits, or this total plus commercial bank time deposits, or a still broader total.

For the United States in particular, exchange rates are an undesirable guide. It might be worth requiring the bulk of the economy to adjust to the tiny percentage consisting of foreign trade if that would guarantee freedom from monetary irresponsibility—as it might under a real gold standard. But it is hardly worth doing so simply to adapt to the average of whatever policies monetary authorities in the rest of the world adopt. Far better to let the market, through floating exchange rates, adjust to world conditions the 5 per cent or so of our resources devoted to international trade while reserving monetary policy to promote the effective use of the 95 per cent.

Of the three guides listed, the price level is clearly the most important in its own right. Other things the same, it would be much the best of the alternatives—as so many distinguished economists have urged in the past. But other things are not the same. The link between the policy actions of the monetary authority and the price level, while unquestionably present, is more indirect than the link between the policy actions of the authority and any of the several monetary totals. Moreover, monetary action takes a longer time to affect the price level than to affect the monetary totals and both the time lag and the magnitude of effect vary with circumstances. As a result, we cannot predict at all accurately just what effect a particular monetary action will have on the price level and, equally important, just when it will have that effect. Attempting to control directly the price level is therefore likely to make monetary policy itself a source of economic disturbance because of false stops and starts. Perhaps, as our understanding of monetary phenomena advances, the situation will change. But at the present stage of our understanding, the long way around seems the surer way to our objective. Accordingly, I believe that a monetary total is the best currently available immediate guide or criterion for monetary policy—and I believe that it matters much less which particular total is chosen than that one be chosen.

A second requirement for monetary policy is that the monetary authority avoid sharp swings in policy. In the past, monetary authorities have on occasion moved in the wrong direction—as in the episode of the Great Contraction that I have stressed. More frequently, they have moved in the right direction, albeit often too late, but have erred by moving too far. Too late and too much has been the general practice. For example, in early 1966, it was the right policy for the Federal Reserve to move in a less expansionary direction—though it should have done so at least a year earlier. But when it moved, it went too far, producing the sharpest change in the rate of monetary growth of the postwar era. Again, having gone too far, it was the right policy for the Fed to reverse course at the end of 1966. But again it went too far, not only restoring but exceeding the earlier excessive rate of monetary growth. And this episode is no exception. Time and again this has been the course followed—as in 1919 and 1920, in 1937 and 1938, in 1953 and 1954, in 1959 and 1960.

The reason for the propensity to overreact seems clear: the failure of monetary authorities to allow for the delay between their actions and the subsequent effects on the economy. They tend to determine their actions by today's conditions—but their actions will affect the economy only six or nine or twelve or fifteen months later. Hence they feel impelled to step on the brake, or the accelerator, as the case may be, too hard.

My own prescription is still that the monetary authority go all the way in avoiding such swings by adopting publicly the policy of achieving a steady rate of growth in a specified monetary total. The precise rate of growth, like the precise monetary total, is less important than the adoption of some stated and known rate. I myself have argued for a rate that would on the average achieve rough stability in the level of prices of final products, which I have estimated would call for something like a 3 to 5 per cent per year rate of growth in currency plus all commercial bank deposits or a slightly lower rate of growth in currency plus demand deposits only.[5] But it would be better to have a fixed rate that would on the average produce moderate inflation or moderate deflation, provided it was steady, than to suffer the wide and erratic perturbations we have experienced.

Short of the adoption of such a publicly stated policy of a steady rate of monetary growth, it would constitute a major improvement if the monetary authority followed the self-denying ordinance of avoiding wide swings. It is a matter of record that periods of relative stability in the rate of monetary growth have also been periods of relative stability in economic activity, both in the United States and other countries. Periods of wide swings in the rate of monetary growth have also been periods of wide swings in economic activity.

By setting itself a steady course and keeping to it, the monetary authority could make a major contribution to promoting economic stability. By making that course one of steady but moderate growth in the quantity of money, it would make a major contribution to avoidance of either inflation or deflation of prices. Other forces would still affect the economy, require change and adjustment, and disturb the even tenor of our ways. But steady monetary growth would provide a monetary climate favorable to the effective operation of those basic forces of enterprise, ingenuity, invention, hard work, and thrift that are the true springs of economic growth. That is the most that we can ask from monetary policy at our present stage of knowledge. But that much—and it is a great deal—is clearly within our reach.

8

Controversy over the effectiveness and timing of monetary policy continues among professional economists. A prominent former member of the Council of Economic Advisers reviews two conflicting views of the role of money. He points out that complexities of the economic system make it difficult to demonstrate the real importance of money as a causal factor in changing economic activity and that, therefore, varied economic policy responses are necessary in managing the economy.

TWO VIEWS OF THE ROLE OF MONEY

James Tobin

James Tobin is Sterling Professor of Economics at Yale University and a former member of the Council of Economic Advisers.

From *Controlling Monetary Aggregates,* Federal Reserve Bank of Boston, 1969, pp. 21–24.

. . .

I will concentrate on the question of evidence, which is crucial to the great debate.

[5] In an as yet unpublished article on "The Optimum Quantity of Money," I conclude that a still lower rate of growth, something like 2 per cent for the broader definition, might be better yet in order to eliminate or reduce the difference between private and total costs of adding to real balances.

One kind of evidence, which has been presented at some length, is timing evidence: namely, the leads of changes in stock of money, or of changes in the rate of change of the stock of money, or of other monetary aggregates over income, or over the rate of change of income or over other measures of economic activity. A large amount of the work of Friedman and Schwartz in their

Monetary History of the U.S. 1867–1960 and in their article, "Money and Business Cycles," is concerned precisely with pinning down these timing patterns. Dave Meiselman [has] mentioned timing evidence . . . also. Now I think it is clear that timing evidence—leads, lags and so on—is no evidence about causation whatsoever. This is argued very eloquently, and I think correctly, by Solow, Kareken, and Brown in their CMC paper.

I have engaged in a little irreverent exercise which constructs two models: on the one hand, one of these British models that Paul Samuelson was referring to, an ultra-Keynesian model where money has no causal relationship to anything, and on the other hand, a Friedman-like model in which money is the driving force of the business cycle. I have then compared the timing patterns of money and the change in money relative to money income and the change in income implied by these two different worlds. As it turns out, the Radcliffe world, the ultra-Keynesian world, produces a pattern of leads and lags in business cycles that superficially looks much more like money causing income than the Friedman world in which money actually is causing income. Moreover, the ultra-Keynesian model produces patterns of leads and lags in business cycles which coincide precisely with the summary of empirical results about such timing that appears in the Friedman-Schwartz article, whereas the implications of Friedman's and Schwartz's own theory diverge considerably from their own empirical findings.

Milton Friedman has responded that he knows better than to think that timing evidence has anything to do with causation. If this is stipulated, we can regard as descriptive but irrelevant detail all those pages about timing that an unwary reader might think were there for the purpose of making some point about causation.

There is a related point about evidence, which has to do with the effects on the data of the sins of the Federal Reserve and other monetary authorities in the past. Now let me give you a ridiculous example to make the point. Don't take it too seriously. Suppose that some statistician observes that over a long period of time there is a high association, a very good fit, between gross national product and the sales of, let us say, shoes. And then suppose someone comes along and says, "That's a very good relationship. Therefore, if we want to control GNP, we ought to control production of shoes. So, henceforth, we'll make shoes grow in production precisely at 4 per cent per year, and that will make GNP do the same." I don't think you would have much confidence in drawing this second conclusion and policy recommendations from the observed empirical association.

Over the years, according to the monetarists, the Federal Reserve has been acting like the producers and sellers of shoes. That is, the Fed has been supplying money on demand from the economy instead of using the money supply to control the economy. The Fed has looked at the wrong targets and the wrong indicators. As a result, the Fed has allowed the supply of money to creep up when the demand for money rose as a result of expansion in business activity and to fall when business activity has slacked off. This criticism implies that the supply of money has, in fact, not been an exogenously controlled variable over the period of observation. It has been an endogenous variable, responding to changes in economic conditions and credit market indicators via whatever response mechanism was built into the men in this room and their predecessors.

The evidence of association between money and income reflects, to a very large degree, this response mechanism of the Federal Reserve and the monetary authorities. It cannot be used simultaneously to support the reverse conclusion: namely that what they have done is the *cause* of the changes in income and GNP. Perhaps the monetarists will be sufficiently persuasive of the Federal Reserve and of Congressional committees to bring about, in the future, a controlled experiment in which the stock of money is actually an exogenous variable.

Much evidence has been presented purporting to show the superior power of monetary variables over fiscal variables and private investment measures in explaining changes in GNP. This evidence comes in what I call pseudo-reduced-forms.

The meaning of the term *reduced-form* is this: If you think of the economy as really a complex set of equations—basic structural relationships describing business investment, demands for loans, demands for money, the consumption function and so on—conceivably you could solve such a system and relate the variables in which you are ultimately interested, such as GNP, to the truly exogenous variables including the instruments of the monetary and fiscal authorities. Such a solution of a big complicated model you would call a *reduced-form*. And then one possible way of estimating a model of the system would be not to estimate the structural equations, the building blocks of the system, but to estimate the condensed equations which relate the ultimate outputs like GNP to the ultimate causal factors. That would be reduced-form estimation.

There are a lot of difficulties in that procedure. Therefore, most builders of big and small models of the economy do not proceed in that way; but, instead, try to estimate the individual structural equations one by one. What I mean by a pseudo-reduced-form is an equation relating an ultimate variable of interest, like GNP, to the supposedly causal variables, but one which doesn't come out of any structure at all. Instead, the investigator just says, "Here are the effects and here are the

causes, let's just throw them into an equation." The form and content of the equation—the list of variables and the lag structure—are not derived from any structural model. That is what we have had presented to us as the main evidence for the supposed superiority of monetary variables in explaining GNP.

When, in contrast, we try to take a *theory* of how money affects the economy and test it in the form it is presented, we have to look at one of two things: either a demand for money equation, or some complicated set of linkage equations through which changes in the money stock affect investment demand, consumption demand, etc. As far as the demand for money equation is concerned, as Paul Samuelson mentioned, the crucial assumption of some monetarists is that interest rate variables are of no importance, so that there is a tight linkage between the stock of money and GNP. If real GNP and prices, current and lagged, are the only important factors in the demand for money balances, then we know that control of money stock is uniquely decisive, and we don't have to look elsewhere in the system. However, all the tests that I know in which interest rates are allowed to enter demand for money equations, indicate that interest rates have important explanatory power.

If we do not really know that the demand for money is exclusively determined by income, then things other than income may absorb changes in money supply. There is no short cut. We have to look for the effects of changes in the stock of money, and it is hard work. We have to look through the system of structural equations to see how money enters directly and indirectly into investment demand and consumption demand and so on. We have to examine long chains of causation. In those chains there could be many slips, and there could be many structural changes, innovations in markets and institutions.

That is the purpose, I suppose, of the hard work involved in large econometric models, work which these other attempts to find evidence try to short-circuit completely.

9

MONETARY POLICY

G. L. Bach

Professor Bach, noting that the links between monetary actions by the Federal Reserve and economic outcomes are unclear at best, argues for a flexible approach to the use of monetary policy. Money would normally be allowed to grow at a roughly stable rate, but growth of the money supply would be altered to fit particular circumstances, such as excessive unemployment or shifts in the liquidity demand for money.

G. L. Bach is Frank E. Buck Professor of Economics and Public Policy at Stanford University, and a frequent adviser to the Federal Reserve on monetary policy.

From *Making Monetary and Fiscal Policy* (Washington, D.C.: Brookings Institution, 1971), pp. 201-5. Reprinted by permission.

. . .

In acting to meet national economic goals, the Federal Reserve cannot operate directly on aggregate demand, output, employment, and commodity prices. Monetary authorities conduct open market operations and change reserve requirements and discount rates, working through intermediate policy variables—the money stock (M_1), money plus time deposits (M_2), the monetary base, free reserves, interest rates, and money market conditions.

In principle, monetary policymakers should be able to forecast the course of aggregate demand in the absence of policy changes, and should know the lags and the impact of Federal Reserve measures operating through the intermediate policy variables. But the links between ultimate goals, intermediate variables, and Federal Reserve actions are not completely clear; nor is it possible to forecast the economy's performance with a satisfactory degree of accuracy. Despite these uncertainties, in reaching policy decisions the monetary authorities must decide, explicitly or implicitly, which of the intermediate targets are pertinent, the probable effects on ultimate goals, and what lags to assume.

1. *Pending further clarification of the link between money and the "real" economy, the Federal Reserve should operate on the principle that there should be roughly stable growth in the monetary aggregates (the monetary base or the money stock).*

2. *Nonetheless, it should have substantial discretionary authority to adjust monetary policy to particular circumstances, which authority may require deviations from the stable growth rule.*

The Federal Reserve has substantial (but not complete) power to control the money stock through the monetary base; and empirical evidence shows a reasonably close, though somewhat variable, relationship between growth in the monetary aggregates and money gross national product (GNP). At least in big depressions and big inflations, changes in the monetary base and money (M_1 or M_2) clearly play an important independent causal role, an essential reinforcing role, or both. In lesser fluctuations, the evidence is less clear as to whether changes in M_1 and M_2 are the cause or the effect of changes in aggregate spending. Clearly, other intermediate variables (interest rates, free reserves, and money market conditions) are jointly affected by actions of both monetary policymakers and the private sector of the economy. They are therefore only partly controllable by monetary policymakers. In terms of monetary theory, there may be important shifts in the demand for money, which would be destabilizing in the absence of offsetting actions by the Federal Reserve, and these shifts affect the impact of any action by the Reserve authorities to change the stock of money.

Most economists argue that monetary changes affect aggregate demand through interest rates, yields on, and prices of, other assets, and changes in the availability of credit. This reasoning suggests that interest rates, multiple credit flows, and free reserves of banks are important intermediate variables for policymakers. Other economists suggest that changes in M_1 or M_2 *directly* affect consumer and business spending, though how this effect occurs is not entirely clear. This reasoning suggests that the Federal Reserve should watch primarily the monetary aggregates and focus on stabilizing their growth. Both groups agree that in periods of substantial inflation, quoted market interest rates lose a substantial part of their validity as indicators of monetary tightness, because an uncertain inflation allowance is added to the "real" rate by both borrowers and lenders. Both agree, further, that it will be impossible for the monetary authorities simultaneously to stabilize interest rates *and* the growth rate of M_1 or M_2 if the public's demand for money shifts. And both agree that, while the Federal Reserve can more or less closely control the nominal money stock (M_1 or M_2), it cannot thereby necessarily control

real output and *real* interest rates. If it issues more money than the public wants to hold at prevailing prices, increased public spending will produce inflation until the *real* purchasing power of the money stock (what economists call "real money") is at the level the public wants to hold.

To choose one intermediate variable (such as stable growth in M_1 or M_2) as the *sole* guide to monetary policy, given these uncertainties, would be irresponsible. Different intermediate variables may be important at different times and under different circumstances; there is no reason to expect simple one-channel relationships among the economic variables in a complex world. Both monetary history and theory present a strong case for at least reasonably stable growth in the monetary aggregates, roughly parallel to growth in the economy's aggregate production potential, as a protection against massive depressions or inflations. But, since the demand for money may shift for a variety of reasons, the Federal Reserve needs to be prepared to offset such shifts if they threaten to be seriously destabilizing.

Therefore, pending further theoretical and empirical clarification of monetary policy—real economy linkages, Federal Reserve officials should operate with a strong but rebuttable presumption that the monetary aggregates should be increased at a stable growth rate. But they should also keep a sharp eye on other potentially important target variables and exercise their best judgment on the basis of this continuing analysis. And they should be prepared to let the money growth rate vary, if there is a convincing reason to do so, with the changing conditions.

This policy would not guarantee a stabilizing monetary policy, given the authorities' imperfect forecasting ability and uncertainty as to the lags involved. It would move monetary policy to a more stable base, however, while preserving flexibility for the authorities to act counter to the presumption of stable growth of *M* in case of clear need.

This flexibility is essential for several reasons: (a) There is no guarantee that fiscal policy miscalculations will not require Federal Reserve counteraction to maintain overall stability. (b) Even with good fiscal policy, international disturbances may re-require monetary policy offsets, as may fluctuations in spending on business plant and equipment and inventory spending in the private sector. (c) Shifts may occur in the public's demand for money that would destabilize spending if *M* were held constant. (d) Conceivably a massive liquidity crisis like that of 1929–33 could develop again, with an enormous increase in the demand for money. In such an event, the Federal Reserve should be free to, and expected to, pour into the economy whatever amount of base money (liquidity) is needed to check the contraction; this is the most important monetary lesson learned from the great depression. And (e) "defensive" Federal Reserve open market operations are often useful in offsetting temporary minor disturbances to the financial markets from Treasury financing, variations in float and international flows of funds, erratic flows in particular domestic credit markets, and the like—although the Reserve authorities have been overly concerned with financial market stability in the past.

. . .

10

Economists disagree about the relative merits of various theories of the effects of money, and construct elaborate mathematical models to prove their point. Here, one Federal Reserve policymaker describes how he uses economic models in policy decisions, and makes a strong case for models that trace the consequences of actual monetary actions rather than models that examine nonoperational economic relationships.

THE USEFULNESS OF APPLIED ECONOMETRICS TO THE POLICYMAKER

Darryl Francis

Darryl Francis is President of the Federal Reserve Bank of Saint Louis.

From the *Federal Bank of Saint Louis Review*, Vol. 55 (May 1973), pp. 7–10.

. . .

Since I am not a builder of econometric models or a practicing econometrician or statistician, I shall speak today as a consumer of the results of econometric models. In broad terms I shall discuss what I expect from my research staff and how I fold the products of their labors into my policy recommendations.

Policymakers' stabilization actions are arrived at through their judgment about the general course of economic activity and the effectiveness of various tools available to them. All policymakers have some view of how the economy operates and how their actions affect the economy. This concept or hypothesis is usually based on years of experience and generally is not formulated as rigorously as an econometric model.

I believe that the concepts policymakers form about the operation of the economy should be constantly subjected to rigorous scientific analysis. Econometric models provide a valuable means of formulating and testing our hypotheses about the economy that can then be subjected to statistical analysis. In other words, we can determine whether our beliefs hold water or have big holes in them.

Before getting into specifics, let me make a few general remarks about the context within which I see a role for scientific research. Most of what has been done by our staff over the years has begun with the formulation of testable, and therefore deniable, statements or hypotheses. Specifically, we frequently begin merely with the statement of a policymaker to the effect that if a specific event should occur, then certain subsequent events will occur. We then seek to formulate such a statement into a hypothesis in such a way that it is not a truism. To do so, we state the conditions which would be acceptable as a denial or rejection of the hypothesis.

Let me illustrate the importance of this by doing the opposite. Suppose someone makes a statement such as "More rainfall may or may not result in a larger corn crop." That statement is empty of content since there is no event which would falsify it. In a nutshell, to engage in worthwhile research, we must be willing to be wrong. This has been the underlying philosophy of our research efforts. We seek to pursue our theoretical formulation and empirical testing in a professional manner, and then to present our results for all to examine. If subsequent events should prove us wrong,

then we will accept it. In this manner economic knowledge is advanced.

As a Federal Reserve policymaker I must live in the real world. Therefore, advice from my staff that I should support a policy that would shift the LM curve is of very little use to me. As a member of the Federal Open Market Committee, I know that the actions I can vote for are changes in Federal Reserve holdings of Government securities. As President of a Federal Reserve Bank, I can recommend to our Board of Directors that they should submit a change in our Banks' discount rate. I cannot recommend to the Open Market Committee that the LM curve should be shifted one way or another. I can only recommend actions in terms of the instruments at hand. The justification for my position must be couched in terms of the probable effects on prices and employment.

In recent years, especially with the advent of computers, there has been a great surge in the amount of mathematics and statistics used by economists. Although the mathematical trappings of economics may not seem too impressive to trained mathematicians, to most policymakers, who have only a limited background in math, they pose a formidable barrier to understanding how economists derive their results. The bewildering struggles that occur between model builders over specification errors, structural versus reduced-form models, recursive versus non-recursive systems, etc., are meaningless to most policymakers.

This is not meant to deny the usefulness of math and statistics. These are very powerful tools, and their use has helped to advance knowledge in many fields of science. However, math is not an empirical science. When it comes down to the time of making a policy recommendation, I must still have a concrete interpretation in terms of open market operations. Also, beyond being told what to expect from a given policy action, I want to have some understanding of how the results are obtained.

The type of economic models that policymakers use depends largely upon the goals of their business. For example, the goal of General Motors is to produce and sell automobiles in order to maximize the net wealth of their stockholders. Therefore, GM policymakers would be interested in understanding the factors influencing the demand for autos and being able to forecast such demand.

The goal of the Federal Reserve, at least as I view it, is to promote high-employment growth without inflation. As a monetary policymaker, I am interested in what the Fed can do to achieve these goals. Therefore, I have directed our research staff to investigate the process by which Federal Reserve actions influence economic activity.

First, I wanted to determine what measure of Federal Reserve actions was most closely related to aggregate economic activity. Through extensive research we have concluded that changes in the money stock provide a highly reliable means of gauging the effect of monetary actions on total spending. However, recognition of this fact alone was only half the battle. To be at all useful in policy recommendations, it was necessary to determine whether, with its available policy instruments, the Federal Reserve could control the growth rate of money. Study of other economists' work, as well as our own investigative efforts, has proved conclusively that the money stock *can* be controlled with a relatively high degree of accuracy.

I think it is important at this point to make a distinction between monetary *actions* and monetary *policy*. For my purposes I am not solely interested in a measure of the intentions of policymakers. I am primarily interested in the results of their

actions. If the effect of monetary actions is to accelerate money stock growth and hence accelerate inflation, that is of interest to me even if the *intent* of policy was to keep interest rates from rising.

If his research is to be of use to a policymaker, an economist must be able to tell me the results to be expected from a particular course of action. For example, if the Open Market Committee takes some action, such as directing the Trading Desk at the New York Federal Reserve Bank to slow money stock growth, I would like to know what this means in terms of the growth of total spending, output, and prices. There are two extreme situations that are not very useful to policymakers. One involves magnitudes they control absolutely, but that have no effect on, or any relationship to, an ultimate policy objective. The other involves magnitudes that seem to be good causal predictors, but which are completely outside the control of the policymakers.

An economist must state his recommendations in a form that has empirical content. I am not primarily interested in statements that express relationships in abstract terms. I want to know what operations to direct the Desk to perform and how and when the performance of these operations will affect the prices people pay for goods and services and the number of people employed.

Therefore, it is not enough for my research staff to tell me that the Fed *can* control the money stock. As a member of the Open Market Committee, I know the Federal Reserve buys and sells Government securities; it does not fly a blimp across the land dumping out money. The assertion "the Fed can control the money stock" must be given empirical content in terms of what the Fed can directly control. The result of this demand for an operational procedure has led us to the use of the monetary base concept and the development of a procedure for determining the effects of a growth rate of base on growth of the money stock.

Here, I feel it necessary to say that I think it should be required of others who recommend that the Federal Reserve control different variables, such as interest rates, that they also provide policymakers with an operational means of achieving this control. It is wrong to accept at face value the statement "the Fed can control interest rates" without the corresponding explanation of *how* the Fed can do this, and what the consequences would be of doing so.

As a policymaker, I am primarily concerned with projection of where the ultimate goals are tending and what will be the effect on these goals if, for instance, the rate of growth of the money stock is altered. Therefore, we build models to help us understand the effect of growth of the money stock on policy goals.

As an example of our attempts to use models to understand the effects of monetary policy on the economy, I could mention the so-called "St. Louis Model." The original equation of this model was developed to test competing conjectures about the relative strengths of the growth of the money stock and fiscal actions. How do monetary and fiscal policy actions interact? Does money matter? Can the Fed continue an expansionary policy and force fiscal policy to bear the burden of restraint? As you can see, these are questions of great importance to a policymaker.

Once the computers have stopped running and my research staff has analyzed the results, I consider these results in my policy recommendations, keeping several points in mind. First, I am aware that no model is the absolute truth. All models have had their hours of glory in addition to their periods that their creators would prefer not to mention. Second, when attempting to see into the future, it is useful to compare the results of more than one model. When the results diverge substantially, this is frequently of more value than when all models give pretty much the same results. A divergence forces us to examine the reasons for the discrepancies and carefully think about the implications of the causes of these differences. Third, all the results of models must be examined to see if they are consistent with our accumulated evidence from history, theory, and practical experience.

My personal preference is for small models, rather than large models. This stems partly from my view that the Federal Reserve should be concerned with the aggregate effects of policy, and should leave the allocative effects to the operation of the market place. Also, not being a practicing econometrician, I prefer models whose operation I can understand. I am willing to trade some so-called "structural richness," much of which refers to matters I do not consider to be the proper concern of monetary policymakers, for an ability to understand the process by which the model arrives at its results. I have never been willing to simply accept the results of any model. As a policymaker, I want to know as fully as possible the basis for my policy recommendations.

In addition to forecasting, policymakers are also interested in planning. Forecasts give us some idea of where the economy is headed, given past policy actions. However, our job does not end with attempts to analyze the effects of policy actions on the economy and to forecast subsequent events. We must also engage in planning. This involves determining desired future values for prices and employment and deciding how to achieve these goals. At the planning stage, both understanding of the economic process and forecasting future developments must blend together. When we seek to influence the course of prices and employment, our research staff is required to use all of its knowledge about forces influencing the economy in order to monitor forecasts of the effects of changes in policy.

These forecasts, upon which we depend in deciding our course of action, involve some assessment of the pattern of developments to be expected following a certain action. Let me be more specific. It is not sufficient for an economist to tell us that a slower growth in money will eventually result in a slower rate of price increase. As a policymaker, I would like to have better information as to the specific open market transactions that would achieve, with a high probability, a desired growth of money. I am also vitally concerned with the time distribution to be expected with regard to changes in prices and output for a given change in the rate of growth of money. Then I want to know how some tangible results can be expected with regard to prices and output, and how the pattern will appear in the data subsequently reported.

Economic research can never tell policymakers what are "good" or "just" policy goals. However, by giving the policymakers an indication of the expected results of different policy actions, economic research can provide a valuable service.

As much as politicians hate to admit it, we live in a world of trade-offs. One of the gravest diseases afflicting rational policymaking is the refusal to accept the fact that we cannot always "have our cake and eat it too." I well remember a couple of years ago the recommendation of the Joint Economic Committee of Congress that called for the attainment of a 2 per cent rate of inflation and a 3 per cent unemployment rate in a short period of time. All accumulated economic research indicated that these two goals were mutually incompatible in the foreseeable future.

Frequently in the past six years we at the Federal Reserve have found ourselves perched on the horns of a dilemma where failure to slow money growth meant accelerating inflation, but slowing money growth meant rising interest rates. Unfortunately, rather than recognize the short-run trade-off implied by economic research, we have ended up with both accelerating inflation and higher interest rates, rather than less inflation *and* lower interest rates that longer-range policy planning could have provided.

Monetary policy cannot "fine-tune" out all fluctuations in economic activity. However, given the current state of economic knowledge, monetary policy can avoid inducing a high rate of inflation or a recession in the economy. Thus, I would like policy to remain neutral with regard to cyclical movements in economic activity rather than run the risk of reinforcing them. I believe econometric models have been an aid to policymakers in outlining the available alternatives, and, therefore, have added to rational policymaking.

. . .

11

THE NEW LOOK IN TAX AND FISCAL POLICY

Conflicting policy goals confront the government's economic policy makers at every turn. A leading economist
suggests how we may be able to achieve apparently conflicting ends by using a proper "mix" of fiscal and monetary policies.

Paul A. Samuelson

*Paul A. Samuelson is Professor of Economics at Massa-
chusetts Institute of Technology.*

From U.S. Congress, Joint Economic Committee, *Federal Tax Policy for
Economic Growth and Stability;* papers submitted by panelists appearing
before the Subcommittee on Tax Policy, Joint Economic Committee on
the Economic Report, 9 November 1955, pp. 229–34.

I

There is much talk about taxes. When I flick on the dial of my radio in the morning, I hear a congressman quoted on how our high level of taxes is ruining the Nation or a senator's tape-recorded alarm over the unfair burden the poor man has to carry because the administration has been favoring big business. My morning paper at breakfast brings me the view of its editor that the United States has been pursuing unsound fiscal policy for the last 25 years. Scratch the barber who cuts my hair and you find a philosopher ready to prescribe for the Nation's monetary ills.

This is as it should be. We expect sweeping statements in a democracy. We hope that out of the conflict of extreme views there will somehow emerge a desirable compromise. Yet such sweeping statements have almost no validity from a scientific, or even from a leisurely common-sense point of view: spend as little as a year going over the factual experience of American history and of other economies, devote as little as a month to calm analysis of probable cause and effect, or even spend a weekend in a good economics library—and what will you find? Will you find that there breathes any-

where in the world an expert so wise that he can tell you which of a dozen major directions of policy is unquestionably the best? You will not. Campaign oratory aside, the more assuredly a man asserts the direction along which salvation is alone to be found, the more patently he advertises himself as an incompetent or a charlatan.

The plain truth is this, and it is known to anyone who has looked into the matter: The science of economics does not provide simple answers to complex social problems. It does not validate the view of the man who thinks the world is going to hell, nor the view of his fellow idiot that ours is the best of all possible tax systems.

I do not wish to be misunderstood. When I assert that economic science cannot give unequivocal answers to the big questions of policy, I do not for a moment imply that economists are useless citizens. Quite the contrary. They would indeed be useless if any sensible man could quickly infer for himself simple answers to the big policy questions of fiscal policy. No need then to feed economists while they make learned studies of the obvious. It is precisely because public policy in the tax and expenditure area is so complex that we find it absolutely indispensable to invest thousands of man-years of scholarly time in scholarly economic research in these areas.

Make no mistake about it. The arguments that we all hear every day of our lives on the burning partisan issues have in every case been shaped by economists—by economists in universities, in business, in Government, and by that rarest of all birds, the shrewd self-made economist. What economists do not know about fiscal policy turns out, on simple examination, not to be known by anyone.

II

With this necessary preamble out of the way, let me record the general views that studies have led me to, about the current state of our fiscal system. This will clear the way for a more detailed analysis of taxes and growth, taxes and stable full employment, taxes and equity, taxes and the level of public expenditure programs.

Here then are the major facts about our system as I see them.

1. The postwar American economy is in good shape. There is nothing artificial or unsound about its underpinnings. For more than a decade we have had generally high employment opportunities. Our production efficiency has been growing at a steady rate that compares well with anything in our history or in the history of countries abroad. For all this we must, in our present-day mixed economy, be grateful to both public and private institutions.

2. The existing structure of Federal, state, and local taxes is in its broad features highly satisfactory. Repeatedly at the polls and through all the legitimate processes of government the citizens of this Republic have indicated that they want our present type of fiscal structure—its substantial dependence at the Federal level on personal and corporate income taxes, its eclectic dependence on selective excises, on payroll

levies for social security, on property and sales taxes at the local levels. If the consensus of citizens in our democracy were to be other than it is—toward less or more equalitarianism, toward less or more local autonomy—there is no reason that the careful analytic economist can see why our fiscal system is not capable of being altered in the desired direction. In other words, there is nothing in the mechanics of a modern economy which makes it impossible or difficult for the citizenry to get the kind of a tax system that they want; our tax system has plenty of give, plenty of room for adaptation and change.

All the above does not imply that we are living in a new era of perfection. The American economy now faces, and will continue to face, many tough problems, many hard decisions. And, to be sure, there are numerous imperfections, inconsistencies, and loopholes in the present tax structure; these do need improving.

What the optimistic diagnosis of the modern-day economist does contradict is the following:

1. The view that America has long since departed from an orthodox fiscal policy and that it is only a matter of time until a grim Mother Nature exacts retribution from us for our folly in departing from the narrow line of fiscal rectitude. (This is a philosophical position that any dissenter from current trends is free to assume; but it is not a factually verifiable view about reality that dispassionate study of statistics and facts can substantiate.)

2. The view, shared in by the extremes of both left and right wings, that our economy generally is moving in unsound directions so that we must ultimately end up in some unnamed disaster or convulsion. (In terms of business-cycle stability and efficient growth, the United States has in the last dozen years dramatically refuted the sour expectations both of those who look

back on a fictitious past golden age and of collectivists who look forward to a golden age that only a revolution can usher in.)

III

Turning now to the goals of any tax system, we can ask: What tax structure will give us the most rapid rate of growth? What tax system will give us the highest current standard of living? What tax structure will make our system most immune to the ups and downs in employment and prices that make American families insecure? What tax structure will realize most closely the community's sense of fairness and equity? What tax structure will have the least distorting effects on our use of economic resources, instead of maximizing the efficiency with which we produce what our citizens most want?

Upon careful thought it will be obvious that there cannot exist a tax system which will simultaneously maximize these five quite different goals of social life.

It is easy to see that high current living standards and rapid growth of our ability to produce are conflicting ends: you have only to look at a collectivized society like the Soviet Union, which decides to sacrifice consumption levels of the current generation in favor of a crash program of industrialization; you have only to reflect that historically in the slums of Manchester working families might have lived longer in the 19th century if England and the other nations had during the industrial revolution slowed down their rates of material progress; you have only to consider the problem of conserving scarce exhaustible natural resources to realize that every society must all the time be giving up higher future resource potentials in favor of keeping current generation consumption as high as it is.

You can imagine a society that decides to devote its income in excess of the bare physiological existence level 100 per cent to capital formation. You can imagine it—but there never has been such a society. Nor would any of us want to live in such a one. It should be obvious, therefore, that no sane person would ever seek a tax program which literally maximized our rate of economic growth. (Yet how many times over the chicken a la king have we all heard speakers reiterate this nonsensical goal.) It is just as obvious that no sane person would want to maximize present living levels if this meant eating up all our capital on a consumption bender that would leave us an impoverished Nation.

There is no need to go through all the other pairs of the five listed goals to show their partial incompatibility. If we are willing to frame a tax system that strongly favors thrifty men of wealth, we may thereby be able to add to our rate of current growth; if we encourage a gentle rate of inflation, we may be able to increase the profits in the hands of the quick-reacting businessman, perhaps thereby stepping up our rate of growth. So it goes, and one could easily work through the other permutations and combinations.

But not all of our five goals are necessarily competing. Some, when you realize them, help you to realize the others. If we succeed in doing away with the great depressions that have dogged the economic record, we may thereby add to our rate of growth. If we shape a graduated-tax system that enables lower income groups to maintain minimum standards of life, we may ease the task of stabilizing business activity. If we replace distorting taxes by less distorting alternatives, the fruits of the resulting more efficient production can add to our current consumption and to our rate of progress in capital formation.

I shall not prolong the discussion of the degree to which the diverse goals of tax policy are competing or complementary. For it will turn out that we can formulate proper policies without having to measure these important, but complicated, relationships.

IV

Upon being told by the economist that it is absurd for Congress to aim at the most rapid rate of growth possible and that it is equally absurd for Congress to aim at the highest possible current level of consumption, the policymaker may be tempted to say: "I understand that. Won't you therefore as an economist advise us as to just what is the best possible compromise between these extremes?"

A good question but, unfortunately, not one that the expert economist can pretend to give a unique answer to. If he is honest, he must reply: "The American people must look into their own hearts and decide on what they consider to be the best compromise rate of growth."

Just because I have advanced degrees in economics and have written numerous esoteric works in the field, I am not thereby empowered to let my personal feelings, as to how much the present generation ought to sacrifice in favor of generations to come, become a prescription for society. It would be as presumptuous for me to offer such specific advice as to let my family's notions about dental care determine how much the typical American family ought to spend on toothpaste. But it is legitimate for me as an economist to say this: Whatever rate of capital formation the American people want to have, the American system can, by proper choice of fiscal and monetary programs, contrive to do. This can be shown by an example.

Suppose the vast majority of the American people look into the future or across the Iron Curtain at the rate of progress of others. Suppose they decide that we ought to have a more rapid rate of capital formation and technological development than

we have been having recently. Then the economist knows this can be brought into being (a) by means of an expansionary monetary policy that makes investment funds cheaper and easier to get. Admittedly, such an expanded investment program will tend, if it impinges on an employment situation that is already full and on a price level that is already stationary, to create inflationary price pressures and overfull employment—unless something is done about it. What would have to be done about this inflationary pressure? Clearly (b) a tight fiscal policy would be needed to offset the expansionary monetary policy: By raising taxes relative to expenditure, we would reduce the share of consumption out of our full employment income, releasing in this way the real resources needed for investment. (It should be unnecessary to go through the reverse programs which would be called for if the national decision were to slow down the rate of capital formation as compared to that of recent years.)

From these remarks it will be clear that economic science is not only neutral as to the question of the desired rate of capital accumulation—it is also neutral as to the ability of the economy to realize any decided-on rate of capital formation.

I repeat: With proper fiscal and monetary policies, our economy can have full employment and whatever rate of capital formation and growth it wants.

V

The optimistic doctrine that our economy can have stability and the rate of growth it wants may seem rather novel. Perhaps even a little shocking. But there are worse surprises yet to come.

The reader may think that my argument rests on something like the following reasoning:

Suppose that political party R is more

concerned with progress than political party D, which shows a greater concern for the little man, with security, and with current consumption. Then if the Nation gives its approval to the general policy goals of R, the Government will have to change its emphasis away from reducing taxes on individuals—particularly rapid-spending lower-income people; and it will have to change its emphasis toward reducing taxes on business, in an attempt to bolster the incentives toward investment. In short, it is by changing the qualitative pattern of taxation, by sacrificing equity to incentive, that the community succeeds in getting higher levels of capital formation when it desires such higher levels.

I predict that much of the testimony before this subcommittee will proceed along these lines. Certainly much of the political discussion of the last three years, when it has had the courage to be frank, has been along these lines.

But this is not at all the train of thought that I wish to emphasize in my testimony. I want to cap the daring doctrine that an economy can have the rate of capital formation it wants with a doctrine that may seem even more shocking. Naturally, I cannot here develop all of the underlying reasoning, nor give all the needed qualifications. But I do in advance want to stress the earnestness with which I put it forward and to underline that it does spring from careful use of the best modern analyses of economics that scholars here and abroad have over the years been able to attain. The doctrine goes as follows:

A community can have full employment, can at the same time have the rate of capital formation it wants, and can accomplish all this compatibly with the degree of income-redistributing taxation it ethically desires.

This is not the place to give a detailed proof of the correctness of this general proposition. It will suffice to illustrate it with two extreme examples.

In the first, suppose that we desire a much higher rate of capital formation but stipulate that it is to be achieved by a tax structure that favors low-income families rather than high-income. How can this be accomplished? It requires us to have an active expansionary policy (open-market operations, lowering of reserve requirements, lowered rediscount rates, governmental credit agencies of the FHA and RFC type if desired) which will stimulate investment spending. However, with our taxes bearing relatively lightly on the ready-spending poor, consumption will tend to be high at the same time that investment is high. To obviate the resulting inflationary pressure, an increase in the overall tax take with an overly balanced budget would be needed.

Alternatively, suppose the community wants a higher level of current consumption and has no wish to make significant redistributions away from the relatively well-to-do and toward the lower income groups. Then a tighter money policy that holds down investment would have to be combined with a fiscal policy of light taxation relative to expenditure. But note that in this case, as in the one just above, any qualitative mix of the tax structure can be offset in its effects by appropriate changes in the overall budget level and in the accompanying monetary policy.

12

This selection reviews the controversy over how much of a "trade-off" between employment and prices exists in a dynamic economy—the so-called "Phillips curve" controversy. It concludes that under some circumstances increased employment can be achieved only at the cost of rising prices, but that in the long run it is far from clear that more inflation will help reduce unemployment.

THE RELATION BETWEEN PRICES AND EMPLOYMENT: TWO VIEWS

Roger W. Spencer

Roger W. Spencer is a business economist with the Federal Reserve Bank of St. Louis.

From *Federal Reserve Bank of St. Louis Review,* March, 1969, pp. 16–21. Reprinted by permission.

. . .

THE STABILITY OF THE PHILLIPS CURVE

An issue of particular importance to policy-makers is the stability of the prices (wages)-employment relationship. Most Trade-Off View studies, by holding constant those factors other than unemployment which determine wages, do not stress fluctuations within a Phillips curve, shifts of the curve itself, or changes in the critical high-employment range. These studies, which rely heavily on regression analysis, often imply that the economy is operating on a single curve, and stabilization actions directed toward guiding the economy to some point off the curve may prove unsuccessful. Such studies, strictly interpreted, indicate that the Phillips curve is a stable relationship.[1] This implication is refuted by Michael Levy, who found that "during the

[1] Stability exists, technically, when the parameters computed for various time periods appear to be drawn from the same underlying population.

postwar years, the basic (Phillips curve) relationship for the U.S. economy between wage rate advances on the one hand, and the unemployment rate, the corporate profit rate, and cost-of-living increases on the other, has been highly unstable." [italics omitted]

Although the relationship may be technically unstable, a plotting of the wage and price changes and the unemployment rate reveals that Phillips' hypothesis—regarding the association of declining unemployment with rapidly rising wages (prices) and rising unemployment with slowly changing wages (prices)—has been generally observable over the past sixteen years. A simple correlation between two variables, as given here by a plotting of points on a two-dimensional graph, does not demonstrate causality, however. The relationship between the rate of change of manufacturing wages and the unemployment rate for the 1953–1968 period is plotted in Figure 1. The curve, which is similar in shape to the curve determined by Phillips, has been arbitrarily drawn to fit the data from 1961 to 1968, a period of uninterrupted eco-

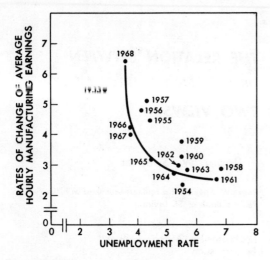

Curve has been arbitrarily fitted to 1961–1968 data.
Data shown are in percentages.

Fig. 1. Rates of change of manufacturing wages and rates of labor unemployment

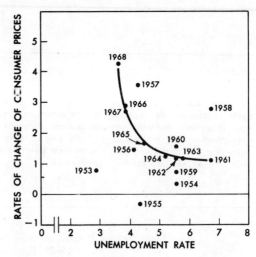

Curve has been arbitrarily fitted to 1961–1968 data.
Data shown are in percentages.

Fig. 2. Rates of change of consumer prices and rates of labor unemployment

nomic expansion.[2] The shape of the curve would be altered to some extent if fitted to the 1953–1960 period. For the sixteen-year period, the curve would be shifted slightly to the right.

Graphical trade-off analysis usually focuses on the wages-unemployment relationship, but it has also been extended to

[2] The 1961 to 1968 curve for the United States mirrors more closely the relationship found by Phillips than do other possible subsets of the sixteen observations. Moreover, the fitting of the curve to the last eight years emphasizes the present position on the "low unemployment-rising wages" portion of the curve. Annual data were used in keeping with Phillips' original work. The problems inherent in using annual data in the Phillips curve relationship are well known. ". . . we regard the construction of a plausible Phillips curve from annual data for a long period as a tour de force somewhat comparable to writing the Lord's Prayer on the head of a pin, rather than as a guide to policy. This is because it is highly probable that the relationship has changed during the period . . . and because of the large changes in some of the variables that take place during the course of a calendar year and are blurred in the annual data." Albert Rees and Mary T. Hamilton, "The Wage-Price-Productivity Perplex," *Journal of Political Economy*, Vol. LXXV (February 1967), p. 70.

the prices-unemployment relationship as has been done in Figure 2. The overall fit for the sixteen-year period would not be as satisfactory as in the previous chart, but there is a close parallel for the past eight years. In some earlier years, sharp price increases occurred at varying rates of unemployment. Unemployment averaged slightly above 4 per cent of the labor force in the 1955 to 1957 period, more than 5 per cent from 1959 to 1960, and a little less than 4 per cent in the 1965 to 1968 period. This evidence suggests that the critical high-employment range has varied, perhaps reflecting the changing nature of the labor force in particular and the economy in general.

Phillips curves derived from regression analysis are based on rather specific assumptions, and the shape can vary substantially when minor modifications of the behavioral assumptions are made, as illustrated by the two following examples. A basic curve derived by George Perry relating consumer prices and unemployment was constructed from an equation in which prices were allowed to respond freely to market pressures. By assuming instead that half of the price increases were autonomous, Perry found that the curve, fairly steeply sloped in the first instance, became relatively flat. In fact, the slope of the curve was less than half of that calculated originally.

Ronald Bodkin determined a near-horizontal linear relation between wages and unemployment. Rees and Hamilton, utilizing the same data and nearly the same assumptions as Bodkin, found a much steeper curve. Their results precipitated the remark:

> Our final caution is that we have been astounded by how many very different Phillips curves can be constructed on reasonable assumptions from the same body of data. The nature of the relationship between wage changes and unemployment is highly sensitive to the exact choice of the other variables that enter the regression and to the forms of all the variables. For this reason, the authors of Phillips curves would do well to label them conspicuously *"Unstable. Apply with extreme care."*

This conclusion implies that the usefulness of such statements as ". . . 4 per cent unemployment is consistent with a 2 per cent rate of inflation if profit rates are at 11.6 per cent. . . ." is limited by the validity of the assumptions which underlie the model.

. . .

THE LONG-RUN EQUILIBRIUM VIEW

The Long-Run Equilibrium View considers the trade-offs between wages or prices and unemployment as transitory phenomena and that no such trade-off exists after factors have completely adjusted to the trend of spending growth. In the short-run there can be a discrepancy between expectations and actual price or wage changes, but not in the long-run. After the discrepancies between expected and actual values have worked themselves out, the only relevant magnitudes are "real," or price-deflated ones.

To illustrate the view, consider the following hypothesized sequence of events in the upswing of a business cycle, beginning with an initial condition of significant unemployment. Monetary or fiscal actions may start an upturn of business activity. Spending occurs in anticipation of a continuation of the price levels which had prevailed in the downswing. Employers begin actively seeking workers to accommodate the rising demand, but wages increase only moderately since a large number of unemployed are seeking jobs. Output and employment rise more rapidly than wages or prices. The remainder of the scenario is outlined by Milton Friedman:

> Because selling prices of products typically respond to an unanticipated rise in nominal demand faster than prices of factors of production, real wages received have gone down—though real wages anticipated by employees went up, since employees implicitly evaluated the wages offered at the earlier price level. Indeed, the simultaneous fall *ex post* in real wages to employers and rise *ex ante* in real wages to employees is what enabled employment to increase. [The nontechnical reader may wish to substitute "anticipated" for *"ex ante"* and "actual" for *"ex post."*] But the decline *ex post* in real wages will soon come to affect anticipations. Employees will start to reckon on rising prices of the things they buy and to demand higher nominal wages for the future. "Market's unemployment is below the "natural" level. There is an excess demand for labor so real wages will tend to rise toward their initial level.

As real wages approach their original level, employers are no longer motivated to hire workers as rapidly or bid up wages so much as in the earlier portion of the upswing. Moreover, rising wages may encourage employers to utilize more labor-saving equipment and relatively fewer workers. As the growth of demand for labor slows, the unemployment rate declines to its "natural" level. Economic units come to anticipate the rate of inflation, and are no longer misled by increases in money income—the so-called "money illusion." The unexpected price increases which accompanied the original expansion of total demand and production caused a temporary reduction of unemployment below the long-run equilibrium level. Only accelerating inflation—a situation in which actual price rises continue to exceed anticipated rises—can keep the actual unemployment rate below the "natural" rate.

Inflation has not been allowed to rise uncontrolled for sustained periods in this country, so little empirical evidence can be amassed to support the contentions that no permanent trade-off exists. In other countries such as Brazil, however, it has been found that sustained inflation does not generate continuous employment gains; in fact, recessions and high unemployment rates have occurred as secular inflation continued. Unanticipated price increases have, in those countries as well as in the United States, generated increased temporary employment, just as unanticipated declines in the rate of price increase have caused temporary rises in unemployment. But if inflation is "fully and instantaneously discounted, the Phillips curve becomes a vertical line over the point of 'equilibrium unemployment.' This is the rate of unemployment where wage increases equal productivity gains plus changes in income shares. The unemployment-price stability trade-off is gone."[3] In other words, there is no particular rate of price change related to a

particular rate of unemployment when the price changes are fully anticipated. Unemployment shifts to its equilibrium value and is consistent with any rate of change of prices. A low rate of unemployment can no longer be "traded-off" against rapidly rising prices, nor can a high unemployment rate be "traded-off" against slowly changing prices.

. . .

Enactment of policies oriented toward eliminating or reducing market imperfections (adjustment costs) will cause the short-run Phillips curve to shift to the left and down. Policies which increase these costs move the short-run Phillips curve upward and to the right. Different forces are at work at different times, causing the curve to shift frequently. Expectations of higher prices will cause the curve to shift upward, and expectations of lower prices move the curve in the opposite direction. The optimal stabilization policies, therefore, would be those which would reduce market adjustment costs and expectations of higher prices. Enactment of such policies would at first move the short-run Phillips curve to the left and downward, and in time, as expectations are fully realized, cause the curve to become a vertical line over the "natural" rate of unemployment.

A hypothetical, long-run relationship between prices and unemployment is presented in Figure 3. Point D represents the "natural" or equilibrium rate of unemployment before market imperfections or adjustment costs are reduced. Curve A represents one of many possible short-run Phillips curves that exist before price changes are fully anticipated. After the rate of inflation becomes fully discounted, the unemployment rate will shift from some point beneath curve A to point D, regardless of whether prices are rising at some slow rate, X, or a rapid rate, Z. The shift may occur along any of an infinite number

[3] Henry C. Wallich, "The American Council of Economic Advisers and the German *Sachverstaendigenrat:* A Study in the Economics of Advice," *The Quarterly Journal of Economics,* (August 1968), pp. 356–57.

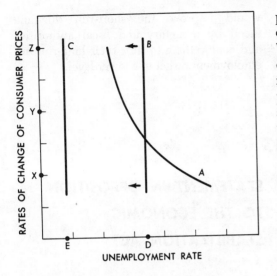

Curve *"A"* is a short-run prices–unemployment relationship.

Vertical line *"B"* is the long-run relationship between prices (fully anticipated regardless of the rate of change) and the "natural" rate of unemployment, *"D"*, before reduction of market "imperfections."

Vertical line *"C"* is a similar long-run relationship between prices and unemployment after assumed reduction of labor and product market imperfections.

Fig. 3. Hypothetical relationships between prices and unemployment

of Phillips curves. The vertical line above point D indicates that no economic units—workers or employers, sellers or consumers, borrowers or lenders—are surprised by price changes. If programs to reduce labor and product market imperfections are implemented, vertical line B will shift, after a transitory period, to the left. Vertical line C represents the new long-run relationship between prices and employment above point E.

. . .

POLICY IMPLICATIONS OF THE TWO VIEWS

Unemployment declined from 5.2 per cent of the labor force in 1964 to 3.5 per cent in 1968. The annual rate of increase in consumer prices rose from 1.3 per cent to 4.2 per cent for corresponding years. These data indicate, according to the Trade-Off View, that stabilization authorities must decide to accept either high rates of price increases in order to maintain low unemployment rates or adopt deflationary measures and accept relatively high levels of unemployment. Only significant reductions of imperfections within the product and labor markets could prevent employment declines in the face of deflationary policies.

Proponents of the Long-Run Equilibrium View point out that even in the absence of structural improvements, monetary and fiscal policies need not be limited by a short-run trade-off between prices and employment. Continuation of expansionary developments will generate either (1) a high, steady rate of inflation which will eventually become fully anticipated and confer no net additional employment benefits (unemployment will gradually return to its "natural" rate), or (2) an accelerating rate of inflation which will permit unemployment to remain below the "natural" rate. Neither expansionary policy alternative appears economically or politically desirable. Deflationary actions would produce increased unemployment (as expectations of price changes are slowly revised) but only temporarily, according to the Equilibrium View. As soon as a new price trend becomes stabilized and fully anticipated, nominal and real wages will coincide, and unemployment will fall to its "natural" rate. An inflationary policy is neither a necessary nor a sufficient condition for the attainment of high levels of employment. Since price expectations seem to change only slowly, actions to reduce the rate of inflation should probably be applied gradually to minimize the transition cost in terms of reduced output and increased unemployment.

Both views recognize the merits of structural measures in complementing monetary and fiscal actions. Policies which reduce the costs of obtaining employment information, improve labor mobility and skills, and eliminate product and labor market monopolies will lower the optimal level of unemployment. Adoption of such policies would improve the short-run dilemma faced by monetary and fiscal authorities and enable them to shift their long-run unemployment target to a lower level.

13

STATEMENT IN OPPOSITION TO THE ECONOMIC STABILIZATION ACT

Leonard Woodcock

During hearings on the Economic Stabilization Act of 1970, Leonard Woodcock, President of the UAW, strongly opposed extension of the Act on grounds that direct controls have never been effective in controlling inflation and probably never will be. His preference is for a voluntary system of wage-price reviews and reliance on the weight of public opinion to restrain inflationary increases.

Leonard Woodcock is President of the United Auto Workers union (UAW).

From U.S. Congress, Senate, *Hearings before the Committee on Banking, Housing and Urban Affairs,* (*Economic Stabilization Legislation—1973*), 93rd Cong., 1st sess., February 1, 1973, pp. 125–128.

. . .

I would like to say on behalf of the UAW that I am here this morning in 1973 to oppose extension of the Economic Stabilization Act.

This has been our consistent position. We opposed the act when it was first suggested in 1970 and we opposed its extension in 1971 and we oppose it at the present time.

It is not because we are inflation-prone. The record of the UAW down through the years shows that we have had a wage and benefit policy which has been consistently counterinflationary.

Of course, we are deeply concerned about inflation. First, because inflation tends to redistribute income in the wrong direction and, second, because inflation or the fear of inflation has been the main inhibiting factor, more properly the excuse, for the failure of our Government to carry out the national commitment to maximum employment and purchasing power expressed in the 1946 Employment Act.

It is a fact that compared with other industrialized countries our record on the employment front is frankly disgraceful.

The U.S. unemployment rate, starting with 1959, the first year for which comparable data began to be compiled, has averaged approximately two and a half times as high as the weighted average for all other countries except Canada for which BLS publishes figures—but Canada's unemployment, unfortunately for them, is largely imported from the United States.

Now, we do not propose that Congress should ignore the inflation problem when we say we oppose the extension of the act. We do propose, as we have many times before, that on a permanent basis there be created a Price-Wage Review Board which through established mechanisms would invoke the power of informed public opinion in those sectors of the economy where price-leading corporations are setting prices, prices set in corporate board rooms and not through the free play of supply and demand.

We oppose the extension of the ESA because it places in the hands of the Executive huge and largely unrestricted powers to impose controls on wages and prices.

It is our firm conviction that outright controls should not be imposed except in clear emergencies because controls inevitably cause distortions, inefficiencies, and inequities that tend to spread throughout the economy.

We believe that price controls in effect since August 1971 have not significantly altered the course that prices would have taken in the absence of those controls.

The Consumer Price Index, which was rising at an annual rate of 6.3 per cent early in 1970, had slowed to a rate of 3.8 per cent during the first 8 months of 1971 before the controls were imposed.

The annual rate of increase from August 1971 through December 1972 was 3.2 per cent.

So, at best, the controls could claim 0.6 of a point.

Weighing that against the inefficiencies and distortions that have been lodged in the economy, we think it is clearly a negative balance.

Now, price controls, we believe, have been essentially meaningless, but wage controls have been quite effective, obviously so.

In the private nonfarm economy for the latest six-month period for which data are available, productivity was rising at an annual rate of 5.8 per cent, which is far above the normal long-trend rate; but the buying power of average hourly compensation of employees increased only 2 per cent a year.

Now, when the Cost of Living Council on January 11, as Phase III began, changed the base period for applying the profit margin standard from the best two out of three years to the best two out of four, and sometimes the best two out of five depending upon the end date of the fiscal year of the particular firm, the Council also gave corporations the alternative of raising prices to reflect increased costs (on a percentage basis, which yields increased unit profits) by an average of 1.5 per cent a year "without limitation as to profit margin."

Now, the profit margin standard was immediately changed in favor of industry without waiting for suggestions from any advisory body, although the provision for the wage and benefit standards continued unchanged with the setting up of the Labor-Management Advisory Committee to make proposals—advisory proposals with regard to that matter.

We believe that that is a good mechanism and obviously my participation on it shows that we are in support of it as long as we have there regulations.

We believe it would have been equally sensible to have involved labor and consumer representatives in advising on the standards to be applied to prices paid by workers and other consumers and, of course, paid to the corporations.

The purpose of the Economic Stabilization Act was stabilization of prices. We think that what should flow from that is that wage increases should be brought under scrutiny only when their effect is to compel price increases or to prevent price reductions that would otherwise be made.

President Truman in an Executive order following V–J Day, a long time ago, invoked that principle of allowing wages to rise without hindrance, so long as increases in wages and benefits would not be used in whole or in part as the basis for seeking an increase in price ceilings or for resisting otherwise justifiable reductions in price ceilings.

Now, wage increases currently are subject to limitations, even when larger amounts would be completely compatible with existing or lower prices.

Prices, on the other hand, are permitted to rise even in cases where profits are already at exorbitant levels; thus, instead of avoiding inequities that inflation creates, the Economic Stabilization Act has been used to aggravate inequities.

Now, all sides can concede that there are other factors that obviously have an inflationary impact. We are told that part of the fight against inflation has been a determination to hold spending below arbitrarily set budget ceilings and it seems quite apparent that the Federal Reserve Board is moving toward tighter money and higher interest rates. And with the combination of all of these things, instead of viewing ESA control powers as the basis for moving full steam ahead toward full employment, the administration and the Federal Reserve Board seem to be applying fiscal and monetary policies that practically guarantee the continuance of very high unemployment.

Thus we believe that under the Economic Stabilization Act the nation suffers all the disadvantages of controls while gaining none of the claimed advantages, neither price stability nor avoidance of inequities nor removal of obstacles to full employment.

I would like to say again, sir, that the three most recent inflations in the United States, including the present one, began at times when unit labor costs were actually declining, when profit margins, far from being squeezed, were actually increasing. We have not had wage-price spirals, but we have had profit-price-wage spirals.

That is why we continue to advocate a permanent Price-Wage Review Board which would rest on a voluntary mechanism, but which would reveal to the whole of the American people the significant economic facts upon which price determinations should be made.

It would be an easily operated mechanism because it would be concerned essentially with the price-dominant companies of whom we estimate there are in the neighborhood of 100, plus giving the President the means to zero in on other inflationary situations.

If it were alleged by a particular company that an increase in price was made necessary by demands of a labor union or labor unions, then the demands of those unions would be put under similar public scrutiny.

We believe that if the light of public opinion could shine into these dark economic corners, it would have a salutary effect upon the inflation problem, which cannot be achieved through mandated Government controls.

. . .

14

THE EXPERIENCE UNDER
THE STABILIZATION ACT

Contrary to the opinion expressed by the President of the UAW in the previous selection, here a prominent economist argues that the Stabilization Act of 1970 was effective in restraining wages and prices during the freeze of 1971 and the subsequent Phase II Period of controls. He comments favorably on the experience under the Act, and he recommends that it be extended.

Arthur Okun

Arthur Okun, a Senior Fellow at the Brookings Institution in Washington, is a former Chairman of President Johnson's Council of Economic Advisers.

From U.S. Congress, Senate, *Hearings before the Committee on Banking, Housing and Urban Affairs,* (*Economic Stabilization Legislation—1973*) 93rd Cong., 1st sess., February 1973, pp. 264–267.

. . .

The nation owes to the Congress an enormous debt for its wisdom in bestowing upon the President—contrary to his own wishes—the authority of the Economic Stabilization Act of 1970; only because of that legislation was it possible for the President to shift course to a vastly improved economic policy on August 15, 1971. Phase I and Phase II have contributed significantly, in my judgment to a deceleration of inflation in the past year and a half even as the economy moved into a period of vigorous recovery. I should like to underline the following key elements in the performance of the federal anti-inflationary effort during Phase II:

(1) The most important element in the program was the enunciation and enforcement of a general wage standard of 5½ per cent a year increases with only restricted and carefully specified exceptions. That general wage standard changed expectations and attitudes of employers and employees throughout the Nation, and its impact extended far beyond the applications approved or disapproved by the Pay Board. The standard got broad acceptance in practice as an equitable and reasonable adjustment in pay for workers in goods and

service industries, in private and public employment, in union and nonunion sectors.

(2) The program made a distinct contribution to slowing prices and costs in the areas of health care and construction. These sectors are not ones of strong monopoly power, but they lack an organized market place in which demand and supply forces can determine prices (or wages) promptly and reliably.

(3) The program served to some degree as a deterrent to price increases by our largest firms, which were classified in Tier I. But its effectiveness was limited: the Price Commission did not develop the needed rules to define those cost increases that would justify price advances; instead it relied excessively on an arbitrary historical benchmark of profit margins. . . .

(4) The exemption of raw farm products from Phase II price controls was a wise move. Indeed I believe it was a misconceived effort to control the prices of other basic commodities like lumber which are produced by many competitive suppliers and are freely traded in commodity markets. In such cases, efforts to hold prices below market levels must result in unnecessary shortages and the unwholesome marketing practices reminiscent of the black

markets of wartime control periods. The huge rise in food prices was a major disappointment during Phase II, but controls were not the way to deal with that problem. Rather the government's powers in agricultural policy should have been used more promptly to promote larger supplies of farm products. The 5 per cent rise in retail food prices during 1972 is no mystery when the price of raw foodstuffs at wholesale rose 20 per cent; widespread attempts to blame food processors and retailers for that inflation are pure mythology.

(5) As the program worked out, I believe it was reasonably fair as between the incomes of workers, on the one hand, and those of business, on the other. I find no decisive evidence that income shares were shifted by the program in either direction. Both workers and business owners scored impressive gains in real income last year.

OUTLOOK FOR PHASE III

Despite my reasonably favorable assessment of the record of Phase II, I can well understand the Administration's desire to sharpen the focus and reduce the scope of the wage-price control program during 1973. I believe that the coverage of Phase II was unnecessarily comprehensive and unduly cumbersome. In particular, the federal government did little to improve the welfare of the consumer or the overall health of the economy by claiming to control rents and the prices of small businesses. We should always shape government price-wage efforts to put maximum reliance on the private marketplace in areas where it functions dependably and to assure that the government promise no more than it can reasonably deliver.

Phase III can do the job that needs to be done—restraining price and wage decisions that are made by big business and big labor in our society. Let me emphasize

that neither big business nor big labor have generally behaved irresponsibly or contrary to the public interest. In particular it is clear that union settlements actually fell behind the general pattern of wage gains during the late sixties; the very large union settlements of 1970 and 1971 were largely the result of an understandable effort of union workers to catch up from that position. Because those settlements generally provided an equitable catchup, the three-year settlements that are about to be negotiated in 1973 and 1974 should be moderate. Phase III must ensure that they are moderate, and must give labor confidence that subsequent rises in the cost of living will also be moderate. The wage patterns established under collective bargaining in our major industries are highly visible: they set a standard and a pattern for the three-quarters of our labor force that is not organized. The hope of maintaining a pattern of reasonable wage increases in nonunion areas rests on keeping the typical wage increases of union settlements this year in line with the general wage standard of 5½ per cent.

In the case of pricing by major firms, the situation is even more critical. Big business is the area of most rapid productivity growth. Price increases in that area must be below the national average in order to make up for the above-average increases that are bound to take place in the area of lower productivity growth, such as services. Specifically to achieve an overall inflation rate as low as 3 per cent, the wholesale prices of manufactured nonfood commodities must increase no more than 2 per cent and probably no more than 1½ per cent.

Phase III shifts the technique of enforcement for major firms, unions, and large groups of unorganized workers from one of advance clearance to one of remedial action: instead of putting a governor on automobiles entering the roads, the govern-ment is standing watch for speeders. The basic speed limits set forth by the govern-ment under Phase III are nearly identical to those of Phase II. With the extension of the authority in the Economic Stabilization Act, the Cost of Living Council will be able to stop the speeders, if and when violations develop.

Thus I believe that Phase III is poten-tially effective in principle; nonetheless, at the present time I cannot have complete confidence that the program will be im-plemented with full effectiveness in prac-tice. I believe the determination of the Administration to make Phase III work effectively would have been less subject to skepticism by the public if some minor de-tails of the program had been different:

(1) I regret that large economic units are required to report price and wage ac-tion only at quarterly intervals; I would have preferred them to be required to make advance notification—although not to ob-tain advance approval—of major actions.

(2) The flaws of Phase II with respect to the control of prices of major industrial firms should have been corrected—price advances should be justified only by those cost increases that are necessary to the direct production and distribution of prod-ucts and that have already been incurred or obligated under contract. To put it nega-tively, cost increases which firms expect to incur in the future or ones which cover overheads and even frills should never be used to justify a current price increase.

(3) It should have established the prin-ciple that increases in wages that exceed the 5½ per cent wage standard—whether or not these increases are revoked by the Cost of Living Council—should not be included in the calculation of increased costs that would justify increases in prices charged to consumers by major firms. When man-agement agrees to a collective bargaining contract, it should be willing to pay the wages out of income arising from produc-tion, and not to pass the bill on to the con-sumer in the form of excessive price in-creases.

(4) The special treatment of food pro-cessors and distributors under Phase III is a pointless symbol which may distract at-tention from the single overwhelming issue in improving the behavior of food prices—namely that of promoting a significant in-crease in the supply of agricultural products for the domestic market during 1973. I con-gratulate the Administration for its recent actions stressing production and produc-tivity rather than scarcity in our agricultural economy. But the evidence that they have diagnosed this problem correctly makes it all the harder to understand why they chose to treat processors and distributors of food any differently from those of other com-modities.

If the Congress should share my con-victions on these matters, it could reflect that judgment in the form of amendments to the extension of the Economic Stabiliza-tion Act.

· · ·

15

REDUCING INFLATIONARY RATES

Dr. Schultze believes the need for wage-price controls can be reduced and finds a partial solution after looking at the pricing behavior of highly concentrated industries. He believes a more vigorous antitrust policy would be an effective tool for changing structural characteristics of many industries to produce greater price stability.

Charles Schultze

Charles Schultze, a Senior Fellow at the Brookings Institution in Washington, was also Director of the Budget for Presidents Kennedy and Johnson.

From U.S. Congress, Senate, *Hearings before the Subcommittee on Antitrust and Monopoly of the Committee on the Judiciary, (Controls or Competition)*, 92nd Cong., 2nd sess., January, 1972, pp. 91–95.

. . .

In the announcement of these hearings which you sent me, the subject of today's session was entitled, "Are there steps that make sense economically which would erase the need for wage and price controls?"

My short, and I hope, not unwelcome answer to this question is, "No." I am convinced that some sort of intervention by the Federal Government into the setting of wages and prices will for a long time to come be a necessary condition for simultaneously achieving full employment and reasonable price stability in our economy.

On the other hand, if the question were rephrased to ask whether there are economic measures which, while not erasing the need for controls, would reduce their rigor and severity and give them a better chance of success, then my answer would be, "Yes." I think there are economically sound measures which would moderate, even if they could not eliminate, the magnitude of the inflationary problem under high-employment conditions.

In order to be more specific let me list and briefly discuss the major sets of economic conditions and industrial practices which either generate or perpetuate inflationary conditions.

Inflation can be generated and perpetuated by an excess demand for goods and services, a demand for goods and services larger than the economic capacity of the nation to furnish them. When market demands are so high that the unemployment rate is pushed to very low levels; when the supply, particularly of experienced full-time workers in large sectors of the economy, becomes very tight so that employers are forced to bid up wages rapidly to get workers; when output presses hard on industrial capacity, inflation is bound to occur. Wages are bid up more rapidly than productivity gains, raw material prices soar, and on top of this, profit margins begin to widen, especially in competitive industries. But, paradoxically, inflation of this variety is not our major problem.

If inflation only occurred when, for one reason or another, the sum of consumer, business, and Government expenditures was excessive, the standard tools of monetary and fiscal policy could handle the situation by reducing this excessive overall level of demand. Mistakes might be made, and surely would be made, but there would be no reason for wage or price controls or for structural reforms introduced on grounds of inflation control alone. The only need is for better monetary and fiscal policies.

But the really intractable problem in our modern economy is that inflation occurs simultaneously with the existence of underutilized resources. In the current situation, an inflation which did indeed start with the overheated economy of the late 1960s, has persisted for more than two years after the overheating disappeared, and persisted through a period of substantial unemployment. Earlier, in the mid-1950s we had significant inflation which began in the absence of economic overheating and continued for about two years, or slightly more.

In short, if inflation occurred only when the unemployment rate had been pushed very low, and if it promptly disappeared once unemployment had risen to the 3½ to 4 per cent range, the problem we are discussing today would be insignificant. It is the fact that inflation persists, and indeed sometimes begins, when unemployment is at or above 4 per cent that poses real dilemmas for public policy.

There are, I think, five elements in the nation's economic structure and habits which lead to the problem of inflation along with high unemployment:

First, there is the fact that in a large number of industries characterized by a high degree of economic concentration, prices tend to be rigid downward—they often do not fall when economic circumstances in a competitive environment would dictate that they should fall. This leads to two inflationary consequences:

(1) Even under conditions of healthy and not excessive prosperity and economic growth, not all industries will experience the same rate of market expansion. Some markets will be expanding sharply, some moderately, and some will be falling. Costs and prices, we know, are likely to rise in industries whose markets are sharply advancing. If prices on the average are to remain stable, and that is what we mean by having no inflation, if prices on the average would remain stable, these price increases must be balanced by price cuts in industries whose markets are growing subnormally or are declining. This is what would happen in a competitive environment. But if prices in large concentrated industries are sticky, if they resist falling in periods of weak markets, then the price averages cannot fail to rise. In short, since some prices are always rising in a healthy economy, others must fall to preserve overall price stability. Paradoxically, therefore, unless some prices fall, the overall price index will assuredly rise, even when the economy as a whole is not overheated.

(2) Productivity expands at widely differing rates among different industries. Bureau of Labor Statistics studies of productivity gains among individual industries confirm this fact. But the rise in wage rates among the different industries is much more uniform than the rise in productivity. As a consequence, if wages generally are to rise at a noninflationary rate—more or less in line with national productivity gains—then the unit labor costs of industries with greater than average productivity gains will fall. The above-average productivity gains in these industries will be larger than the advance in wages. As a consequence their prices should be reduced. If, however, prices are sticky downward in concentrated industries with higher than average productivity gains, then profit margins will widen. In turn, it is most unlikely that they will be allowed to go on unchallenged. Management will not let the margins rise too far above normal for fear of inviting unwanted new competition into the industry. Unions will seek to take the abnormal gains away and very often will succeed. Their success will be emulated by unions in other industries which do not

have above-average productivity gains. And in turn, this will raise costs and prices in those other industries.

In summary, the failure of prices in concentrated industries to respond to downward economic pressures as they should can generate an inflationary bias in the economy; in part because some price cuts are always needed to balance the inevitable price increases, and in part because the failure to cut prices in response to large productivity gains invites excessive wage advances that tend to be emulated in other sectors of the economy.

The nature of wage bargaining is a second major factor producing inflationary bias. The so-called wage-wage spiral tends to perpetuate inflation once started. Union contracts typically cover periods of more than a year—three-year contracts have become a common practice. A long-term contract signed during a period of economic overheating, say in 1968 or 1969, will usually contain a large wage increase, simply reflecting the inflationary conditions and tight labor market of the period. Subsequently, even when inflationary pressures subside and even if unemployment is rising, other unions signing new contracts will feel a necessity to win wage increases for their numbers equal to the wage won earlier by the first union. Settlements in such large industries as autos, steel, aluminum, aerospace, and can manufacturing influence each other. One large construction settlement, for a particular craft or in a particular locality, acts as a magnet for other crafts and other localities. Such mechanisms as the Davis-Bacon Act and the union contracts for public employees in many cities help spread these construction wage increases widely.

If inflation, once started, is ever to be brought under control, the sheer arithmetic of the situation requires that contracts signed after an inflationary boom is over must contain lower wage advances than contracts signed earlier. But the wage-wage spiral and follow-the-leader union settlements substantially delay this period of adjustment and help perpetuate inflation long after labor markets have loosened up and excess capacity appears.

A third contributor to the current problem of inflation lies in the changing nature of the labor market; fifteen years ago, when the overall unemployment rate was about 4 per cent, about 30 per cent of the unemployed were teenagers and young adults. In 1969, when the overall unemployment rate also averaged about 4 per cent, half of the unemployed, 50 per cent of them, were teenagers and young adults, conversely, and again by the sheer arithmetic of it. Therefore, a smaller proportion of the unemployed are now skilled experienced adults than was true fifteen years ago. To reach an average unemployment rate of 4 per cent today would mean a much lower rate of unemployment among the core of the experienced labor force than was the case in earlier years. And it is the tightness of the labor market among such experienced adult workers which probably has the most significant impact on key wage bargains.

In short, 4 per cent unemployment probably means tighter labor markets and larger wage increases than it did ten or fifteen years ago. Let me be very clear about it. This is not to say that we should abandon our attempts to reduce unemployment to 4 per cent or less. But we do need to face the fact that at this overall unemployment level, 4-percent labor markets may be tighter and wage increases larger than they once were, and that specific manpower training and public employment programs may be needed to reduce the size of the inflationary problems which accompanies this fact.

A fourth set of factors that operates to produce inflationary bias in our economy relates to the price-fixing policies of the Federal Government itself. Transportation rate regulation that discourages rate reductions, expensive farm price supports, import quotas (both legal and voluntary), subsidies to an inefficient merchant marine, Davis-Bacon wage provisions in Government contracts, and many other similar cases, all operate in a generally inflationary direction, by reducing competition and putting relatively high floors under prices that contribute to the downward stickiness. . . .

The fifth element of inflationary bias lies, I believe, in the case with which highly concentrated industries pass on wage and other cost increases. Many observers have noted that these industries tend to follow target-rate-of-return pricing. During periods of economic overheating, they may raise prices by somewhat less than would be characteristic of competitive industries. But once monetary and fiscal policies succeed in throttling down the overheating in the economy, there is a tendency for inflationary price rises to be perpetuated by target-rates-of-return pricing. Despite weakening markets, firms with substantial market power continue to pass along cost increases fully. They do not absorb them very much or as much as they should. Their resistance to wage demands based on market conditions that no longer exist is weakened, because of their propensity to raise prices to cover the higher costs. Moreover, as sales level off while additional capacity continues to be installed, these industries sometimes attempt to recover their target return at a lower rate of capacity utilization. This occurred quite extensively during the 1956–57 inflation, fifteen years ago. It is another factor that tends to perpetuate an inflation well past the period of economic overheating, and produce the paradox of general price increases during periods of less and sometimes substantially less than full employment.

All of these five features of our economic system interact with and reinforce each other. Follow-the-leader wage settlements help spread to other industries the inflationary wage gains that arise when high productivity growth industries refuse to cut prices. The target-rate-of-return pricing helps perpetuate price increases long past the end of an economic boom and feeds back into wage increases through its effect on the cost of living. The total impact of these structural characteristics is greater than the sum of the individual parts.

What can antitrust policy do about these problems? I do not pretend to be an expert in antitrust policies and can, therefore, only offer some highly tentative suggestions which follow from an analysis of the nature of inflation.

Let me first get out of the way what I believe is a spurious issue. In general, I do not believe that there is much evidence, if any, that concentrated industries generate inflation by arbitrary increases in their profit margins during periods of high unemployment and weak markets. Aside from the possible case of the steel industry in the middle 1950s, this kind of behavior does not appear to have been a major inflationary factor. But the first and fifth factors I mentioned above do appear to represent practices by which concentrated industries impart an inflationary bias to the economy:

By often failing to reduce prices in the face of either weak markets or above-average productivity gains;

By target-rate-of-return pricing that results in a full pass-through of cost increases even in the face of weak product markets, and in some cases preserves profit margins or tries to preserve profit margins, by raising prices to cover the costs of unutilized capacity.

Industries characterized by large numbers and low concentration ratios are less likely to exhibit this kind of behavior. Their prices and the wage increases they are willing to grant respond more closely to the forces of the market. As a consequence, fiscal and monetary policies, by regulating the strength of market demand, can more promptly choke off incipient inflationary pressures. Inflation may indeed still occur if monetary and fiscal policies goof and permit excessive demand pressures to build up. But the correction of these errors would be swifter and the tendency for inflation to persist while unemployment increases would be less.

An antitrust policy that concentrated explicitly on helping to reduce the inflationary bias in the economy would require important changes, I think, in traditional approaches. Anticompetitive behavior would have to be judged in terms of its departure from competitive pricing policy, particularly in terms of how prices in an industry behave in the face of softening markets or extra large productivity gains. Downward price rigidity would become a prima facie reason for viewing the industry structure with suspicion. The desirability of divestiture and the breaking up of large scale units would be judged in terms of its likely effect on price flexibility, not in terms of the particular practices by which bigness had been attained or price rigidity maintained. I am not enough of an expert in antitrust matters to determine the extent to which this approach would require changes in the antitrust laws or could be carried out by a different execution of existing laws.

Let me close as I began. I believe that the current inflationary bias in the economy stems from a number of structural characteristics in our society. Not all of those structural characteristics can realistically be corrected by antitrust policy. If we are to have both full employment and reasonable price stability, some form of income policies will have to be around for the foreseeable future. But antitrust policy can attack some of the structural distortions in the economy; it can lessen, although not eradicate, the inflation which accompanies full employment; it can increase the likelihood that incomes policies will work. It can, therefore, help rescue economic policy from the cruel dilemma that it has been facing in recent years. A nation and its leaders should not be put in the terrible position of choosing between price stability and full employment. Both justice and economic efficiency require that we have both. Antitrust policy can help us have them.

·   ·   ·

16

EDUCATION, POVERTY, AND THE THEORY OF THE DUAL ECONOMY

Some "radical" economists, including the author, believe that there are really two labor markets, the "primary" labor market, which includes most workers, and the "secondary" market, which includes basically the poor, the minorities, women, and youth. Workers in the "secondary" market exhibit high job turnover rates, have low productivity and wages, and are prevented from moving out into the more stable "primary" labor market because of their low incomes, their lack of education, and discriminatory practices.

Bennett Harrison

Bennett Harrison is Associate Professor of Economics and Urban Studies at MIT.

From U.S. Congress, House of Representatives, *Hearings before the Select Subcommittee on Labor of the Committee on Education and Labor,* (*The Employment and Manpower Act of 1972*), 92nd Cong., 1st sess., October, 1971, pp. 102–118.

. . .

Dual market analysts believe the economy to be stratified into what Barry Bluestone calls a "core" and a "periphery." . . . The division is functional and not simply semantic; workers, employers, and even the underlying technologies in the two strata behave very differently in important qualitative ways. The central institution of the "core" has been called the "primary labor market," and this is the part of the core which we shall study here. In the primary labor market, the attributes of jobs and the behavioral traits of workers interact (for example, by mutual reinforcement) to produce a structure characterized by high productivity, nonpoverty wages, and employment stability.

The high productivity of primary labor is a function not only of the knowledge and skills (that is, the "human capital") of the workers, but also (and perhaps more fundamentally) of the capital equipment with which they generally work. The market power of the typical primary firm, and the relatively high degree of profitability which is the usual corollary of such power, enable the employer to invest in modern capital equipment (frequently embodying "leading edge" technologies), to maintain that equipment, and to replace it when necessary. The same factors make it possible for such firms to invest in the "human capital" of their employees, so that the equipment will be used efficiently. While this is, of course, an ideal construct, it does seem to be broadly descriptive of the technical conditions of production in the leading, highly concentrated industries in the American economy, and provides a plausible (albeit partial) explanation of the relatively high average productivity of the core of the American labor force.

Primary employers typically pay nonpoverty wages. This may be partly explained by the aforementioned high average and marginal productivity of core labor, but most dual market theorists prefer a more institutional explanation. The very economic power that underlies the profits that enable primary employers to make productivity-enhancing investments also permits them to pass along a share of wage (and other cost) increases to their customers. In other words, their oligopoly position *permits* them to maintain nonpoverty wage levels without seriously eroding their profit margins. At the same time, the economic power of concentrated primary industries has induced the organization of what Galbraith calls "countervailing power" by labor unions. The evidence on how unions have affected the American wage structure is surprisingly ambiguous; there is, however, no question about the ability of unions to prevent employers from paying poverty-level wages.

There is an important feedback mechanism at work here. In conventional ("neo-classical") price theory, profit-maximizing employers are assumed to set the wage rate for all workers equal to the value of the marginal product of labor: the contribution of the last worker hired to the firm's revenue. Some economists believe that the relationship between wages and productivity is more complex, that (in particular) work effort (and therefore measured productivity) may well be an increasing function of wages. If this view is correct, then the relatively high wages that primary employers are able to pay (and that primary unions "encourage" them to pay) in turn induce the productivity increases by labor that (coming full circle) generate the profits out of which those nonpoverty wages are paid.

Workers in the primary labor market tend to be relatively stable. There are at least three plausible explanations of why primary employers value work force stability. First, their investments in the "specific training" of their workers—training highly specific to the particular conditions of this particular firm (or plant) and not easily transferred to other work environments—represents a "sunk cost" which they naturally wish to recoup. . . .

A second and somewhat more controversial explanation has to do with the development within large firms of . . . the "internal labor market." . . . Firms can go into the external labor market at times when conditions (such as excess supply) favor the firm in the wage-bargaining process (an obvious example is the extent to which corporations flood college campuses at graduation time each year). Since the employer-employee relation in the core of the economy is often characterized by the use of fairly long-term contracts, firms can then retain (or "hoard") this relatively cheaply bought labor against those times when external labor is more expensive. Such internal labor markets are, therefore, institutional manifestations of the employers' desire for work force stability.

A third explanation of firms' demand for stability is derived from the work of Kenneth Arrow, who observed that most of what workers learn about the equipment and systems with which they work is probably really learned "on-the-job;" it is "learning by doing." [1] The more complex the job, that is, the more intricate or subtle the technology and the equipment, the longer it takes the average worker to "learn" the job and to reach the point where—for all practical purposes—he has obtained his peak of efficiency. . . .

. . .

THE "SECONDARY LABOR MARKET"

Research—much of it concerned with the study of ghetto labor markets—has indicated the existence of a class of jobs that contrasts sharply with the primary labor market along each of the three dimensions we have discussed.

Secondary workers tend to display relatively low average and marginal productivity. Until recently, one explanation for this was the dearth of "human capital"

---

[1] Kenneth Arrow, "The Economic Implications of Learning-by-Doing," *Review of Economic Studies,* June, 1962.

(particularly formal education of at least average quality) possessed by these workers. While this continues to provide a partial explanation, it is becoming increasingly less convincing as even ghetto blacks gradually close the education gap between themselves and the average American. By 1970, the gap between the median schooling of young whites and blacks had fallen to less than half a year. . . .

Table 1

| Age | Median years of school completed | |
	Blacks	Whites
21 to 21 years	12.4	12.8
22 to 24 years	12.3	12.7
25 to 29 years	12.2	12.6
30 to 34 years	12.0	12.5

SOURCE: U.S. Department of Commerce, Bureau of the Census, Current Population Reports, series P–23, No. 38 (BLS report No. 394), "The Social and Economic Status of Negroes in the United States, 1970," Washington, D.C., July 1971, table 65.

In any case, the importance of formal education in determining worker productivity is itself now in some doubt, as we have seen. Probably more important is the absence of economic power in this segment of the periphery of the economy. With little or no oligopolistic market control, and with small profit margins, secondary firms tend to use more antiquated capital, which of course, tends to diminish productivity. Finally, the jobs themselves often do not *require* skills of any great consequence, involving instead the kind of routine unskilled tasks that attract (and at the same time reinforce the life styles of) casual laborers.

. . .

Annual wage income is the product of an average wage *rate* and the number of hours, days or weeks during the year in which a person works. The instability of secondary labor (discussed shortly) drives down the duration of work, while the economic structure of the peripheral firm causes it to pay a low wage rate. Taken together, these factors guarantee that workers will be forced to subsist on a poverty level income—to the extent that they rely for income entirely on what they can earn in the secondary labor market. Low productivity contributes to the explanation of these low wages, but so does the lack of market power among peripheral employers. Moreover (as indicated earlier), dual labor market theorists believe that these factors are interdependent: the marginal firm, by paying low wages and by not providing its workers with adequate complementary capital, discourages its labor force from taking those actions or developing those attitudes that would lead to increased productivity, which, if capitalized, could increase the firm's capacity to pay higher wages. The lack of economic power that characterizes peripheral firms (as reflected, for example, in the relatively high elasticity of their output demand curves) also makes it impossible for them to raise wages and other input costs without eroding profit margins, perhaps to the shutdown point. Finally, the low wages found in the secondary labor market are partly the result of the relative simplicity of the technologies in secondary industries: since skill requirements are minimal, the opportunity cost of secondary labor is low, given the large pool of readily available substitutable workers out "on the street."

Although the primary labor market is characterized by a mutual employer-employee "taste" for stability, both firms and workers in the secondary labor market seem to benefit from unstable work force behavior. That secondary labor is significantly more unstable than primary labor is incontestable.

. . .

Secondary employers have several reasons for placing a low value on turnover, in sharp contrast to their fellows in the primary labor market.

They can, as a rule, neither afford nor do their technologies require them to invest heavily in "specific training." Instead, they tend to rely on the "general training" (for example, literacy, basic arithmetic) provided socially. With minimal investment in their current labor force, and given the ready availability of substitute labor outside the firm, such employers are at the very least indifferent to the rate of turnover. Moreover, these firms lack the size and wealth necessary for the development of internal labor markets. Nor have they any reason to want to develop such institutions; since their skill requirements are minimal, they are unlikely to encounter periods when the labor they need is scarce and therefore expensive to recruit through conventional ("external") labor markets. Finally, everything we have hypothesized about the technology of secondary industries implies that the typical job is easily and quickly learned. . . .

Workers, for their part, seem similarly to have a rational preference for instability in the secondary labor market. The jobs are boring, and do not pay well. Employers seem not to mind—and perhaps even to encourage—casual attitudes toward work. The penalties for poor industrial discipline are generally not severe. Doeringer's studies of antipoverty programs in Boston led him to conclude about the job placement system for ghetto workers that it was seldom able to refer its clients to jobs paying more than they were earning before—"only two dollars an hour or less." This lack of upward mobility in the placement system contributes to the poor work habits and weak job attachment of the "hard-to-employ":

. . .

Thus, whereas primary employers and employees interact in an institutional setting characterized by high productivity, nonpoverty level wages, and high work force stability, the firms and work forces in the secondary labor market tend to organize themselves into production systems displaying low productivity, poverty level wages, and low stability (high turnover). It is interesting to observe that what appears to be "subemployment" or "underemployment" from the conventional perspective of an essentially unified economy is now seen to be the *normal* mode of employment in a backwater of that economy, a sector cut off from the mainstream.

IMPLICATIONS AND CONCLUSIONS

Locked out of existing primary jobs by discrimination, class basis and the institutionalized prerogatives of primary labor, and segregated into the peripheral economy with its secondary jobs and "irregular" means of supporting a family, the urban poor (and indeed the working poor everywhere) need *new jobs*. These jobs must offer adequate pay, promotional opportunities, and attractive benefits. They must be *stable* jobs, and this stability may be exactly what is needed to motivate the development among the disadvantaged of new attitudes toward the "world of work." Finally, the new jobs must be accessible to the poor, in terms of both location and skill requirements. In other words, we desperately need in the United States an explicit economic development policy.

17

CURING HIGH UNEMPLOYMENT RATES AMONG BLACKS AND WOMEN

A well-known woman economist contends that occupational segregation of minorities, women, and youth into jobs having high job turnover rates leads to wage and income discrimination against these groups. She believes this discrimination can be at least partially offset by youth programs, public service jobs, and vigorous affirmative-action programs.

Barbara Bergmann

Barbara Bergmann is Professor of Economics and Director of the Project on the Economics of Discrimination at the University of Maryland.

From U.S. Congress, Joint Economic Committee, *Hearings, (Reducing Unemployment to 2 Per Cent)*, 92nd Cong., 1st sess., October 17, 1972, pp. 41–49.

. . .

We will not begin to take the monetary and fiscal steps necessary to reduce the unemployment rate in the United States toward levels considered respectable in most other developed countries—in the neighborhood of 2 per cent—unless and until progress is made in solving the problem of high unemployment of blacks and women, who now together constitute 44 per cent of the labor force. Women's unemployment rates are currently running 64 per cent higher than men's and black rates are running 110 per cent higher than white rates. Even in times (unlike the present) when the labor market for white prime-age males is tight, and further expansion via monetary and fiscal policy threatens highly inflationary consequences, high unemployment among blacks and women as well as among youths keeps the size of the total group of unemployed people very large.

I will argue that we can bring down the pathologically high unemployment rates among blacks and women by policies that encourage employers to treat members of these groups more as white males are now

treated. I will further argue that such policies would not merely have the effect of spreading the misery around more evenly, but would enable us to move to an era in which unemployment rates could be lower for all groups, without inflationary consequences.

Martin Feldstein [1] has brought together in a very helpful way the evidence on unemployment by race, sex, and age. He shows that women, blacks, and youth tend to have high unemployment rates whether the rate for white males is high or whether it is low. Improvement in the state of aggregate demand changes the unemployment rates for women and young blacks very little. Rates for black men and women and white male youth are reduced by improvement in aggregate demand, but even in the best of times their rates are high.

In explaining this phenomenon of high unemployment rates for blacks, women, and youth, Feldstein attributes great importance

---

[1] Martin Feldstein, "Lowering the Permanent Rate of Unemployment," a report to the Joint Economic Committee, 17 October 1972.

to high labor turnover among these groups —to a tendency to leave jobs. . . .

Although I believe that shortage of demand is even more important than high turnover in causing high unemployment, I do believe high turnover deserves more attention than we have given it. Moreover, I believe Feldstein is right on target in his diagnosis of the cause of high turnover among youths.

The very same diagnosis is to a great degree applicable in the case of high turnover among women and blacks. Women and blacks also suffer from "the types of jobs that are available and the lack of adequate rewards for stable employment." Robert E. Hall put the matter very strikingly when he said,

". . . the whole notion of a career with steady advancement is relevant only for white males . . . Blacks and women seem to be excluded from work that offers an incentive to stay with a job permanently. . . ." [2]

The lack of careers leads to drift from one job to another and to drift into and out of the labor force. It is these drifting people who create the high labor turnover statistics and contribute, along with deficient demand, to the high unemployment rates that Feldstein documents.

Blacks and women do not have careers because they are denied access to jobs of a "career" type. The denial of a career to blacks of both sexes and white women is done through a system of occupational segregation. The occupational segregation of blacks from whites *of equivalent educational experience* . . . shows for twenty-one manufacturing industries the great overconcentration of blacks in service occupations and as laborers, and their gross underrepresentation in occupations where advances in wages and status are more

common. In printing and publishing, for example, we see that blacks had in 1967 only 1.3 per cent of the professional and technical jobs, whereas judging by their educational experience (on which the "target black employment share" is based) they should have 4.7 per cent of those jobs. In the same industry, blacks had 1.6 per cent of the craft jobs, as opposed to a "target" of 9.6. On the other hand, the share of blacks in jobs as laborers was double what might have been expected, judging by their educational experience, and their share of service jobs was triple the target level.

. . .

The occupational segregation of women from men is even more extreme than the occupational segregation by race. Its extent has been documented by Harriet Zellner, to whom is owed the figures in Table 1.[3] Zellner has grouped detailed occupations by the extent to which they were segregated by sex. She found that 47 per cent of all women worked in occupations that were almost entirely female, while 87 per cent of all men worked in occupations where women were grossly underrepresented. Only 11 per cent of women and 6 per cent of men work in occupations where women have fair representation. The lack of a meaningful career for most women that occupational segregation entails is well illustrated by the familiar figures of the young executive trainee (male) and his secretary (female) both of whom may have gone to the same college, taken the same courses, and achieved identical grades.

The kinds of jobs to which most women and blacks are consigned tend to be repeti-

---

[2] Robert E. Hall, "Why Is the Unemployment Rate So High at Full Employment?" *Brookings Papers on Economic Activity,* 3: 1970, pp. 393, 396.

[3] Harriet Zellner, "Discrimination Against Women. Occupational Segregation and the Relative Wage." Paper delivered at the Meetings of the American Economic Association. New Orleans, December, 1971. A condensed version of this paper appeared in the *American Economic Review,* May 1972.

Table 1

DISTRIBUTION OF WOMEN AND MEN AMONGST OCCUPATIONS GROUPED BY
SEGREGATION LEVEL, PRIVATE SECTOR, 1960 [1]

	Females	Males	Percent distribution		Females as percentage of total
			Females	*Males*	
Total employed	16,370,285	36,709,582	100	100	31
Occupation group:					
I. Occupations with 80 to 100 percent women	7,673,389	578,057	47	2	93
II. Occupations with 50 to 79 percent women	3,664,547	1,730,629	22	5	68
III. Occupations with 33 to 49 percent women	1,731,389	2,320,730	11	6	43
IV. Occupations with 0 to 33 percent women	3,300,960	32,080,166	20	87	9

[1] Based on data from the U.S. Bureau of the Census, "1960 Census of Population," PC(2) 7A, occupational characteristics, table 21.

SOURCE: Harriet Zellner, "Discrimination Against Women, Occupational Segregation and the Relative Wage," paper delivered at the meetings of the American Economic Association, New Orleans, December 1971. A condensed version of this paper appeared in the *American Economic Review*, May 1972.

tive, boring, and without interesting human contact. These kinds of jobs may be tolerated by the less talented or imaginative. Even those of ability may tolerate such jobs if they are seen as possible stepping stones to higher things. But where these jobs are dead ends, as they are for most blacks and most women, incentive to stay in any particular job is low. To go in exasperation from one boring job to another, even at the cost of a spell of unemployment, may be better than staying on one particular boring job, especially if nothing is to be gained by staying in terms of salary, responsibilities, and advancement. An occasional retreat from a boring job into unpaid household work is undoubtedly refreshing for women who can afford such a luxury. I would conjecture that much of the job leaving is done—and therefore much of the associated unemployment is suffered by—those blacks and female workers with the most ability, to whom the system of occupational segregation is least tolerable and most galling.

I know there is a great temptation in some quarters to attribute the poor labor market position of blacks and women and their high unemployment to the inferior characteristics of the sufferers rather than to the discriminatory action of employers in restricting access to certain jobs to white males. Blacks, it is said, lack aptitude, and women lack labor force attachment. Whatever truth there is to these assertions will not be uncovered until employers begin giving a square deal to those blacks *with* aptitude and those women *with* labor force attachment. Only then will we begin to see whether the present labor force behavior of blacks and women, particularly their higher turnover rate, is not merely a reaction to employer discrimination.

There is considerable evidence already that implicates discrimination as the reason for higher turnover rates for women and blacks. Relative labor turnover, rates by occupation, based on unpublished data of the Bureau of Labor Statistics are shown in Table 2. The rates of turnover for laborers, service workers, and clerical workers are two to three times as high as turnover rates among professionals, technical workers, and craftsmen. But where is cause and effect here? Are rates for blacks and women high because they are overrepresented in

Table 2

ESTIMATED INDEX OF TURNOVER RATES BY OCCUPATION, 1967–70

Professionals, technical workers, managers	1.00
Sales workers	2.36
Clerical workers	1.83
Craftsmen and foremen	1.16
Operatives	1.80
Service workers	3.14
Laborers	3.86

SOURCE: Unpublished data of the U.S. Department of Labor.

high turnover occupations, or do these occupations have high turnover because they are peopled by blacks and women? I have made calculations that indicate a considerable part of the large difference in job leaving between blacks and whites is due to the fact that blacks tend to have jobs in occupations in which both blacks and whites leave jobs relatively frequently. A calculation by Isabel Sawhill indicates that about one-half of the 18 per cent difference in turnover between men and women can be accounted for by the fact that women tend to be employed in industries and occupations in which both men and women leave jobs frequently.

What this means is that the reduction of occupational segregation would tend to reduce the difference in the turnover and unemployment rates of whites and blacks and reduce the difference in the turnover and unemployment rates of men and women. But would such a development—justified on equity grounds alone—leave the total rate of turnover and unemployment as high as ever? I believe that the effect of lower rates of turnover for women and blacks would not be cancelled out by higher turnover for white males. There are four reasons for this:

(1) Labor would be better distributed across occupations according to aptitude. Many women and blacks of above average ability find themselves, because of race and sex discrimination, in jobs in which their full talents are not utilized. These people are surely major contributors to the turnover statistics. If nondiscriminatory hiring were the rule, fewer individuals would find themselves mismatched in their job.

(2) A higher proportion of the total work force would realistically consider themselves in the running for promotions in their current places of work. Here the analogy of a sweepstakes is useful. By cutting discrimination, the number of tickets in the promotion sweepstakes would be increased, although the chance of any ticket paying off would be reduced. A disproportionate amount of the turnover comes from those who have no ticket in the promotion sweepstakes whatever. Therefore increasing the number of tickets, even while somewhat debasing their value, should reduce total turnover.

(3) Certain types of occupations—laborers, service occupations, some clerical occupations—which now contribute disproportionately to the turnover statistics, would tend to fall in size. These occupations are now overcrowded and hence underpaid because they have a "captive" labor supply—women and blacks who because of discrimination have no place else to go. If discrimination were eased, part of this labor supply would go to other occupations.

(4) In all probability the laborer, clerical, and service occupations would improve in terms of pay and working conditions, just to meet the competition for labor. This might in turn reduce turnover in these occupations, even as they were falling in size.

Let me emphasize again that I do not believe that relatively high turnover is the entire explanation for relatively high unemployment among women and blacks, or even the most important reason. These groups have been growing in size relative to the size of the group of white prime-age males. Yet women and blacks continue by and large to be restricted to the same occupations they were restricted to twenty or thirty years ago. As a result, these occupations have tended to become overcrowded. This overcrowding, which accounts for the low wage levels in the occupations given over to women and blacks, also is a cause of high unemployment for these groups.

I have attempted in a very simple way to estimate the amount of unemployment that can be attributed to turnover and the amount which must be ascribed to deficient demand. These estimates appear in Table 3. Although estimated unemployment among black men due to turnover (1.1 per cent of the labor force) is higher than the amount of unemployment due to turnover among white men (0.6 per cent), most of the difference in the white and black rates seems attributable to a lower demand for black men as compared with white men. About 15 per cent of the difference in the two rates is due to differences in turnover between blacks and whites. Similarly, about 4 per cent of the difference in unemployment rates among men and women is due to differences in turnover. Thus, although the high turnover of women and blacks does contribute to their higher unemployment rate, the most important source of high unemployment for these groups is deficient demand due to occupational crowding and generally slack conditions.

Feldstein, Hall, and others trace high unemployment rates back to high labor turnover in youth, blacks, women. We have traced the chain of causation back another step, from high turnover rates to occupational discrimination and have added another factor which seems considerably more important—occupational overcrowding. Only a great curtailment in occupa-

	Male		Female	
Age	White	Black	White	Black
16 to 19	0.8	1.3	0.9	1.6
20 and over	.6	1.1	.7	1.2

Table 3, Part A

UNEMPLOYMENT ESTIMATED AS DUE TO TURNOVER
[Percentage of the labor force]

Part B
UNEMPLOYMENT RATES—AUGUST 1972

16 to 19	13.0	22.4	13.4	31.2
20 and over	3.2	6.5	5.6	8.8

Part C
RESIDUAL UNEMPLOYMENT ESTIMATED AS DUE TO DEFICIENT DEMAND

16 to 19	12.2	21.1	12.5	29.6
20 and over	2.6	5.4	4.9	7.6

SOURCE: See text.

tional discrimination will bring down the turnover, reduce the overcrowding and hence the unemployment rates of these groups. There is good cause to believe that such a curtailment would also bring down total turnover and would permit total unemployment to be reduced safely by increases in aggregate demand.

IS PROGRESS BEING MADE?

It would be pleasant to report that the problems of women and blacks with unemployment and occupational segregation are being relieved at a respectable pace, but I believe the evidence now available points the other way.

Our research group is planning an extensive study of the results of the 1970 Census focused on just this question. The evidence we have now, based on older data, seems to indicate that progress for blacks is quite slow and that women may be going backwards rather than forwards.

An essential in reducing black unemployment rates and raising black incomes relative to white incomes is the achievement of a better occupational mix for blacks. Our research group has made some projections to the year 1977 of the share blacks will have in various occupations in manufacturing industries, based on hiring practices in these industries in the late 1900s. . . . Comparing these projections with actual black shares in 1967, we see that the projected shares of blacks in occupations in 1977, although something of an improvement over the 1967 shares, are really very little of an improvement. Blacks will continue to be overrepresented in occupations with high labor turnover (and lower pay as well) and underrepresented in the "career" occupations. In no manufacturing industry are blacks on the path to achieving an occupational distribution that would substantially lower their average turnover and reduce their unemployment rate.

When we turn to the developments for women, we see a retrogression. In the period between 1950 and 1970, women in the labor force increased by 70 per cent, as compared with a 15 per cent increase for men. Largely because of employer discrimination, vast numbers of these women crowded into the already overcrowded clerical occupations, which more than doubled in size. Women in these occupations lost ground relative to the rest of the economy in terms of salary, a way of saying that the price the economy paid for increasing the size of clerical occupations was to put these women to lower-priority (and no doubt more alienating) tasks. It is no wonder that such a situation should lead to high turnover and high unemployment among women.

WHAT POLICIES FOR REDUCING TURNOVER AND UNEMPLOYMENT?

Martin Feldstein has proposed we set up a Youth Employment Service and Youth

Employment Scholarships that would have the effect of getting more on-the-job training for youth, and encouraging young people to stay on in particular jobs.[4] I would wholeheartedly endorse that suggestion, but only on condition that care be taken to ensure that young people have access to the federally subsidized jobs without regard to race or sex. The Federal record in ensuring nondiscriminatory entry to its youth programs is quite poor, the most shameful case being the programs of the Bureau of Apprenticeship. I think that a federal youth program that would help to perpetuate present occupational segregation by race and sex would do more harm than good. After all, the labor market problems of young white males very soon solve themselves through the process of aging—the employment problems of young black women and men and of young white women are not so easily conquered.

To a nondiscriminatory youth program, I would add two other programs as essential: an expanded program of public service jobs and a strengthened program of affirmative action by nondiscriminatory hiring by private employers, enforced by the Federal Government.

Public service employment is a necessary tool for breaking down patterns which have led to high turnover and high unemployment for youth, blacks, and women, simply because it is too much to expect the private economy to solve this problem all by itself. The public service already plays a role in giving blacks and women a better deal than does the private labor market. Its role must be expanded, and whatever patterns of discrimination remain within the government service must be broken up.

.   .   .

---

4 Feldstein, "Lowering Unemployment," p. 38 ff.

18

Mr. King argues that construction unions have systematically discriminated against blacks. In order to redress the balance, he believes affirmative-action hiring quotas for minorities must be adopted and cites legal precedent for such action.

DISCRIMINATION IN EMPLOYMENT

Paul King

Paul King is Executive Director of the United Builders Association of Chicago.

From U.S. Congress, House of Representatives, *Hearings before the General Subcommittee on Labor of the Committee on Education and Labor,* 92nd Cong., 2nd sess. Hearings held in Chicago, Illinois, October 21–22, 1972.

. . .

Let me move along and suggest to you that a strong and definitive position on the matter of quotas must be developed and supported. An elementary law of physics states, in essence, that if an undue stress is applied to one part of a system, so as to create an imbalance, force of equal magnitude must be applied to the remainder of the system in order to restore the initial balance.

Whether we attribute that to Newton, Galileo, or any other physical scientist, it is pretty widely accepted. The current furor over quotas is an attempt to distort the valid concepts to be found in establishing numerical goals. This is no more than an attempt at establishing a very necessary Federal force being applied to relieve the distortions in the construction system created by the racist and discriminatory practices of the construction labor unions. For the sake of added support to my analysis, I refer the committee to court decisions that reflect the thinking that racially oriented harm requires racially oriented relief.

I won't cite all of these court cases, but let me just bring out the essence of these cases:

Citing *Norwalk Core* v. *Norwalk Rede-*

velopment Agency, the court has stated, and this is the court's degree:

What we have said may require classification by race. That is something that the Constitution usually forbids, not because it is inevitably an impermissible classification, but because it is one that usually, to our national shame, has been drawn for the purpose of maintaining racial inequality. Where it is drawn for the purpose of achieving equality, it will be allowed, and to the extent that it is necessary to avoid unequal treatment by race, it will be required.

Calling your attention to the Pittsburgh case involving *Childress* v. *Plumbers Local 27* in 1969, this black plumber claimed that the union's membership restrictions violated the 1964 Civil Rights Act. The court had Childress admitted and required the union's testing patterns changed. The court decreed:

Local 27 will maintain a separate referral list for black journeymen. Black referrals will be made on a one-to-one basis with one black journeyman referred for each white journeyman. Referrals by this method shall continue until the black list is exhausted and shall recommence when any black journeyman is laid off, or otherwise listed. The dual referral system shall continue during the life of this decree, after which time the lists shall be merged.

Another case, *Watson* v. *Limbach*, a Columbus, Ohio, case, reaches specifically into areas involving the Joint Apprenticeship Committee of the Plumbing and Pipefitting Industry of that city, and I think, Mr. Chairman and members of the committee, that it is important for you to pick up these points.

The decree indicated that:

(1) The 1972–73 apprenticeship class shall be chosen as follows: I, the first ten accepted shall be black; II, thereafter, blacks and whites will be selected on a one-to-one ratio.

(2) Apprenticeship classes for the next four years shall be selected according to a one-to-four black-white ratio.

(3) The above system shall continue until the EEOC has indicated to the JAC that whatever future selection criteria are utilized have been validated.

(4) Lowering the high school graduation requirements to completion of the tenth grade.

(5) The placement of one black member on the Joint Apprenticeship Committee.

These and other court decisions validate, in my mind, the legality and necessity of goals and timetables often called quotas. What is now necessary is that the disadvantaged blacks throughout the country be encouraged, and joined by our elected officials, in waging a war in the courts to achieve racial balance in the construction unions.

Now, you will note that the *Watson* v. *Limbach* case referred to the Joint Apprenticeship Committee. It should be noted that these committees are usually made up of an equal number of labor union representatives and contractors. This labor-management duo is responsible for the selection of apprentices, administration of the apprenticeship program, arbitration in disputes involving apprentices, and, in general,

overseeing all affairs involving new and incoming trade union members.

Though the contractors contribute to the JAC, labor unions generally control them. In practically all cases we've examined, there are no blacks on either side of the JAC. Neither labor or management has any black men making decisions on the future of black youngsters seeking to gain livelihood in the respective crafts.

The importance of black participation in these apprenticeship matters must be clearly understood. Except for the isolated crafts that have the "trainees" category, the only way for an outsider to enter the unions, which allow them to work, is to be trained through the particular craft's apprenticeship program.

The current guidelines generally require persons with certain levels of education, usually between the ages of seventeen and thirty years. These rules clearly discriminate against educationally deprived men thirty-five to forty-five years old. Should the man over thirty-five, who may very well be the father of a family, be told that he is too old to be trained for a job in an apprenticeship program? Can you imagine the chagrin he must feel when he sees construction sites inundated with old nonproductive foreigners fifty and sixty years old, who never were apprentices but who, in fact, got their training on the job "learning while they were earning." These men had the advantage of friends and relatives who would sponsor them. The older black man has none of these, and the younger blacks must be accepted, taught, judged, in practically all cases, by an all-white Joint Apprenticeship Committee.

Construction unions have taken advantage of the socioeconomic needs that the construction industry must meet. They have allowed the union's attrition rate to exceed the number of entrants, driven the wages up to a point where the purchaser of construction services must pay in excess of $12 to $13 per hour, and convinced their present membership that blacks who opt for entry into the crafts are threatening to take away their (meaning the current white membership's) jobs.

I ask you, is it fair, or by any means just, to allow a white union worker to gain 1,600 hours of work per year at eight dollars per hour, while the black worker has no hours of work at zero dollars per hour?

In areas such as Chicago, where the non-white population approximates 50 per cent of the total, 1600 hours should be divided up so that black Americans get at least 800 of these hours along with the opportunity to be trained and upgraded so that they can perform satisfactorily.

. . .

Allow me to call your attention to the subject of "plans", developed to increase black and other minority participation in the construction industry.

The Philadelphia Plan is a governmental, "imposed" plan. It is a valuable and necessary device in forcing contractors to develop meaningful and productive affirmative action programs.

It was announced earlier this month by Assistant Secretary of Labor Richard Grunewald that a Pennsylvania plumbing contractor was barred from further government work because the firm was found to be in noncompliance with the Philadelphia Plan and to have failed to make good faith efforts to comply with the goals and timetables for hiring minorities.

Debarrment took place in connection with a HUD-assisted Turnkey Housing Project in Pottstown, Pa. This action was concurred in by HUD.

The biggest problem with the Philadelphia Plan is that it is not exercised more in the Philadelphia area; and similar plans, which can result in debarrment, are not in effect in other areas of the country. I must

say that it is encouraging to see this kind of action being taken when there is so much pressure from organized labor and other so-called "liberal" groups against it.

Contractors facing these kinds of sanctions often throw before us their dilemma of having signed collective bargaining agreements with unions that restrict their hiring to union referrals only. Hence, they conclude that the unions, not the contractors, are at fault when no blacks are on the job. This is only partly true.

Federal laws, Presidential Executive orders, and the civil rights acts take precedence over any agreement, and those who sign to illicit covenants are guilty, if no more than by association.

Unions will attempt to use the excuse that there is not enough work for their present members; hence, they can only agree to additional hiring "when economic conditions permit." This argument must also be wiped away. The very institutions who speak out against big business have created a racist elite working group that, in essence, says that blacks can get an opportunity to work only when they, meaning the unions, have as many full work weeks and as much overtime as they decide they need.

This preposterous attitude must be attacked by all political leaders who would call themselves concerned with black people. The irony of it all is that blacks are not trying to "bust" unions, but to join in order to "build" unions. Blacks are not trying to dismantle apprenticeship programs, but to participate in them in order to become qualified craftsmen. If those who control unions don't see it, I shall tell them and you, as well.

The job picture with its bleak future outside of construction, is such that unions ought to save their energy in fighting off blacks and pool the resources of white and black workers in an effort to bring respect, dignity, and stability to the construction worker group. This effort is needed, not in any utopian "black and white together" social effort, but in the pure self-interest of each man seeking to provide for his family and himself, and attempting to insure that means of provision.

The Chicago Plan, referring to the one of 1970, was the first of the "hometown" solutions. I had an opportunity to participate in the closing of millions of dollars in construction sites, and I might add that the only violence in these actions did not come from the black "teen nations," but from the white union members who violently prevented the Assistant Secretary of Labor from conducting Federal hearings.

It should be noted that there were two important positive features of our activity: First, it was the first time that a sustained formalized relationship between the black community, the construction contractors, and unions was developed.

Second, this effort evoked certain commitments from the contractors, heretofore not present, and, in general, increased the awareness of Chicago's leaders and citizens as to the importance of the black construction issue.

The fundamental weakness of the plans was that black people did not have an adequate voice in the policy and implementation of the program, and there was never an unqualified commitment from the individual craft unions. I would hope that future plans in this city or elsewhere would not suffer from these inadequacies.

Construction contractors and unions should not be the only targets discriminatory practices in construction hiring. I must also call your attention to the vast maintenance construction done by major office buildings, hospitals, schools, and hotels who, by virtue of their receipt of Federal funds, or in the case of some hotels, because their parent corporation does business with the Federal Government, are required to comply with Executive Order 11246 and other affirmative action efforts.

If you were to take a careful look at the maintenance construction personnel employed by the hotels of Chicago, you would find few, if any, blacks. As Congressman Parren Mitchell's Subcommittee on Economic Development points out, hotels award miniscule jobs, if any, to black contractors, do not demand black employees of their white contractors, but continue to benefit from millions of dollars spent by black people.

. . .

For added support, we might note a major action by the Justice Department in May of 1971 in California. In this case, the Justice Department filed a suit against eight Ironworker locals and nine joint apprenticeship committees for discriminatory hiring practices. Nine employer associations, Bethelehem Steel, Kaiser Steel, and U.S. Steel were also named as defendants.

The settlement lays down specific guidelines to integrate the union, which was reported to have fifteen blacks out of a total 9,000 membership. Under these steps, apprenticeship committees must take a minimum of 170 blacks each year for the next five years, with half between the ages of eighteen and thirty, and the remainder over thirty.

Let me just cite here, as I close, some of the content of this suit filed in California: (1) that employer associations take steps to see that black apprentices are provided with a reasonable level of employment, (2) that unions recruit by advertising once a month for six months, and then quarterly in black community newspapers and by contacting black organizations, and (3) that unions report on a quarterly basis to the government and to the court the steps they've taken to comply with the order.

With these precedents and courses of

action, the Congressional Black Caucus can initiate a victorious battle for blacks and other minorities in this Nation's construction industry.

So, members of the committee, what does it all mean? It can best be stated by sharing with you a portion of the transcript of one of the labor hearings I chaired on behalf of the National Association of Minority Contractors.

This hearing was held in Seattle, Wash., in January 1971. This is the testimony of a young black lad who had gotten into the union, and over several months had worked less than 100 hours, while white boys worked regularly. He went to the hiring hall each day only to be told there was no work. He was sent all the way to Olympia to work at some times (over seventy-five miles of travel), when work was going on in the city proper. He could not make proper contact or receive proper assistance from the Apprenticeship Committee.

This is, in fact, a portion of his testimony with questions being asked by one of the members of the committee:

"How do you support yourself? How do you live? You are not working enough time to support one individual. So you have a family?"

The answer was "Yes."

"Are you married?"

The answer was "Yes."

"Do you have children?"

The answer was "Yes."

"How do you support them?"

The answer was "The best way I can, you know. United Construction Workers are offering a few jobs."

A question, "What about your friends? How do they support themselves, those that are in the construction industry if their work habits are much the same as yours? How do you live?"

At that point, I stopped the questioning and had the young man's statement stricken from the record; I said at that time that he ought to invoke the fifth amendment, because the question was kind of sticky.

The essence of his answer was that he would not let his family suffer or starve, and that he would do "whatever was necessary" to prevent those eventualities from occurring.

A few months ago, I found out that the man was in jail for theft or burglary. A man in jail—not because he was too lazy to work, not because he was a hardened criminal, a hustler, or a pimp—but in jail because he was denied the opportunity to work.

And who are the victims of this racism? Certainly he and his family. Certainly the total black community. Ironically, though, the same people who deprived him of the opportunity will have to absorb the weight of another inmate in a corrective institution in their community; a mother and child who may go on welfare; and a man who may end up with a hopeless feeling toward this racist society, which could result in a potential lifetime criminal in that community's midst.

MARKET SYSTEMS

PART THREE

19

Who gives direction to the marvelously intricate and efficient economic machine that is the American free enterprise system? Mr. Randall argues cogently that businessmen, motivated by financial gain, but tempered with a high sense of social responsibility, perform this function and perform it well.

WHO GIVES FREE ENTERPRISE ITS SENSE OF DIRECTION?

Clarence B. Randall

Clarence B. Randall is a former President of Inland Steel Company. He has also held several high government posts.

American businessmen are being driven these days to take a hard second look at the philosophy and the practices of free enterprise.

This system of accumulating private capital under single control—and risking it for gain simply because of individual initiative—has come to businessmen as instinctively as the act of breathing. In fact, until recently, some of them lacked even a rudimentary awareness that there *are* in the world other systems for the production and distribution of goods.

All this is changing, thanks to the Russians. Instead of concealing their strength until they could choose their time to strike, they rather naively rang the alarm bell by rocketing Sputnik into orbit and by putting the first man into space. Now the American businessman knows that the way of life to which his entire effort is dedicated is under severe challenge nearly everywhere in the world, and that he must either justify it by his conduct, or face the grim prospect that his grandchildren may lose it. He is staggered by the sudden realization that free enterprise does not automatically export itself, and that new nations, when given an opportunity for a free choice, are apt to reject it, and to accept the Communist program. Vigorous person that he is, he resents this incredible phenomenon, and a highly creditable determination to do something about it is seizing him.

When he takes this hard second look at himself and his way of life, what does he find? What are the "truths" which he holds to be "self-evident"?

His first truth is that the principle of freedom, upon which our form of democracy must irrevocably be based, is indivisible. There are no separate freedoms that may be specifically allocated to particular groups or institutions. The right to make private decisions with respect to the production of goods is precisely the same right exercised by the professor at the university who insists upon teaching whatever economic doctrine he believes to be true. Each must fight to the death to protect the right of the other, or all will be betrayed together. Whatever restricts one restricts both, and all who believe in freedom must jointly resist limitation wherever it appears, without immediate thought of self. We need all hands on deck all the time if "life, liberty, and the pursuit of happiness," the national goals proclaimed in our Declaration of Independence, are to be preserved.

FILLED WITH FREEDOM

It is this freedom, applied in industry to the point of saturation, which has given the American economy its enormous vitality and resiliency, and which the businessman is determined to see preserved at all cost.

This is so because no other system of production has yet been conceived which so effectively releases the full creative effort of each individual involved. Our industrial way of life dignifies the worth of the individual, first, by preserving for him full choice as to what calling he will embark upon, and, second, by rewarding him in direct ratio to the contribution he makes to society.

We believe that the incentives created by monetary compensation are both effective and moral. We have proved by our long history that the sum total of all effort when given freely, and with enthusiasm, in our form of society, is greater than the resultant of total effort that is brought forth by compulsion under collectivism. And we see not the slightest wrong in doing well by those who try, and not so well by those who do not. We believe that in granting rewards that are proportionate to effort we are merely giving recognition to the fact that in a free society the goals of the individual and those of society are not in conflict, but parallel.

In support of these truths, powerful testimony is now coming from behind the Iron Curtain. Of all people, the Communists are the most thorough-going of pragmatists. A thing has to work or it will be discarded. They boastfully began the reorientation of their industry on the starry-eyed theory that society would take from every man according to his ability, and grant him his share of the total production in strict accordance to his need, regardless of his effort. Now they know better. Quietly, they have dropped that theory and now employ a wide range of group bonuses, and of individual incentives accomplished through both salary and emoluments. In a land that has few automobiles, a limousine and chauffeur can create powerful motivation. Add a *dacha* on the Black Sea, and the upward surge of production can be pronounced. In fact, incredible as it seems, the spread between the compensation of the manager of a steel plant in Russia and that of the lowest paid worker is unquestionably greater than the comparable difference in the United States.

We apply this principle of freedom that saturates not only to the production of goods, but to their sale and distribution as well. We have no lonely commissar pontificating by himself as to what quantities and qualities of merchandise we should turn out. We vote all day every day as to what they should be. Every time a housewife goes into a supermarket and buys a package, she casts a ballot, as does her husband when he makes the down payment on an automobile. By totaling the resultant from an infinite number of such free choices, we arrive at consensus as to our goals.

In fact, the basic concept that underlies everything we do is the idea that the wisdom of the many is at all times more to be trusted than the wisdom of the few. There is always the chance under communism that a commissar may display great genius, but there is a still greater chance that he may display colossal ignorance and stupidity, and only fools would knowingly take such risks.

We employ the same principle of freedom that saturates in the formulation and gathering of the capital required in building and equipping our industrial plan, and in financing our operations. We rely on no other force than the incentive of intelligent self-interest for providing our funds. No individual is required to save. He may eat today and starve tomorrow, if he so elects. No part of that share of the product of his toil which has been allocated to him will ever be taken from him against his will in order that capital may be accumulated. But as a rational being, he soon senses that there is a future, and that for him and his family it will be a better future if he with-

draws a part of his earnings from immediate consumption, and risks it for further gain by buying common stock of his company, or of another if he prefers.

This broad diffusion of ownership does two things. First, it keeps management on its toes; unless industry fully measures up and gives full value in terms of return on investment, the flow of capital will stop; people will spend and not save. And, second, those who own want to understand, and a means of communication is established by which people everywhere acquire insight into the problems of the national economy.

The powerful magnetic force which keeps the compass of industry pointing true north, to the welfare of society as a whole, is competition. The rule of survival of the fittest, the counterpart of freedom of enterprise, sternly demands that each separate unit of production put forth its utmost effort at all times, and that is social gain of a high order. We speak of ours as a profit system, but actually it is a profit and loss system, and the two forces of hope and fear operate in parallel to eliminate those whom in America we call the "free riders."

DANGER SIGNS

When one businessman enters into a secret agreement with another businessman to restrict competition, he is either guilty of moral turpitude or ignorant of the enterprise system. The pegging of prices, the arbitrary dividing of territories, the withholding for a fixed period of advances in technology, and all similar devices which evil minds can think up to fatten profits at the expense of the consumer are a denial of our heritage. And they will destroy the enterprise system if they are allowed to persist. Such power over society cannot be lodged in private hands, and an angry public, when fully roused, will punish us all by withdrawing the privileges which it has bestowed in the field of private endeavor.

This, of course, raises the whole question of the importance of moral attitudes in the preservation of the enterprise system. It is actually more important that we be right than that we be effective. The very highest standards of ethics must henceforth govern the conduct of industrial leaders if society is not to turn against us; and we in the United States now comprehend this clearly.

We still have areas of weakness, however. Take executive salaries, for example. It is urgent and right that men who bear great responsibility should be generously compensated, but when moderation yields to avarice, hostile social forces are swiftly set in motion.

Here are some of the danger signs. When the top man has the highest salary in his industry, he may be justified, for someone has to be the high man, but he should be put upon great caution to be sure he is right. And when the top man submits his proposed compensation to no one but an "inside board," namely a group of directors who work for him, he is clearly vulnerable.

We have erred, too, with respect to expense accounts. Under our law, legitimate entertaining may be deducted as a cost for purposes of computing the corporate income tax. But when the company president gives a champagne party at a night club, or uses the company airplane to take his friends on a duck-hunting trip, he steps far over the line of propriety. His conduct poses a threat to the survival of the entire private enterprise regime. His subversion and the Communist's differ only in degree.

On the other hand, there have been great advances in general probity during the years of the present generation. In my day, for example, I have seen commercial bribery all but completely eliminated. Time was that one company would place an industrial spy in the research department of a competitor, or when a supplier would buy the favor of a purchasing agent, but those moral lapses have been cleaned up—and cleaned up by industry itself, without the necessity for new laws.

In fact, the outstanding characteristic of the entire business community in the United States today, and the one which holds the greatest promise for the future, is its high sense of social responsibility. We now see clearly that the welfare of a particular enterprise and of the area in which it is located are inseparably linked, and we see further that the welfare of industry as a whole and of our country are likewise indivisible. It has taken a long time for this full sense of social mission to become the dominant philosophy of our industrial leadership, but such is now the unquestionable fact.

NEW ROLE FOR BUSINESSMEN

And it is right that this should be so. It is merely the logical extrapolation of a principle which, once accepted, could lead to only one conclusion: for every privilege bestowed upon individuals in a democratic society there is a corresponding obligation. Such is the essence of freedom. In the past, we have heard too much about our rights, not enough about our responsibilities. All this is now undergoing revolutionary change, and the businessman is assuming an important role in this significant transformation as he takes his hard second look at the enterprise system.

Nearly all leading American firms, for example, now set aside a part of their profits for philanthropy. Most of them do this by establishing a charitable foundation, which is administered by a special staff, and not by the board of directors. Through this medium they give support to hospitals, homes for the aged, child welfare institutions, health programs, and a wide variety of social agencies. This is only the beginning, however, and in large corporations literally hundreds of worthy causes will be assisted. Education stands high on the list, and liberal arts colleges are supported in parity with those which turn out technically trained graduates. Above all, the motive behind the allocation of such funds is not to help the company, but solely to serve the community and the nation. That is industrial statesmanship of the highest sort. We had a little trouble with the lawyers on this at the start, but it is now entirely clear that under our law a corporation may use its funds for the common good, as, of course, it should.

Moreover, businessmen in the United States now give themselves in addition to their money. You will find them lending their management skills to community institutions by taking unpaid executive posts, or by serving on boards of trustees, and you will find them employing their promotional gifts in leading fund-raising campaigns for charitable purposes. They are establishing by their conduct the proposition that free enterprise not only receives from society but gives full value in return.

You will find businessmen in our government these days, too, at every level, carrying heavy responsibility at substantial financial sacrifice, and doing so with distinction. When, unexpectedly, a corporation officer is asked to close his desk for a term of years and go to Washington, or to his state capital, he does so in a high spirit of dedication. He knows that in this world of crises the demand for talent in government has greatly exceeded the supply, and he answers the call in the spirit of his new philosophy of social mission. Actually, the combination of the mature executive from business, paired with a career officer, makes a strong team. The professional provides the indispensable familiarity with the subject matter and the knowledge of how government operates; the amateur brings awareness of the state of public opinion and the courage to take a fresh approach, inasmuch as his own future is never at stake in anything he does. His greatest desire is to get the job done worthily and go home.

Leaders in American industry are thus in many ways rising magnificently to the challenge of a world in torment and distress. They believe fervently that the forces of private initiative as released into the field of production in a free and democratic society bring greater good to more human beings than is possible under communism. But they also know that freedom brings responsibility, and that production as such is not a goal in itself. They are fully aware of their social obligations and are determined to fulfill them abundantly.

20

PUBLIC AFFAIRS:
THE DEMANDING SEVENTIES

What are the responsibilities of American corporate business In the 1970s? Mr. Llnowltz, former president of one of the most technologically progressive of modern corporations, discusses the relationship of corporate management to the complex problems of social needs in the United States.

Sol Linowitz

Sol Linowitz is the former President of the Xerox Corporation; he has since served the federal government in several capacities.

From *Public Affairs in National Focus,* National Industrial Conference Board, 1966, p. 117. Reprinted by permission.

. . .

CORPORATE IDENTITY AND GOALS TO TAKE ON NEW DIMENSIONS

The first tenet which I would like to put forward this evening is simply this: *The responsibility of business to society in the future cannot be and will not be discharged in the same way we have been discharging it in the past.* It is also my belief that American business and industry will in the future be confronted with a challenge unlike any they have yet had to face. The problem will be, if you will, one of identity: What should a corporation be? Which goals can it best seek to pursue? What meaning does it have for people and for the society of which it is a part?

My own thesis is this: *To realize its full promise in the world of tomorrow, American business and industry—or, at least, the vast portion of it—will have to make social goals as central to its decisions as economic goals; and leadership in our corporations will increasingly recognize this responsibility and accept it.*

An enormous amount of economic power is today vested in American corporations. Corporate decisions influence fully half of our national income and affect the employment of more than 30 million people —almost as much as all other institutions and services combined.

A corporation's economic responsibility alone is awesome. A top corporate officer, if asked to define his most important function today is apt to say: "Finding meaningful goals for the use of economic power." And his emphasis would be on the word "meaningful," because goals are obviously irrelevant unless people believe in their importance.

In recent years, the corporate community has been searching far and wide for creative and talented people, for managers with imagination, for innovators. The search has intensified to the point at which companies unblushingly promote the weather, the scenery—and even the proximity to ski slopes. Yet it gets more and more difficult—not to find people, but to find good people.

A far lesser number of young men are planning business careers these days. At Harvard, for example, only 14 per cent of 1964 graduates entered business, as compared with nearly 40 per cent five years earlier. Last year a much discussed *Wall Street Journal* story began: "The word on the campus is that business is for the birds." The conclusion is inescapable that in defining goals that are meaningful for a nation, the majority of whose population will soon be under the age of 25, the corporate world is having more and more difficulty.

Nor do the more common and popular explanations of that difficulty seem to me very satisfying. I do not believe, for example, that young people today really resent corporate life as a kind of "suburban serfdom" in which the only alternatives are crushing conformity or lasting frustration. Such mythology has been effectively destroyed too often. Nor am I implying that the corporation itself needs a totally new *raison d'être.* The challenges of supplying the world's best-developed economy are obvious and undisputed.

But in the very fact that our economy is developed so well—that we have proven the capability to build houses and highways, to produce toothbrushes and baseballs, and to satisfy our material needs—lies the clue to the future of young people and to the most significant goals for private enterprise.

ENTREPRENEURIAL BRILLIANCE ESSENTIAL TO ELIMINATION OF SOCIAL PROBLEMS

Whether we like it or not, the youth of America simply does not believe that the larger portion of American business and industry has yet come to grips with what they regard as the dominant, motivating force of today. In a world in which the overriding concerns are social rather than material, they feel that the greatest challenge before us lies in the banishment of problems which have been plaguing the world for centuries. Their vision of a great society—whether you spell it in large or small letters—is by no means an accident or a phenomenon which, like a comet, flashes into view for a few months or a few

years and then disappears. Nor is it for them just a political phrase or the invention of one man or one group. At its heart is the widespread, and still growing, belief that for the first time in history we have the tools and the capabilities and the resources to obliterate poverty, illiteracy, disease, and social and physical stagnation—not only in our own country, but wherever the peoples of the world will permit us to reach.

Why have the young people in our colleges and universities turned their backs on a business career? Men such as Peter Drucker, who have studied the problem, believe that to a significant extent they have done so in disenchantment and because they have felt a failure on the part of business leaders to evolve concepts of social and moral responsibility that keep pace with the changing conditions of our world. Leaving aside the question as to whether this impression is a fair one and a correct one, the important fact is that American youth today apparently does have this impression and is, therefore, making its commitment elsewhere in an effort to find fulfillment and to become involved in the world around them. For the young people today do want to be deeply involved with their world. Nearly 10,000 of them are working in the most backward areas of the world trying to make life more productive to people who have no concept of the meaning of the word "comfort." What we have seen happening with the Peace Corps has been dedication to the cause of human welfare on the part of thousands of young people who are eager to work and build for a world of peace and freedom.

I think what the youth are seeking from American business and industry is a sure indication that it, too, feels their sense of responsibility and commitment—that it, too, recognizes it has a stake in the conquest of war, disease, hunger, and poverty. I am by no means proposing that American industry take upon itself a solitary crusade for the conquest of the world's burdens. What I am suggesting is that a systematic and intimate understanding of the dominant social problems of our day, combined with a firm dedication to public service, will lead to the discovery by businessmen of innovations that will satisfy their direct corporate goals and simultaneously make a contribution to the most pressing human needs.

. . .

Naturally, there is no single or sure solution to any of these problems anywhere in the world; but I firmly believe that the imagination and entrepreneurial brilliance that has met our physical needs so well in the past can and will be adapted in fresh, new measure to help in finding answers.

By the same token, I think American business and industry can and must reveal its concern with such problems as the war against poverty here at home. For at the heart of the antipoverty program is the future of those on the slag heap of our society whose development can constitute an immensely valuable human resource for the future of American industry. Industry is already helping with the Job Corps program and with some community action efforts. But it can do a great deal more. Industry might, for example, announce that an employee who indicates his willingness to volunteer a year of his life to fighting poverty by joining the VISTA Corps, or some other phase of the antipoverty program, should have the opportunity to do so. I believe that policies should be developed so that he can take a leave of absence from his corporate career without jeopardizing his future. Even more, I believe that a company policy should be evolved which would make clear that such positive action on his part would be regarded as a plus on his record. For the fact is that at the heart of the antipoverty program is the future of

millions of Americans, and American industry has a vital stake in what is going to happen to them—for good or for ill.

In short, I feel that the corporate goals of tomorrow—which can appeal to the leadership we need and must have will have to be both worldwide and "soul-size."

. . .

It seems to me that in order to develop the kind of business leaders we must have, promising young men should be rewarded with jobs of increasing responsibilities and different functions—a progression which would be neither lateral nor vertical but diagonal. This would give a man scope, sustain his interest and curiosity, challenge his ability and—most importantly—equip him in a far better way with the diversified knowledge necessary for executive leadership in the company of tomorrow.

An integral part of this development would certainly be responsibility for dealing with public affairs. Today involvement with questions of public policy is generally the prerogative of top management and the staff of a specialized department. It is at least worth considering whether it would not be wiser for corporations to assign specific public problems to management at all levels. Not only would the exposure be invaluable, but the complexity of the problems of the times seems to call for precisely such a course.

For if one thing is certain, it is that both the number and the difficulty of public issues will increase.

Entirely apart from the activities at the federal level, we know that demands on education will increase, the need for more and more highways will become pressing, new methods of retraining industrial workers will have to be explored, and the demands on the states will thereby become greater than ever.

The compounding problems of our cities will also be pressing in upon us. In many respects, industry has in the past tended to ignore urban problems until they have reached emergency proportions. (Air and water pollution are good examples.) But we will simply not be able to take the same risks in the future. Some two-thirds of our total population now live in urban areas. The megalopolis is a distinct force in our lives, whether running from Boston to Washington or San Diego to San Francisco. All this will mean staggering challenges and profound social and political implications.

The businessman who will be called upon to lead his company intelligently will have to be prepared to understand the meaning of such changes, to adjust to them, and to contribute meaningfully to the performance of local, state, and federal government in dealing with them. Therefore, it becomes critical for corporations in the Seventies to search out ways and means to make public affairs an integral part of the experience of management at all levels, and in as many functions as possible. Unless the industrial leader of the future is now given an opportunity to familiarize himself with our rapidly evolving social and political situations, he will not be ready to cope with them, or even perhaps to understand them, when we ask him to assume leadership. If we truly believe that contribution is a major adjunct of profit, then we must follow where the argument leads and develop people who can with judgment, wisdom, and understanding translate that belief into fact.

. . .

21

PRICING IN ELECTRICAL APPLIANCES

Different firms set prices in different ways. Three economists describe in detail how the prices of consumer appliances were established by some leading firms.

A. D. H. Kaplan, Joel B. Dirlam, and Robert F. Lanzilotti

A. D. H. Kaplan was a senior economist for The Brookings Institution. Joel B. Dirlam is Professor of Economics at the University of Rhode Island. Robert F. Lanzilotti is Professor of Economics and Dean of the College of Business Administration at the University of Florida.

From *Pricing in Big Business* by A. D. H. Kaplan, Joel B. Dirlam, and Robert F. Lanzilotti (The Brookings Institution, 1958), pp. 13–23, 55–65. Reprinted by permission.

STEEL

The pricing process in steel reflects the industry's history of price leadership and the influence of vertical integration. Earlier studies of steel pricing have concentrated on such factors as the forward integration of the major steel producers, the method of price quotation, the heavy investment and overhead costs, and the peculiarities of demand.[1] In the present context, however, interest is focused on the determinants of policy as they appear to a leading firm. Hence, little purpose would be served by attempting a detailed summary of factors that may affect steel pricing. Nevertheless, certain aspects of the price history of steel that are directly relevant to an interpretation of the views of management require consideration.

The quoted base price for basic steel and steel products tends to be uniform among firms following the lead of United States Steel. Finished steel is sold mostly by specification—this being true not only of highly fabricated pieces like structural steel, but also of the general run of sheets, plates, bars, rods, etc. Extra charges, which are imposed for variations in alloy and other specifications, are important in the final delivered price. Up to the Second World War, the industry apparently agreed on uniform extras to tie in differences in specifications with a uniform base price; but in recent years, this practice seems to have become less prevalent.[2] Room is left for differentials among companies in the final price, despite the fact that most standard products are quoted at base prices plus extras showing no appreciable spread from the quotations of U.S. Steel. There still remains the freight advantage or disadvantage of location in relation to particular market outlets.

[1] E.g., Carroll R. Daugherty, Melvin G. de Chazeau, and Samuel S. Stratton, *The Economics of the Iron and Steel Industry* (1937).

[2] Special prices are made for large contracts, and there is evidence that charges for extras are less uniform than they once were. In this connection, there is strong opinion among producers that discrimination and secret price cuts are not characteristic in the industry. The reason offered by one steel executive is that virtually everyone knows everyone else's costs; in effect, that the industry operates in a goldfish bowl. Also "the price cuts of the thirties taught everyone a lesson."

Mechanics of Pricing

United States Steel states that it employs a "stable margin" price policy, that is, in general it aims at maintaining margins despite variations in sales volume. In so doing it uses standard costs,[3] computed on the basis of 80 per cent of capacity as normal, and including an assignment of overhead burden to every product. Although the company continuously watches actual costs, it follows standard cost logic for pricing purposes. Standard costs are revised annually to account for such factors as increased labor costs, rising markets, new machines, new processes, new kinds of coal used, and similar factors affecting actual costs.[4]

[3] Standard cost may be defined as "predetermined cost for each operation, or each unit of finished product . . . intended to represent the value of direct material, direct labor, and manufacturing burden normally required under efficient conditions at normal capacity to process a unit of product." E. A. Green, National Association of Cost Accountants Bulletin, Vol. 16, cited in *Accountants' Handbook* (1944), p. 225.

One of the main purposes of employing standard costs is to avoid the presumption of significant changes in profits or efficiency when these may be due in a particular instance to a temporary change in the cost or market situation respecting a specific item. To provide for these shifting situations, cost standards are used to make the stated costs of parts, assemblies, and finished products accord more closely with planned objectives. A common objective to which standard costs are frequently geared is a break-even point regarded as normal or optimum—e.g., 70 or 80 per cent of capacity. Another purpose of standard costs is to control plant operations by developing and analyzing variances or differences between standard and actual costs; or by developing cost ratios or trends which use the standard costs as measuring rods.

[4] The market against which U.S. Steel measures adequacy of its capacity and its hoped-for share of sales is the projected total national market (including imports), broken down by individual product groups, by regions and mills. On the basis of these figures and the amount of various products the company feels it can and wishes to sell, the company's "operating plan" for the year is determined.

Standard costs are determined for each mill, but these individual standards are used primarily for gauging efficiency and for stimulating incentive at the local level. For pricing purposes, the standard cost used is an average, weighted by the volumes at respective mills. This means that in addition to changes in the factors mentioned above, as occasioning revisions in standard cost, allowance is also made for higher capital costs of new facilities. Thus, high capital costs exert an upward push on company-wide weighted standard costs and prices.

The company stresses the distinction it makes between what it calls "price structure" and "price level." Price structure involves "a hard-boiled application of standard costs in pricing individual products"; price level is concerned with the general or average level of prices for the corporation, which in the final determination of prices involves much more than standard costs. The distinction can be seen more clearly by a discussion of the use of standard costs in connection with the mechanics of an actual price change, such as occurred following the wage settlement of 1956.

General Price Revision, August 1956

The average increase of $8.50 per ton in steel prices on August 7, 1956 was determined essentially as follows: With the wage negotiations as a backdrop, the Executive Vice-President, Commercial, directed his Price Division to recommend price schedules on the basis of hypothetical wage settlements.[5] According to a tradition in the steel industry, each cent-per-hour increase in direct labor costs adds another

cent to steelmakers' nonwage costs per ton of steel. This working figure has been derived from experience in earlier wage settlements. With this labor-to-total cost ratio, the anticipated wage settlement is roughly doubled and multiplied by a traditional figure of twenty man-hours (more recently a figure of fifteen has been used to reflect higher efficiency) to yield the expected cost of a new wage package per ton of steel. Since the new contract (July 1956) was estimated to add 24 cents to the company's hourly labor cost per ton, an increase of $9.60 per ton was indicated.[6]

The Price Division bases its recommendations on more than this rule of thumb. It also makes a product-by-product analysis in which it considers proposals of the various product departments regarding changes in individual products. Whenever a product section of the company feels a change in base price is needed, it makes such recommendations in writing to the Commercial Department. The form used for this purpose calls for a detailed justification of the recommendation in terms of the pricing history and competitive information on the product and the expected impact of the proposed revision on specific company accounts or industries. The recommendation is accompanied by financial information prepared by the comptroller showing on a per-ton basis the present and proposed cost, together with the present and expected profit or loss.

These recommendations and attached supporting information are presented to the

---

[5] The Price Division consists of four or five price analysts charged with the responsibility of continuing examination of the price problem from many different angles (demand, costs, competition, market strategy, etc.).

[6] The custom of using this crude method of estimating price increases largely explains the expectation of the "trade" generally that prices would go up by at least $9.60 per ton. Some estimates ran as high as $12 per ton on the average, since in 1955 the industry used a 2.5 to 1 basis of estimating the total cost impact of the wage settlement. *Business Week* (Aug. 11, 1956), p. 25.

director of the Price Division for his evaluation and in turn are submitted to the Vice-President, Commercial, for final action. It is important to note the kinds of information before the price makers at this level of management (which actually evaluates proposed price changes and determines the changes to be made, when, and by how much). The changes are considered in terms of profit return on *sales*, not investment. This illustrates, as in the case of other companies in the sample, the way in which pricing officials view their product pricing problems, in contrast to the top level management, which views price policy primarily in terms of return on investment, but which does not actually determine prices.

Although the 1956 general price revision increased the composite average 6.25 per cent ($8.50 per ton), the prices of different

pitious time for a complete revision of prices; the labor cost factor in the given product; the company's leadership position in the product; expectations of the trade (and the potential pressure from congressional committees and the public) With the 1956 three-year contract, management expected to make more selective price changes as it deemed appropriate, rather than follow its earlier practice of general annual changes.[7]

Cost-Price Relationships

That standard-cost doctrine has not been rigidly followed by the company in pricing is suggested by price changes that do not seem to conform to the usual varieties of standard-cost plus target-return pricing. Standard-cost pricing is designed to avoid the necessity for making short-run changes in burden that would result if adjustments

	Aug. 7, 1956 Price (Per ton)	Previous Price (Per ton)	Per Cent Increase
Alloy steel			
Billets, blooms, slabs	$107	$ 96	11.5
Hot-rolled strip and sheet	155	144	7.6
Wire—Premier spring, high carbon	168	152	10.5
Wire products			
Nails	167	152	9.9
Barbed wire	187	175	6.9
Carbon steel			
Cold-finished bars	137	125	9.6
Light rails	120	113	6.2
Plates, high strength (Man-Ten S)	127	120	5.8

products were not raised uniformly. Many products were raised more than 6.25 per cent, some less. The items tabulated . . . taken from U.S. Steel quotations announced immediately after the wage settlement illustrate the variations in the price increases.

These differences show, among other considerations, such factors as: holding back on changes during the year, the post-wage settlement being regarded as the most pro-

were continuously made for temporary changes in volume. Actually, U.S. Steel has not been able to ignore short-term shrinkage of demand. Moreover, it has not been able to carry its "fair return" logic to the point of forcing price increases in depressions to offset higher unit costs at low volume, because its competitors would not fol-

[7] This selective policy apparently was not followed in the general price increase of $6 per ton announced by U.S. Steel on July 1, 1957.

low. Nor has it cut prices in boom periods, which would be the corollary of price increases in depressions.

Differences in margins among products were not demonstrated by the corporation in terms of cost and price data on given product lines but were assumed to be generally recognized in the industry. Mill prices cannot be directly related to costs for U.S. Steel or its competitors, whose prices, with certain exceptions noted below, are generally designed to meet the corporation's prices. United States Steel has the same prices at Pittsburgh and in Ohio, Illinois, Indiana, and Alabama, and apparently averages mill costs to get such equalization.[8]

The Competitive Impact on Pricing

The intensity of competition from other steel companies varies with the effectiveness of U.S. Steel's price leadership. With swings in the business cycle, there has been some modification of the "full-cost stable-margin" pricing philosophy of U.S. Steel and its leading competitors. Competitors of the corporation are more likely to take premiums in periods of prosperity, while U.S. Steel appears to demand no more than its published prices. In recession, however, the company has followed the trend toward concessions initiated by competitors. United States Steel has tended to be the laggard in recognizing the price cuts of its rivals. The ostensible regularity and comparative rigidity in steel prices have been appreciably modified by the policies of steel companies other than U.S. Steel. From 1946 to 1950 the prices of many steel producers were substantially higher than those of U.S. Steel.

When pricing through the basing point

system was in effect, there were apparently fewer exceptions to the leader-follower pattern. Yet, even in 1936 U.S. Steel had to cut its base prices to reflect levels prevailing generally in the industry but not yet "official." With all mills on an f.o.b. basis, when demand is heavy, there is perhaps less of a disposition on the part of competitors to follow U.S. Steel. The corporation's public announcement of October 1953, reiterated in its *Annual Report* for 1953—that when necessary to get the business, it would meet the lower delivered price of a competitor—suggests that when rivals expect operation will be less than capacity, they are more disposed to undercut U.S. Steel.[9] There is no indication that the October 1953 policy resulted in U.S. Steel's having to match price reductions that yielded its competitors a lower base price than U.S. Steel had set.

Opportunities to differentiate prices to take advantage of locations within a given natural market may vary with the particular products and sections of the country that are involved. In the East, for example, where Bethlehem Steel has four mills, the mill prices for semifinished steel plates, bars, and sheets are the same at all its mills and identical with Pittsburgh prices. Structural prices are slightly higher than Pittsburgh, but are the same at all its mills, even

---

[8] According to one pricing official, "standard costs on most products are much closer among mills than is commonly supposed: the variations run about five per cent." The Fairless Works is evidently an exception.

[9] "Under the revised policy, U.S. Steel will continue to quote prices f.o.b. its mills, or, if the customer so desires, it will quote delivered prices which reflect full transportation charges from shipping mill to destination. The revised policy, however, permits the meeting of a lower delivered price of a competitor when necessary and commercially desirable in order to participate in the business of an individual customer. This change in policy is consistent with the stand long taken by U.S. Steel—that it has the right to compete in good faith in any market for the business of any consumer. This provision for meeting the lower delivered price of a competitor does not constitute a return to the so-called multiple basing point pricing method which was abandoned by the steel industry in 1948." U.S. Steel Corporation, *Annual Report, 1953*, p. 12.

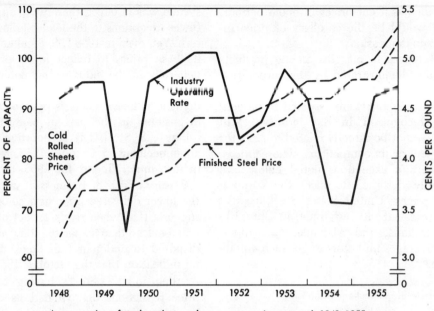

Average prices of steel products and average capacity operated, 1948–1955

Johnstown, which is near Pittsburgh. Yet, Sparrows Point prices are higher than Pittsburgh on wire rods, wire, and tin mill products. Some of these are made at the Johnstown mill, but for these products Pittsburgh prices are applied. Similarly, U.S. Steel's Fairless Works enjoys a $3.00 per ton price differential over other mills on standard bars, small shapes, and special quality and concrete reinforcing bars, and a $1.00 differential on hot- and cold-rolled sheets. Farther west, National Steel's Great Lakes plant near Detroit has enjoyed a differential over Pittsburgh of $2.00 (formerly $4.00) per ton on sheets. It is a moot question whether such differentials could be maintained in conditions of slack demand and underutilization of plant capacity by other steel producers, such as prevailed in 1953–54.

It also seems clear that firms will quote outside their natural territory and absorb freight. United States Steel management indicated in interviews that the 1953 announcement regarding its intention to meet the delivered prices of competitors should

not be taken to mean that it will shade its base prices to meet individual situations. An officer explained that the company "is committed to a one-price policy; if it is deemed desirable to change price, it will be an across-the-board change." The management stated that it will do no more than equalize the freight disadvantage, even in those instances when U.S. Steel's base price is higher than a competitor's.[10] The company's determination to implement this policy strictly has been spelled out in a memorandum to all sales offices, with specific instructions respecting the conditions under which freight absorption cases would be considered by the Commercial Department.

[10] This would appear to be somewhat inconsistent with the earlier announcement about "meeting the delivered prices of competitors." Also, it is difficult to understand how customers could be gained or held (except in periods of steel shortage) if it meant that U.S. Steel's delivered price (with freight equalized) would still be higher than that of a rival steelmaker. It would appear that U.S. Steel will not *initiate any price shading*, but if threatened with loss of customers will retaliate as necessary to keep them—*e.g.*, by freight absorption.

Competitors, meanwhile, complain that prices on many steel products, even after the broad price readjustments carried through in 1956, have not been high enough to stimulate the desirable level of new investment in the industry. Generally, the assertion takes the form of the specific accusation that U.S. Steel is pricing as though new capacity cost $100 instead of the current $300 a ton. United States Steel has joined in complaints of an insufficient return, yet apparently does not intend to relieve the pressure on its competitors.[11] A campaign by steel men to boost prices was dampened when U.S. Steel would not go along with a general price increase in the fall of 1955.

Although steel producers have complained, it is evident that the "art of followership" is still deeply embedded in the philosophy of pricing in the steel industry. National Steel has been a price follower in every line in which it engages, in two of which (tin plate and light sheet steel) it has been an important producer. Despite former President Weir's adoption of the position that steel prices should be based on full cost of the most efficient firm, the company nevertheless has rested profitably under the umbrella of U.S. Steel prices during a large part of its history.[12] National's price has generally followed the Pittsburgh price, with freight allowed when necessary. While the company unhesitatingly meets price cuts—and does so by reducing the

base price rather than the extras—it makes no effort to lead in price reductions.

Thus, U.S. Steel's competitors, except to the extent that they produce specialities or otherwise tailor their services, feel forced to go along with the U.S. Steel base price plus transportation cost in "normal" times when demand is heavy. By concentrating in those areas of steel making, particularly tin plate, where it can operate at low cost and raise technical standards, National appears to have been a successful operator. Indeed, one officer of U.S. Steel who has been with the corporation for many years has expressed the opinion that companies like National and Bethlehem, with more centrally located facilities, have been able to improve those facilities at the same location. United States Steel, by contrast, was disinclined to abandon its original locations and less adaptable steel capacity "because of long-continued obligations to community and to staff." Hence, it has had greater overhead burdens and lower margins in comparison with other steel companies. These disadvantages have been offset in part by the advantages accruing from "a very broad product line and also complete geographic coverage."

Patently U.S.. Steel's policies pervade the pricing structure and price levels for all steel products. Even with products numbered in the thousands, and customers exceeding 100,000, the company has sought to apply a uniform, universally applicable pricing policy. Its price policy was characterized by one of the senior officials interviewed as follows: "U.S. Steel has never tried to price to maximum profit not only in the short run but even in the long run." It appears that U.S. Steel holds the philosophy of cost-plus pricing. Nonetheless, even such a company has difficulty in following a formula in pricing steel products—partly because of the differences in costs among plants and the heavy overhead

---

[11] Since 1940, according to a statement made by Mr. Fairless in 1953, U.S. Steel had not, in ten out of twelve years, recouped "a dime of added profit on the millions of extra tons of steel that [it] produced for the people of this nation," nor earned "one cent of increased return on the billon and a half of additional capital that has been poured into [its] business." *New York Times*, Apr. 26, 1953, p. 5.

[12] Recently the pinch of higher costs has led to industry criticism of prices under U.S. Steel's leadership as being inadequate to provide for depreciation and new capacity. National Steel Corporation, *Annual Report, 1955*, p. 6, and *1956*, p. 5.

factor, and partly from the desire to hold customers.

The corporation has given evidence of limiting profits and refraining from exploitation of shortages, which can be viewed as manifestations of awareness of its responsibilities and vulnerability as the largest and dominant firm in the industry. In the past, according to U.S. Steel, it has refrained from cutting off its semi-integrated customer-competitors in periods of shortage when it could make higher profits by sharply raising prices or by finishing the steel products itself—a problem that is not so important today with increased integration of smaller mills. President Fairless testified that the company has checked with its customers before raising prices and has held off in reducing published prices, in the interest of customers with heavy inventories. Moreover, on occasion it has accepted orders for certain items at a loss to keep its regular customers. Competitors, on the other hand, even when they believe that U.S. Steel's prices are not high enough, will not ordinarily go above them. The period following the Second World War was an exception. When U.S. Steel has suffered a decline in volume, as in 1954, its pricing philosophy has predisposed it to resist significant cuts. The relative regularity of steel prices through marked changes in operating levels occurring since 1947 seems to bear out the traditional tendency to resist price revisions in steel until action is unavoidable.

. . .

CONSUMER APPLIANCES

There are several stages in the pricing process of a major consumer appliance. During the early period of development of the new piece of equipment—automatic washing machine, refrigerator, TV set— prices differ widely as experience accumulates to determine the most wanted type. After the experimental years, when the consumer has come to know the general character of the product, the result of continuing surveys of dealers' experiences and consumers' reactions is to produce a consensus on what constitutes the "right" price for retail distribution. In the case of 1954 models of automatic washers, there was apparently a general understanding that $300 was the "right" figure to aim at in producing the standard model, for among twenty-four leading manufacturers' brands of automatic washing machines two out of three were priced at $299.95, or within a dollar of that figure. The list price being accepted as the starting point, the problem shifts to a consideration of what the manufacturer can profitably put into the product.

The information on consumer appliances (as with other electrical equipment) has for the most part been supplied by General Electric, the only electrical equipment company in the sample; but in the case of the automatic dishwasher, the cost and price breakdown given below was provided by a large appliance manufacturer not interviewed for this study. It will serve, nevertheless, to illuminate several aspects of pricing policy enunciated by General Electric representatives in respect to consumer appliances.

Starting from the retail list price of $299.95, the manufacturer deducts 40 per cent for the retailer's margin and about 7½ per cent for the wholesale distributors' margin, leaving roughly $156 out of which the manufacturer must get his cost plus profit. With all manufacturers having a similar target to work on, the competition appears to turn mainly on whether one manufacturer can put into the $156 more appeal value than another.

The competition can be shifted to greater emphasis on price by carrying in addition to the standard "de luxe" models more or less stripped models, which eliminate certain automatic controls or trims featured in the former. At this lower level ($239.95 was a common figure), the manufacturers' standard brands encountered the private label brands of the mail order houses and the brands of various manufacturers catering to price-conscious buyers.

General Electric does not follow cost-plus pricing in the sense that it would determine the selling price from a calculation of its own costs. It prices for the market, actual or estimated. In pricing a new item, it prefers to go directly by market surveys to the consumer buyer where a controlled pricing experiment offers the same product with different prices in different areas and also, where feasible, through different channels of distribution.

In the opinion of a General Electric executive, the firm's experience shows that neither distributors and dealers nor the company's salesmen and executives are fully dependable in their guesses of what the consumer will pay for a product. Direct access to the consumers, confronting them with a real choice in a realistic selling environment, is the way to get answers to questions concerning the price-quantity relationship. Dealers can be more helpful in other aspects of marketing than pricing and determination of the features a product should have. This executive believes that in the future G.E. will pay more and more attention to the housewife in determining price and product features.

General Electric, like the other leading manufacturers, carried a $299.95 model among its 1954 automatic washers. But, unlike its competitors, G.E. featured its $349.95 model and treated its $299.95 as a partially stripped version of its standard model.

General Electric's approach to pricing a new consumer product can be illustrated directly by its development for the market in 1949 of a portable dishwasher. The dishwasher was tested in three markets, and the following three prices were set: $149.50; $169.50; $189.50. Each of these prices represented a different method of distribution, ranging from home demonstration at the top price to orthodox department store distribution without demonstration. (Several hundred dishwashers were made by essentially hand processes for this test.) The company thus learned about the relative effectiveness of various distribution methods and what needed to be improved in the product, particularly in styling, to make it more salable. General Electric price policy does not stress, indeed G.E. does not consider desirable, the use of low price in the early stages of development of a product as the means of tapping new markets and expanding uses. For example, when the new dishwasher was sold at $200 instead of $250, no more than 5 per cent of additional sales was believed to result. This was because the "service" idea of an automatic electric dishwasher was not yet so fully accepted as to make a price concession expand sales significantly. When the service idea caught on so that the sales reached about 15 per cent of the market potential, demand became very responsive to price. Similarly, in this early stage the stripped models of dishwashers were not particularly effective. The new portable dishwasher, for example, "looked too cheap." Another $5.00 spent on streamlining and in embellishment made it look like another $30 to the customer.

In its present policy on appliances, G.E. apparently exercises a degree of independence associated with maintenance of quality prestige for its products. Thus G.E. itself adheres to quoted prices. At the end of a year, when a new model is coming out, G.E. gives notices to distributors and dealers and expects them to work off their inventory before the new model comes along.[13]

At the level of distributors, and more importantly at the level of dealers, it is recognized that quoted prices are as a rule not strictly adhered to. General Electric does not fair trade its major appliance lines. Executives explain that the techniques of indirect price concession on "big ticket" items have been so finely developed "that it would take a large staff of lawyers to police fair trading in 40 states." Evasions through trade-ins and wiring charges are hard to detect and harder to prevent. These General Electric products, however, have been fair traded in a few states where distributors make the decision. While G.E. has no right to tell distributors to whom to sell, and at what price, it does believe in maintenance of the margins considered necessary to perform adequate service. It is interested in seeing that service does not deteriorate.

Whether to advertise prices of major appliances nationally has been a moot question at G.E. During the immediate postwar inflation, the policy of advertising prices nationally was abandoned because of unsettled conditions, in which production of the advertising frequently lagged behind the rising cost level.[14]

The experience with television sets, which in 1948 and 1949 were selling at about a 20 per cent markup in New York City rather than the larger margin allowed for in the suggested list price, illustrated the difficulty of preventing price shading at the dealer level. The irregularities were related to the mortality rates of independent dealers in different areas. From the standpoint of General Electric, a fair estimate is that a dealer who carries major appliances and electronic items needs about 2,000 wired homes. This is probably a factor in its selection of dealers. The company likes to see dealers big enough to have at least two outside salesmen.

Although G.E. does not regard itself as operating on a cost-plus basis in the field of consumer appliances, its realizations nevertheless do not change drastically over time, partly due to the tendency noted above for manufacturers to settle through experience on a customary price and then adjust cost to price with a "normal" profit margin in mind. What changes there are would not be mainly attributable to departure of actual prices from quoted prices but rather to variations in the proportions of long and short margin products. This type of variation is not regarded as very important. However, there is a broad secular downward change in percentage of net profit to sales as well as cyclical fluctuation.

Small portable appliances, which are sold by G.E. to a great variety of dealers, were generally fair-traded in the interest of maintaining profitable margins for the dealers. The small appliance fair-trading unit of General Electric has pointed out that the number of small appliances it is possible to dispose of is largely dependent on ability to attract dealers. Up to a point, sales volume may be determined by consumer elasticity of demand, but as soon as the retail price is reduced to the point at which the dealer's profit margin begins to be undermined, there is a progressive decline in the number of dealers willing to carry the article and in the extent to which they will push its sale. The problem of the manufacturer, therefore, is to set the "optimum" price, which is the one that combines

[13] This was contrasted with the practice of some rivals of making early price cuts on the old model. One manufacturer has been known to make large additional quantities at the end of the model year and to dump the old model at low prices, while simultaneously selling the new. The general impression is given that large companies typically adhere to quoted prices of major appliances and that small companies with less well-established brands are less punctilious on this score; but this was not explicitly stated to the interviewer.

[14] However, on small appliances under $25, which were fair-traded until 1958, prices have been nationally advertised.

attractiveness to the consumer with a profit margin satisfactory to the dealer, and ensure it through fair trading. Since many of these items are supplied as gifts, their biggest sales occurring before Christmas and on other gift-giving occasions, the company may concentrate on building consumer prestige through attractiveness rather than on an effort to be the lowest-priced producer in the line.

General Electric has supplied the following case history of a small specialty item that is not fair-traded, as an example of the tests applied to determine the "right price" to be suggested to retailers.

Adjustable Night Light

The market for night lights has been well established in the American retail economy. Introduced more than twenty years ago, these small lights have increased in sales until today the annual sales volume is several million units. General Electric played a dominant role in introducing the original night lights and has enjoyed a satisfactory market position ever since. Several retail channels handle the sale of these lights. Variety chains were among the first actively to promote the item, but hardware stores, drug stores, and more recently food stores have all successfully merchandised night lights.

Recently General Electric looked for product innovations which would help:

1. Expand the market.
2. Add features to better suit the customer needs.
3. Secure larger share of available market.
4. Improve G.E.'s profit position.
5. Enhance the value of the entire G.E. Wiring Device Consumer Line.

General Electric recognized that if they were to find such a product it would be necessary to employ the "double profit" system, a profit for the manufacturer and a larger profit or benefit for the customer. The question arose as to what additional features, performance, or attractiveness could be added to the present product to increase the appeal to the customer. Actually, performance and attractiveness of the present night lights left little to be desired so it appeared that the solution must involve the matter of product features.

The Marketing Section had long realized that customers' comments concerning the present night lights were centered on two general areas:

1. *Quality of Light*—Some customers complained that there was too much light—others too little. There was no control of the intensity of the light in the present products. Light intensity control was particularly desirable in a sickroom.
2. *Position*—Two forms of night light were available. In one form the light was essentially parallel to the wall where it was out of the way and could not easily be disturbed in passing. However, since some outlets are mounted vertically and the remainder horizontally, some customers would find the night light in a vertical position and others in a horizontal position. Customers generally preferred the light to be vertical. In the second type, the light protruded straight out from the wall. This light was adjustable so that light always shone down but had the disadvantage that it was easily disturbed by persons passing by.

Product planning specifications. The Marketing Section decided that if they could have a "de luxe" item with the above two features at the "right price," they would have a product that would satisfy the requirements. But what was the "right price"? The earlier night lights had a retail price of about 59 cents. How much would the customers pay for the additional features? The Marketing Section concluded that since this was largely an impulse item, a top price of 98 cents was desirable. Further, since more and more retail outlets were going to self-service, the package became more important since it must do the selling job to a large extent.

A preliminary investigation indicated that an attractive number of customers were willing to pay this premium for the "de luxe" item. A Product Planning specification was prepared describing the desired features, performance and attractiveness of the product. It was recognized that color was important since the item must attract attention on the counter. Conventional night light colors are brown, ivory, pink, and blue. Ivory was rejected because it was too translucent to achieve desired lighting effect (see below); brown was rejected because it was relatively unattractive; pink and blue were selected for their attractiveness on the counter as well as their nursery appeal. G.E. felt that the higher-priced item would be more attractive as a gift than the conventional 59 cent item. Further, it was hoped that the new item would not only appeal to the new customers but would also be sufficiently attractive to cause persons who had previously purchased night lights to purchase the new, more desirable one.

Engineering problem. The major engineering problem consisted in finding a suitable means of dimming the light that would not be too costly. Conventional methods of dimming by the use of variable resistors or variable auto transformers were rejected because of cost and size. Finally, an ingenious means of dimming the light by a mechanical shutter was devised and this was designed into a light using the "Moon and Stars" as the motif. For full brightness the shutter was adjusted mechanically to "Full Moon" effect. For lowest brightness the shutter could be adjusted so that only the "Stars" gave off light. This design was found to be patentable.

The cost estimates, based upon this design, were somewhat disappointing. Since a lower than normal return would be realized at the previously considered retail price of 98 cents, the entire price question was reopened.

Setting selling price. In the final determination of price it was necessary to review the objective of the development.

1. The new light was not intended to replace existing lights but rather to upgrade a portion of the market. Even though the total annual volume of night lights was several million units, the sale of anything over 100,000 units would be considered satisfactory for the new product. Costs were essentially constant after this volume was achieved.

2. This new light was originally conceived as a 98 cent item because this is the generally considered top price for "impulse" items. However, with price inflation, customers were conditioned to seeing items of this type move up beyond the dollar figure. Also, because this was conceived as being a gift item, the higher retail price might attract more customers. Since there was no competitive product, the customer had no direct method of establishing value and could only compare it to the then available but less desirable products selling at 59 cents. However, one difficulty with even the 98 cent price was that this item was designed to be sold on the electrical counter of the retail outlets previously mentioned. Since most items on this counter sold for a much lower price, there was the question of customer resistance to a product of this price being sold on this counter.

[It was noted that from the standpoint of the retailer the item must produce a profit compatible with the counter space required to display it. A higher priced item might produce for him more dollars of profit than one selling at a lower price with higher volume. Consequently a lower sales volume (with a higher price) could justify the necessary counter space as against a drive for volume through low margin pricing.]

3. A study was made of volume-selling price relationship required to achieve the same dollar profit to the Department. These data were calculated at 99 cents, $1.09, $1.19, and $1.29 selling prices. The study disclosed that it was necessary to sell twice as many at 99 cents as was necessary at $1.09 to achieve the same dollars of profit for the manufacturer. It was necessary to sell twice as many at $1.09 as at $1.29 to achieve the same dollar profit. Four times the volume was required at 99 cents as was required at $1.29 to produce the same dollar profit. Furthermore, since costs were estimated to vary only slightly with volume above 100,000, the higher selling price provided a better return on investment.

4. Items of this type often require special pricing for special promotions. The selling price was established high enough to allow for this type of promotion on a profitable basis.

5. The final question was the effect of pricing on volume in actual test situations. If the higher price reduced sales much below 100,000, it would not be considered despite the reasons cited above. Tests were conducted in various retail outlets in selected cities to test the effect of price on sales. These tests indicated that price was not a particular factor up to and including $1.29 but that sales fell off above this figure. Consequently, the item was introduced with a suggested retail of $1.29. However, since none of our wiring devices is fair-traded and no effort is made to control or establish retail prices, we have no assurance that the price was followed in all instances.

22

THE REVENUE MAXIMIZATION HYPOTHESIS

William J. Baumol

Economists traditionally explain that businessmen try to maximize profits. Professor Baumol believes that, although profits are important, most businesses are more concerned with expanding their total sales.

William J. Baumol is Professor of Economics at Princeton University.

Excerpted from *Business Behavior, Value and Growth.* Rev. ed. by William J. Baumol, © 1959, 1967, by Harcourt Brace Jovanovich, Inc. and reprinted with their permission.

Before turning to the substantive material of this brief chapter, it is necessary to explain the limitations of the evidence on which its allegations, and some of those which occur later, . . . are based. Essentially, the assertions are no more than impressions gathered through casual observation of the operation of a number of business firms. In my work I have had occasion to examine in detail some of their decisions and the data on which they were based. Perhaps equally illuminating have been management's reactions to our own recommendations. These reactions certainly seemed indicative of the nature of management's objectives and, in particular, its attitude toward profit maximization. As we shall see, this will play an important part in the sequel.

It must be emphasized, then, that the empirical observations which are reported here were highly unsystematic and represent a sample which, as statistical studies go, must be considered extremely small. Their only and peculiar virtue is that they can lay claim to having come, as it were, from the inside.

Let us return now to the real matter of this chapter. . . . I shall take the position that, *in day-to-day decision-making*, management often acts explicitly or implicitly on the premise that its decisions will produce no changes in the behavior of those with whom they are competing. . . .

Of course, . . . in making its more radical decisions, such as the launching of a major advertising campaign or the introduction of a radically new line of products, management usually does consider the probable competitive response. But often, even in fairly crucial decisions, and almost always in routine policy-making, only the most cursory attention is paid to competitive reactions. This apparently dangerous attitude does not usually lead the businessman into serious difficulty because, I believe, his more ordinary decisions are rarely met by prompt aggressive countermoves of the sort envisaged in many of our models. There are several reasons why this should be so.

1. Complexity of Internal Organization

The modern industrial giant is a mammoth organization almost always engaged in many activities—some of them highly diverse in character. Its great size and complexity have been accompanied by a correspondingly large and involved managerial organization. Proposals are charac-

teristically inaugurated at points in the organization far removed from the makers of the final decisions. Moreover, because of the multiplicity of departments usually involved, and the uneasy truce between highly centralized control and departmental autonomy, responsibility is frequently divided and is rarely well defined. As a result decision-making is often a lengthy process whose outcome is fairly unpredictable.

This decision-making apparatus is too clumsy and slow-moving for effective interplay of strategy and counterstrategy among competing firms. A move by one of them, *provided it is not too radical*, may just be ignored by the others, simply because divided responsibility invites each decision-maker to shift the responsibility onto others. Even if some countermove is proposed, the suggestion is likely to be watered down as it passes through various echelons and committee meetings. What finally does come through is very likely to come only after a very considerable lapse of time.

2. The Use of Rules of Thumb

Top executives are usually too busy, and their computational skills are sometimes too limited for them to be able to probe very deeply into every business problem. Management's difficulty is that it must retain some measure of control over the operations of the firm without, at the same time, tying itself up in operational detail. This problem is solved by the frequent use of rules of thumb—prices are set by applying a standard markup to costs; advertising expenditures are determined by setting aside a fixed percentage of total revenues; and inventories are required to meet a preset turnover norm.

These rules of thumb do not work out too badly. They translate hopelessly involved problems into simple, orderly routines. They save executive time and permit a degree of centralized control over the firm's farflung operations. By and large, they probably contribute considerably to overall operating efficiency. Most executives appear to recognize these rules for what they are—imperfect expedients designed to cope, in a rough and ready manner, with a difficult control and decision problem.

But rules of thumb tend to reduce competitive give and take among oligopolistic enterprises. Because they must be relatively simple in order to be useful, these rules do not make provision for a variety of contingencies. For example, an average cost pricing rule takes no explicit account of recent trends in the decision patterns of other firms in the industry. It provides no elaborate directions for adaptation to each of the many possible moves of competitors.

In one rather typical case, the manufacturer of a fuel kept his price just slightly above that of the nearest competing fuel because his large overheads made his average cost rather high. When it was pointed out to him that a lower price could reduce his average costs substantially through an increase in his sales volume, he accepted the suggestion with apparently little concern for the possibility that his rival would retaliate by also cutting his price. Moreover, his confidence seems to have been justified by the results. It should be added that in this industry firms in many other cities seem to have had the same experience. Very likely, the manufacturers of the competing fuels failed to meet these price cuts because they too were using average cost pricing procedures.

3. Desire for the Quiet Life

In recent years the managers of large firms have displayed signs of a desire for respectability and security. To avoid difficulties with public regulatory authorities as well as with their own stockholders, man-

agements have veered away from the rough and tumble. But firms who wish to live and let live are not likely to be anxious to make life unpredictable for one another. And it is my impression that business organizations have, to some extent, come to depend on each other to be well-behaved. In fact, they frequently seem to expect others to go along with their decisions and, if anything, to adjust their policies in a cooperative spirit. In some cases I have even seen the possibility of competitive countermoves considered as a sort of breach of etiquette —as a slightly shocking contingency.

4. Reservations

In making a case of this sort it is quite easy to exaggerate and, no doubt, I have somewhat overstated the point. It is not true that a reign of perfect and universal mutual inattention has descended upon our oligopolies. Among many firms there are unsettled border disputes that lead to occasional forays. For example, in one industry where pricing seems otherwise to be conducted on a gentlemanly basis, there is mutual suspicion of the discounts that are offered (for advertising purposes) for the use of their products by nonprofit organizations! One firm undertook a sort of cloak-and-dagger investigation to find out what rebates were really being offered, and indicated that it was prepared to do whatever was necessary to get its products displayed through this channel.

Moreover, it must be recognized that while it does not usually consist of a series of strategic moves and quick responses, vigorous competitive activity does take place. The oligopolist has a fiercely tender regard for his share of the market and, if ever he finds himself losing out, energetic steps may be expected. I will discuss some implications of this attitude later in the book. But for the moment I simply take note of its existence and reassert my belief that in its day-to-day pricing and output decisions, the oligopolistic firm nevertheless takes only the most cursory glance at the probable reactions of its competitors in the confident expectation that their unresponsiveness (so long as there is no large change in market share) will continue very similar to its own.

It must be emphasized that there still remains a very important role to be played by the theory of oligopolistic interdependence and its analysis with the aid of tools like those provided by game theory. For decisions relating to radical changes in policy interdependence is usually as important as our theory has always supposed. However, the ordinary problems of value theory, the routine pricing, and advertising decisions are generally not beset by these complications. This has been the burden of the argument of this chapter. . . .

5. The Logic of Oligopolistic Decision-making

If interdependence is demoted from its central role in the theory of oligopoly, some alternative must be chosen to replace it. The obvious candidate is the premise that each firm tries to maximize its profits as though it were in isolation.

However, the consequences of such an assumption are not particularly satisfying. As I shall point out later, it leaves unexplained some frequently noted features of oligopolistic behavior. Moreover, my experience, and apparently that of some others who have worked with business firms, is that profits do not constitute the prime objective of the large modern business enterprise. It must be made clear that I am not trying to reopen the tired and tiresome argument against the economic man. Surely, he never existed and does not now, but he is still a very useful approximation. On the contrary, I believe the businessman can usefully be viewed as a

calculating individual, but one whose calculations take account of profits in a manner that differs somewhat from the standard view.

. . .

. . . But first, to lay the ground for some of the later analysis, and to help supply plausibility to my hypothesis, I shall argue in the next chapter that even to the profit maximizing firm the scale of its operation can become an important proximate objective.

THE REVENUE MAXIMIZATION HYPOTHESIS

Though businessmen are interested in the scale of their operations partly because they see some connection between scale and profits, I think management's concern with the level of sales goes considerably further. In my dealings with them I have been struck with the importance the oligopolistic enterprises attach to the value of their sales. A small reversal in an upward sales trend that can quite reasonably be dismissed as a random movement sometimes leads to a major review of the concern's selling and production methods, its product lines, and even its internal organizational structure.

Before going on I must make an important terminological point. In ordinary business parlance the term "sales" refers not to the number of physical units of one of its products that has been sold but, rather, to the *total revenue* obtained by the firm from the purchases of its customers. In the near universal multiproduct firm any measure of overall physical volume must involve index number problems, and the adoption of a value measure doubtless is to be expected. In any event, in the sequel I shall adhere to the businessman's practice and use the terms "sales" and "total revenue" as synonyms. As a reminder, however, I will frequently employ "dollar sales" or "sales revenue" or some other such expressions.

1. Disadvantages of Declining Sales

There are many reasons why the businessman should show such concern about the magnitude of his sales. Declining sales can bring with them all sorts of disadvantages: there is reason to fear that consumers will shun a product if they feel it is falling in popularity, though their information on these matters is certainly often spotty. Banks and the money market will tend to be less receptive to the desires of a firm whose absolute or relative sales volume is declining. Perhaps even more important in this connection is the very real danger that firms whose sales are falling will lose distributors—a major marketing setback. Management also is not unmoved by the fact that in a declining firm personnel relations are made much more difficult when firing rather than hiring is the order of the day. The firm that declines (or which remains small when others expand) can lose monopoly power and the power to adopt an effective competitive counter-strategy when one is called for. And it may become more vulnerable to a general deterioration in business conditions. For all these reasons the executive may reasonably conclude that maintenance of as large a sales volume as possible is the only way to succeed in business.

Even if size did not promote profits, personal self-interest could well induce the managers of a firm to seek to maximize sales. Executive salaries appear to be far more closely correlated with the scale of operations of the firm than with its profitability. And in the modern corporation, which is characterized so often by separation of ownership from management, many executives find it prudent to avoid an absolute or relative decline in their operations.

Here, management's concern with the volume of sales is compounded of its very conscientious concern with the responsibilities of its trusteeship and a desire to play good stockholder politics. In any event the effects are the same—the volume of sales approaches the status of a prime business objective.

2. Sales as an Ultimate Objective

Up to this point, in essence, I have been arguing that the firm may be expected to promote sales as a means to further its other objectives—operational efficiency and, ultimately, profits. So far, there is no necessary clash with orthodox analysis.

But now I propose to take the next step and suggest that the businessman has gone still further in his regard for sales volume. I believe that to him sales have become an end in and of themselves.

It must be made clear to begin with, that this hypothesis in no way conflicts with an assumption of rationality. People's objectives are whatever they are. Irrationality surely must be defined to consist in decision patterns that make it more difficult to attain one's own ends, and not in choosing ends that, for some reason, are considered to be wrong. Unless we are prepared to determine other people's values, or unless they pursue incompatible objectives, we must class behavior as rational if it efficiently pursues whatever goals happen to have been chosen.

The evidence for my hypothesis that sales volume ranks ahead of profits as the main object of the oligopolist's concern, is again highly impressionistic; but I believe it is quite strong. Surely it is common experience that, when one asks an executive, "How's business?" he will answer that his *sales* have been increasing (or decreasing), and talk about his profit only as an afterthought, if at all. And I am told the requirements for acceptance to membership in the Young Presidents Organization (an honorific society) are that the applicant be under 40 years of age and president of a company whose annual volume is over a million dollars. Presumably it makes no difference if this firm is in imminent danger of bankruptcy.

Nor is this failure to emphasize profits a pure rationalization or a mere matter of careless phrasing. Almost every time I have come across a case of conflict between profits and sales the businessmen with whom I worked left little doubt as to where their hearts lay. It is not unusual to find a profitable firm, in which some segment of its sales can be shown to be highly unprofitable. For example, I have encountered several firms that were losing money on their sales in markets quite distant from the plant where local competition forced the product price down to a level that did not cover transportation costs. Another case was that of a watch distributor whose sales to small retailers in sparsely settled districts were so few and far between that the salesmen's wages were not made up by the total revenues they brought in. When such a case is pointed out to management, it is usually quite reluctant to abandon its unprofitable markets. Businessmen may consider seriously proposals which promise to put these sales on a profitable basis. There may be some hope for the adoption of a suggestion that a new plant be built nearer the market to which current transportation costs are too high, or that watch salesmen be transferred to markets with greater sales potential and a mail order selling system be substituted for direct selling in little populated regions. But a program that explicitly proposes any cut in sales volume, whatever the profit considerations, is likely to meet a cold reception. In many cases firms finally do perform the radical surgery involved in cutting out an unprofitable line or territory, but this usually occurs after much heart-searching and delay.

3. The Role of Profits

It is tempting to object that along this road lies bankruptcy; and so it would if management were prepared not only to subordinate profit considerations to sales, but to disregard profits altogether. After all, maximum sales might require prices so low that the costs would nowhere be covered. It is quite true that there is some conflict between the firm's sales goal and its profit objectives, and, as is to be expected, the matter is settled by compromise. The compromise is, of course, usually tacit, its terms are ill-defined, and doubtless, it varies from case to case. But I think it is, nevertheless, possible to set up a formal relationship which is analytically useful and, at the same time, provides us with a reasonably close approximation to the facts.

The nature of this approximation is again best suggested by an illustrative experience. A manufacturer of a new synthetic yarn indicated that he was reluctant to promote sales by introducing his product at a price that would not cover the cost of his small initial outputs. The firm's usual rate of return on investment played an explicit and very fundamental role in these deliberations. It was made clear that management was not concerned with obtaining profits higher than this. Once this minimum profit level was achieved, sales revenues rather than profits became the overriding objective.

I suspect that the much publicized practice of average-cost pricing is a crude attempt to achieve just this sort of goal. Prices are set at a fixed markup above average costs, not only because this is a convenient rule of thumb, but also because the practice appears to set a floor under the rate of return. Of course, it does not always work out in that way because volume can be miscalculated and cost estimates may therefore turn out to be incorrect. But the objective of the procedure seems clear nevertheless.

I am prepared to generalize from these observations and assert that the typical oligopolist's objectives can usefully be characterized, approximately, as sales maximization subject to a minimum profit constraint.

Doubtless this premise overspecifies a rather vague set of attitudes, but I believe it is not too far from the truth. So long as profits are high enough to keep stockholders satisfied and contribute adequately to the financing of company growth, management will bend its efforts to the augmentation of sales revenues rather than to further increases in profits.

. . .

23

The large firms of the drug industry have often been accused of padding prices to increase profits. The drug firms say the prices and resulting profits are necessary to finance research. After reading this testimony, what do you believe?

COMPETITIVE PROBLEMS IN THE DRUG INDUSTRY

William S. Comanor

William S. Comanor is Associate Professor of Economics in the Graduate School of Business, Stanford University.

From U.S. Congress, Senate, *Hearings Before Subcommittee on Monopoly of Select Committee on Small Business.* 90th Cong., 1st sess., part 5, pp. 2043–55.

. . .

The core of this paper is a statistical analysis of the relationship between advertising and profit rates across a wide range of consumer goods industries. Our analysis was limited to this sector of the economy for it is only here that advertising seems to have a major competitive impact.

Even among consumer goods industries, advertising seems far more important in some industries than others. In most industries, advertising expenditures account for a relatively low proportion of total revenues while in a handful of others, they reach very high proportions. Thus, in the 41 consumer goods industries examined in our study, 25 had advertising-sales ratios below 3 per cent, eight had ratios between 3 per cent and 6 per cent, and only six industries had ratios which exceeded 6 per cent.

In the latter group, perfumes had an advertising-sales ratio of 15 per cent, cereals and drugs were approximately 10 per cent each, soap 9 per cent, beer 7 per cent, and soft drinks slightly more than 6 per cent.

At lower levels, cigarettes and wines had advertising-sales ratios of about 5 per cent.

These findings suggest that the economic effects of advertising expenditures are not likely to be felt generally throughout the economy but rather are limited to a small subset of industries.

Senator Nelson: Doctor, I notice that

you comment on this later on in your testimony, but the figure that you use for expenditures for advertising of drugs is 10 per cent of sales.

What you are saying is that the total expenditure for advertising for drugs equals 10 per cent of the total sales of drugs, is that correct?

Dr. Comanor: That is right.

Senator Nelson: And in this figure, you are using both prescription and nonprescription; that is, proprietary drugs.

Dr. Comanor: That is right.

. . .

Dr. Comanor: The 10 per cent figure applies both to proprietary as well as prescription drugs. As I note later in my statement, it applies to the average values for the years 1954 through 1957. So we are dealing with a period over 10 years ago.

. . .

Senator Nelson: The reason it seems to me that it would be valuable to have the statistics separated out with a separate set of statistics for proprietary and prescription drugs is that they present two very different problems in terms of the difficulty in entering the marketplace that you talk about. It seems to me that it is one kind of problem to get into the marketplace and compete in the sale of a prescription drug when all of the advertising of that drug is aimed solely at the medical profession and quite another problem to get into the marketplace with a proprietary drug where all the advertising, or almost all of it, is aimed at the general public.

Dr. Comanor: I agree with you completely. I think these two separate industries create very different problems for public policy. This figure was used because the data was obtained from the Statistical Division of the Internal Revenue Service and the IRS publishes data for the two industries combined. The only tax return

data that are available to the general public for this particular industry combine both proprietary and prescription drugs. So that although for public policy purposes, I agree with you completely, for the purposes of our study, we were forced to use the combined industry.

. . .

Dr. Comanor: In most industries, even in the consumer goods sector, advertising probably plays a relatively minor role, although it appears to play a major role in a few others.

One further feature of these statistics is that the subset of industries with high advertising-sales ratios is comprised entirely by those which produce consumer nondurables rather than consumer durables. Industries which produce electric appliances or radio and television sets spend relatively little on advertising as a proportion of total sales. And yet, it is precisely these industries which are generally considered to produce highly complex products about which consumers might need considerable information.

In the statistical analysis, we examine the joint effect of advertising, together with a number of other market structure variables, on profit rates. The additional variables are the degree of market concentration, the rate of growth of demand, and estimates of two entry restricting factors: the extent to which production economies of scale exist in the industry, and the total amount of capital required for entry. These additional variables were introduced into the analysis although our primary attention was directed at the impact of advertising outlays because they are generally considered to influence profit rates and we wished to examine the net effect of advertising on profits after the influence of these other factors had been accounted for.

The statistical analysis is founded largely on tax return data which are compiled by the statistical division of the Internal Revenue Service. It is based on industries as defined by the IRS and refers to average values for the years 1954 through 1957. Averages were taken so that the results would not be influenced by the particular business conditions which happened to exist in a given year, and the years chosen refer to a complete business cycle.

The statistics on profit rates and advertising-sales ratios which are used in the empirical analysis are presented in Table 1 attached to my statement.

Dr. Comanor: A significant correlation exists between these two variables. While high profit rates may be and frequently are associated with relatively low advertising-sales ratios, such as instruments which include cameras, industries with high advertising-sales ratios almost without exception have relatively high profit rates. And this refers specifically to the six industries that have advertising-sales ratios which exceed 6 per cent.

Thus, the average profit rate for those six industries was 11.9 per cent which is 65 per cent greater than the average return for the 35 remaining industries of 7.2 per cent.

Senator Nelson: When you say "average profit rates," are you talking about after-tax profits?

Dr. Comanor: I am talking about after-tax profits.

While motor vehicles has the highest profit rate of any industry in the sample, and at the same time has a relatively low advertising-sales ratio, the next three most profitable industries—cereals, drugs, and perfumes—are all those with very high levels of advertising expenditures.

Senator Nelson: Does the automobile industry fit into the picture you describe later of an industry that has some very difficult entrance barriers—that is, the vast investment it takes to get in?

Is advertising a factor there?

Dr. Comanor: I think most economists

Table 1

AVERAGE PROFIT RATES AND ADVERTISING-SALES RATIOS IN 41 CONSUMER GOODS INDUSTRIES, 1954–57

(In per cent)

	Profit Rate	Advertising-Sales Ratio
1. Soft drink	10.0	6.2
2. Malt liquors	7.2	6.8
3. Wines	7.3	5.2
4. Distilled liquors	5.0	2.1
5. Meat	4.6	.6
6. Dairy	7.9	2.2
7. Canning	6.4	2.9
8. Grain mill products	7.0	1.9
9. Cereals	14.8	10.3
10. Bakery products	9.3	2.9
11. Sugar	5.8	.2
12. Confectionery	10.6	3.5
13. Cigars	5.3	2.6
14. Cigarettes	11.5	4.8
15. Knit goods	3.8	1.3
16. Carpets	4.5	2.0
17. Hats	1.6	2.2
18. Men's clothing	5.9	1.2
19. Women's clothing	6.1	1.8
20. Millinery	−1.3	.8
21. Furs	5.7	1.0
22. Furniture	9.7	1.5
23. Screens and venetian blinds	9.3	1.6
24. Periodicals	11.7	.2
25. Books	10.1	2.4
26. Drugs	14.0	9.9
27. Soaps	11.7	9.2
28. Paints	9.9	1.5
29. Perfumes	13.5	15.3
30. Tires and tubes	10.2	1.4
31. Footwear	7.6	1.5
32. Handtools	11.4	4.2
33. Household and service machinery (not electrical)	7.3	1.9
34. Electrical appliances	10.3	3.5
35. Radio, TV, and phonograph	8.8	2.2
36. Motorcycles and bicycles	5.2	1.1
37. Motor vehicles	15.5	.6
38. Instruments	12.0	2.0
39. Clocks and watches	1.9	5.6
40. Jewelry (precious metal)	5.3	3.2
41. Costume jewelry	1.4	4.0

would agree that the automobile industry has very high entry barriers, but that these are not accounted for by advertising expenditures as much as by the important scale economies which exist in the industry, as well as by the very high absolute capital requirements. In addition, the current franchise system does tend to restrict entry. While important entry barriers exist, I think most economists would not stress the effect of advertising in this particular industry, although firms in the industry spend very large absolute sums on advertising, since after all, it is one of our largest industries. But these large absolute sums account for a relatively small percentage of sales.

Senator Nelson: Would you agree that there is a distinction between the automobile and the prescription drug industry on at least a couple of grounds relative to the advertising question, the automobile industry having a relatively low advertising ratio to sales, with the drug industry having a high advertising ratio to sales? Would you agree that one of the reasons for the distinction there is that there is a multiplicity of drugs and the person who makes the determination about what drugs will be used and what brand will be used is the doctor, whereas in the automobile industry, there are only four major companies in this country and the consumer, by looking at the product, makes the decision about what he will buy?

Dr. Comanor: While this factor is certainly important, I would emphasize a somewhat different factor, which is that in the motor vehicle industry, factors such as high absolute capital requirements inhibit entry so that the auto firms do not feel compelled to allocate further sums to restrict the entry of new firms.

In addition, while advertising promotes product differentiation in the automobile industry, there are various other factors besides advertising which are at least as important, if not more important, in creating product differentiation, such as the annual model changes.

In the pharmaceutical industry, where products which embody the same chemical compound but which are produced by different firms are now similar to one another, advertising plays a much more important role. It is in this context that it is interesting to note that high advertising outlays generally are concentrated in the nondurables field, where product differences are probably much less. Advertising is very high, for example, in the detergent industry, although detergents are probably less different from one another than automobiles.

In addition, we know that in the proprietary drug field, there are very high advertising outlays for products such as aspirin, although aspirin is aspirin.

Therefore, what we find is that advertising expenditures tend to be highest where real product differences are not pronounced. And advertising tends to be relatively low where real product differences in tact exist.

. . .

Dr. Comanor: These preliminary observations were corroborated by our statistical analysis where the influence of the additional market structure variables was also considered. We found that advertising has a statistically significant impact on industry profit rates and that this effect is stronger than that of any of the other variables examined.

Furthermore, the magnitude of the effect is surprisingly high. Industries with high advertising outlays earned, on average, profit rates which exceeded those in other industries, after correcting for the other variables, by nearly 4 percentage points. This difference represents, moreover, a 50 per cent increase in profit rates. Since profits represent the difference between prices and costs, and since advertising outlays is a cost to the firm making the outlay, these findings suggest that high advertising expenditures have a double effect on price levels. Not only do they represent higher costs, but also they are associated with higher price-cost margins.

. . .

In the consumer goods industries where advertising is relatively important, we frequently observe unbranded products which sell at prices substantially below those of highly advertised products even though there may be little real difference between them. Because products which are little advertised must sell at far lower prices than those of their established rivals, the latter can raise prices above costs and earn high profits without fear of enticing the entry of new firms and of the resulting effect on price levels.

High advertising outlays create effective entry barriers through a number of routes. In the first place, high current levels of advertising expenditures create additional costs for new entrants which will generally exceed those for established firms. Because of buyer inertia and brand loyalty, more advertising messages per prospective customer must be supplied to induce brand switching as compared with repeat buying. And therefore, new entrants must be prepared to supply more advertising messages per prospective customer than do their established rivals.

. . .

Although this study refers to the entire consumer goods sector of the economy, we can note that the drug industry is one of those in the sample with both high profit rates and high advertising-sales ratios. During the period between 1954 and 1957, this industry stood in third place out of 41 in both respects. As defined in this analysis, however, the drug industry refers to both prescription and proprietary products.

In the prescription drug industry, advertising accounts for only a portion of the firm's total selling and promotional budget. Detail men and other forms of direct sell-

ing also are important, and therefore figures on advertising alone understate the total effort in persuasion which is carried on by the drug companies.

Senator Nelson: In your figures on advertising, you did not include any of the costs of the detail men?

Dr. Comanor: That is correct.

Senator Nelson: What did you include?

Dr. Comanor: We included expenditures on advertising as reported in tax returns.

Senator Nelson: You reported what the industry claimed as advertising and what the IRS accepted as advertising?

Dr. Comanor: That is correct.

Senator Nelson: Do you know what that included?

Dr. Comanor: That includes expenditures on printed advertisements, direct mail advertisements, and also advertisements in medical journals. It does not include salaries for detail men, for samples, or things of this sort.

Senator Nelson: It did not include samples?

Dr. Comanor: It did not include samples.

Senator Nelson: Even though samples had some advertising material with it?

Dr. Comanor: I think that is correct.

Senator Nelson: Did you include other expenditures such as material furnished to medical students, stethoscopes, that sort of thing?

Dr. Comanor: I am not absolutely certain, but I think not. I would have to check with the IRS before I could answer these questions completely.

Senator Nelson: I do not know what these expenditures amount to, but we have had testimony that medical students get a considerable amount of material, some advertising and promotional, some of them stethoscopes and so forth.

Do the firms deduct this as a business expense?

Dr. Comanor: This is surely a business expense. I am not certain whether it is included in these advertising figures. My wife is a medical student, and I am forced to admit that she has received a stethoscope and a black bag.

Something that you might be interested to know is that one of the drug companies provides every second-year medical student with a black bag which is plastic. The same company in their fourth year provides the medical student with a black bag of real leather. She is now going around with her plastic one.

Senator Nelson: They have somewhat less confidence in the prospects for the second year student than the senior student?

Dr. Comanor: That must be it.

. . .

Given the rapid pace of new product introduction, it is not surprising that doctors have been open to the persuasion and influence of the drug companies. At a 1959 medical conference on the evaluation of new drugs, it was reported that "physicians are frightened, confused and puzzled by advertising material which pushes as many as a thousand new drugs or combinations of drugs every year . . . several practitioners at the session said they felt a void of information about the proper use of new drugs."[1] The simple pace of new product introduction has been a major factor which has increased the effectiveness of heavy advertising and promotional expenditures.

[1] Herman Somers and Anne Somers, "Doctors, Patients, and Health Insurance," p. 100.

Furthermore, most new products have received patent protection. Thus, in 1961, of the 656 single chemical entities which were used for therapeutic purposes, 377 were sold only by a single firm, which amounted to about 57 per cent of the total.[2] The impact of the patent system, however, has not been to create tight monopoly positions, since patented products are often highly substitutable and compete with one another. But rather, it has been to foreclose, to a great extent, rivalry between identical chemical entities or standardized commodities about which price competition might develop. It has strengthened and encouraged a form of chemical product differentiation. In the majority of cases, therefore, advertising has been able to exploit and emphasize the chemical differences which do in fact exist among products.

When doctors are forced to choose between different chemical compounds which purportedly do the same thing, a large measure of uncertainty is certain to exist. Even though a doctor might believe that different compounds have similar therapeutic effects, he is never quite sure, and the prudent course of action is to prescribe the drug which has become well-known. And becoming well-known is, of course, the function among other things of the level of advertising and promotional expenditures.

. . .

[2] Hugh P. Walker, "Price Levels and Market Power in the Ethical Drug Industry," paper presented at the December 1967 meetings of the Econometric Society, Washington, D.C., table 3.

24

Agreements among producers to fix prices and market shares are illegal and inconsistent with the principles of a competitive society. This article discusses the development of an industrial conspiracy in the electrical equipment industry, and it provides some insight into the problems and attitudes of the executives who were involved.

THE ELECTRIC CONSPIRACY CASE

From the *Wall Street Journal*, January 10, 12, 1961. Reprinted by permission.

THE PROBLEMS OF PRICE FIXING

For a number of years various electrical companies and individuals successfully evaded the antitrust laws. They periodically met to fix prices, divide up markets, and otherwise cartellize their industry.

But examination of court records of the cases indicates the conspiracy was not a very successful one. Prices were not fixed except temporarily—some one of the conspirators was forever evading the intent of conspiracy.

Markets were divided somewhat more successfully, but here again the planners of the market were always running afoul of new circumstances which did not fit into the master plan. Certainly the attempt to evade the give and take of the market place meant for the people and companies involved a good deal of unforeseen trouble—the law aside. Red tape flourished; bureaucracy, unofficial and perhaps illegal though it may have been, grew apace. The need for conspiratorial gatherings mounted, all as man-made rules were substituted for competition.

For example, the circuit breaker conspiracy involving General Electric, Westinghouse, Allis-Chalmers, and Federal Pacific ran into this problem in 1958—what to do about the entrance onto the scene of a new company? While a new competitor is never an easy matter for an individual company, it was also quite complex for the conspirators.

What happened was that I-T-E Circuit Breaker Co., a factor in other aspects of the electrical equipment business, in 1958 bought out a small company and wanted to enter the circuit breaker field where prices were being fixed and markets allotted on a percentage basis.

"Now, room had to be made for I-T-E," Antitrust Chief Bicks noted in remarks at the arraignment of the defendants. "So a series of meetings began in January of 1958, at which I-T-E indicated its desire for some business. I-T-E had bought a company; it wanted to get into the business.

"The knowledge by I-T-E that it was entering into a preexisting conspiracy is clear beyond doubt from the pattern of events in early 1958. I-T-E began meeting with the four conspirators that had been going, going more or less smoothly, it's true, with greater or less success, with greater or less mutual confidence that each of the conspirators was living up to his part of the deal, but, nonetheless, one constant conspiracy I-T-E sought to get in.

Overall Policy

"In early 1958 I-T-E secured an agreement as to the overall pricing policy leaving the allocation aside.

"The nature of that agreement arrived at in early 1958 at a series of meetings was roughly this, that general pricing would be tied to G.E.'s book price, that I-T-E in the southern part of California would be allowed 15 per cent off, that I-T-E nationally would be allowed 5 per cent off. . . . Remaining to be finalized was I-T-E's allocation share of the sealed bid business. This was discussed. . . . I-T-E was cut in for a share of 4 per cent following a series of conferences, and so from 1958 on everybody cut back a bit except Federal Pacific. . . .

"The three big companies, G.E., Westinghouse, Allis-Chalmers . . . cut down their percentage. Federal Pacific came up from 10 to 15. I-T-E was cut in for 4. That was roughly the pattern of the conspiracy that kept on until the date of the indictment."

I-T-E, seeking to plead no contest in this case, said among other things that it was charged with being only a small factor in the industry for a short period of time. It has told its men to stay away from competitors, that if they're caught in such activities again they'll be fired.

It was one thing, as in the circuit breaker case, to agree that a certain company would get a specific piece of sealed-bid business. It was something else again to see that the designated company actually got the job. Here, again according to Mr. Bicks' statement to the court, is how that worked, amid burgeoning red tape.

"At a working level meeting where a particular big job was up for discussion the percentages initially would be reviewed in light of what was known as the ledger list, which had on it recent sealed-bid jobs given to the other defendants. In light of that ledger list it was decided which of the companies, to keep the percentages constant, would get the job. Now if that company was prepared to say the price at which it was going to bid, then the other companies could discuss among themselves

what they would bid, add on for accessories, to make sure to give . . . the company . . . whose turn it was to get the job, the best shot at it.

Numbers Code

"If the company, whose job the particular rigged job was supposed to be did not know the price, there would be later communication, either by phone to homes with just the first names used, or by letter to homes with just first names of senders, with no return address, and this wonderful code. . . . The numbers were 1, General Electric; 2, Westinghouse; 3, Allis-Chalmers; and 7, Federal Pacific. What happened to 4 or 5 and 6 until I-T-E came in remains a mystery."

One of the great ironies of the conspiracies was that no matter how hard the participants schemed, no matter how friendly their meetings and communications might be, there was an innate tendency to compete. Someone was always violating the agreements to get more business, and this continually called for new illegal plans. For example, price-cutting in sales of power switching equipment to government agencies was getting out of hand in late 1958. This led to the "quadrant" system of dividing markets.

"So," declared Baddia Rashid, chief of the trial section of the antitrust division, "at a meeting in November of 1958 at Philadelphia . . . they decided that the best way to handle the sealed-bid market was to allocate the business; however, since there were sixteen companies involved in this particular conspiracy it would have been difficult to try to allocate the business as in other cases on a percentage basis, and therefore it was decided that it would be best to divide the country into four separate geographical areas which were called quadrants—the northwest quadrant, the southwest quadrant, the southeast quadrant, and the northeast quadrant.

"Four companies were assigned to participate in each quadrant, and one of the company representatives in that quadrant was designated as a secretary for the purpose of handling the allocation within the particular quadrant." For example, ". . . in the northeast quadrant . . . meetings were held, and it was decided that the business within that quadrant would be allocated in an alphabetical rotation . . ."

This plan did not work to everyone's satisfaction, but rather than fall back on the give and take of the market place, which the law requires, the conspirators formulated another plan.

"In September of 1959, however, there were some complaints that had arisen because some companies felt they were not getting a sufficient share of the business . . . it appeared that certain of the quadrants were obtaining more sealed-bid business than other quadrants. Therefore, they held a meeting in Pittsburgh . . . in September, 1959 . . . and they discussed this situation. . . . After some discussion it was finally decided that perhaps the best way to do it would be to go back to a national allocation scheme at which each company would be allotted a certain percentage of the business. They all agreed to that plan, and each company was then asked to indicate what percentage of the sealed-bid market it felt it should obtain. . . . An individual from one of the . . . companies was designated to act as secretary. . . ."

But the basic problem, in this industry where price fluctuations were sometimes drastic, was "stabilizing" prices, and efforts to bring this about spawned many a difficulty.

Reviewing the Books

In one case one conspirator sneaked in a bid on a product below the price level which had been agreed upon, the government said. Discussions among the conspirators followed, and the offending company was asked to bring in its books so they could be checked. The representatives of the other companies reviewed them and decided "that this company had deviated from the established prices. So the representative from this company indicated that henceforward he would try to control it a little better." Such meetings to keep the co-price-fixers in line were frequent in other cases.

In a case involving industrial controls these meetings became quite numerous. The government characterizes this case as perhaps the most serious price-fixing case encountered in the "past five or ten years." It counted 31 separate meetings from 1955 until the date of the indictment by the defendants, General Electric, Westinghouse, Square D Co., Cutler-Hammer Co., Clark Controller Co., and Allen-Bradley Co. Mr. Rashid spelled out some of the details for the court.

"The first [meeting] occurred in August of 1955, in Maine. At this meeting all of the defendants except a representative of General Electric were present . . . the individuals present agreed to increase the prices of industrial control equipment by 10 per cent and to put this price increase into effect the following September. They mutually agreed that Cutler-Hammer would be the first to announce the price change and that the rest would follow thereafter.

"There was another meeting in November of 1955 at Atlantic City, New Jersey, in which again all the defendants except General Electric met to discuss the effect this recent price increase was having on the market.

"This was followed by a meeting in April of 1956 at Cleveland, Ohio. Between the November, 1955 meeting and the April, 1956 meeting, General Electric had unilaterally put into effect a price increase. The rest of the companies therefore met in April of 1956 to decide what they would do. . . . They had a discussion and decided that with respect to some products they would all follow G E.'s prices, with respect to other products they would not follow it.

"When this was agreed upon General Electric thereafter retracted its price increase with respect to those products that the other companies did not agree to.

Mutual Complaints

"There was another meeting in May of 1956 at Hot Springs, Virginia, which was a so-called price-cutting-discussion meeting at which the companies got together to complain against each other when they were cutting prices from those that had been agreed upon."

In a framework of fixing prices, there arose also the problem of how to price a new product. In some cases the pricing problem evidently stymied introduction of the product.

At a meeting in May of 1957 at Hot Springs, Mr. Rashid declared, there was discussion of the Double O starter that Cutler-Hammer wanted to market. After general discussion there was a "consensus" reached "that it should sell for about two-thirds of the price of the starter then in existence. They tentatively agreed that this new product should be put on the market . . . on or about January 1, 1960."

The following November some of the conspirators met in the suite of Allen-Bradley at the Traymore Hotel in Atlantic City, the government alleged.

"Cutler-Hammer at this meeting wanted to put on the market a low-quality starter; the other defendants (G.E. was not present) were complaining to Cutler-Hammer that that was a bad practice, that what Cutler-Hammer should do should be to put

on the market a high-quality standard and that the price of that product should be comparable to the price of existing starters, so that as Cutler-Hammer was contemplating reducing the price of this new starter by about 20 per cent or 25 per cent, that would have cut into the market of the starter that was then being marketed."

Then at a meeting on January 9, 1958, the government said, ". . . they resumed a discussion of the Double O starter, and they again criticized Cutler-Hammer for wanting a low-quality starter, and in the end the other companies won, and it was agreed that Cutler-Hammer would put out a high-quality starter."

At the same meeting, "Square D Co. was criticized for having put out a new oil-type pushbutton enclosure. . . . The reason they were criticized . . . was the price . . . was lower than the prices of comparable products then in existence."

These then are some of the unexpected tangles that developed from the electrical equipment conspiracies. No matter how diligently plans and schemes were laid, they somehow could not defeat the basic economic factors, which insisted on responding to the inherent forces of the free market.

. . .

Potentials for Trouble

Certainly the climate in which the individuals and companies in the heavy electrical equipment industry operated was loaded with potentials for trouble, and these may well have been the genesis of the legal difficulties which came to afflict a large segment.

The industry is a relatively compact one. Its members range from very large enterprises to relatively small ones. For example, among those indicted in the case were General Electric with $4 billion annual sales and Joslyn Manufacturing and Supply Co. of Chicago with annual sales of less than $2 million and only 45 production employees.

The industry is tightly-knit with many friendships among executives of competing firms; indeed, officials of smaller firms sometimes are former General Electric or Westinghouse Electric executives. The men involved oftentimes had similar educational backgrounds also—college graduates in engineering with a rise through technical ranks into the world of sales. There sometimes existed on the part of the men with the bigger companies an almost protective, big brother attitude toward the smaller companies; this was reciprocated.

And the friendships were not only professional but often quite personal. Trade association meetings fostered these. It was perhaps easy in the camaraderie of these meetings at upper-bracket hotels, amid speeches typical of any association lauding the industry's members and "mission," to draw even closer than business and background indicated. It was perhaps easy, with wives and children present, and acquainted from past conventions, to drift into the belief that nothing could be very wrong in such an atmosphere.

Darkening Grays

Indeed, many of the meetings took place at the conventions of the National Electrical Manufacturers Association and other trade groups. Rather typically, after a conventional and perfectly lawful meeting of some kind, certain members would adjourn for a rump session and a few drinks in someone's suite. It seemed natural enough that mutual business problems would be discussed—specifications, for example— and like as not prices would come up. In time it was easy enough to drift from general talk about prices into what should be done about them—and finally into separate meetings to fix them for everyone's mutual benefit.

Thus purely legal gatherings might have drifted into ones with increasingly dark shades of gray and finally into ones that were pretty black; more than one moralist has noted that it isn't the blacks and whites of situations that get initially law-abiding citizens into trouble; rather it is a progressive inability to distinguish between shades of gray.

It was especially easy in this industry to get into price discussions.

The economic position of the various companies has often been one of feast or famine—large orders or none at all for the gigantic pieces of equipment manufactured. Widespread overcapacity after World War II brought intermittent price warring. In 1955, for example, there occurred a price war, known throughout the industry as the "white sale," which saw some prices cut as much as 50 per cent. Profit losses resulted and in some cases red ink. Again in 1957 there was a lesser wave of competitive cutting. At least during the "white sale" General Electric and Westinghouse wound up with most of the business. By reports then current some smaller companies were seeking government intervention under the Sherman Act's antimonopoly provisions.

The case has a number of ironic aspects, but one of the great ones is that men in the large companies believed they had to protect the position of the smaller companies or run the risk of antitrust prosecution. Another is that much of the overcapacity underlying the "need" to fix prices was government spurred. Fast tax write-offs, growing out of two wars in two decades, brought the greater capacity for defense that the government wanted, but they also left the manufacturers with an embarrassing amount of plant.

As a result of this industry makeup, the friendships, and the price-capacity situation, there evidently developed in wide segments the philosophy that collusive activity was ethical, illegal though it might be.

Perhaps an extreme exponent of this view, though expressing a widespread one, is F. F. Loock, president, general manager, and sales manager of Allen-Bradley Co. of Milwaukee, who has pleaded guilty.

Looking back on what happened, he says: "No one attending the gatherings [in the electrical controls industry] was so stupid he didn't know [the meetings] were in violation of the law. But it is the only way a business can be run. It is free enterprise."

Price fixing is not usually associated with the idea of free enterprise, with the idea that the market mechanism is to be the ultimate controlling factor, and that this mechanism must remain unimpaired either by individuals or governments. But there is a rationale for the cartel system which permits the general type of collusive activity the electrical men were engaged in. According to it, markets are divided and prices fixed so everyone involved can "get along." Even the consumer is supposed to benefit because stable markets aid stable production and supposedly costs can thus be stabilized.

"Protection Against Buyers"

Price competition is anathema to such a setup. Mr. Loock says one reason for the gatherings in his industry was "we also need protection against buyers" and the "illegal meetings gave us such protection."

Elaborating on the need for "protection," Mr. Loock cites one instance in which the purchasing agent of a major Detroit manufacturer told the electrical manufacturer another one had offered a lower price. "By discussing the matter, which was not true, among ourselves, we were able to iron out the problem." He concludes: "I believe that in an industry where money is necessary to continue research and development of products, we should have some protection against the crookedness of some buyers."

There was also a feeling in the industry that the antitrust laws were unjust. With a rationale developed of friendly live and let live among competitors, laws designed to force competition seemed "government interference." The question was also asked in the industry: If such getting together was all right under the old N.R.A., why isn't it all right now? Of course the N.R.A. of the 1930s was declared unconstitutional by the Supreme Court, but some say the industry's philosophy of "getting together" has roots in that era.

But if illegal "stabilization" was an industry way of life, it should not be assumed that relations were continually rosy among competitors, or that all authority in the industry was bent on collusive activity.

Getting together to fix prices did not alter the basically competitive situation prevailing in the industry's markets. Indeed, it often seems some attendance at the collusive meetings was with tongue in cheek as to stabilizing prices, with a real reason of finding out what the rest of the industry was up to in order to get the jump in the next price cutting wave. Too, some of the conspirators pretty much inherited their roles from predecessors, older men who may have felt more of a tug from the industry's "way of life" than they did. In fact there was personal dislike among some of the individual conspirators; perhaps an individual who did not like himself for conspiring had little respect for others also so engaged.

. . .

25

Antitrust policy in the United States has been characterized by a two-sided approach, with one set of policies for protecting competition against monopolistic activities of other firms, and another looking to the structure of markets and the size of firms. This article explores the consequences of our present antitrust policies in an era characterized by rapid change and growth of the financial conglomerates, and it suggests that the antitrust laws be amended to clarify national policy toward bigness and competition.

ANTITRUST IN AN ERA OF RADICAL CHANGE

Max Ways

Max Ways is Associate Managing Editor and on the Board of Editors of Fortune Magazine.

From *Fortune* (March 1966), p. 128. Reprinted by permission.

Our sacred cow was born two-headed. Any serious examination of antitrust must start by recognizing that two distinct—indeed, contrary—policies have existed side by side. One policy has protected competition against such practices as conspiracies between firms to fix prices or limit production; this side of antitrust, exemplified by the Addyston Pipe case of 1899 and the very similar electrical conspiracy cases of 1961, has played and should continue to play a helpful part in the ever increasing liveliness and flexibility of the American market. The other antitrust policy has been fearful of change; it has frowned upon the growth of firms, especially by merger; it has sought to preserve the specific structure of markets on the assumption—long since demonstrated to be groundless—that the degree of competition is directly proportionate to the number of competitors and inversely proportionate to their average size; it has impaired the legitimate scope of freedom of contract and introduced arbitrary rigidities into the market through which we allocate our resources.

During the last fifteen years the second policy has become more and more dominant in antitrust enforcement. Essentially, this other head of antitrust is anticompetitive and reactionary. Instead of relying upon the market to protect consumers and encourage progress, it substitutes the preferences of public administrators and judges as to how production and distribution should be organized. By trying to shield specific competitors against the effects of competitive innovation, it tends to reverse—or at least to inhibit—that long line of social evolution which has been described as the movement "from status to contract."

Because our economy is so resilient, the measurable practical damage done by this second kind of antitrust policy has not been great—yet. But what of tomorrow?

We can know very little about the business specifics of 1986 or 1996. But some general statements about the next twenty or thirty years can be made with a high degree of confidence. Among them: (1) the pace of change, which broke through a sort of sound barrier around 1950, will continue to accelerate; (2) change will be made up of millions of innovations; many will be based on scientific discoveries and technological inventions; there will also be significant innovations in merchandising, finance, and corporate structure, and those patterns of coordination and decision making that we sum up in the word "management." In short, what we know of the next twenty years is that corporations will need the utmost flexibility because in each year our economy will be more and more involved with innovation. It is this prospect that urgently requires the U.S. to abandon the anticompetitive side of antitrust.

TRAUMATIC MEMORIES

Serious debate of antitrust policy is drowned out by a kind of litany. "What makes the American business system superior to the British and all others?" "Antitrust." "What slakes the public resentment of big business?" "Antitrust." "What preserves us from direct government regulation and maybe even socialism?" "Antitrust." . . .

But this thing, as they used to say in Hollywood, is bigger than all of them. The reactionary side of antitrust has a momentum that is built into court decisions, congressional investigations, and the clichés of public discussion. This trend has picked up speed during the terms of such dissimilar Presidents as Truman, Eisenhower, Kennedy, and Johnson. A White House "friendly to business" cannot reverse the way antitrust has been going. The place to clarify a fundamental national policy is Congress. . . .

Much more is at stake than the level of corporate profits, or the efficiency of the aggregate economy, or its rate of growth. The *quality* of the American future depends on the flexibility of the market framework. If our business system continues to be haunted by hallucinations lingering from American capitalism's traumatic childhood, we will deal clumsily—and perhaps disastrously—with an era of radical change. . . .

BRYAN, BRANDEIS, BIGNESS AND BADNESS

A glance back at the origins of antitrust may help clarify the choice that now con-

fronts the U.S. In both its good and bad aspects, antitrust was a response to the great change that began in the last third of the nineteenth century. The good side—the confidence in competition and the resolve to foster it—was a brave leap in the dark by a nation that could not be sure of the direction in which modern capitalism would evolve. The bad side—the fear of large business units, new methods, new patterns of trade—was a timid, if understandable, clinging to the circumstantial patterns of an older America. Both elements, side by side, can be clearly seen in the discussion of "the trusts" that rolled through the U.S. between 1880 and 1917.

Many words conspicuous in that discussion—including "trust," "monopoly," and "competition"—had split meanings; antitrust history is an exercise in unscrambling unintentional puns. "Trust," for example, meant originally a quite specific device by which stockholders in competing companies ended competition by pooling their voting stock in the hands of a board of trustees. But "trust" was also widely used to mean *any* large business corporation. "Trusts" in the first meaning—along with price-fixing agreements and other anticompetitive practices—were regarded by many lawyers and businessmen of the day as "conspiracies in restraint of trade," which had been illegal under common law. A practical difficulty was that the courts of the states, which normally enforced such common-law principles, could not readily get their hands on these huge new combines; they leapt across state lines and operated a nationwide business system. Without an act of Congress, federal courts had no solid authority to enforce the common-law prohibition against agreements in restraint of trade. Many who supported the Sherman Act of 1890 saw it as plugging a loophole in the federal-state structure. They reasoned that in the new business world, as in the old, competition would protect the public and stimulate progress. The good side of present antitrust policy is descended from this position.

But their interpretation of antitrust fell a long way short of satisfying that part of the public clamor which used the word "trust" to mean everything that was large, new, and different in business. Theodore Roosevelt understood—perhaps sooner and better than anyone else—the political dilemma involved in the two usages of the word "trust." In 1900, as governor, he told the New York Legislature: "Much that is complained about is not really the abuse so much as the inevitable development of our modern industrial life. We have moved far from the old simple days when each community transacted almost all its work for itself and relied upon outsiders for but a fraction of the necessaries, and for not a very large portion even of the luxuries, of life. Very many of the antitrust laws which have made their appearance on the statute books of recent years have been almost or absolutely ineffective because they have blinked the all-important fact that much of what they thought to do away with was incidental to modern industrial conditions, and could not be eliminated unless we were willing to turn back the wheels of modern progress by also eliminating the forces which had brought about these industrial conditions." As a politician, T. R. was responsive to that element in popular antitrust feeling which was simply resentment of change. But when it came to practical antitrust policy he moved very cautiously because he believed that at bottom the people wanted progress even more than they wanted "the old simple days."

. . .

. . . Louis Brandeis, one of the most influential voices in developing the reactionary side of antitrust, never really believed that, under the stimulation of increasing competition, corporate management was reducing administrative inefficiencies; instead, he seemed to feel that a thousand nail kegs would be hidden behind a thousand pickle barrels. Brandeis believed that in very big corporations inefficiencies would be multiplied; therefore, if big corporations made profits this fact could be explained only by assuming that size gave them illegitimate "market power" to insulate them from their small competitors.

THEY RAN HARDER

This sort of thinking widened the split that had opened between two meanings of the word "monopoly." Originally, it had meant an exclusive right, granted or protected by the Crown, to do business in a certain commodity in a defined area. (All enduring European cartels were to have this element of government protection.) In the U.S. of 1880–1917, however, monopoly began to take on a very different meaning, which is at the root of many of our present antitrust difficulties. Section 2 of the Sherman Act is directed against "every person who shall monopolize, or attempt to monopolize or combine or conspire with any other person or persons, to monopolize any part of the trade or commerce among the several states. . . ." Does "monopolize" refer to a set of practices intended to erect artificial walls against competition? Or does the statute forbid a company to attain in the course of the competitive race a large share of a line of trade? Under the influence of the Bryan-Brandeis type of "conservatism," the word "monopolize" has tended to move more and more toward the latter meaning. *Fortune's* proposition is intended to move it back toward the first meaning.

The greatest source of confusion, however, lay in the different applications of the word "competition." When in the late nineteenth century the U.S. entered a genuine market economy, businessmen were not immune to the general feeling of insecurity. The late nineteenth century's notorious conspiracies in restraint of trade were efforts to flee the rising uncertainties of intensified competition. These conspiracies all broke down, either because they had been outlawed by Section 1 of the Sherman Act or because of technological developments.

. . .

THE GREAT SCOURING-PAD CASE

Don Quixote wasn't exactly crazy; he had just arranged his mental life so that he could see what he wanted to see. Sometimes events in the actual world of business intrude abruptly upon antitrust's *La Mancha*. The government had no sooner won the Paramount Pictures case, after years of complicated market analysis, than television came on the scene to prove that the movie industry as a whole was not exactly immune from competition. Within a few years television not only changed the structure of the entertainment industries but also caused an upheaval throughout the world of advertising. Television is the biggest and best-known postwar example of the effect of innovation on the U.S. economy. But every year there are tens of thousands of smaller examples of how innovation can transform a relatively stagnant business situation into one marked by agitated competition. Frequently, the increased liveliness is triggered by a merger.

Consider the great scouring-pad case pending, as this was written, before the Federal Trade Commission. For many years two medium-sized companies, S.O.S. and Brillo, doing a nearly equal business, accounted for more than 95 per cent of the steel-wool pads sold to housewives for cleaning pots and pans. During this period the competition between Brillo and S.O.S.

does not appear to have been intense; there were few important changes in product design or in production or merchandising methods. At the end of 1957, General Foods, which had not previously been in the household cleanser business, bought S.O.S. No challenge came from Washington. During the next two years sales of S.O.S., relative to Brillo's, slumped.

General Foods then took several steps to revive its ailing property, steps that did not depend upon General Foods' vast size or market power but simply on its managerial brains. It turned the S.O.S. account over to a different advertising agency; then it followed the agency's recommendations for some changes in the product and the advertising pitch. Because investigators found that housewives associated the red soap in S.O.S. pads with rust, the soap was changed to blue; to call attention to the sizable amount of soap in S.O.S., a TV commercial showed a soap pad being whipped into a sort of meringue in an electric mixer. Brillo fought back with a plastic pad called "Dobie" and a disposable pad called "Paddy." General Foods, after a fumble with something called "Handigrips," countered "Paddy" with "S.O.ettes." General Foods' tactics worked. S.O.S. overtook Brillo and spurted ahead, even making big gains in the New York market, where Brillo's share had run as high as 84 per cent.

Clearly, competition was heating up in scouring pads. But the F.T.C. was not pleased. In 1963 it issued a complaint charging that the six-year-old merger of General Foods and S.O.S. violated the Clayton Act because it "tended to create a monopoly." In its complaint the FTC had little to say about what was actually going on in scouring pads. Instead, it stressed the size of General Foods and carried on about such matters as the company's possession of more than 50 per cent of the markets in coconut and "edible gelatins (excluding ready-to-mix desserts)." The FTC displayed its solicitude for the status quo ante by asserting that the merger had "upset and realigned adversely, and threatens to upset and realign further, the competitive structure of the household steel wool industry." This fell deed, said the complaint, had been achieved through General Foods' "economic power, merchandising prowess and extensive advertising and promotion." S.O.S.'s share of the steel-wool scouring-pad market had risen from 51 per cent at the time of the merger to 57 per cent at the time of the complaint. The FTC asserted that monopoly was on the march.

But was it? At the initial hearing before the FTC's examiner, evidence showed that innovation had been breeding in another part of the teeming forest of American business. Scouring pads made with materials *other than steel wool* were attracting a rising share of the housewife's money. General Cable had a copper pad called "Chore Girl"; Kurly Kate Corp. had a plastic pad called "Flip" and two copper pads called "Kurly Kate" and "Kopper Kate"; Du Pont was in there with "Combo," made of nylon; Colgate-Palmolive had test-marketed a nylon pad called "Colgate-Ajax"; General Mills had a plastic pad called "Ocelo"; Minnesota Mining & Manufacturing was marketing "Scotch-Brite" and building a plant to make "Rescue" (both of nylon). Lever Brothers, Procter & Gamble, American Home Products, and a host of small firms were reported considering getting into the cleaning-pad free-for-all. Some monopoly!

The FTC's examiner was not impressed. He defined the market in which S.O.S. was sold as that for "steel wool scouring pads." He cited the indubitable fact that the physical properties of steel-wool pads are different from those of nonsteel pads. But do their *uses* differ? The FTC's lawyers say

"we must conclude" that nonsteel pads are used only for cleaning china and glassware, but the lawyers did not produce evidence to back this up. General Foods denies that it is the case. Store managers, who probably know more about housewives than do FTC lawyers, mingle steel-wool pads and nonsteel pads on their shelves, indicating that they think it's all one market. Advertising for the nonsteel pads directly attacks steel pads as out of date. Prices of several nonsteel pads are obviously set up to compete (on a per-time-used basis) with steel pads. In short, against a mountain of evidence that all scouring pads compete with all other scouring pads in an exceedingly lively market, the FTC's lawyers and the examiner, intent on showing monopolistic concentration, decided that steel wool stands impregnably alone in its ability to clean pots and pans. If so sweeping a claim were publicly made on behalf of S.O.S. or Brillo, the FTC would probably crack down on it for deceptive advertising.

ON THE POINT OF A NEEDLE

Many government briefs and judicial opinions contain ingenious economic analysis and show an impressive ability to relate old legal precedents to new sets of facts. Yet these admirable exercises are suffused with unreality. Everybody now laughs at the medieval schoolmen who engaged in complicated speculation on how many angels could dance on a needle's point. The schoolmen did this as a kind of mental calisthenics; they were not attempting to regulate a seraphic oligopoly. The FTC, the Antitrust Division, and the federal judges, however, aren't kidding.

The trouble is that the sophisticated analytical techniques they employ, though impressive in a purely academic sense, are being hopelessly outstripped by the increasing fluidity and complexity of the U.S. economy. . . . The mind reels at the prospect of antitrust lawyers and economists arguing over whether X's lasers really compete with Y's masers.

It is significant that market structure analysis as used in antitrust cases always distorts the facts in one direction—toward a simpler, more primitive, more stagnant economic picture than the situation that actually exists. In the present state of the science, economic analysis cannot handle more than a small fraction of all the variables and contingencies needed for a sound *legal* judgment on changing market structure in any particular "monopoly" case. And the analysis tends to ignore the element around which competition in fact increasingly centers—managerial brains.

THE CREATIVE GALE

The economist who best appreciated the central role of management in the modern economy was Harvard's great Joseph Schumpeter. Writing in the 1930s and 1940s, he foresaw that the future U.S. economy would live in a self-generated "gale of creative destruction." He believed that the excellence of an economy would and should be measured by its innovative capacity rather than its size. As Schumpeter used the term, innovation did not mean the ability of science to discover new truths or of technology to invent new things. His "innovation" is an *economic* act by which a new product or a new service or a new production or merchandising method is introduced to actual use. One of management's most important functions is calculating the relative risks and rewards of possible innovations. At any point in time there are millions of potential innovations, many of them arising from advances in science and technology. These compete with one another for birth. A decision to attempt a

certain innovation is based on calculations about how it will fare in competition with other offerings, old and new. Before and after the decision, management assembles and coordinates the work of scientists and technicians from many specialized fields, along with the judgments of merchandisers and of men who deal with the markets for capital. Rivalry between corporations centers on management teams that compete with one another to find new ways of cutting costs, increasing volume, modifying old products and introducing new ones. The general market "allocates resources" by awarding different levels of profits to the winners and losers of this race.

Given Schumpeter's views about the decisive role of management, it is not surprising that he expressly foresaw the importance of mergers for American business. He understood, of course, that some operations require heavy capital investment under a unified management; but his thought on mergers went much further than a justification of bigness. Schumpeter's view of the innovating society puts the accent on flexibility. The merger technique is one that a management can use to develop the abilities it has, or to acquire abilities it needs to take advantage of new opportunities, or to protect itself by product diversification when the "gale of creative destruction" blows hard upon its existing business. In the innovating society, no company can expect to maintain indefinitely a given product line or a given market position or a given technology or a given set of marketing methods or a given set of financing arrangements.

Here is an example of a merger where present antitrust policy would play down the socially valuable motives while imputing "monopolizing" motives.

Company A has a group of scientists and engineers who have developed a narrow line of products in a specialized field of electronics. Starting from scratch six years ago, company A has achieved a profitable volume of $20 million a year. Its product line looks safe over the next three or four years—but beyond that, who knows? Its research and development people, still fecund with ideas, may come up with another series of inventions; but this second series, unlike the first, may not find an avidly waiting market. The second series may require vigorous selling, a skill that company A has not needed to develop. The second series may require financing on a scale unknown to the brief history of company A. It may require a great increase in numbers of employees, bringing problems of union negotiations of which company A is innocent.

Company B is also in electronics. It is older and bigger—say, $250 million a year. Some of its products compete directly with the present products of company A. Company B thas a vigorous merchandising arm and a good reputation in the markets for capital. Its present product line looks fairly safe over five or six years. But its R&D seems tired, sterile. It decides that acquisition of company A will stimulate its research, while it can supply the broader managerial deficiencies of company A.

Antitrust policy, as now practiced, would tend to ignore all these considerations of managerial balance and efficiency and concentrate upon one fact: A and B are competitors in certain markets; therefore a merger between A and B is a horizontal merger that would "reduce competition"—meaning only that it would reduce the number of competitors in a narrowly defined market. Antitrust policy would say that if company A needs merchandising and financing expertise, let it go into the executive market and hire the men *individually*; if B needs scientists, let it do the same. This answer displays an ignorance of how work is organized in this society. A first-rate R&D department is far more valuable than the sum of the individual skills

that make it up. So is a first-rate sales department or a treasurer's office. Company A's inventiveness might be aborted long before it could build, man by man, its merchandising and financial skills. And company B's capacity for introducing innovations might be wasted for lack of technological inventiveness.

Merger of A and B can be defended as socially desirable on grounds of efficiency. In a static economy this desideratum might be overbalanced by the danger of monopoly. But on the actual line of this economy's movement the danger that a merged A and B could garner the fruits of monopoly approaches zero.

. . .

THE "SOCIAL AND MORAL" ARGUMENT

The trustbuster has in his arsenal one reserve weapon that transcends economics. When he fails by economic analysis to show that some company, escaping the competitive discipline, has damaged the public, he can always shift his ground to the "social and moral" argument against bigness—an argument that goes all the way back to the William Jennings Bryan era. This argument rests upon one interpretation of "equality" as a social goal. It prefers a society of many small producers because it fears "the concentration of political or social power in the hands of a few men."

In antitrust law the classic expression of this fear of bigness is a passage in Judge Learned Hand's opinion in the Alcoa case. He brushed aside as irrelevant Alcoa's attempt to show that it had not *acted* as if it were a monopoly, that it had not engaged in "predatory practices" or gouged the public. Moving to the "higher" ground, Judge Hand said: "Congress . . . did not condone 'good trusts' and condemn 'bad' ones; it forbade all. Moreover, in doing so it was not necessarily actuated by economic motives alone. It is possible, because of its indirect social or moral effect, to prefer a system of small producers, each dependent for his success upon his own skill and character, to one in which the great mass of those engaged must accept the direction of a few."

This quotation encapsulates fundamental mistakes about the nature of the modern corporation. It assumes that today's business unit is simply a magnification of the village general store where the proprietor "directed" his obedient clerk; this way of looking at modern business inevitably results in a picture of concentrated power.

But the regimentation and loss of freedom that Hand feared is not a characteristic of large-scale business. The actual development of the modern corporation disperses power to many individuals within a unified decision-making structure. The head of a modern corporation is hedged about with new limitations upon his power. He is rarely, for instance, in any significant sense the owner of the business. The rise of professional management, distinct from the shareholders but answerable to them, has created a fundamental check-and-balance situation unknown to early capitalism and to the old law of private property. A more recent and equally important trend has been the dispersal of power *within* management. In a complex modern organization a subordinate is not the "agent" of his boss. Managers far below the top level of a large contemporary corporation have power that inheres in their skills, rather than in the delegation of a superior. They are not so much "directed" as given respon-

sibility and opportunity to initiate, to decide, and to coordinate activities that a chief executive officer would be quite helpless in handling. More and more work that is entirely "directed" from above is performed by machines and computers. Millions of little managers within large modern corporations have more actual scope for individual choice and decision than the "independent" small farmers, artisans, and small tradesmen of the nineteenth century had.

The U.S. public, which may be more in touch with reality than antitrust lawyers, seems to sense that business power is not being concentrated "in the hands of a few men." Once upon a time every banker and bootblack knew the names of Vanderbilt, Rockefeller, Morgan, Harriman, Carnegie. He knew what business each was in and what kind of man each was. These men were giants in the land and their tremendous concentration of economic power carried with it a threat of inordinate political and social influence. But the man in the street today is not likely to know the names of Frederic G. Donner, Michael L. Haider, Fred J. Borch, Albert L. Nickerson, and Donald J. Russell, who are the chief executive officers of companies doing an annual business in excess of $40 billion—a sum that makes the sales of the old Standard Oil Trust look like a hot-dog stand. If your barber can identify the companies headed by the names above, he should stop cutting hair and come write a gossip column for *Fortune*.

. . .

26

MARKET POWER: ALTERNATIVE TREATMENTS

The concentration of market power in a few giant firms persists in many American industries, and, according to the author, this type of concentration leads to market inefficiencies. Correction of these inefficiencies requires a redefinition of national priorities and an eclectic use of government policies designed to foster greater competition.

William G. Shepherd

William G. Shepherd is Professor of Economics at the University of Michigan.

From U.S. Congress, Joint Economic Committee, *Hearings,* (*Price and Wage Control: An Evaluation of Current Policies*), 92nd Cong., 2nd sess., part 2: *Studies of Selected Aspects,* 1972, p. 263 ff.

· · ·

THE SCOPE OF THE PROBLEM

It is now apparent that the U.S. economy contains a core of industries with a high degree of market power. The central problem is the firm with a high market share in a large market. IBM and Xerox, with market shares of about 70 per cent, are obvious examples. There is now a broad expert consensus, with a good scientific basis, that shares over 30 per cent usually involve appreciable market power and affect performance. The same is true, but more loosely, when several firms (the conventional number is four) have a combined share (or "concentration ratio") above about 50 per cent. Market power ranges from pure monopoly (90 to 100 per cent), to near-monopoly (70 to 90 per cent), tight oligopoly (four firm concentration above 50 per cent), and on down to loose oligopoly and perfect competition.

Monopolies are anciently known as an economic and social bad; tight oligopolies are now also recognized as usually behaving like shared monopolies. The behavior is simple; hold price above competitive levels, which would otherwise be at the level of costs. The resulting profit on investment will exceed the competitive profit rate (nowa-days about 8 per cent), in some cases going as high as 30, 40, even 100 per cent, or higher. These profit flows convert into wealth for the few lucky owners, and there are other bad effects to be noted shortly below.

Monopolies and shared-monopolies are often short-lived and trivial. It is the others, the relatively few chronic cases in large industries, that are the real concern. The instinct to focus on the "big industries" is a sound one, for a high market share in a very large industry obviously does have more total effect than the same share in a small market.

In perspective, these chronic cases form the core of what is a serious but not critical problem. How much market power is there? Answer: a lot. In manufacturing industry, about 50 per cent of activity is in markets concentrated above 60 per cent. There are more cases of near-monopoly than we usually admit; Xerox, IBM, Western Electric (in AT&T), Campbell Soup, many drugs, General Motors buses and locomotives, for example.

Is market power rising? Not sharply, but the trend is clearly not down. Does it persist? Yes, in many important cases. Autos, telephone equipment, computers, soaps, electrical equipment, and others are part of an industrial scene that—despite rhetoric about dynamic change—has hardened in the last twenty-five years. The same is true of the utility sectors—power, communications and transport—where regulation has created monopolies. It holds also for the crucial financial sector, where banks, insurance firms, stock exchanges, and underwriters maintain fraternal traditions long since vanished elsewhere. Finally most professions—law, medicine, even morticians—also maintain market power under "self-regulation."

In short, the patient is not getting worse fast, but his sickness is serious and accu-rately diagnosed. A selection of the main cases is given listed in rough order of importance in Table 1. The disease is also probably more—*not less*—serious in the U.S. than in other industrial economies. Abroad, international trade plays a larger role, and governments have developed a richer variety of treatments for monopoly. In Britain, for example, nearly all major cases of market power are more recent and unstable than their U.S. counterparts.

This market power has several main effects, which have been measured with reasonable accuracy. First, it raises prices—

Table 1

PRIMARY KNOWN CASES OF MARKET POWER IN MANUFACTURING

Company and industry	Probable market share in relevant markets (approximate percent)	Size assets 1971 (million)	Profit rate 1960–71 (percent of invested capital)	Basic position has been held since approximately	Special entry barriers
Western Electric (communications equipment)	98	$4,012	10	Before 1913	Near-exclusive A.T. & T. supplier
IBM (computers)	70	9,576	17	Before 1930	
General Motors (automobiles)	55	18,242	19	1928	
Xerox (copying equipment)	75	2,156	23	1963	Basic patent
Eastman Kodak (photographic supplies)	55	3,298	20	1895	
General Electric (electrical equipment	45	6,888	16	1900	User loyalties
DuPont (industrial chemicals)	40	3,999	17	1930's	
United States Steel (steel and products)	35	6,409	6	1930's	
Standard Oil (N.J.) (oil products)	25	20,315	13	1930's	
Procter & Gamble (soaps)	35	2,013	16	1920's	Advertising
Campbell Soup (soups)	75	677	13	1920's	
Coca-Cola (beverage syrup)	50	1,108	20	1920's	Brand name
Aluminum Co. of America (aluminum)	30	2,665	7	1955	
Gillette (razors, etc.)	65	555	31	1920's	
Kellogg (cereals)	45	378	21	1920's	Advertising

NOTE: Certain drug, copper, and glass companies would also be included if sufficient data were available.

SOURCES: Shepherd, *Market Power and Economic Welfare: An Introduction* (New York: Random House, 1970); op. cit.; "The Elements of Market Structure," *Review of Economics and Statistics,* (February 1972); and various other sources.

once, not repeatedly. This in turn makes excess profits available; roughly, each added ten points of market share is associated with an added 2.5 points to the rate of return on investment. For market shares in the forty to seventy range, this is a fine harvest, ten to fifteen points or more above the competitive rate of return. Thus General Motors has been at about 20 per cent, IBM at 17, Xerox in the 22 to 30 per cent range, Gillette at 25, and many drug companies are above 20 per cent.

Second, the effect of wealth inequality is large. Much large family wealth traces back to major monopolies (Rockefeller, du Pont, Mellon), and the process continues. Worse, the turnover of family wealth has probably slowed in recent years, because the present industrial structure has hardened.

Third, efficiency suffers. Most firms with high degrees of market power must struggle to avoid slackness and waste, often with less than success. Frequently the torpor soaks up all of the monopoly profits; more often it adds 2, 3, or 5 per cent to costs and cuts the innovative effort of the firm appreciably. Large-share firms commonly become imitators, and new technology flows primarily from smaller firms.

Fourth, opportunity is narrowed and disequalized. There are fewer points of responsibility and opportunity, both for managers and innovators. The network of financial and old-boy ties is tighter. One effect is that minority groups are more thoroughly excluded. My research shows that both blacks and women fare poorly in big business and financial management, compared to more competitive firms.

Good sense and scientific findings therefore establish a rebuttable presumption that monopoly and shared monopoly are costly, perhaps extravagantly so. The economic burden of proof favors revising them into loose oligopolies or constraining their market power by other means. The problem cases fall into three main categories:

(1) Market power with inefficiency: such as steel, copper, glass, rubber, aluminum, tin cans, electric power, telephones, hospitals, railroads.

(2) Market power with excess profits: such as General Motors, Ford, IBM, Xerox, Eastman Kodak, Procter and Gamble, du Pont, Gillette, and a variety of drug firms.

(3) Government dependents: such as aircraft and engines, milk, sugar, oil.

Market forces are not correcting the underlying structural problems in these industries. In a few cases, modern technology may dictate the structure, and so the monopoly losses may be balanced by gains in efficiency. But in the rest of the cases, there are net losses, some of them running into billions of dollars.

The losses can be defined for each case. The losses also cumulate in the economy to cause much of the recession-inflation problem, which the British call stagflation. If in fact the U.S. is catching the "British disease," market power is one of the causes.

Viewed another way, there are rich yields to be had from better industrial policies toward the core cases. These gains would be widely spread; nearly all would gain, even many who were presently most openly against effective actions. Granted, industrial policies cannot hope to redress the core social problems, such as the deeper structure of unequal family wealth. Yet they can do much to improve economic performance and widen opportunity for deprived groups, including the mass of white lower-middle class working people.

GENERAL POLICY GUIDANCE

The basic need is to reestablish priorities. Antitrust is presently out of balance and overloaded with tasks. Certain traditional tools should be pressed harder, others dropped, and other new treatments need developing.

J. K. Galbraith is quite right that antitrust policies shield the leaders by bearing down on lesser competitors. The Antitrust Division works mainly on conduct, under Section 1 of the Sherman Act. Section 2 actions to change structure have gone deep into limbo since 1952. The FTC also spends most of its resources policing smaller firms and lesser industries. An increasing variety of sectors are exempt under regulation, which commonly neither controls nor permits potential competition. Other sectors under self-regulation (banks, law, health services) are even more insulated from competition.

The result is a trap. Even in the narrow area where antitrust has jurisdiction, we won't use the effective tools, and we are not developing new ones. So poor industrial performance backs us into such bad expedients as price controls, import controls, and subsidies. Other countries (Britain, Japan, Germany) are not so euphoric about traditional antitrust nor lacking in creative alternatives.

A word on methods. Good policies are clinical in approach, based on a careful weighing of costs and benefits. In each instance one estimates costs (disruption, agency costs) and benefits (better efficiency and equity) and applies the treatment with the best yield. One must discount the amounts for delay and uncertainty, and multiply for precedents. The burden of proof about gains and losses needs to be set evenly rather than, as now in the courts, strongly against changes in the *status quo*. Treatments must be well-designed and strategic, as well as adequately funded. And since action takes time, often years, treatments must anticipate changes. Delay is the cancer of antitrust: there must be deadlines and time incentives.

As a matter of content, treatments must deal with the deeper financial ties and controls on firms, not just with their surface forms. In most markets, the bankers give intimate counsel and set limits on what their client firms may do. Effective policies will have to mobilize such insider talents and incentives, and citizen motives via class-action suits, rather than rush headlong up against the best financial and legal talent. In short, grass-roots support must be wedded with first-class strategists who can induce compliance rather than try brute force. The older Taft had a brilliant strategist in George Wickersham, a Wall Street lawyer who won Standard Oil, du Pont, and American Tobacco in 1911. Now we will need that brilliance plus new treatments, that neutralize resistance.

A certain amount of realigning and reorganizing of market structures may ultimately be needed. But that is only part. On a larger plane, what is needed is a clinical learning process; it need not be disruptive or obsolete. Rather than turning back the clock, the proper objective is to release the potential of modern industry from its nineteenth century fetters.

27

ON THE CREATION OF CONSUMER WANTS

In traditional economic analysis, free choice and consumer "dollar votes" lead to an optimal allocation of productive effort. In this article, three "radical" economists argue that capitalistic (for example, American) consumerism fosters ever-increasing emphasis on induced consumption; and that, as a consequence, the system does not follow consumers' "real" desires and free choice becomes a myth.

Richard Edwards, Michael Reich, and Thomas Weisskopf

At the time this was written, the authors were young economists at Harvard University, and leaders of the "radical economics" movement.

Source: Edwards, Richard C., Michael Reich, and Thomas E. Weisskopf, *The Capitalist System: A Radical Analysis of American Society;* Prentice-Hall, Inc., Englewood Cliffs, N.J. (1972), pp. 374-76.

• • •

The "dollar votes" of buyers in the market represent the principal force determining production priorities in a capitalist society. The market system for deciding what goods are produced leads to many forms of irrationality: for example, the whims of the wealthy take precedence over the needs of the poor (since the rich have many times the "dollar votes" of the poor), and consumers can express only private, individual consumption wants. Furthermore, even the conscious consumption decisions of the individual consumer do not necessarily reflect his or her real needs.

In this section we will explore the reasons why the consumer cannot be regarded as the final arbiter of production priorities in a capitalist system.

We begin by noting that consumers' wants in our society are not god-given nor simply "human nature" but are instead the product of a specific historical context. As Richard Lichtman put it,

Every society, in order merely to survive, must satisfy the basic subsistence needs of its members for food, shelter, clothing, and human recognition. There is a level of productivity that must be achieved by any social group; for human beings have fundamental needs whose violation brings social disorganization or death. That is one half of the truth. The other is that human needs are satisfied through specific means of production that shape and alter the original needs and give rise to new needs whose satisfaction depends upon new technical instruments and new forms of social organization. Every society, therefore, in struggling to satisfy fundamental human needs, shapes these needs in distinctive ways and produces new needs which were not part of any original human nature.[1]

The capitalist mode of production conditions the needs and wants of consumers: the extreme emphasis placed on consumption, variously referred to as "consumerism," "consumptionism," or the "ethic of consumption," pervades both the consumption patterns and the production priorities of capitalist society.

Consumerism derives first of all from the alienated nature of work under capitalist relations of production. Work is eliminated as a potential arena for the worker's ex-

---

[1] Richard Lichtman, "Capitalism and Consumption," *Socialist Revolution* 1, no. 3 (May–June 1970), p. 83.

pression and self-fulfillment; that the principal incentive to work is wages—external to the work process and useful only during the nonwork part of the day or week—testifies to the depersonalizing content of work and the reasons for people's consequent "escape" into consumerism.

The alienation of the worker from production thus leaves only the sphere of consumption as an arena for expressing one's individuality, asserting one's humanity, and simply escaping the debilitating effects of one's job. Ellen Willis points out that:

> As it is, the profusion of commodities . . . is a bribe, but like all bribes, it offers concrete benefits—in the average American's case, a degree of physical comfort unparalleled in history. Under present conditions, people are preoccupied with consumer goods not because they are brainwashed, but because buying is the one pleasurable activity not only permitted but actively encouraged by the power structure. The pleasure of eating an ice cream cone may be minor compared to the pleasure of meaningful, autonomous work, but the former is easily available and the latter is not. A poor family would undoubtedly rather have a decent apartment than a new TV, but since they are unlikely to get the apartment, what is to be gained by not getting the TV? [2]

Furthermore, the commodity fetishism inherent in capitalist production relations reinforces this emphasis on consumption; for commodity consumption is seen not as a means but as an end in itself. Capitalism asserts that the best and indeed the only

proper means for achieving greater happiness or a better life is by increased consumption. To solve one's problems, to find happiness, to "lead the good life," one need only have the money to buy the right things or to go to the right places. Thus, increased consumption, a higher "standard of living" (that is, more goods), and economic growth become goals of society and unquestioned ends in and of themselves.

Capitalist firms take an active role in stimulating consumption demand. Many commodities are purposely designed and constructed in order to wear out or fall apart very quickly, insuring that consumers will periodically have to buy a new model of the product. Automobiles are one of the most blatant examples of such planned obsolescence, but they are by no means atypical. Unnecessary frills are often attached to products such as automobiles and forced upon the consumer in need of the basic good. Needless to say, the embodiment of superfluous accessories onto basic goods is a convenient way to stimulate consumption demand.

Firms also stimulate consumption demand by undertaking a tremendous sales effort, exemplified by massive advertising. This advertising attempts to convince people that the acquisition of commodities, for which they otherwise would not have any use, will result in greater happiness. In a society based on alienated labor, the effect of so much propaganda for consumption is bound to be significant.

For all of the above reasons, it is simply false to assert that production priorities in a capitalist society follow the dictates of consumers. . . .

[2] Ellen Willis, "Consumerism and Women," *Socialist Revolution* 1, no. 3 (May–June 1970), p. 70.

28

The editors of *Socialist Revolution*, a part of the radical "underground" press, argue that capitalistic (that is, profit-directed) production and economic organization lead to economic and political structures that dictate consumer choices and lifestyles. Radical economists perceive this situation as leading to "irrational" choices in the name of "rationality," with the end result being an impoverished, insensitive society.

REVOLUTIONARY POLITICS AND THE REDEFINITION OF WELL-BEING

the editors of *Socialist Revolution*

Excerpted from *Socialist Revolution*, Vol. 1, No. 2, pp. 10-15. Reprinted by permission.

• • •

The imperatives of expanding and realizing surplus value are today generating social relations within the proletariat and between capital and the proletariat that are experienced in ways that engender radical and potentially revolutionary politics. Capitalist development is producing a need for a politics oriented around the issue of alienated labor and around the revolutionary struggle for socialism.

This revolutionary potential is rooted in a proletariat that has been transformed according to the bourgeoisie's need to expand and realize surplus value (that is, profits). The expansion of surplus value has required both an expansion of the proletariat and the general technical and cultural upgrading of the proletariat. On the one hand, the quantitative growth of the labor forces has required the uprooting of the rural population, the mass migration of Southern black and poor white population to the cities, the destruction of small-scale industry and farming, and the mass entry of women into factory and office employment. In brief, the development of twentieth-century capitalism has been based on the proletarianization of the great majority of the population.

On the other hand, the expansion of surplus value has required rapid advances in productivity, which, in turn, has required an increasingly skilled proletariat. Advanced capitalism has produced not only a larger working class but also a new working class—not simply in the form of a stratum of technical workers or "mind workers" but rather in the form of an entire work force that compared to previous work forces in history is increasingly educated to complex techniques of production processes, communications, and economic and social control. Advanced capitalism has become more "rational," that is, more efficient, productive, and profitable. The need to expand surplus value has necessitated the development of new productive processes, new synthetic materials, new rational forms of work organization, efficient control of raw materials supplies, a "systems" approach to production, distribution, and economic control. These, in turn, require an upgrading of the technical level of the proletariat as a whole.

The *realization* of surplus value has required new, expanding markets, the substitution of values in exchange for values in use, and the creation of new needs, both domestically and internationally. Abroad, imperialism has transformed traditional, semifeudal, and semicapitalist modes of production. At home, commodity production has replaced pre- and semi-capitalist production in small-scale industry, on the farm, and in the home. In most of the nineteenth century, factory production replaced basic commodities traditionally produced by artisans and craftsmen; the problem of finding new markets for the products of large-scale industry was minimal. In the twentieth century, the market for traditional "wage goods"—food, clothing, shelter, and the related demand for capital goods—has been too thin to absorb the product of large-scale industry. To supplement the market for "wage goods," capital has been compelled to manipulate the production of the entire range of human needs.

The realization of surplus value requires the ruling class to direct the proletariat's search for the satisfaction of its needs, its unconscious motivations and desires, to the marketplace. Modern advertising exploits people's need for accomplishment, status, prestige, even affection and love; it focuses their awareness of these needs upon commodities in the market rather than upon their relations with one another. The ruling class is also compelled to manufacture new needs by increasing the general level of expectations and hammering away at the theme that commodities are indispensable for the "good life," a "happy home," "good marriage," and, in general, "success" in all spheres of life. And this requires product differentiation, advertising, sales, public relations, entertainment, commercial sports—industries and activities that are need-producing. The realization of surplus value depends upon surveys of consumer behavior, motivational research, psychological depth studies, a greater emotional knowledge of the proletariat, the use of the mass media to educate the proletariat that commodities will satisfy their deepest emotional needs. Modern capitalism thus produces a kind of sensitivity, the sensitivity of the salesman, the copywriter, the sports promoter, the television director.

Both of these tendencies—the expansion and upgrading of the proletariat and the search for new markets—have led to the interpretation of the economic base and superstructures, not merely in the form of an expanded rule of government in the economy, but also in the integration of all secondary institutions and activities into production itself. The state, especially the education system, petty commodity production, the farm, and the home are all sources of labor power and exploitable markets. Recreation, leisure time, and cultural activity all constitute growing markets. And accompanying the spread of commodities and commodity culture into all spheres of life is the spread of instrumental social relations and new forms of social antagonism from the sphere of direct production into the secondary institutions.

Advanced corporate capitalism also requires the development of a political system designed to maintain the social order by politically containing and integrating the proletariat into a corporate liberal consensus. Keynesian and neo-Keynesian planning is impossible without cost-of-living indexes, budgetary control, balance-of-payments analyses. Production and distribution planning is impossible without an extended government apparatus that serves to coordinate corporate policies. Social planning is impossible without city planning, welfare departments, "humanistic" approaches to child care, education, family counseling, schools of psychology. Military planning is impossible without an elaborate science apparatus. And all of these activities rest on the development of an information industry, an information explosion, which includes "presentation depots" and "interpretation networks." The development and consolidation of the corporate liberal social order also engenders a kind of rationality and a kind of sensitivity—the rationality of the economist, urban planner, "systems" expert, and cost accountant, and the sensitivity of the social worker, public health nurse, psychotherapist, and teacher.

These changes taken together produce the conditions for a new kind of human being: first, "rational man," with an ability to conceptualize, analyze, and synthesize. By educating itself to the operation of the economy and society, the ruling class, at times deliberately and at times inadvertently, educates the proletariat as well. Second, "sensitive man," with an ability and need to empathize with others, to feel deeply. By educating itself to the emotional state of the proletariat, the ruling class also educates the proletariat, a proletariat that can potentially identify well-being with a social order in which both men and women can afford intimacy, spontaneity, and joy. Modern capitalism produces *awareness*—both of a cognitive and emotional kind—partial and distorted as it is, including the potential awareness of the irrational character of capitalism itself.

On the one side, capitalist society gives birth to a technically skilled, curious, aware, and understanding proletariat—a proletariat that is potentially equipped to rule. At the same time, the ruling class further consolidates its own rule by concentrating economic power, monopolizing the science apparatus, deepening its control over the education system and taking control of the state budget from the Congress.

Capitalism teaches that production is rational and then hires people to waste and destroy it. It programs students in school to perform as "human capital" and then hires them to design, build, program, and control machines and to create systems approaches to production, sales, and social problems. Capitalism educates people to new consumption horizons and then shortens these horizons by producing wasteful and destructive objects.

Material production is defined as well-being, and then the bourgeoisie orders the production of objects whose usefulness is subordinated to the need to sustain aggregate demand, to maintain the corporate liberal social order at home, and to firm up the imperialist system abroad. Bourgeois thought teaches people to respect nature and then capitalist development wastes and destroys the productive forces by polluting the air and water, fouling the land, poisoning the food, the wild life, and man himself.

In these ways, advanced capitalism produces new experiences for which it has no satisfactory explanation, new promises of personal liberation and happiness that cannot be fulfilled, new hopes that it shatters, a new rational, sensitive man reproducing himself in a society that is increasingly irrational and insensitive. It teaches that men and women are historical subjects and treats them as objects. It defines people as ends and treats them as means. Needing historical understanding, the proletariat finds ideology, which constrains its intellectual development and historical consciousness. Needing emotional understanding, the proletariat finds manipulation, coercion, and oppression, which constrains its emotional development and self-consciousness.

Thus, people increasingly perceive and experience capitalist society as impoverished, not prosperous, as irrational, not rational, as insensitive, not sensitive. Capitalism produces the idea that well-being consists simply of material production and consumption, and an experience that contradicts this idea. Thus, there arises the possibility of a redefinition of well-being, the opposition of bourgeois ideology by critical thought, an opposition of bourgeois social relations by potentially socialist relations, and, ultimately, the opposition of bourgeois production relations by the struggle for socialist production.

. . .

29

Some—not all—advocates of collectivist societies believe income should be distributed equally among individuals. A leading economist, who is a strong advocate of freedom of choice and the market system, examines some of the factors affecting income distribution and the ethical grounds underlying them.

THE DISTRIBUTION OF INCOME

Milton Friedman

Milton Friedman is Professor of Economics at the University Chicago.

From *Capitalism and Freedom* (Chicago: University of Chicago Press, 1962). Reprinted by permission.

A central element in the development of a collectivist sentiment in this century, at least in Western countries, has been a belief in equality of income as a social goal and a willingness to use the arm of the state to promote it. Two very different questions must be asked in evaluating this egalitarian sentiment and the egalitarian measures it has produced. The first is normative and ethical: What is the justification for state intervention to promote equality? The second is positive and scientific: What has been the effect of the measures actually taken?

THE ETHICS OF DISTRIBUTION

The ethical principle that would directly justify the distribution of income in a free market society is, "To each according to what he and the instruments he owns produces." The operation of even this principle implicitly depends on state action. Property rights are matters of law and social convention. As we have seen, their definition and enforcement is one of the primary functions of the state. The final distribution of income and wealth under the full operation of this principle may well depend markedly on the rules of property adopted.

What is the relation between this principle and another that seems ethically appealing, namely, equality of treatment? In part, the two principles are not contradictory. Payment in accordance with product may be necessary to achieve true equality of treatment. Given individuals whom we are prepared to regard as alike in ability and initial resources, if some have a greater taste for leisure and others for marketable goods, inequality of return through the market is necessary to achieve equality of total return or equality of treatment. One man may prefer a routine job with much time off for basking in the sun to a more exacting job paying a higher salary; another man may prefer the opposite. If both were paid equally in money, their incomes in a more fundamental sense would be unequal. Similarly, equal treatment requires that an individual be paid more for a dirty, unattractive job than for a pleasant rewarding one. Much observed inequality is of this kind. Differences of money income offset differences in other characteristics of the occupation or trade. In the jargon of economists, they are "equalizing differences" required to make the whole of the "net advantages," pecuniary and nonpecuniary, the same.

Another kind of inequality arises through the operation of the market is also required, in a somewhat more subtle sense, to produce equality of treatment, or to put it differently to satisfy men's tastes. It can be illustrated most simply by a lottery. Consider a group of individuals who initially have equal endowments and who all agree voluntarily to enter a lottery with very unequal prizes. The resultant inequality of income is surely required to permit the individuals in question to make the most of their initial equality. Redistribution of the income after the event is equivalent to denying them the opportunity to enter the lottery. This case is far more important in practice than would appear by taking the notion of a "lottery" literally. Individuals choose occupations, investments, and the like partly in accordance with their taste for uncertainty. The girl who tries to become a movie actress rather than a civil servant is deliberately choosing to enter a lottery; so is the individual who invests in penny uranium stocks rather than government bonds. Insurance is a way of expressing a taste for certainty. Even these examples do not indicate fully the extent to which actual inequality may be the result of arrangements designed to satisfy men's tastes. The very arrangements for paying and hiring people are affected by such preferences. If all potential movie actresses had a great dislike of uncertainty, there would tend to develop "cooperatives" of movie actresses, the members of which agreed in advance to share income receipts more or less evenly, thereby in effect providing themselves insurance through the pooling of risks. If such a preference were widespread, large diversified corporations combining risky and nonrisky ventures would become the rule. The wildcat oil prospector, the private proprietorship, the small partnership, would all become rare.

Indeed, this is one way to interpret governmental measures to redistribute income through progressive taxes and the like. It can be argued that for one reason or another, costs of administration perhaps, the market cannot produce the range of lotteries or the kind of lottery desired by the members of the community, and that progressive taxation is, as it were, a govern-

ment enterprise to do so. I have no doubt that this view contains an element of truth. At the same time, it can hardly justify present taxation, if only because the taxes are imposed *after* it is already largely known who have drawn the prizes and who the blanks in the lottery of life, and the taxes are voted mostly by those who think they have drawn the blanks. One might, along these lines, justify one generation's voting the tax schedules to be applied to an as yet unborn generation. Any such procedure would, I conjecture, yield income tax schedules much less highly graduated than present schedules are, at least on paper.

Though much of the inequality of income produced by payment in accordance with product reflects "equalizing" differences or the satisfaction of men's tastes for uncertainty, a large part reflects initial differences in endowment, both of human capacities and of property. This is the part that raises the really difficult ethical issue.

It is widely argued that it is essential to distinguish between inequality in personal endowments and in property, and between inequalities arising from inherited wealth and from acquired wealth. Inequality resulting from differences in personal capacities, or from differences in wealth accumulated by the individual in question, are considered appropriate, or at least not so clearly inappropriate as differences resulting from inherited wealth.

This distinction is untenable. Is there any greater ethical justification for the high returns to the individual who inherits from his parents a peculiar voice for which there is a great demand than for the high returns to the individual who inherits property? The sons of Russian commissars surely have a higher expectation of income—perhaps also of liquidation—than the sons of peasants. Is this any more or less justifiable than the higher income expectation of the son of an American millionaire? We can look at this same question in another way.

A parent who has wealth that he wishes to pass on to his child can do so in different ways. He can use a given sum of money to finance his child's training as, say, a certified public accountant, or to set him up in business, or to set up a trust fund yielding him a property income. In any of these cases, the child will have a higher income than he otherwise would. But in the first case, his income will be regarded as coming from human capacities; in the second, from profits; in the third, from inherited wealth. Is there any basis for distinguishing among these categories of receipts on ethical grounds? Finally, it seems illogical to say that a man is entitled to what he has produced by personal capacities or to the produce of the wealth he has accumulated, but that he is not entitled to pass any wealth on to his children; to say that a man may use his income for riotous living but may not give it to his heirs. Surely, the latter is one way to use what he has produced.

The fact that these arguments against the so-called capitalist ethic are invalid does not of course demonstrate that the capitalist ethic is an acceptable one. I find it difficult to justify either accepting or rejecting it, or to justify any alternative principle. I am led to the view that it cannot in and of itself be regarded as an ethical principle; that it must be regarded as instrumental or a corollary of some other principle such as freedom.

Some hypothetical examples may illustrate the fundamental difficulty. Suppose there are four Robinson Crusoes, independently marooned on four islands in the same neighborhood. One happened to land on a large and fruitful island which enables him to live easily and well. The others happened to land on tiny and rather barren islands from which they can barely scratch a living. One day, they discover the existence of one another. Of course, it would be generous of the Crusoe on the large island if he invited the others to join him and share its wealth. But suppose he does not. Would the other three be justified in joining forces and compelling him to share his wealth with them? Many a reader will be tempted to say yes. But before yielding to this temptation, consider precisely the same situation in different guise. Suppose you and three friends are walking along the street and you happen to spy and retrieve a $20 bill on the pavement. It would be generous of you, of course, if you were to divide it equally with them, or at least blow them to a drink. But suppose you do not. Would the other three be justified in joining forces and compelling you to share the $20 equally with them? I suspect most readers will be tempted to say no. And on further reflection, they may even conclude that the generous course of action is not itself clearly the "right" one. Are we prepared to urge on ourselves or our fellows that any person whose wealth exceeds the average of all persons in the world should immediately dispose of the excess by distributing it equally to all the rest of the world's inhabitants? We may admire and praise such action when undertaken by a few. But a universal "potlatch" would make a civilized world impossible.

In any event, two wrongs do not make a right. The unwillingness of the rich Robinson Crusoe or the lucky finder of the $20 bill to share his wealth does not justify the use of coercion by the others. Can we justify being judges in our own case, deciding on our own when we are entitled to use force to extract what we regard as our due from others? Or what we regard as not their due? Most differences of status or position or wealth can be regarded as the product of chance at a far enough remove. The man who is hard working and thrifty is to be regarded as "deserving"; yet these qualities owe much to the genes he was fortunate (or unfortunate?) enough to inherit.

Despite the lip service that we all pay to "merit" as compared to "chance," we are generally much readier to accept inequalities arising from chance than those clearly attributable to merit. The college professor whose colleague wins a sweepstake will envy him but is unlikely to bear him any malice or to feel unjustly treated. Let the colleague receive a trivial raise that makes his salary higher than the professor's own, and the professor is far more likely to feel aggrieved. After all, the goddess of chance, as of justice, is blind. The salary raise was a deliberate judgment of relative merit.

THE INSTRUMENTAL ROLE OF DISTRIBUTION ACCORDING TO PRODUCT

The operative function of payment in accordance with product in a market society is not primarily distributive, but allocative. The central principle of a market economy is cooperation through voluntary exchange. Individuals cooperate with others because they can in this way satisfy their own wants more effectively. But unless an individual receives the whole of what he adds to the product, he will enter into exchanges on the basis of what he can receive rather than what he can produce. Exchanges will not take place that would have been mutually beneficial if each party received what he contributed to the aggregate product. Payment in accordance with product is therefore necessary in order that resources be used most effectively, at least under a system depending on voluntary cooperation. Given sufficient knowledge, it might be that compulsion could be substituted for the incentive of reward, though I doubt

that it could. One can shuffle inanimate objects around; one can compel individuals to be at certain places at certain times; but one can hardly compel individuals to put forward their best efforts. Put another way, the substitution of compulsion for cooperation changes the amount of resources available.

Though the essential function of payment in accordance with product in a market society is to enable resources to be allocated efficiently without compulsion, it is unlikely to be tolerated unless it is also regarded as yielding distributive justice. No society can be stable unless there is a basic core of value judgments that are unthinkingly accepted by the great bulk of its members. Some key institutions must be accepted as "absolutes," not simply as instrumental. I believe that payment in accordance with product has been, and, in large measure, still is, one of these accepted value judgments or institutions.

One can demonstrate this by examining the grounds on which the internal opponents of the capitalist system have attacked the distribution of income resulting from it. It is a distinguishing feature of the core of central values of a society that it is accepted alike by its members, whether they regard themselves as proponents or as opponents of the system of organization of the society. Even the severest internal critics of capitalism have implicitly accepted payment in accordance with product as ethically fair.

The most far-reaching criticism has come from the Marxists. Marx argued that labor was exploited. Why? Because labor produced the whole of the product but got only part of it; the rest is Marx's "surplus value." Even if the statements of fact implicit in this assertion were accepted, the value judgment follows only if one accepts the capitalist ethic. Labor is "exploited" only if labor is entitled to what it produces. If one accepts instead the Ruskinian premise, "to each according to his need, from each according to his ability"—whatever that may mean—it is necessary to compare what labor produces, not with what it gets but with its "ability," and to compare what labor gets, not with what it produces but with its "need."

The achievement of allocation of resources without compulsion is the major instrumental role in the market place of distribution in accordance with product. But it is not the only instrumental role of the resulting inequality. The role that inequality plays in providing independent foci of power to offset the centralization of political power, as well as the role that it plays in promoting civil freedom by providing "patrons" to finance the dissemination of unpopular or simply novel ideas should also be noted. In addition, in the economic sphere, it provides "patrons" to finance experimentation and the development of new products—to buy the first experimental automobiles and television sets, let alone impressionist paintings. Finally, it enables distribution to occur impersonally without the need for "authority"—a special facet of the general role of the market in effecting cooperation and coordination without coercion.

FACTS OF INCOME DISTRIBUTION

A capitalist system involving payment in accordance with product can be, and in practice is, characterized by considerable inequality of income and wealth. This fact is frequently misinterpreted to mean that capitalism and free enterprise produce wider inequality than alternative systems and, as a corollary, that the extension and development of capitalism has meant increased inequality. This misinterpretation is fostered by the misleading character of most published figures on the distribution of income, in particular their failure to distinguish short-run from long-run inequality. Let us look at some of the broader facts about the distribution of income.

One of the most striking facts which runs counter to many people's expectation has to do with the sources of income. The more capitalistic a country is, the smaller the fraction of income paid for the use of what is generally regarded as capital, and the larger the fraction paid for human services. In underdeveloped countries like India, Egypt, and so on, something like half of total income is property income. In the United States, roughly one-fifth is property income. And in other advanced capitalist countries, the proportion is not very different. Of course, these countries have much more capital than the primitive countries but they are even richer in the productive capacity of their residents; hence, the larger income from property is a smaller fraction of the total. The great achievement of capitalism has not been the accumulation of property, it has been the opportunities it has offered to men and women to extend and develop and improve their capacities. Yet the enemies of capitalism are fond of castigating it as materialist, and its friends all too often apologize for capitalism's materialism as a necessary cost of progress.

Another striking fact, contrary to popular conception, is that capitalism leads to less inequality than alternative systems of organization and that the development of capitalism has greatly lessened the extent of inequality. Comparisons over space and time alike confirm this view. There is surely drastically less inequality in Western capitalist societies like the Scandinavian countries, France, Britain, and the United States, than in a status society like India or a backward country like Egypt. Comparison with communist countries like Russia is more difficult because of paucity and unreliability of evidence. But if inequality is measured by differences in levels of living between the privileged and other classes, such inequality may well be decidedly less in capitalist than in communist countries. Among the Western countries alone, inequality appears to be less, in any meaningful sense, the more highly capitalist the country is: less in Britain than in France, less in the United States than in Britain—though these comparisons are rendered difficult by the problem of allowing for the intrinsic heterogeneity of populations; for a fair comparison, for example, one should perhaps compare the United States, not with the United Kingdom alone but with the United Kingdom plus the West Indies plus its African possessions.

With respect to changes over time, the economic progress achieved in the capitalist societies has been accompanied by a drastic diminution in inequality. As late as 1848, John Stuart Mill could write, "Hitherto [1848] it is questionable if all the mechanical inventions yet made have lightened the day's toil of any human being. They have enabled a greater population to live the same life of drudgery and imprisonment, and an increased number of manufacturers and others to make fortunes. They have increased the comforts of the middle classes. But they have not yet begun to effect those great changes in human destiny, which it is in their nature and in their futurity to accomplish."[1] This statement was probably not correct even for Mill's day, but certainly no one could write this today about the advanced capitalist countries. It is still true about the rest of the world.

The chief characteristic of progress and development over the past century is that it

has freed the masses from backbreaking toil and has made available to them products and services that were formerly the monopoly of the upper classes, without in any corresponding way expanding the products and services available to the wealthy. Medicine aside, the advances in technology have for the most part simply made available to the masses of the people luxuries that were always available in one form or another to the truly wealthy. Modern plumbing, central heating, automobiles, television, radio, to cite just a few examples, provide conveniences to the masses equivalent to those that the wealthy could always get by the use of servants, entertainers, and so on.

Detailed statistical evidence on these phenomena, in the form of meaningful and comparable distributions of income, is hard to come by, though such studies as have been made confirm the broad conclusions just outlined. Such statistical data, however, can be extremely misleading. They cannot segregate differences in income that are equalizing from those that are not. For example, the short working life of a baseball player means that the annual income during his active years must be much higher than in alternative pursuits open to him to make it equally attractive financially. But such a difference affects the figures in exactly the same way as any other difference in income. The income unit for which the figures are given is also of great importance. A distribution for individual income recipients always shows very much greater apparent inequality than a distribution for family units: many of the individuals are housewives working part-time or receiving a small amount of property income, or other family members in a similar position. Is the distribution that is relevant for families one in which the families are classified by total family income? Or by income per person? Or per equivalent unit?

---

[1] *Principles of Political Economy* (Ashley edition; London: Longmans, Green & Co., 1909), p. 751.

This is no mere quibble. I believe that the changing distribution of families by number of children is the most important single factor that has reduced inequality of levels of living in this country during the past half century. It has been far more important than graduated inheritance and income taxes. The really low levels of living were the joint product of relatively low family incomes and relatively large numbers of children. The average number of children has declined and, even more important, this decline has been accompanied and largely produced by a virtual elimination of the very large family. As a result, families now tend to differ much less with respect to number of children. Yet this change would not be reflected in a distribution of families by the size of total family income.

A major problem in interpreting evidence on the distribution of income is the need to distinguish two basically different kinds of inequality; temporary, short-run differences in income, and differences in long-run income status. Consider two so-cieties that have the same distribution of annual income. In one there is great mobility and change so that the position of particular families in the income hierarchy varies widely from year to year. In the other, there is great rigidity so that each family stays in the same position year after year. Clearly, in any meaningful sense, the second would be the more unequal society. The one kind of inequality is a sign of dynamic change, social mobility, equality of opportunity; the other, of a status society. The confusion of these two kinds of inequality is particularly important, precisely because competitive free-enterprise capitalism tends to substitute the one for the other. Noncapitalist societies tend to have wider inequality than capitalist, even as measured by annual income; in addition, inequality in them tends to be permanent, whereas capitalism undermines status and introduces social mobility.

. . .

30

GOOD PROFITS PROMOTE PROGRESS

What role do profits really play in our economy? Mr. Kappel argues that realized profits, not just the profit motive, are essential and that profits are essential for efficient management.

Frederick R. Kappel

Frederick R. Kappel was Chairman of the Board and is currently Chairman of the Executive Committee of the American Telephone and Telegraph Company.

From Business Horizons (Winter 1961), pp. 21–28. Reprinted by permission of Business Horizons and the University of Indiana.

A few years ago, a group of Bell System managers made an intensive study of the relationship between profits and performance in American industry. They started with two questions: "Does profit do anything? Is it only a result or does it also cause things to happen that affect our economy?"

Their broad conclusion was that good profit, good business performance, and healthy economic progress all go together. But the men who made the study went further. Good profit, they suggested, does much more than parallel good performance. It is one of the essential factors in bringing good performance about. (The other essentials named were good management and a good product.) In other words, good profit is by no means merely a result; it is also causative, dynamic, and energizing.

These conclusions were based on the group's study of the actual case histories of companies in several industries. The weight of the evidence was that where profits have been relatively good, performance has also been relatively good, measured by several important criteria. Of the businesses analyzed, those that earned well had better growth records—with all that connotes of value delivered to consumers—than those that earned poorly. The more profitable companies put more investment (including more retained earnings) into new and improved equipment; they did more research and more innovating; they offered better job opportunities; and they contributed more to community well-being.

Thus, the study group suggested that good profit should be regarded as a prime *cause* of economic and social progress. Profit, they felt is not merely an end result of the business process, but a lively functional element that does indeed "cause things to happen."

CONCEPTS OF PROFIT

The idea has had a mixed reception. Many people have said to me that they think it

makes excellent sense; others have been critical. They have argued that, while good performance may indeed produce good profit, it is not demonstrable that good profit will generate good performance. Our study group, they contend, must have been putting its carts before its horses.

This critical reaction is not surprising. It is, after all, a new thought that profit can be causative in the sense suggested. For generations, profit has been regarded mainly as a result, a residue, a remainder, and this is still the popular notion. It is a notion derived, perhaps, from nothing more complicated than the classroom illustration that if a man grows an apple for eight cents and sells it for ten, he is left with two cents' profit. Or it may be that the classical economists of the last century are partly responsible. As they saw the matter, according to the *Encyclopaedia of the Social Sciences:*

> There was first a separation between rent and a kind of gross income of the capitalist, as the businessman was then more or less correctly called; subsequently the latter fund was divided between the capitalist and the laboring classes. Wages were supposed to be determined independently, the final share of the capitalist being left as a residuum.

Residuum—there is something lifeless and inert about the very word. It gives linguistic support to the view that the figures on the bottom line belong also at the bottom of our scale of values; and perhaps the typical form of income statement, showing profit at the bottom, further encourages this view. This is too bad, for as I see it, the fact that profit is something left over does not in any sense define its character. Its appearance as a remainder merely reflects its place in time, which is necessarily after the transactions that produced it. But this is no clue to its nature or potential.

Thinking about this, I was interested when someone the other day called to my attention the views of Francis Amasa Walker, as discussed by John Chamberlain in his book *The Roots of Capitalism*. According to Chamberlain, Walker, a Civil War general, teacher at Yale, and later president of M.I.T., "isolated profit as the driving force of industrial progress." While Walker too saw profit as a result, he saw it also as something more. Profit, said Walker, is the special creation of the gifted enterpriser. He produces it "by his comprehension of the demands of the market; . . . by his organizing force and administrative ability; by his energy, economy, and prudence." Thus, profit is more than a result; it is the instrument of dynamic change.

The classical concept of profit as mere residue suggests that when profit has been gained, its vitality ends. It is not useful to society; rather, it is likely to serve only the convenience and comfort of those who have possession of it. All this fits in with many people's feeling that while a little bit of profit may do no harm, profits for the most part are bad. To what degree public distrust of business profits may be derived from the concept of profit as a residue or any other economic theory, I am not able to say. More important is the fact that there is at present little or no theory of the kind that might dispel distrust. So far as I can see, profits are distrusted largely because the public sees them as a manifestation of economic power; because there is evidence every now and then that certain profits have not been honestly earned; and because of the belief that profit is often a reflection of the ability of some people to gain at others' expense. But these are political, ethical, and emotional considerations. They have nothing to do with any principle of business profit as such. It will be a pity, therefore, if we cannot gain acceptance for some view of profit other than one that, implicitly at any rate, deprecates its social usefulness. From the concept of profit as mere residue it is only a step to the moral contention that paucity of profit is a demonstration of virtue, and only one more step to the proposition that if scant profit is a mark of high integrity, then no profit at all must be a mark of the highest.

The danger is that noneconomic considerations may in the end determine what is to be done about profit. We need, on the one hand, a clear understanding that aberrations in business practice, unwarranted exercise of power, and the like are in no sense indicators of the function of profit. On the other hand, we need a concept of profit so satisfying that it will be impossible to identify ethical failure with failure of the profit principle.

Let us go back a moment now to Walker, who found in profit the driving force of industrial progress. Today one hears countless voices that seem to be saying much the same thing. I have in mind all the economists and journalists who echo and reecho the refrain that "the profit motive" is the dynamo of enterprise. But for some reason, at least in this country, it seems to me there is much more applause for the profit motive than there is for profits. It is almost as though there were two kinds of thought: One has something in common with Walker's views, except that the modern stress, as I have said, is on the motive alone, whereas Walker did not stop there; the other, which is strengthened by the residue theory, if not derived from it, appraises profit with a wary eye, as something acceptable only when it is scant.

THE PROFIT DILEMMA

In short, we are seriously at odds with ourselves about profits. Our attitude is: Hurrah for the profit motive and down with profits. Or as a Latin might put it, "Motive *si*, profit *no*." We want people to work for profits, but we are not at all sure that we want them to be earned. This is economic schizophrenia. It is absurd to hold that profit is a desirable incentive but a poor achievement. Men cannot work on the basis that it is right and necessary for them to pursue a goal that, when they reach it, will prove a sterile thing at best, and at worst a harmful one.

The Russians, I may remark, are in no such dilemma. They want profits, the genuine article, and not just "the profit motive." Witness this statement from the draft program of the Soviet Communist party as translated by Tass and printed in *The New York Times* on August 1, 1961: "It is necessary to promote profitable operation of enterprises, to work for lower production costs and higher profitability."

Wouldn't it be interesting some day to see a platform of the Republican or Democratic party calling for higher profitability? I am sure we can count on both parties to continue advocating prosperity, but it would be a great thing for the country if we might also find included—say in 1964— a recommendation in favor of higher profitability, the necessary ingredient of that prosperity.

THE BENEFITS OF PROFIT

I have a good many reasons for believing that a plus in business profits fairly earned is a plus for everybody. *The profitable business has freedom to do what is right.* I did not say has freedom to throw money around. The business that is profitable can operate much more economically than the one that is not, for the profitable operation does not have to defer current expenditures that will improve long-run performance. The company that puts off doing what it ought to do, because it cannot afford it at the time, inevitably sacrifices long-run economies.

I could sum up much of what is in my mind by saying that good profits facilitate

good management judgment, but since this statement needs particularizing, I shall try to illustrate.

Training

Let us look first at the training of people. This is essential to the vitality of any business enterprise and its ability to contribute to economic progress. The selection of able people is a crucial task requiring thought, time, and money, and it is but the start of the long-range development process that calls for more of all three. I am not thinking of formal training procedures alone, but of the whole complex of effort needed to bring about conditions that encourage personal growth, inspire quality performance, and enable the individual to realize deep satisfaction in his work. The business that has adequate means available is far more likely, I think, to make the conscious and continuous effort needed than the business that is hard up.

There is growing conviction that the best way to test managerial talent is to give young people from the start assignments that truly challenge their capacity—in preference to training routines that impose a minimum of responsibility, fail to offer the trainee any sense of having a real job, bore him unutterably, and give him sore feet from standing around. One of the good arguments in favor of testing men early in their careers is that they will learn from their mistakes. In saying this, I am not advocating mistakes at any time; we have, however, to be realistic. If we are going to give people responsibility in this way, there are bound to be some errors, and they are bound to cost money (albeit less than the cost of bigger errors the same people might make in later years if they did not have the judgment gained from making little ones). But if we cannot stand the cost of the small errors, we are not going to assign the responsibility. In other words, we are not going to do what we know we ought to do to build the future.

It may be said that these examples hardly provide all the evidence needed to support the case for healthy profit. I agree. Before offering more illustrations, however, let me remind the reader that these I have mentioned lie in an area of special importance for the future. With the advance of technology, there is an ever-growing need for the training and retraining of men and women in almost every phase of industry. People must learn to use new arts effectively, find new markets for new products and services, and function to best advantage in new forms of organization. In short, industry in the years ahead faces a tremendous task in education, and if industry cannot earn the means, the task is simply not going to be done well. To put it another way, the country is well aware that the schools face a problem of unprecedented scope. But as we all know, education is not completed at school; it only begins there. This is the recurrent theme of every college commencement, and with good reason. Starting where the schools leave off, industry must shoulder a considerable part of the total responsibility for future education —quite apart from its financial contributions to the schools.

Physical Plant and Engineering

Another aspect of what I choose to call the vital or causative function of profit lies in the area of engineering and building plant facilities. Let us look at an example drawn from the telephone business, which must make heavy investment in physical plant in order to serve its customers.

A telephone engineer is called on to decide what size of telephone cable should be installed to serve a growing neighborhood. He knows it must serve perhaps 200

homes immediately. He is also reasonably confident that, in another couple of years, possibly 200 more homes will want service. Putting in a cable today that is big enough to serve all 400 homes will obviously cost more now than putting in one that will serve only 200. The carrying charges will be higher, too, of course. But if the engineer puts in the cable today that will serve only 200 homes, and another of equal size is needed two years later, the total cost and carrying charges will be considerably more in the long run.

So what will the engineer do?

If the company he is working for is hard up, he will have to put in the smaller cable because that is cheaper *now*, even though it is obvious that this course will be more expensive in the end. If, however, the company is in good financial shape, if it can readily get the capital needed for investment in the larger cable, and if the general level of earnings permits absorbing the higher carrying cost of the bigger cable until its full capacity is utilized, then the engineer will be encouraged to install the bigger cable. Again I point out that good profit favors doing what ought to be done.

It is a commonplace that profit or the prospect of profit is necessary to attract capital. Less emphasized, but no less important, is the fact that healthy profit in countless instances promotes capital's effective and efficient application. The example I have cited is not an isolated instance; telephone people, and no doubt others in many different lines of business, have to make thousands of decisions like the one mentioned above. In the making of all such decisions, reasonable present prosperity helps to promote long-run economy and progress.

In the last year or so, much public attention has centered on the fact that a large proportion of America's industrial plant is growing old. Surveys that have been made indicate that about a third of it is now so old and inefficient that it ought to be scrapped. The Secretary of the Treasury has said that the average age of the nation's plant is twenty-four years, and the President has observed that some two-thirds of our machine tools are more than ten years old.

Aging plant is progressively more inefficient. We need to modernize our productive facilities to compete more effectively in world markets, help balance our international payments, and create job opportunities for our growing work force. Why then does industry retain so much old and inefficient plant? One important reason is that our tax laws do not allow industry enough depreciation expense, either in total or year by year. The result is understatement of true costs, corresponding overstatement of income, and, in consequence, a tax on capital. (Any levy on a proper expense that the law requires to be mislabeled as income must be a levy on capital; it cannot be anything else.) In any event, adequate depreciation plus adequate real profit has been made impossible.

I have been arguing my conviction that good profit works in favor of productive efficiency. It seems to me that the apprehensions about inadequate depreciation and the movement to find some remedy support this argument. In essence, what we have here is a growing concern that capable and effective businesses should be able to earn the real profits they need in order to become more productive. Maybe some people in government have not thought the matter through in this way; if they have not, I wish they would. Knowing the problem for what it really is might lead also to better understanding of the function of profit in other respects.

Lean Leavings Not Enough

The main effort in this article has been to suggest the meaning of a concept that

says that profit is not something merely residual, but is causative and energizing. At this point, however, someone may well say, "Look here, this is all very well, but are you really talking about profit per se and how much of it there ought to be? It seems to me you are talking rather about some of the things a well-managed business needs to do *before* it makes a profit—before it is able to deposit that residue. There are other accomplishments that are also important: good wages and working conditions, for instance, safe working practices, research and development, the introduction of new products and services, alertness to consumer needs, and so on. So long as you accomplish these and still have something left over, this is what really counts, isn't it? And where is your proof that the residue, the profit, needs to be more than minimal?"

I can only answer that last question from actual experience as a manager, and this experience has convinced me that the quality of management performance is influenced in every aspect by the prospect of good earnings on the one hand, or of lean leavings on the other. For evidence, I have to turn again to events in the Bell System. This is not intended as special pleading, and I hope it will not be so interpreted. The fact is simply that to speak from experience, it is necessary to refer to it.

Our overall earnings situation in the years soon after the war was poor. In the early 1950s, there was a slight improvement, and in the last few years there has been further improvement. What one may trace rather easily, as earnings have risen, is an acceleration of projects that markedly increase the quality, dependability, and convenience of the service rendered.

For example, we measure the quality of telephone transmission in terms of how people might hear each other if they were conversing in a quiet open field. In 1950, transmission on the average long distance call was as though the talkers were standing 15 feet apart. In the ten years following, this distance was reduced some 20 percent—to about 12 feet. But with a better profit margin at hand, we are now working on a program to cut the distance down to less than 5 feet by 1970. This will make an enormous difference in the ease of conversation.

Perhaps it has been noticed also that as Bell System earnings improved in the later 1950s, there came a succession of new telephone instruments and systems for homes and offices. Direct distance dialing spread rapidly so that today about three-quarters of all our customers can dial their own calls to all parts of the nation. Ocean telephone cables to Europe, Alaska, and Hawaii have resulted in a great improvement in overseas services.

Today a program is under way to sharply reduce the occasions when people wanting to telephone in the busier periods of the day will find no circuits available. Another important project is construction of a bomb-resistant underground communications system across the continent. Our direct distance dialing program is proceeding on a schedule that will make such calling available to nearly every Bell System customer in the next four years. Means for automatically identifying the calling number are being installed under an accelerated program. Data-Phone services, which enable machines to communicate with other machines through the regular nationwide telephone network, are being rapidly extended. Millions of dollars are being spent for the development of communications satellites that may permit global communications, including television and data as well as voice transmission, on a scale hitherto impossible.

Were the profits of the Bell System today no better than they were in the 1940s and well into the 1950s, it would be impossible for us to push ahead with anything like the same vigor. And if we could not

maintain good earnings, we would necessarily have to put a checkrein on forward undertakings. Prudence would demand this.

Not that profit can or ever should be assured. It must be worked for and earned in every sense of the word. But if the ultimate end in sight is meager, few managers will bend extra effort to develop and proceed with new and useful long-range projects that increase current costs, or build additional excellence into their product, or take special pains with their maintenance, or spend either a million dollars or a hundred to make their plant and facilities more efficient. More likely, they will feel pressed to move in the reverse direction. They may compromise on quality; they may skimp on maintenance, or even do none for as long as possible. They may rely protractedly on the outmoded and outworn. Against his better judgment, against all his instincts to do the job well, the manager is pushed into ill-advised corner-cutting, into expedients and substitutes, into deletions and omissions that may not show immediately but will ultimately sap the long-run vigor and strength of the enterprise. In short, if he has no hope of prosperity by the means that will most benefit his customers and his company, which is to give real value and earn an equivalent reward, he is forced into the situation of trying to keep integrity in his financial statements by taking it away from his business.

THE BROADER VIEW

Earlier in this article I put some stress on the difficulties we get into if we admire profit as a goal but deplore it as an achievement. We cannot be half for profit and half against it. I wonder if the reason some of the critics of profit get into this situation may not be that they see business managers as dedicated *solely* to profit. Perhaps some managers are so dedicated. However, my observation is that most of them have a broader view. In a business like the one I am in, the question is ever present, "Which comes first, service or profits?" Our license, of course, is only to serve, nothing else. But to answer the question by separating the one from the other is difficult indeed. Years ago, the answer was given in these words, and I find it hard to improve them: "We must serve well to prosper. We must prosper to serve well."

I have omitted from this discussion such an obvious point as the fact that prosperity pays taxes. All it appears necessary to say is that if the government wants revenues, the government will do more than give lip service to the profit goal—it will really encourage the making of real profits and rejoice in the result.

No discussion of business profits can be conclusive. But to refer again to the study mentioned at the start, where there is overwhelming evidence that profit, perfor-mance, and progress are intimately linked, may there not be wisdom in accepting the likelihood that profit is in fact an essential contributing factor? I realize that economics is not an exact science. By the same token, however, it seems necessary to say that no theory that denies a causative, creative role to business profits can be taken as definitive. From experience and observation, I am persuaded that good profits not only accompany and make manifest sound progress, but do in fact make important contributions to it, and must be regarded as essential to promote economic growth and the achievement of desirable economic goals. Only an economy in which industry and government see eye to eye on this, and work in harmony to nourish business profit, will realize its full potential in creating productive efficiency, in delivering the greatest value to the consuming public, and in raising living standards.

31

Collective bargaining is a complex and often mysterious process. Professor Dunlop explains some of the major functions of collective bargaining and some of the conflicting issues involved in evaluating it.

THE SOCIAL UTILITY OF COLLECTIVE BARGAINING

John T. Dunlop

John T. Dunlop is Professor of Economics at Harvard University.

John T. Dunlop, "The Social Utility of Collective Bargaining," in Lloyd Ulman, ed., *Challenges to Collective Bargaining*, © 1967 by The American Assembly, Columbia University. Reprinted by permission of Prentice-Hall, Inc., Englewood Cliffs, New Jersey.

. . .

. . . The American public does not well understand the role of collective bargaining. It is dangerous for a society to distort and misconceive so widely the purposes, operations and limitations of so basic an institution. It is no less inimical to the future of organized labor and management.

John Mitchell, the great leader of the miners at the turn of the century, wrote: "In the long run, the success or failure of trade unions will depend upon the intelligent judgment of the American people." Alfred Marshall concluded his analysis of trade unions in the early 1890s: "Public opinion, based on sound economic and just morality, will, it may be hoped, become ever more and more the arbiter of the conditions of industry." These judgments are no less relevant today in shaping the future of collective bargaining and highlighting the decisive role of public opinion.

The social utility of collective bargaining, or any institution for that matter, is to be appraised fundamentally by reference to alternative ways of performing the same functions in the society. What are the central purposes of collective bargaining? What are the major alternatives in our industrial society for achieving these purposes? How is collective bargaining to be judged in comparison to other institutions which involve conflicting interests of individuals and groups, such as local governments, the press, medical care, universities, and Congress?

In our industrial relations system, collective bargaining purports to accomplish three major functions: (a) it is a system to establish, revise and administer many of the rules of the work place; (b) it is a procedure to determine the compensation of employees and to influence the distribution of the economic pie; (c) it is a method for dispute settlement during the life of agreements and on their expiration or reopening, before or after, resort to the strike or lockout. These are basic purposes which every industrial society and economy must somehow perform.

The major competitors to collective bargaining are three: these decisions may be made unilaterally and posted by management subject to competitive and political limitations; they may be imposed by a labor organization which specifies the conditions on which it will furnish or maintain labor services; they may be decided in one form or another by governmental fiat. Even when decisions are made unilaterally, they are influenced by a variety of constraints: managements must accommodate within limits to the labor market, and government decrees must meet the tests of acceptability and the market within limits in order to survive. There are various combinations or compromises among these three broad alternatives, and our present system of collective bargaining is one.

There is no doubt a role today as always for the prophet wailing against the evils of the system and the reformer who reminds us how far our institutions fall short of perfection. Every conspicuous strike brings forth a rash of editorials and articles. Wrote A. H. Raskin in 1959:

> The steel companies and the United Steelworkers of America have become standard-bearers in what amounts to an outbreak of class warfare—low-voltage, non-violent, but none the less destructive in its implications for industrial democracy and an economy calculated to serve the consuming public, as well as its dominant power blocs. . . . And these potential explosions are merely the most dramatic in a series of equally dismaying indications that something is seriously awry in the system of collective bargaining that is our main reliance in keeping labor disputes from wrecking our free economy.

There is much in contemporary collective bargaining, as in other aspects of American life, which generates frustration, alarm and disenchantment. But we would do well to concentrate upon the hard questions of the alternatives, the realistic choices, for major changes or for continuing tinkering with our system of industrial relations.

THE DEBATE: PRO'S AND CON'S

The popular debate about collective bargaining has been conducted with reference to five main issues, or five groups of charges and defenses:

1. Strife vs. Peace—The charge is made that collective bargaining exhausts the parties and the community in strife and conflict. Unions are depicted as the most powerful organizations in the community in that they, and they alone, can deprive the community of essential goods and services.

The defense is made that the extent of strife in collective bargaining is declining, and there is even talk of the withering away of the strike. The average level of strike activity in the six years 1960–65, as a percentage of working time, was one-half the level of the preceding decade. The extent of violence in labor disputes has been very materially reduced over the past generation. The occasional withdrawal of services or a lockout is said to be inherent in the free market, a refusal to buy or sell. In fact, the community has never been seriously hurt by a work stoppage. The alternatives to collective bargaining are likely to prove of greater mischief to the community.

2. Economic Distortion vs. Standardized Competition—The detractors of collective bargaining contend that it leads to labor and management combining against the public interest. Producers combine to push up wages and prices against the interests of the consumer. Moreover, the allocation of resources in the economy is distorted so that there are too few workers at too high wages in organized sectors and too many workers at too low wages in sectors without collective bargaining. The national product for everyone is lower as a result.

The defenders argue that collective bargaining "takes wages out of competition" and compels employers to compete among each other on the basis of managerial efficiency rather than on their capacity to depress wage rates. It places competing employers on an equal basis and assures that competitors are confronted with the same price for labor services.

3. Disruptive Inflation vs. Plea of Not Guilty—Charles E. Lindblom wrote that "Unionism is not disruptive simply because it causes inflation and unemployment, for these are problems in a nonunion economy as well. Rather it is disruptive because it will cause an amount of lasting unemployment or a degree of continuing inflation which will become so serious that the competitive price system will be abandoned in the search for remedies." The experience with incomes policies in Western countries suggests that free collective bargaining, full employment and a reasonable degree of price stability are incompatible.

The proponents of collective bargaining plead not guilty to the charge of constituting a significant independent influence creating inflation. The finger should be pointed rather to monetary or fiscal policy of governments or to high profits which may appropriately stimulate larger wage demands. The relative stability of labor costs in manufacturing over the past five or six years is cited to support this defense.

4. Stifle vs. Stimulate Management—The indictment is made that collective bargaining constricts management with a variety of artificial rules leading to excessive manning, inefficient operations and loss of prerogatives essential for an enterprise to grow and adapt in a dynamic economy. In the absence of collective bargaining management would be more efficient and productivity would grow faster. On the other hand, according to the late Sumner Slichter,

Unions have greatly improved the management of American enterprises by accelerating the shift from personal management to management based upon policies and rules, and they have given the workers in industries the equivalent of civil rights. The strong upward pressure of unions on wages has been an important influence stimulating technological change and raising real wages—though other influences have been even more important.

Collective bargaining procedures facilitate orderly introduction of change.

5. Union Dictatorship vs. Industrial Democracy—The advent of the union at the work place is seen by its critics as installing an arbitrary union boss over the members to replace the management boss over the employees. The union officer is depicted as having vast powers over the member in disposing of grievances and setting wages and other conditions of work.

Collective bargaining is described, in contrast, as the introduction of industrial democracy at the work place. Through elected representatives, the individual worker participates in the determination of wages and working conditions. Our labor organizations are among the most democratic of institutions in the society; indeed, they may be much too responsive to the immediate wishes of the rank and file on wage and technological displacement issues. The Landrum-Griffin law has accentuated these problems by making union officers even less willing to take unpopular positions with the rank and file.

· · ·

These conflicting views on collective bargaining are not readily reconciled. There are no doubt individual collective bargaining relationships which can be found to fit each of the above conflicting categories. In a large country with more than 150,000 agreements diversity should not be surprising. Some of these pro's and con's arise from inherent conflicting tendencies within collective bargaining. Some tension and inner conflict is normal to institutions as well as to personalities. Some of these opposing appraisals involve appeals to contending social and economic values—price stability, economic growth, full employment, industrial peace, union democracy, distributional equity and freedom from government regulation. These goals are scarcely entirely compatible, and a degree of one can be achieved only at the price of giving up a degree of another. Finally, some of the popular views sketched in apposition are simply in error or are gross oversimplifications.

It is perhaps foolhardy for anyone to state an overall appraisal in capsule form. Professor Slichter once put it this way:

> Our system . . . gives the American worker better protection of his day-to-day interests than is received by workers anywhere else; it puts American employers under greater pressure than the employers of any other country to raise productivity; and, though it gives unions a wonderful opportunity to whipsaw employers, it gives employers a freedom to bargain which they like and for which they seem willing to pay a big price. Hence, we seem justified in being grateful that we have been favored by fortune and perhaps also in taking modest pride that we have pursued opportunist policies with considerable flexibility and good sense.

My own summary appraisal would state that our collective bargaining system must be classified as one of the more successful distinctive American institutions along with the family farm, our higher educational system and constitutional government of checks and balances. The industrial working class has been assimilated into the mainstream of the community and has altered to a degree the values and direction of the community, without disruptive conflict or alienation and with a stimulus to economic efficiency. This is no mean achievement in an industrial society. The institution faces, however, new challenges in the generation ahead; the discussion considers these questions in a final section.

The Unappreciated Contributions of Collective Bargaining

The public vision of collective bargaining highlights the large strike, the public debate and invective and the legislative investigation. The routine negotiations, the smaller scale and local relationships, the parties who shun publicity, and technical developments escape all but the specialists. Moreover, the press does not report or interpret, and the public does not understand, many of the most significant functions which collective bargaining performs. It would be remiss not to call attention to a few of these unappreciated contributions.

1. One of the major activities of collective bargaining involves the determination of priorities *within* each side in the bargaining process. The view that a homogeneous union negotiates with a homogeneous management or association is erroneous and mischievous. A great deal of the complexity and beauty of collective bargaining involves the process of compromise and assessment of priorities within each side. In an important sense collective bargaining typically involves three coincidental bargains—the rejection of some claims and the assignment of priorities to others within the union, an analogous process of assessing priorities and trade-offs within a single management or association, and the bargaining across the table. The same processes are involved in the administration and application of the agreement.

A labor organization is comprised of members with a conglomeration of conflicting and common interests. A gain to one may involve a loss, or preclude a gain, or distort past relationships with another. The skilled and the unskilled, the long service

and the junior employees, the piece workers and the day workers, workers in the expanding departments and contracting jobs may not have the same preferences. As George W. Taylor has put it: "To an increasing extent, the union function involves a mediation between the conflicting interests of its own membership." Similarly, even in a single management the production department and sales department may assess differently the consequences of a strike; the financial officers may see an issue differently from the industrial relations staff. In an association in multi-employer bargaining there are often vast differences in financial capacity, concern over specific issues and philosophy toward the union.

One of the major reasons that initial demands of both sides often tend to diverge so far from final settlements is that neither side has at the outset established its priorities or preferences. Indeed, these relative priorities are established during the bargaining process since they are not independent of the rankings established by the other side. This view of the bargaining process also helps to explain the sense of comradeship that experienced labor and management negotiators reflect in treating with their respective committees and constituents.

This internal accommodation is at the heart of collective bargaining. It is not to be dismissed or denigrated by snide references to internal politics on either side. In working at these internal adjustments in a viable way collective bargaining is serving a social purpose of enormous significance. Moreover, the responsibility for working out the solution by internal processes is essential to the strength of leadership and to the continued vitality of the management or labor organization. This adjustment process is not ordinarily visible to the public but needs to be understood and appreciated.

2. It is strange indeed that public opinion in an industrial society would appear to understand so little of the problems and opportunities of the immediate work place —the factory machine, office desk, airplane cockpit, the construction site, the truck cab, etc. The handling of grievances is decisive both to labor costs and earnings or income; it is basic to morale and efficiency. The day-to-day administration of incentive systems and job evaluation, the flow of workers in the internal labor market by promotions, transfers, layoffs and retirements, the adjustment to technological and market changes and thousands of other types of questions arise each day. These processes have little public glamour but they are vital to management, workers and labor organizations; they are decisive to an industrial society.

Our decentralized collective bargaining system has developed grievance procedures with resort to private arbitration that have contributed materially to industrial peace and to both private and social efficiency at the work place. The wild cat strike is not in many places a serious problem; most grievance procedures work well, although there is, of course, still room for improvement; private arbitration is an established system of last resort except in a few situations where the parties have deliberately reserved a special-purpose strike as the last resort. The adjustments to changing labor markets and shifting product demands and technology work reasonably well. Indeed, any international comparison of industrial relations at the work place supports the conclusion that American managements generally retain wide powers of initiative (there are exceptions), and American workers have clearly defined procedures which operate well to seek redress. The connection of the union to the worker at the work place is direct. Moreover, these arrangements appear to evolve and adjust reasonably well to changing conditions.

Collective bargaining contributes much to what has been called the "permanent efficiency of the nation." In comparison to its principal competitor, government regulation, the system of decentralized collective bargaining at the work place must be ranked definitely superior.

3. At the market or industry level collective bargaining also performs a variety of functions. (Some of these points may apply in some cases to the plant level as well.) The method of wage payment is a significant problem which may seem unimportant. The joint development of the job evaluation plan in basic steel, for instance, and its continued revision, is central to orderly operations. The review and revisions of methods of wage payment have fundamental consequences for labor costs and earnings as experience with any demoralized incentive plan will indicate. The development and administration of apprenticeship and training programs is typically a locality or nationwide function of collective bargaining in an industry or a sector. The establishment of health and welfare and pension plans has often been at the industry level. The development and spread of supplementary unemployment benefits and other approaches to more stable earnings is a contribution of collective bargaining above the level of plant administration. Any approach to decasualization and seasonality in industries such as longshoring and construction requires a market-wide or industry-wide approach.

The relative competitive position of different firms as far as labor costs or the price of labor (wage rates and benefit structure) is concerned has been a major preoccupation of collective bargaining from its earliest days. This role has been particularly significant in highly competitive industries such as clothing, garments, construction, trucking, service trades and other local market oriented industries. Any individual enterprise, in a highly competitive industry, is narrowly constrained as to what it can do in the labor or product market. A variety of structural reforms relating to compensation methods, training, manpower use, dispute settlement procedures and the like require a market-wide approach to be effective.

While syndicalism is an appropriate concern in some few situations, the market or industry level of collective bargaining more typically provides a restraint and a check in our pluralistic society to the growing formal and informal regulation and influence of governmental agencies. A continuing interaction is essential in my view for regulatory policies and for procurement policies. Unpolicied and unwatched bureaucrats are no less perilous to the public weal than combinations of labor and management.

. . .

32

LABOR-MANAGEMENT RELATIONS IN THE PUBLIC SECTOR

Theodore Kheel

Increasingly, public employees—including college professors—are turning to collective bargaining to further their goals. Although many states have laws that grant public employees the right to bargain collectively, these laws often bar strikes. The author contends that the right to strike is the essence of effective collective bargaining strength and that public employees will strike when they feel threatened. In fact, many public employees do strike, though sometimes such a walkout is euphemistically referred to as "a withholding of services."

Theodore Kheel is a prominent labor arbitrator and mediator.

From U.S. Congress, House of Representatives, *Hearings before the Special Subcommittee on Labor of the Committee on Education and Labor,* 92nd Cong., 2nd sess., May 3, 1972, p. 505.

. . .

Now, as employees in the public service began to organize, began to join together for what the Wagner Act calls mutual aid and protection, but not with the rights given under the Wagner Act, they began to petition their employers in groups.

The employers would hear them, would discuss matters with them. They would consider what they said, but then make a decision, which was the final decision. Now, that did not seem to cause any problems until the question arose about whether where the employees did not like the final decision, they could strike.

This matter came up very sharply in New York State in 1947 as a result of a strike by teachers in Buffalo. Mr. Thomas E. Dewey was then the Governor, and he put through the legislature of our State a law known as the Condon-Wadlin law which specifically forbad strikes by public employees.

It contained no alternate procedure for the resolution of their rights, than existed at that time. Mr. Dewey, in a very interesting message which he issued in connection with the signing of the bill, pointed out that employees had the right to petition their Government, to be heard, to present, whether they did that with a lawyer or with a union as a representative, in a collective way, but that the decision of the employer was final.

If they did not like it, they could go to the electorate and campaign to get somebody else elected in place of the employer who had made the decision.

Now, both because of the success of the National Labor Relations Act with private employees, and because of the expansion of services rendered by Government, and the growth in the number of public employees —as is so well pointed out in the statement I have here about the three bills before you, regarding the purpose of the bills— because of this expansion, the discussions began and were being pressed to give public employees rights similar to those in the private sector.

I might say that almost simultaneously with Mr. Dewey's Condon-Wadlin law, President Roosevelt made a statement saying that strikes by public employees were intolerable, and could not be allowed to take place. That is the statement very frequently cited by people who feel to this day that public employees should not have the right to strike under any circumstances.

In 1965 or 1966, as a result of negotiations in 1965, there was a horrendous strike of the transport workers in New York City, perhaps the most devastating strike in a municipality in the history of labor relations. Of course, that created quite a stir, and immediately led to the appointment of a committee headed by Dr. George Taylor, formerly of the University of Pennsylvania, and a great expert in labor relations.

The committee also included four other distinguished experts in this field. They came in with the document known as the Taylor Committee report which in turn led to the Taylor law in New York City.

If you will pardon me, I make references frequently to the experience in New York State because I happen to live in New York State, but I do believe that the experience has been the most intensive, and therefore the most revealing in terms of what the problems are.

Dr. Taylor and his committee came to grips with what is the essential question, that is the right to bargain collectively. They started out with the premise that they believed in sincerely, and I think that there was surely room for argument on both sides to say the least, that public employees should not have the right to strike under any conditions.

Now, starting out with the premise, they realized that you cannot have collective bargaining by definition. Now, that does not mean for this reason alone that there should not be a total ban on strikes by public employees, but it does mean that we make a mistake if we think simultaneously that we can have such a ban and have collective bargaining as we know it.

. . .

Now, joint decision-making means, in a bargaining relationship, that both sides must have the right to say no, which is the essence of bargaining.

If you go to buy 100 shares of stock and the price is too high, you say no. If the price you offer to the seller is too low, he says no. When you agree on a price, you have a bargain. If you can't say no, you cannot bargain.

If, therefore, you say that employees should have the right to bargain collectively, which is merely joining together and bargaining as a group, rather than individually, unless they have the right to terminate the relationship for a period of time, the service that they are rendering continues, and there can be no opportunity to say no.

It would be just as if you were to go to a used car dealer, and say, "I would like to buy a car. Let me have it and I will drive it around. Then, we will talk about the price." You have the car, and you can use it for the next several years. When incentive is there for you to come to a conclusion with him. You only get that incentive when you can't get what you want.

Now, ironically, that opportunity to arrive at an agreement jointly is one that belongs to the employer as well as the employees, but in the case of the employer, in some instances, it is not the right to strike, obviously, but the right to take a strike. That is the corresponding right of employers, the right to strike, because the strike is used when the union is the demanding party and wants a change to reflect whatever it is that requires a change to take place.

The cost of living has gone up, so—they want a wage increase, and the employer has a right to take a strike, instead of agreeing, if he is unable to say yes, or unwilling to say yes. The right to lockout is used by the employer where he wants a change such as a cut in wages, or a change in the manning scale.

The union's right to take a lockout is the opposite right in those circumstances. Now, if you ban that right for some reason of public policy, and there are surely reasons of public policy why the right to strike, or the right to take a strike, or the right to lockout, and the right to take a lockout, should be banned in certain instances where there is an impact on the public, when you do that, the consequence is that you cannot have collective bargaining. Now, if you say, therefore, nonetheless that the employee should have the right to discuss or the right to consult but not the

right to bargain, then you must do one of two other things when you deprive them of the opportunity to participate in the decisionmaking process.

You must either say, the employer should make the final decision, or that a third party should. Third party decisionmaking is, of course, arbitration. If it is compelled, it is compulsory arbitration.

I think that it is very important to understand, when we are talking about organization of employees for collective bargaining, that we are talking about either such collective bargaining with the right to strike, or we are saying that they shall have the right to discuss and to consult with the employer making the final decision. We can also say as we do in some instances that the decision shall be made by a third party.

The Taylor law designed a new term called "collective negotiations." Obviously they used that term instead of collective bargaining, because they recognized a difference, but they never defined what the difference was.

However, Dr. Taylor being a very astute student of the subject matter put in his report, the other committee members also, that if there could not be an agreement through discussion or through negotiations, as distinguished from bargaining, that the final decision would be made by the legislature, the appropriate legislative body involved.

Ironically enough, that meant in the case of authorities which were wholly autonomous, that the authority was the final legislative body.

In other instances it meant the legislative body of the municipality, or the legislative body of the State. The legislators were reluctant to have this final decisionmaking vested in them. They had visions of picketlines in front of the capitol building in Albany.

So they lopped off that recommendation,

and the law as passed originally said, "Collective negotiations followed in impasses with fact findings and recommendations, and a submission of the report to the legislature," but with no recommendation that the legislature do anything about it.

This led to all kinds of confusion in a variety of ways. First of all, cases arose in which a board made a recommendation which the union accepted, and the employer rejected. Now, that was the end of the line, there was no other place to go. Or, as happened in most instances, the union rejected the recommendation, and the employer accepted. The recommendations, by definition, were not binding, they were merely recommendations so that the right to reject was implied as a legal right under the law.

Nevertheless by rejecting, the union came to the end of the line, and the question arose, what do you do then? In many instances, unfortunately, they took what appeared to them to be the only alternative, and that was to strike.

However, some organizations were more ingenuous and they introduced various forms of work interference. Perhaps the most ingenuous was devised by the police officers of the Long Island expressway who undertook to enforce the letter of the law that said, anybody who exceeded 60 miles an hour should be ticketed.

It had been a common practice to let drivers at certain times of the day, go to 70 maybe even more. They began to enforce the law as required, and they issued so many tickets in such a short time that the courts were crowded to capacity. They were required to go to court, and there was in effect a strike, not by disobeying the law, but by complying literally with it.

Also what happened, and ironically this did produce collective bargaining in the public service, the union threatened to strike, or they implied a threat, and the implication was sufficiently scarey to be real, and the employers bargained. But, instead of bargaining as private employers do, in an atmosphere in which the U.S. Government says, "Collective bargaining is a policy of this country which everybody endorses, and is a wholesome, healthy thing," they were producing bargaining by threatening to violate the law.

Not only that, but when you have a law that says no, you can't do something, you have to have a penalty system. The next question is, what kind of a system of penalties do you impose for violations? That also raises the question of who is the violator, when the strike takes place. Is it the union leadership? Is it the union itself, which is an imaginary, but very real entity with money sometimes although sometimes it is broke, or is it the employees that belong to the union?

We have gone back and forth on that in New York. In 1966, the law that came out of the subway strike was predicated on the assumption that Mike Quill was responsible for that strike. I don't think that this was entirely correct, but that is an irrelevant matter.

Therefore, the penalty was placed on the leadership, and that resulted in jail sentences. Then it became a matter of necessity for leaders who were concerned about reelection to accept the jail sentence, rather than compliance. So, the oracles began to say, "Don't impose jail sentences, that will only make martyrs out of these fellows."

The editorials poured forth from the New York Times, and other such respectable publications, about that. Then along came a situation in which the leadership made an agreement with the public employer, and the rank-and-file in its wisdom overturned it. The leader of the union had a very difficult choice. Should he repudiate the democratic vote of the members and defy them, or should he lead them?

If he defied them, somebody else would lead them, not him. So, he took the very practical course of saying, if this is what you want, I will lead you. He wound up in jail as a result.

The officials of government who wished at this point to bring about the settlement had nobody to deal with, and the Governor of our State found it necessary to get the head of the union, who had originally reached an agreement and was anxious to maintain an agreement, released from jail so that he could negotiate with him.

As soon as they reached a new agreement, they put him back in the jailhouse. Out of that came the belief that maybe it should be the employees who should be penalized. So the law contains provisions that say, "If you don't work, if you partake of this, you will lose so many days' pay." That happened to be the law also in Condon-Wadlin in 1966 when the subway strike took place.

In the course of the ten days that the strike persisted, there were efforts, in which I participated, by the mayor, the Secretary of Labor, the President of the United States commented on it, and others including editorial writers, to bring about a settlement.

Finally, on the tenth day, a settlement was reached at city hall with flashing bulbs and television cameras, and congratulations, and handshakings. A few days later, a taxpayer brought a suit to prevent the settlement from being carried out.

By this time, unfortunately, Mr. Quill had died, and his place was taken by the present head of the union, Mr. Matthew Guinan, who was very anxious not to have to call another strike.

He was in the unfortunate position of being the successor-president who was being asked to forego the benefits of the agreement that had been negotiated with the mayor, and approved under kleig lights by the negotiators.

He sought help from people in public life, and the Governor responded by sending a special message to the legislature proposing repeal of the penalties retroactively, in the case of the transit workers alone. That law was passed.

We have an example there of a law that was violated, that contained penalties for its violation which was repealed after the law was broken, and the penalties by court decision had become due and payable.

That was hardly the way to engender respect for law, although it was probably, under the circumstances, about the only thing that could have been done without creating another strike situation.

Now, the question is, where are we and what do we do about it? We want two things that, unfortunately, are in conflict with each other. Unless we think the problem through clearly, we will continue to be schizophrenic. We have a split in our objective.

We want collective bargaining for public employees. But we also want them not to have the right to strike. We have to face that problem, and devise a solution. In my judgment, we must also recognize that if we decide to prohibit the strike, we can only have an alternate procedure that winds up in a final decision, and that only alternate procedure is compulsory arbitration.

I think we must also recognize that compulsory arbitration is a very difficult process to impose effectively, that it is a kind of a copout for people who do not want the responsibility of decision-making, and that it presents some very severe constitutional questions, both the State and Federal, in the case of employees with demands that affect the legislative process and the obligations of executive personnel under laws which they are sworn to obey.

It seems to me that what we have to do is, either review our belief that employees should have the right to bargain collectively, under all circumstances, and in place impose some other mechanism that calls on the employees to accept the decision of the employer as the final decision, or we have to review the question of whether the right to strike, and the right to take a strike, should be banned.

I don't think that you can answer that question categorically. It does seem to me that we must think the problem through clearly, if we are to arrive at a satisfactory decision.

There is one other point I wish to make before I conclude this opening statement and that is a comment on what I believe is the major fear that underlies much of the opposition to the right to strike by public employees.

I think the fear is, not so much that it will give them collective bargaining and joint decision-making, but that they have too much muscle, and as a result will get an unfair share of the pie in the competition for what is available in public funds, as compared with the commuter, the person who needs health care, people on welfare, and so forth.

If this is our concern, and it may be a legitimate one, we ought to say that and examine it for what it is, because there is an opposite side also to that concern, that is, the employee, public or private, who does not have the muscle, whose rights are so low, and whose work is so easily replaced or not missed, that he has no leverage.

That is not only the highly unskilled worker. It was, for example, the employees of Consolidated Edison in New York who struck that great utility. If they had been successful in shutting it down, we would have had the most calamitous situation in the history of labor relations in our city, far worse than the subway strike, because it would have shut down the subway as well as everything else.

That strike failed because the equipment was automated, and supervisors could handle it. The telephone workers just concluded a six- to eight-month strike in New York. Insofar as most people were concerned, they were saying, "we think that the service has improved during the strike." They were not affected.

The people who were affected were those who needed new telephones, who could not get them installed, but even those were being taken care of in emergency situations.

We had a ferryboat strike, but the ferryboat workers lost. The welfare workers have struck several times, and nobody gives a damn, because all it means is that people on relief will not get paid, except those who made it before the strike who are sent their check by mail. Some of those stay on relief, when they might otherwise have gone off.

On the other hand, there are situations involving as a classic example, police and fire, where the consequences can be horrendous.

. . .

The question is, "If the city, the country, the State, or the Nation is about to collapse, and people are about to die, and hospitals are prevented from functioning, do you say under those circumstances that workers should have the right to strike?" The answer is, "Of course, not."

There is a right of the people to be protected. There is a right to bargain collectively. Many times, rights that the Constitution recognizes are in conflict with other rights that the Constitution recognizes, and we have to make a balance and decide which right is superior.

Let us not throw the baby out with the wash, let us not destroy the bargaining process in the process of either protecting the public's legitimate right not to be injured, or the public's concern that maybe the organizations are too strong, and are demanding too much.

Now, in that regard, I think that perhaps at the moment the most pressing problem we face is the inability of public employers to come to the bargaining table as effectively, as completely prepared, and as effectively constituted to deal with organized labor as their counterparts in the private sector.

The one thing that American industry did when it was faced with the obligation to bargain collectively under the Wagner Act, is, it tooled up for it. It got experts or experts appeared and after a while they learned enough to become experts. They learned from their mistakes, each time they were a little smarter than they were the time before.

Today, in most situations, there is what the law seeks in the National Labor Rela-tions Act, that is, an equality of bargaining power. At any one moment, there is going to be a difference in the scale, but in some instances it favors the union, and in some instances it favors the employer. And it readjusts from year to year.

The one thing you learn, if you are in the business for a long time, and that is, a victory in 1972 may not be worth a lot in 1974. These things have a way of evening up over a period of time, not necessarily at the particular bargaining session, but there are measures that employers take such as moving to other areas, or automating, or going out of a particular business and into another business, which is their way to offset what they think are excessive demands. There are measures that unions take also.

If we don't have that give and take, we have to set up a machinery for making all of these decisions, which is not the kind of society we want, but this does not rule out the necessity of taking such action with all of its consequences, and unsatisfactory though they may be, when there is a right that we believe needs greater protection than the right to bargain collectively.

. . .

URBAN
AND SOCIAL
PROBLEMS

PART FOUR

33

New York City's welfare population increases by the month as newcomers pour in, mostly from the South. This article describes these welfare recipients and the often debilitating effects on them of the welfare system.

A PORTRAIT OF NEW YORK'S WELFARE POPULATION

Julius Horwitz

Julius Horwitz is a novelist who has worked in government and social welfare agencies.

From *The New York Times Magazine* (January 26, 1969). © 1961/ 1969 by The New York Times Company. Reprinted by permission of William Morris Agency, Inc.

. . .

FOR SOME, WELFARE IS A "BANK"

The traditional pattern of welfare as a form of paternalism began to change with the influx of low-income Puerto Rican families in the nineteen-forties and fifties. They used welfare as an economic stabilizer, a guaranteed income in case low-paying restaurant, hotel, nursing-home, hospital, garment-industry jobs could not support a family, or if the exorbitant rents in the West Side slums ate up the take-home pay. They paid little attention to the caseworkers. They saw welfare as a source of money, nothing else.

Similarly, the low-income Negro families who come to New York City from the South in search of the American experience of opportunity use welfare as a "bank." They know that they have "on deposit" in

New York City enough money to take care of them—to compensate for the lack of jobs, the lack of enough money on a job.

In a welfare center on 14th Street off Fifth Avenue, a Negro man of 20, waiting to see his caseworker, told me, "I don't find welfare a shame. I paid my taxes even if they didn't believe it in Alabama. I heard about welfare being a kind of bank in New York. This is only tax money they're giving out. I lost my job at $85 a week. I can make out on the $66 they give me every two weeks. It really worked like a bank when I applied at the end of July. I filled out an application no more complicated than a short income-tax form, and that same day they gave me money for rent and food because my money ran out."

New York City is an open city: No passport or identity card is required to take up residence. As a result, it is almost impossible to measure the so-called in-migration to New York from the South and Puerto Rico. At best, there are only estimates and they are dated. From 1960 to 1965, according to the Community Renewal Program, the net addition of nonwhites in New York City was 154,120 persons; the net addition of Puerto Ricans was 36,692—and the out-migration of whites was 450,115. But these are estimates based on population projections—not hard data.

Nor is there any way of knowing how many of these in-migrants are motivated by the higher welfare payments in the North. But the hard fact is that while Mississippi, for example, estimates that a family of four requires $201 a month to meet basic needs, including rent, Mississippi actually pays an A.D.C. family of four only $55—meeting 27 percent of the family's basic needs. Alabama has a similar standard of $177 a month, but pays $89. New York, where living costs are higher, pays 100 percent of the budget deficit—an average of $278 a month for a family of four, including rent. It is a situation that prompted a task force appointed by President Nixon to recommend that the Federal Government set uniform minimum standards and take over a larger share of the costs.

I went out to talk to men who had made the migration. On a stoop on West 103d Street I found Mr. Williams, who came to New York from Georgia in 1959, and found himself on welfare in August, 1968. He said to me, "You don't want to go up to my room. Some junkie might hit you over the head. They stole all my clothes when I came out of the hospital."

"What did they take?"

"They took three shirts, two pants, one pair of shoes, six pairs of underwear, tops and bottoms, a razor, a comb. They left me one dirty pair of underwear. The shoes were brand-new. They cost me $14.81. But I've also got some clothes in pawn. They're out in Long Island. When the pawn shops closed in Harlem during what I call the so-called riots—they weren't the real riots—my clothes went there. You can't find a pawnshop now in Harlem; they're closing up."

"What do you need from welfare?" I asked.

"Mostly money to get my clothes out of pawn." Mr. Williams took a card out of his wallet and showed me a job referral he had as a messenger for a Madison Avenue firm. "I'm supposed to go to work on Tuesday," he said. "I want to go on the new job looking like a gentleman. I don't have to take the job, you know. I can stay on welfare. But I want to see how they treat me, if they give me the money I really need to get back to work. I don't want to become a welfare addict."

. . .

The most tragic group among welfare recipients is the children. There are 600,000 welfare children in New York, and 445,300 of them are fatherless.

The basic rule in New York is that a man can be in the home but he must contribute whatever income he has toward the support of his family. This applies to married and unmarried men. Nobody knows how many men "abandon" their families so the families can receive welfare payments to "supplement" low-paying jobs. Nor does anybody know how many men desert their families because they are afraid of fatherhood.

But the results are clear. The children, whatever their age, become adults before they ever have a childhood. They leap from infancy into a fatherless world. They suffer a grade retardation twice as great as non-welfare school children. As many as 60 percent of the referrals to mental retardation institutions come from welfare families. In more than 85 out of 100 cases the retardation results from environmental deprivation rather than organic brain damage. These children, except for the few who live in families where there is a link to stability, are exposed to a world that no child can survive without damage. They see adults as enemies. They understand perfectly their status as welfare children but they are helpless to change what they understand. How can any child be expected to stand up against the American way of seeing welfare recipients as the living dead?

In a welfare center in Harlem I talked to a father who had deserted his children. I asked him why he never went once to look at the face of the child he had fathered. He told me he had never seen the face of his own father. "So what?" I said. He said, "What good is it seeing the face of my boy if I can't support him?"

"Did your father ever support you?" I asked. "No," he said. "Then you're just repeating history; you're not changing history," I said. He said, "What the hell do I care about history? Whatever I do my boy has a long hard way to go."

"They're going to ask you now to sign a paper saying that you're the father of your boy. Are you going to sign it?" "It won't make me his father." "What will make you his father?" He was silent. He gripped the table as if he might tear it to pieces. He didn't answer my question. He didn't know how to answer it.

Where is welfare heading? In a welfare center on Eighth Avenue I sat down next to a Negro man in his late thirties. His name was Mr. Mitchell. He wore a leather jacket. His slacks were neat. He had a strong quiet face. His eyes studied the room. They had focus; they did not stare inward, which is what you usually see in a welfare center—row after row of people unable to see the world around them or to feel they have a place in it.

I said, "I'd like to talk to you about welfare. What it does for you. What it doesn't do. What kind of hang-ups welfare has for you. Is that all right with you?"

He looked at me for an instant to see if I was out of focus and then he said, "Sure."

"What do you think of welfare?" I asked.

"It's like being in bondage," he said, as though he had spent a lifetime thinking about it. "You can survive, but that's about all. I feel they should abolish welfare. The kids grow up on welfare with the attitude that everything should be free and easy. With parents that work, the kids are different, they look different, they think different, they see things ahead of them, they're moving toward something real in this world. The kids I see on welfare in the neighborhood around the West 140's are looking for a handout. It's killing them. I see kids of 10 and 11 and 12 on dope. They have babies when they're 12 and 13. They're pulling down whatever the rest of the black people are pulling up. These kids need leadership. They need it bad."

"How would you give it to them?"

"Nobody ever asked me that before," he said. "But welfare should let a man in the house. Forget the rules. If he's the kind of man you see around the blocks in Harlem he can't make enough money to take care of a family. But he makes some money. He can't take on the responsibility for a whole family. Some men can't face that kind of responsibility. It drives them away. But let them face whatever responsibility they can take and they might stay on."

"Would it drive you away?"

"No, it wouldn't," he said. "I don't have any children yet but one is on its way. It won't set me running. I wouldn't leave my kids. I take that seriously, having kids."

"What about the men you talk to, what kind of reasons do they give for leaving their children?"

"They say they don't make enough money. They say they don't have enough money for themselves if they have to give to the family. They never grew up in families where they saw a father giving money to the family. They don't know what it means to support a child. They never saw it done. They grew up without support. You can tell the guys who never saw their fathers. Something is cut out of them, like they don't belong to anyone, like everyone is an enemy. They produce babies but they never had any training to be a father. They never saw it done, being a father. They never come around to see their babies, most of them. You got a lot of guys that need to be made into fathers."

"Why are you here today, sitting in a welfare office?" I asked. "You look like you can make out."

"I can. I got on welfare in August because the place where I was working on 38th Street closed down. Then I had to go into Harlem Hospital for two weeks. When I came out I needed money to pay the rent that was due on my apartment. You don't get a chance to save for emergencies on $84 a week. But now I found a job with the Board of Education. I'll be starting work next Monday."

"Then why are you here today?"

"Just to ask them for some money to buy working clothes. I need some winter clothes for this new job."

"Will the job pay you much money?"

"It'll pay me less than what they say a poverty wage is here in New York City. I'll get $2,800 a year for a six-hour day. That's less than poverty. But I need a job. And I got it. After that stay in the hospital I can't take the kind of jobs I used to be able to handle."

"When did you come to New York City?"

"In September, 1957."

"Do you remember how you came, why you came, what made you give up your home in the South?"

"That's something you don't forget," he said. "I was doing construction work in Columbia, S.C. I was making $1.50 an hour. I thought I could make more money in that same trade in New York. Some of my family was living here. I had some cousins, aunts, an uncle. I had a long talk with my mother about going. She said it was my decision. The South was getting worse. The court decisions made the whites begin to go by the rules, and they made all the rules go against you.

"I got on a bus and came to New York. I thought I could go right into construction work. I learned I had to get into a union first. No union would take me. I got a job in a restaurant I didn't want to do. I kept getting jobs I didn't want to do. There was no job I wanted to stick to because I knew that construction was my real job.

"That happens to a lot of guys from the South here in New York. They come knowing what they want, but nobody in this city wants to know it. That sets you drifting.

You keep drifting. One day you find out that the only thing out there for you is welfare. Without welfare you have to kill or steal just to keep alive. I never thought I would end up needing welfare."

. . .

There would be nothing really wrong with the present system of public assistance if America would forget its punitive, deep-rooted, almost hysterical hatred of poor people who speak up before they are spoken to. The legal structure guiding welfare is not inhuman. The intake interview does not *have* to be dehumanizing. The welfare caseworker does not *have* to be faceless. The energy it now takes to destroy welfare children could be used to help the children get through the bleak days of dependency.

Somehow or other, America has to forget its puffed-up image as a righteous, pious, inviolate moral force protecting the aged, the sick and dependent children. The image simply does not square with the facts. The welfare poor are now forcing this confrontation. For the first time in America the poor are throwing off the mask of meekness imposed on them by organized systems of welfare and charity. The Communists could not arouse the American poor. The radicals never did. But now the American poor have surfaced, whatever the historical reasons, and it is unlikely they will permit themselves to be drowned again by the milk of human kindness. . . .

34

LIKE IT IS IN THE ALLEY

Robert Coles

Rats are in the alley, along with cockroaches, flies, maggots, and decay. But above all, there is in the alley a feeling of helplessness—with respect to landlords, city administration, police, the world outside the ghetto. This helplessness is graphically depicted by a psychiatrist working in a major urban ghetto.

Robert Coles is a research psychiatrist at the Harvard University Health Services.

Reprinted by permission from *Daedalus*, Journal of the American Academy of Arts and Sciences, Boston, Massachusetts, Fall, 1968, pp. 1322–26.

. . .

Peter sees rats all the time. He has been bitten by them. He has a big stick by his bed to use against them. They also claim the alley, even in the daytime. They are not large enough to be compared with cats, as some observers have insisted; they are simply large, confident, well-fed, unafraid rats. The garbage is theirs; the land is theirs; the tenement is theirs; human flesh is theirs. When I first started visiting Peter's family, I wondered why they didn't do something to rid themselves of those rats, and the cockroaches, and the mosquitoes, and the flies, and the maggots, and the ants, and especially the garbage in the alley which attracts so much of all that "lower life." Eventually I began to see some of the reasons why. A large apartment building with many families has exactly two barrels in its basement. The halls of the building go unlighted. Many windows have no screens, and some windows are broken and boarded up. The stairs are dangerous; some of them have missing timber. (*"We just jump over them,"* says Peter cheerfully.) And the landowner is no one in particular. Rent is collected by an agent, in the name of a "realty trust." Somewhere in City Hall there is a bureaucrat who unquestionably might be persuaded to prod someone in the "trust"; and one day I went with three of the tenants, including Peter's mother, to try that "approach." We waited and waited at City Hall. (I drove us there, clear across town, naturally.) Finally we met up with a man, a not very encouraging or inspiring or generous or friendly man. He told us we would have to try yet another department and swear out a complaint; and that the "case" would have to be "studied," and that we would then be "notified of a decision." We went to the department down the hall, and waited some more, another hour and ten minutes. By then it was three o'clock, and the mothers wanted to go home. They weren't thinking of rats anymore, or poorly heated apartments, or garbage that had nowhere to go and often went uncollected for two weeks, not one. They were thinking of their children, who would be home from school and, in the case of two women, their husbands who would also soon be home. *"Maybe we should come back some other day,"* Peter's mother said. I noted she didn't say *tomorrow,* and I realized that I had read someplace that people like her aren't precisely "future-oriented."

Actually, both Peter and his mother have a very clear idea of what is ahead. For the mother it is *"more of the same."* One evening she was tired but unusually talkative, perhaps because a daughter of hers was sick: *"I'm glad to be speaking about all these things tonight. My little girl has a bad fever. I've been trying to cool her off all day. Maybe if there was a place near here, that we could go to, maybe I would have gone. But like it is, I have to do the best I can and pray she'll be o.k."*

I asked whether she thought her children would find things different, and that's when she said it would be *"more of the same"* for them. Then she added a long afterthought: *"Maybe it'll be a little better for them. A mother has to have hope for her children, I guess. But I'm not too sure, I'll admit. Up here you know there's a lot more jobs around than in Alabama. We don't get them, but you know they're someplace near, and they tell you that if you go train for them, then you'll be eligible. So maybe Peter might someday have some real good steady work, and that would be something, yes sir it would. I keep telling him he should pay more attention to school, and put more of himself into the lessons they give there. But he says no, it's no good; it's a waste of time; they don't care what happens there, only if the kids don't keep quiet and mind themselves. Well, Peter has got to learn to mind himself, and not be fresh. He speaks back to me, these days. There'll be a time he won't even speak to me at all, I suppose. I used to blame it all on the city up here, city living. Back home we were always together, and there wasn't no place you could go, unless to Birmingham, and you couldn't do much for yourself there, we all knew. Of course, my momma, she knew how to make us behave. But I was thinking the other night, it wasn't so good back there either. Colored people, they'd beat on one another, and we had lot of people that liquor* was eating away at them; they'd use wine by the gallon. All they'd do was work on the land, and then go back and kill themselves with wine. And then there'd be the next day—until they'd one evening go to sleep and never wake up. And we'd get the Bossman and he'd see to it they got buried.

"Up here I think it's better, but don't ask me to tell you why. There's the welfare, that's for sure. And we get our water and if there isn't good heat, at least there's some. Yes, it's cold up here, but we had cold down there, too, only then we didn't have any heat, and we'd just die, some of us would, every winter with one of those freezing spells.

"And I do believe things are changing. On the television they talk to you, the colored man and all the others who aren't doing so good. My boy Peter, he says they're putting you on. That's all he sees, people 'putting on' other people. But I think they all mean it, the white people. I never see them,—except on television, when they say the white man wants good for the colored people. I think Peter could go and do better for himself later on, when he gets older, except for the fact that he just doesn't believe. He don't believe what they say, the teacher, or the man who says it's getting better for us—on television. I guess it's my fault. I never taught my children, any of them, to believe that kind of thing; because I never thought we'd ever have it any different, not in this life. So maybe I've failed Peter. I told him the other day, he should work hard, because of all the 'opportunity' they say is coming for us, and he said I was talking good, but where was my proof. So I went next door with him, to my neighbor's, and we asked her husband, and you know he sided with Peter. He said they were taking in a few here and a few there, and putting them in the front windows of all the big companies, but that all you have

to do is look around at our block and you'd see all the young men, and they just haven't got a thing to do. Nothing."

Her son also looks to the future. Sometimes he talks—in his own words—"big." He'll one day be a bombadier or "something like that." At other times he is less sure of things: "I don't know what I'll be. Maybe nothing. I see the men sitting around, hiding from the welfare lady. They fool her. Maybe I'll fool her, too. I don't know what you can do. The teacher the other day said that if just one of us turned out o.k. she'd congratulate herself and call herself lucky."

A while back a riot excited Peter and his mother, excited them and frightened them. The spectacle of the police being fought, of white-owned property being assaulted, stirred the boy a great deal: "I figured the whole world might get changed around. I figured people would treat us better from now on. Only I don't think they will." As for his mother, she was less hopeful, but even more apocalyptic: "I told Peter we were going to pay for this good. I told him they wouldn't let us get away with it, not later on." And in the midst of the trouble she was frightened as she had never before been: "I saw them running around on the streets, the men and women, and they were talking about burning things down, and how there'd be nothing left when they got through. I sat there with my children and I thought we might die the way things are going, die right here. I didn't know what to do: if I should leave, in case they burn down the building, or if I should stay, so that the police don't arrest us, or we get mixed up with the crowd of people. I've never seen so many people, going in so many different directions. They were running and shouting and they didn't know what to do. They were so excited. My neighbor, she said they'd burn us all up, *and then the white man would have him-self one less of a headache. The colored man is a worse enemy to himself than the white. I mean, it's hard to know which is the worst."*

I find it as hard as she does to sort things out. When I think of her and the mothers like her I have worked with for years, when I think of Peter and his friends, I find myself caught between the contradictory observations I have made. Peter already seems a grim and unhappy child. He trusts no one white, not his white teacher, not the white policeman he sees, not the white welfare worker, not the white storekeeper, and not, I might add, me. There we are, the five of us from the 180,000,000 Americans who surround him and of course 20,000,000 others. Yet, Peter doesn't really trust his friends and neigh-bors, either. At nine he has learned to be careful, wary, guarded, doubtful, and cal-culating. His teacher may not know it, but Peter is a good sociologist, and a good political scientist, a good student of urban affairs. With devastating accuracy he can reveal how much of the "score" he knows; yes, and how fearful and sad and angry he is: *"This here city isn't for us. It's for the people downtown. We're here because, like my mother said, we had to come. If they could lock us up or sweep us away, they would. That's why I figure the only way you can stay ahead is get some kind of deal for yourself. If I had a choice I'd live some-place else, but I don't know where. It would be a place where they treated you right, and they didn't think you were some nuisance. But the only thing you can do is be careful of yourself; if not, you'll get killed somehow, like it happened to my father."*

. . .

35

WORK AND WELFARE

Special Task Force to the Secretary of HEW

There have been many attempts to change our welfare sys-tem, particularly by tying welfare more closely to work. This study examines the relationship between welfare and work, especially with respect to ADC mothers.

From *Work in America*, Report of a Special Task Force to the Secretary of Health, Education and Welfare, December 1972, pp. 140–143.

. . .

In original conception and intent, welfare is an income maintenance program for those who cannot take care of themselves. The main programs provide categorical aid to the blind, the aged, the disabled, and to families with dependent children (a pro-gram originally designed to make it pos-sible for widows and mothers without em-ployable husbands to stay at home and raise their children.)

Increasingly, however, the original pur-poses and definitions of welfare have lost their force, especially with respect to the Aid to Families with Dependent Children. What was originally defined as a popula-tion dependent on the larger community for maintenance and support tends now to be defined in the public's mind as a population of malingerers who ought to be forced to accept work. The result is that persons who cannot take jobs or, by social agreement, should not take jobs, are now the target of programs designed to make them take jobs.

This change in public perception and policy has two main roots. One is the frustration born of the now-certain knowledge that the need for a federal public assistance program will always be with us and will not, as was originally hoped, wither away as a result of the growth of a comprehensive contributory social insurance system. The other is the change from widows and orphans to unmarried mothers and illegitimate children as models or prototypes of the ADC family. ("The ADC example we always thought about," remembers the first Executive Secretary of the Social Security Board, "was the poor lady in West Virginia whose husband was killed in a mining accident, and the problem of how she could feed those kids.") Where the original model of the miner's widow evoked compassion, the new model of the unwed mother evokes deep and widespread resentment.

Underneath the resentment and the frustration, and giving rise to them, are a host of unverified assumptions about the character and composition of the welfare population: most poor people don't want to work; most people on welfare are black; welfare mothers have babies to increase their welfare benefits; people on welfare live well and easy; most people on welfare want to be on welfare; and so on.

Every one of these assumptions is demonstrably false as a generalization, and is true only in the occasional particular. The facts are that most poor people are not on welfare and the majority of poor people not only want to work but do work, year round and full time; black families, though

overrepresented, make up less than half of the AFDC caseload; the average monthly payment per recipient on AFDC is $49.60; most mothers on AFDC do want to work—it is not difficult to add to the factual side of this misunderstood issue.

What is so terribly damaging to the prospect of developing constructive programs for dealing with the problems of welfare is that these false stereotypes of poor people, black people, and AFDC families are widely held by the general public. The negative attitudes of most Americans about welfare thus constrain national leaders in their development of policy. Indeed, the existence of these feelings leads to a situation in which the public's "price" for welfare reform is the inclusion of mandatory work requirements for those on welfare, including mothers.

The variety of recent attempts to reform the welfare system are characterized by the inclusion of mandatory work provisions. These reflect the public's belief that there are many people on welfare who don't belong there, who could and should be working, and that we can deal with "the welfare mess" by forcing these people off the rolls. Realistically, then, we cannot expect a welfare reform program that does not have a work requirement for mothers until there is general public agreement that the great majority of people on welfare belong there (in the sense that they have no other place to go). The only able-bodied adults on welfare are those on the AFDC rolls, but since less than 5 per cent of the families receiving AFDC include an able-bodied man, the only category of recipients with any potential for joining the work force are women with dependent children, the very persons AFDC was designed to assist in staying home.

From the analysis we present in this section, the present public attitudes may very well lead to a worse welfare problem in the future. A welfare program with a compulsory work requirement for mothers will not help the mothers, the children, or the society at large, and, as we will discuss later, it will not enhance the all-important role of the central provider in establishing family stability. We believe that the alternative presented here, that of viewing mothers as working and of making jobs available for central providers, would better achieve the major objectives of the general public—a decreasing welfare caseload in the long run.

SHOULD WELFARE MOTHERS BE REQUIRED TO TAKE A JOB?

The question of whether the mother in a fatherless family (76 per cent of AFDC families) should take a job or not is a complex one. It is not even clear that anyone other than the mother has the legal or moral right to make that decision, or that anyone other than the mother can make the decision that is best for her and her children. Some mothers prefer outside jobs to keeping house and raising children; others prefer to stay home. To force all AFDC mothers to do one or the other is to do violence to what we know about human development and family relationships: mothers who work because they prefer to work, and mothers who stay home because they prefer to stay home, probably make better and happier mothers (and children) than those who do one or the other because of circumstances or coercion. It follows that the public interest and the interests of the mother and her children

will be best served if the mother herself makes the choice. This choice, of course, must be essentially a free one: a decision either way must not carry with it any special penalties, rewards or forfeitures.

The easiest part of the problem has to do with those women now on AFDC—perhaps a majority—who, other things being equal, would prefer to work and support their families. But other things are not equal. They do not take jobs because there aren't suitable child care facilities, or because the costs associated with having a job and paying for child care often leave them with less than they would be receiving on welfare. These women do not need to be coerced into the labor force; they need the freedom to join it: adequate child care facilities and a decent job at a living wage.

The more difficult part of the problem lies with those AFDC mothers who choose to remain home and raise their children themselves. More accurately, the problem lies not with them but rather with our system of public values regarding women and women's roles and our definition of work. When we say to the AFDC mother, for example, "You must go to work or take work-training in order to be eligible for public assistance," we are, in effect, telling her that, from society's point of view, she is not now working, that keeping house and raising children are not socially useful, at least not as useful as "a job." But we are able to make this judgment of the AFDC mother who stays home and raises her children only because we make this same judgment of all housewives.

.   .   .

36

Economists have well-developed theories about the relationship between advanced and "developing" countries. In this article, the author draws a picture of the relationship between center-city ghettos and the rest of society in terms similar to those used for advanced and developing countries. Professor Tabb argues that the "developing country"—the ghetto—is seriously disadvantaged by its "colonial" relationship.

THE BLACK GHETTO AS COLONY

William K. Tabb

William K. Tabb is Associate Professor of Economics, Queen's College of the City University of New York.

From *The Political Economy of the Black Ghetto* by William K. Tabb, W. W. Norton and Co., Inc., New York, 1970, p. 21 ff.

. . .

THE DEVELOPMENT PERSPECTIVE

Introductory chapters of a standard development textbook present a description of the typical less-developed country: low per capita income; high birthrate; a small, weak middle class; low rates of increase in labor productivity, capital formation, domestic savings; and a small monetized market. The economy of such a country is heavily dependent on external markets where its few basic exports face an inelastic demand (that is, demand is relatively constant regardless of price, and so expanding total output may not mean higher earnings). The international demonstration effect (the desire to consume the products enjoyed in wealthier nations) works to increase the quantity of foreign goods imported, putting pressure on the balance of payments as the value of imports exceeds the value of exports. Much of the small modern sector of the economy is owned by outsiders. Local entrepreneurship is limited, and in the absence of intergovernmental transfers, things might be still worse for the residents of these areas.

The economic relations of the ghetto to white America closely parallel those between third-world nations and the industrially advanced countries. The ghetto also has a relatively low per capita income and a high birthrate. Its residents are for the most part unskilled. Businesses lack capital and managerial know-how. Local markets are limited. The incidence of credit default is high. Little saving takes place and what is saved is usually not invested locally. Goods and services tend to be "imported" for the most part, only the simplest and the most labor-intensive being produced locally. The ghetto is dependent on one basic export—its unskilled labor power. Aggregate demand for his export does not increase to match the growth of the ghetto labor force, and unemployment is prevalent. As consumer goods are advertised twenty-four hours a day on radio and television, ghetto residents are constantly reminded of the availability of goods and services that they cannot afford to buy. Welfare payments and other governmental transfers are needed to help pay for the ghetto's requirements. Local businesses are owned, in large numbers, by nonresidents, many of whom are white. Important jobs in the local public economy (teachers, policemen, and postmen) are held by white outsiders. The black ghetto, then, is in many ways in a position similar to that of the typical underdeveloped nation. Can such relationships be termed colonial? And to what extent is the issue one of race and how much one of class?

* * *

THE CHOICES

In many ways the options open to the black ghetto are similar to those of the developing nation. For each the crucial question is how much foreign influence is desirable. A nation may invite foreign capital in, allow for complete foreign control of its key sectors, and permit repatriation of profit and principal at the will of the investors. At the other extreme, a country can forgo foreign capital, management, and markets and opt for complete autonomy. The latter course means a break with past social, political, and economic institutions. It calls for the total mobilization of the energies and resources of the country to substitute for resources that formerly were available from abroad. This has proven a difficult challenge when attempted by nations like Cuba and China. It is questionable whether regions that are part of a nation can successfully develop independent of external controls. The analogy therefore reaches its limit at this point.

Although riots can be seen in terms of "'expropriating the expropriators,'" the black community can gain only a limited independence. Blacks in the final analysis are Americans. They do not live in a territory that could become independent. Giving them their own nation by rearranging white and blacks in an India-Pakistan type of division makes little sense. The blacks would still be poor and still be limited to a dependent status that would be no more than a neocolonialism in which they exported labor-intensive products and imported most sophisticated goods from the

dominant white nation. Blacks must either be integrated into the society or establish a tenuous independence within the white nation. How great the ghetto's autonomy would be would depend on the collective identity of blacks as blacks and their willingness to press demands and obtain political power. However, there are narrow limits to what determined blacks can do, even when they win political control of a whole city. Richard Hatcher, the mayor of Gary, Indiana, commented in a speech that his electorial success had not brought about meaningful black control: "There is much talk about black control of the ghetto," he said. "What does that mean? I am mayor of a city of roughly 90,000 black people, but we do not control the possibilities of jobs for them, of money for their schools, or state-funded social services. These things are in the hands of the United States Steel Corporation and the County Department of Welfare of the State of Indiana. Will the poor in Gary's worst slums be helped because the pawnshop owner is black, not white?"

Black people could run the schools, the libraries, and the local parks, but to get money they would have to go outside the ghetto. Once black leaders are chosen and start dealing with those who hold real power, they will find that in order to get concessions they must first get rid of the militants who are "causing trouble and alienating the whites." This type of political pressure will probably be combined with efforts to create a middle class among blacks: homeowners and black capitalists. Such a group would serve as a bulwark against "those who would tear at the fabric of our society." The argument is often presented: "Give these people a piece of the action, a stake in America." In addition to the carrot of ownership for an enlarged middle class, manpower training for a growing working class, and welfare for the rest, there is still the tactical police force and other counterinsurgency forces.

There are, therefore, strong pressures to work within the system. Arthur Lewis, a prominent black economist, has urged black students to stop pushing for separate black programs and work instead to get more rigorous training as chemists, engineers, and economists. The neighborhood, he believes, is not the important focal point for action. Lewis suggests that black success is measured by how many blacks "become top members of the establishment." [1] Lewis stresses the limits of a movement for neighborhood autonomy. "There will be black grocery shops in black neighborhoods, but in your lifetime and mine," Lewis wrote, "there isn't going to be a black General Motors, a black Union Carbide. . . ." [2] Lewis ignores the reasons blacks attack a free enterprise system that has "chosen" to hire blacks last and fire them first. Entry into better jobs for individual blacks has come only recently, as a result of pressure by black mass action.

The possibilities for change open to a purely black social movement are limited by the minority position of blacks in a white society. For this reason Lewis counsels blacks to obtain better education so they can compete for jobs at General Motors. Through involvement in such powerful economic institutions, blacks can advance their cause. Although Lewis does not accept the colonial analogy, the advice he offers ghetto residents is similar to that often given to newly independent nations—invite foreign business in by giving them advantageous terms, and foster cooperation with these firms so that local entrepreneurship will develop. Critics of this approach

term it neocolonialism. They say that foreign firms will exploit the local economy.

In this country the very large firms project an image of concern. They initiate training programs for ghetto workers. Their presidents serve as chairmen of local Urban Coalition groups. At the same time, black militants are suspicious of these firms. Corporation executives have great political power. They are listened to in the councils of government. Militants ask, "How could the ghetto remain a colony if these men did not permit this to be so?" Like Eldridge Cleaver, for example, they see General Motors not as a bastion of strength that may be entered, but as one that must be destroyed. Cleaver believes corporations know that black strength is not in their interest. "White General Motors . . . knows that the unity of these twenty million ragamuffins will spell the death of the system. . . . At all costs, then, they will seek to keep these blacks from uniting, from becoming bold and revolutionary. These white property owners know that they must keep the blacks cowardly and intimidated." [3]

The dismantling of the colonial barriers against blacks carries with it a challenge to the corporate sector, an implicit threat to the dominant position of the profit motive as the determining factor in guiding production decisions. The black colony is forced to demand just such changes. If the wealth of America is to be shared on a more "equitable" basis, new rationales for distribution will have to be developed. Unlike overseas colonies that can win their freedom and go their own way, blacks must remake the total economic and social system in America if they wish to change their own situation.

An equally important obstacle to black liberation is the working-class white who is

---

[1] W. Arthur Lewis, "The Road to the Top Is through Higher Education—Not Black Studies," *The New York Times Magazine*, May 11, 1969.

[2] *Ibid.*, p. 40.

---

[3] Eldridge Cleaver, *Soul on Ice* (New York: McGraw-Hill, 1968), pp. 136–137.

not too far ahead of the average black. Members of the white working class find that their tax burden has been rising. They resist income transfers to those below them, for they would have to pay for them. Their relative status is also diminished if blacks rise in social and economic position. The working-class white is apt to feel a general discontent, and his cultural background and educational training lead him to accept demonological interpretations for the sources of the evils which afflict him. He is hostile to ideas he views as foreign and often has very strong racial prejudices. He sees his enemy as the blacks who want to take his job and the welfare mother who wants something for nothing, while he pays for her illegitimate children out of his ever-rising taxes. He does not see his enemy as the corporate elite which has sold him on consumerism and taught him to decry "big government" and "wasteful spending." It would seem that the white worker, tired from long hours of essentially meaningless work, wants to escape through the possession of more private goods. When black demands threaten what he has built up for himself and his family, he is unlikely to respond with understanding and generosity. James Boggs, a leading theorist of the black liberation movement, sees white workers as representing "the bulk of the counterrevolu-

tionary force against the Negro revolt." He views white workers as allied with their bosses against blacks at home and Third World people abroad.[4] However, he also sees that as blacks successfully force changes in working conditions and in income distribution, white workers' attitudes may change, even to the point of accepting black leadership around what come to be perceived as essentially class issues.[5]

It seems likely, however, that white society in the 1970s will continue to accept limited numbers of gifted blacks who work their way up. More than this will not come very easily. "Given a choice between a massive freedom budget and a police state, the American electorate is more likely to choose the latter."

The type of policies that will probably get government endorsement in the coming years is likely to be neither a massive reallocation of national resources to serve the needs of our low-income groups, nor the acceptance of a police state. Before the latter is forced on the nation there are a number of reforms that can be attempted.

• • •

---

[4] James Boggs, *Racism and the Class Struggle* (New York: Monthly Review Press, 1970), pp. 14, 53.

---

[5] *Ibid.*, pp. 17, 173.

37

THE FAILURE OF THE PUBLIC SCHOOLS AND THE FREE MARKET REMEDY

Some educators have proposed a "free market" for schooling, where families would be given educational vouchers for each child. Students and their families would then choose schools freely, purchasing the best schooling available to them. Levin explores the consequences of such a free market for education, especially for poor people and minority groups.

Henry M. Levin

Henry M. Levin is Professor in Education at Stanford University.

From *The Urban Review* (June 1968). Reprinted by permission of *The Urban Review*, a publication of the Center for Urban Education.

The American public schools have been severely criticized in recent years, and no schools more so than those responsible for educating "disadvantaged children" in urban areas. The utter failure of traditional schooling to impart even basic reading skills to substantial numbers of youngsters has stimulated a barrage of proposals, from educators and noneducators alike, to change the educational system.

. . .

A MARKET FOR SCHOOLING

The proponents of the market approach believe that by giving students and their families a choice of schools, and by requiring schools to compete for students, massive increases in educational effectiveness and output would result. For, if schools had to compete for students, they would likely be much more responsive to the particular needs of their clientele. That is, the private schools—in order to achieve goals of profit, or in the case of nonprofit ones, capacity enrollments—must provide what appears to be good schooling in order to attract students.

The father of this approach is the Chicago economist, Milton Friedman, and it is Friedman's basic scheme that dominates the proposals of others who would also replace the public schools with a market of choices. Before outlining the Friedman plan, however, it is important to point out that all of the advocates of the market approach view basic schooling as a public function. They do so because at the very least, ". . . a stable and democratic society is impossible without widespread acceptance of some common set of values and without a minimum degree of literacy and knowledge on the part of most citizens. Education contributes both." Thus, because of the social benefits derived from a citizenry which has received some basic level of schooling, the responsibility of paying for this education is considered to be a social burden rather than an individual one. But Friedman would separate the financing, which would be public, from the management and operation of schools, which would be private.

Government could require a minimum level of education which they could finance by giving parents vouchers redeemable for a specified maximum sum per child per year if spent on "approved" educational services. Parents would be free to spend their sum and any additional sum on purchasing educational service from an "approved" institution of their own choice. The educational services could be rendered by private enterprises operated for profit, or by nonprofit institutions of various kinds.

The result would be that:

. . . Parents could express their views about schools directly, by withdrawing their children from one school and sending them to another to a much greater extent than is now possible.

Indeed, the scheme is based upon the plausible premise that:

Here as in other fields, competitive private enterprise is likely to be far more efficient in meeting consumer demands than either nationalized (publicly run) enterprises or enterprises run to serve other purposes.

It is interesting to note that almost two centuries before Friedman, Adam Smith asserted that while the public should pay some of the costs of teaching children of the working class the 3 R's, the teachers would soon neglect their responsibilities if they were fully paid out of public funds.

In summary then, the government would provide families with a voucher for each school-age child, which would guarantee a maximum specified sum of money which could be paid as tuition to any "approved" school. Nonpublic schools would compete among themselves—and perhaps with the public schools—for students by offering a variety of educational choices. Freedom of entry by schools into the market—provided that they met minimum qualifications— would insure efficiency in the production of schooling, and students and their families would be given a market of educational alternatives in place of the present rigid assignment practices. Moreover, such competition would induce innovation and experimentation in that each school would try

to obtain competitive advantages over the others. Thus, the operation of the market would provide far more choices and a greater degree of efficiency in the schooling of all students, especially those pupils who are presently confined to slum schools.

. . .

What, then, are the probable effects of the market approach on the production of both private and social benefits?

In terms of private benefits, it is likely to be true that any measure of competition among schools would lead to increases in their effectiveness. The motive for success- —profit maximization—would require that a school meet the need of its students better than its competitors for any given cost. The fact that existing policies would have to be reexamined in the light of their educational contributions would probably engender thorough changes in the administration of the schools. By increasing the number of decision-making units, the probability of schools innovating to gain competitive advantages would be far greater than under the present system. While many examples of such change can be envisioned, a notable one would be the introduction of those new curricula and instructional aids which showed great promise relative to their costs. Most of the existing public institutions have been loath to adopt any but the most modest changes in their educational strategies.

Another fruit of competition among schools might be more imaginative recruitment policies for teachers. At present, teachers are hired on the basis of a single-salary schedule, one which fixes the teachers' salary on the basis of how much schooling he has had and the amount of his teaching experience. Such factors as the quality of his schooling, his actual teaching ability, his expected performance as reflected in his preservice teaching and personality traits or his field of specialization have no effect on his salary. Under this system, the more imaginative persons—who are often able to reap greater returns outside of teaching—either do not enter the schools or leave after short periods of time. On the other hand, those who have few alternatives in the labor market remain in the schools, protected from dismissal by life-long tenure contracts after only three years of experience. Thus, while there are some expectations, the single-salary schedule fosters mediocrity in teacher selection and retention.

Furthermore, it leads to shortages of teachers with training in some specialties and surpluses of teachers with other training. That is, while mathematics and science majors receive higher starting pay in the market-at-large, they receive the same salaries as do other specialists in the schools. It comes as no surprise, then, to find that schools show a shortage of teachers properly trained in science and mathematics and a surplus of social studies and male physical education teachers. As a result, of course, the social studies and physical education teachers are then often assigned to teach secondary courses in mathematics, physics, chemistry, and other shortage areas. Competitive schools would have to hire on the basis of the realities of the market place rather than on the basis of rigid salary schedules.

Moreover, competitive schools would be more likely to adopt a policy of flexible class size depending upon subject matter, grade level, and type of student, which is a more sensible goal than maintaining uniform class sizes. There would also be more willingness to differentiate staffing by substituting teacher aides, curriculum specialists, and other specialized personnel for classroom teachers wherever accompanied by increases in efficiency *ceteris paribus*.

Most important of all, individual differences among teachers might be utilized as an asset in the educational process by enabling teachers to pursue their own teaching styles and approaches in place of the present attempts of the schools to standardize curricula, syllabi, and pedagogy along narrow guidelines.

. . .

THE EDUCATIONAL MARKET PLACE AND SOCIAL BENEFITS

Our schools shoulder the primary burden for satisfying at least two social goals: Those of imparting minimum levels of literacy, knowledge and the common values necessary for a stable democracy; and of decreasing disparities in incomes and opportunities associated with race and social class.

Friedman considers only the first of these social objectives. Under his plan, schools would be required to meet minimum standards—such as a common content in their programs—much as restaurants are required to ". . . maintain minimum sanitary standards." But Friedman's analogy is a bad one, for requiring a common content in school programs is more like requiring uniform nutritional offerings in restaurants, not just cleanliness. Who would decide what minimum content was, and how would it be assessed? Would the traditional sequence of courses be considered minimal? Would teachers be required to satisfy certain criteria, or could anyone be hired to teach? All of these issues would have to be reconciled, and it is likely that the common content requirements to which Friedman alludes would lead to far more extensive regulation than he suggests. And obviously the greater the requirements which are imposed, the more alike schools would be; and in the extreme, the very animal which we wish to replace might merely be disguised in the new trappings of a highly regulated private industry.

Beyond the social responsibilities of assuring minimal literacy and basic skills, there is also the responsibility of exposing children to fellow students who are drawn from a variety of social, economic, and racial groups. It has also been asserted that slum children become more highly motivated and are likely to develop greater aspirations when they are exposed to children from the middle-class. Our present system of segregating school populations according to the neighborhoods in which they are located does little to achieve the goal of mixed-class schools. Friedman's approach, however, makes no provision for ensuring that students attend schools in racially and socially diverse environments. Indeed, it is likely that social segregation—one of the by-products of the neighborhood school—would increase under the market proposal. For, experience with private schools suggests even greater segregation of student bodies on the basis of religious, ethnic, racial, economic, and other social criteria.

The significance of the probability of increased socioeconomic segregation under a free market system is that such a result would work directly against the second social responsibility of the schools—the equalization of opportunity for all racial and social groups. Friedman asserts that: "The widening of the range of choice under a private system would operate to reduce . . . stratification"; and Jencks agrees with him, but neither gives any evidence to support this contention.

It is interesting to note that at least two Southern states, Virginia and Louisiana, adopted tuition plans to circumvent the court edict requiring them to integrate their public schools. In particular, then, how have the poor fared in the market place?

THE POOR AND THE MARKET PLACE

If the public sector has failed the poor in the efficient production and allocation of social services, the private market can hardly claim a greater degree of success in satisfying their needs. For example, a recent study of the Federal Trade Commission showed that goods purchased for $1.00 at wholesale sold for an average of $2.65 in stores located in poor neighborhoods, but only $1.65 in stores located in the "general market." Geographic mobility, education, income, access to capital (credit)—the very things which the poor lack and the middle class possess—are the characteristics that enable one to operate most successfully in the private market. The failure of the market to give rich and poor equal access to privately produced goods and services should, in itself, make us skeptical about applying it to education.

First, while the private market would likely provide many educational alternatives to middle-class children, there would probably be far fewer sellers of educational services to the children of the poor. It is important to note that schooling must be consumed at the point of purchase; therefore geographical location of schools becomes a salient feature of the market place. But if the previous experience of the slums can be used for prediction, few if any sellers of high quality educational services at competitive rates will locate in the ghetto. Not only is there no Saks Fifth Avenue in Harlem; there is no Macy's, Gimbels, Korvettes, or Kleins.

In part the disparities between the slum markets and markets in other areas are the result of differential costs. Those firms or agencies which did elect to build schools in the "inner cities" would face higher land prices, construction costs, and even teacher costs than those in less congested areas. Thus students attending schools in the slums would receive less education per dollar than those attending schools in other areas.

In addition, the fact that many families could increase their expenditures on schooling beyond the maximum provided by the state would also tend to bid schooling resources away from the ghettos, particularly in the short run. Not only do the poor lack the incomes to add private expenditures to the proposed public vouchers, but on the average they also have more children to educate. Consequently, public funds will be all they will have to spend on the schooling of their children. Given this situation, the schools which now serve the poor could not hope to obtain the better teachers since such personnel would probably prefer to teach for more money in a middle-class school rather than for less money in a ghetto school.

Even if the slum children were accepted at private schools located outside the ghetto—a highly dubious eventuality given the history of private schools—the poor would have to bear the costs of transportation to such institutions. While the monetary costs of transportation represent only part of such a burden, even $5 a week represents $180 over a school year. Thus, the ghetto resident is likely to face a higher cost of educational services whether he sends his child to a school in or out of the inner city.

Jencks asserts that private schools would spring up to serve Negro children if only money equal to what was spent in the public schools were provided for tuition. Unfortunately, experience with this very approach has suggested that such optimism is probably unwarranted. In order to defy the desegregation order provided by the 1954 Brown decision, Prince Edward County, Virginia, abolished its public schools in 1959 and provided tuition grants to students so that they could attend privately operated schools. While a system of private schools did emerge to serve the needs of white students, no private alternatives became available to black pupils. As a result, those Negro children who could not be sent to relatives or friends in other districts received no regular education at all.

. . .

Friedman tacitly assumed that the initial distribution of income among households is appropriate, and he proposes that individual households should consume educational services according to their own demand functions, rather than by requiring all households to accept the formal schooling allocated by the political process. Friedman considers that a "major merit" of the voucher system is that parents with higher incomes and greater desires for education could add their own monies to the standard tuition grant provided by the government. That is, the middle and upper classes—having higher incomes and fewer children—could purchase much better educations for their offspring than could the poor.

This argument ignores completely the crucial role which has been given education in increasing the future opportunities and incomes of youth. True equality of opportunity implies that—on the average—an individual of any race or social class has the same opportunity to achieve a given income or occupation as a member of any other race or class. Of course, it is sham to assert that any such situation exists today; but under the market approach to education, the disparity in income distribution among rich and poor and among Negroes and whites would probably increase.

Educational expenditures represent investment in "human capital," investment that raises the potentialities and increases the future incomes of those receiving the schooling. By increasing the difference in educational investment between rich and poor, middle- and upper-class children would experience even greater advantages over lower-class children than their parents enjoy at the present time. That is, rather than schooling being utilized as a device for equalizing opportunity, the market would enable it to widen the present disparity between the opportunities afforded the privileged and the disadvantaged.

. . .

Thus the free market remedy as Friedman has proposed it would probably have greater private benefits than does the present system. Even the poor might experience some improvement in their schooling from a market which gave them alternatives to their present schools. Yet offsetting these private gains are the social costs imposed by a system which would tend to change the relative distribution of schooling alternatives in such a way that the present disparities in income and opportunities among social and racial groups would increase. Moreover, the free market approach would probably lead to greater racial and social segregation of pupils among schools than presently exists. These are tremendous costs to inflict upon a society which is preaching equality on the one hand and on the other hand is reeling from urban riots that are largely attributable to the frustrations of unequal opportunity.

A SIMPLE MODIFICATION

The Friedman approach might nevertheless be modified to avoid some of its deleterious consequences while taking advantage of the benefits of a competitive system. Since we are particularly concerned with the educational deficiencies of the inner-city schools and their disadvantaged clients, we might inquire into how the market approach might be adapted to the specific needs of ghetto children. The simplest way to implement the market approach without putting the poor at a disadvantage would be to grant tuition payments which are inversely related to family income and wealth. Disadvantaged children might be given vouchers which are worth two or three times the value of the maximum grants given children of the well-to-do. Such a redistributive system of grants would overcome many of the initial market handicaps faced by slum families. Thus, differences in tuition would be based upon relative educational needs, costs, and the family resources for fulfilling those needs.

However, since it is unlikely that this differential voucher plan would ever be adopted by the electorate, we ought to consider other market proposals. One of the most meritorious of these is the plan recommended by Theodore Sizer, dean of Harvard's Graduate School of Education. Sizer would have the state provide tuition payments—and thus schooling alternatives —only for children of the poor. These family allowances ". . . would allow that one section of our population that suffers most seriously from segregated schooling—the poor—to move, at their own initiative, and if they want to, into schools of their choice outside their neighborhoods." This specific application of the Friedman proposal appears to be politically feasible and it is likely to spawn both the private and social benefits that we discussed above.

The voucher plan is not the only way of instituting some measure of competition among schools. James S. Coleman has suggested that school districts might contract with private firms for specific educational services such as arithmetic and reading instruction, and the firms would be reimbursed on the basis of their performances in imparting skills to students as measured by standardized tests. These reading and arithmetic programs would be located throughout the city, and they would represent alternatives to those which are presently offered within each school. "Each parent would have the choice of sending his child to any of the reading or arithmetic programs outside the school, on released time, or leaving him wholly within the school to learn his reading and arithmetic there. The school would find it necessary to compete with the system's external contractors to provide better education, and the parent could . . . have the . . . privileges of consumer's choice."

While this proposal deserves serious consideration, it would have to overcome two obstacles. First, full consumer choice among schooling programs might lead to similar or even greater social, racial and economic segregation among schools than presently exists.

. . .

Moreover, to the degree that there are educational goals which should be implemented into instructional programs but do not necessarily coincide with changes in test performances *per se*, we might find contractors pursuing goals which are so narrow that they are deleterious to the imparting of broader learning skills. After all, a contractor who is rewarded on the basis of test results has a strong incentive to prepare the student *only* for the limited dimension of the performance to be tested.

. . .

A SUMMARY

The replacement of the existing system of publicly operated schools by a market of private ones—supported by government vouchers—would probably yield mixed results. On the one hand, parents would have greater choices among schools and schools would have to be productive in order to survive in the competitive framework. The increase in consumer choice and the resultant competition among schools would be likely to lead to greater educational benefits for many students and their families (private benefits) than those which they receive under the present monopolistic system.

On the other hand, the schools are also expected to fulfill certain social functions. It is in these that a market approach to schooling is likely to yield poor results. For example, basic schooling represents the primary device for equalizing opportunities among racial and social groups. Yet, advantaged children would probably receive far better schooling under the market proposal than would disadvantaged ones, and it is likely that this disparity would lead to larger future inequalities in opportunity between the children of the middle class and those of the poor. Further, it is not clear that a set of largely autonomous schools could provide the common set of values and knowledge necessary for the functioning of a democratic society. Finally, it is likely that the market proposal would increase racial and social stratification of students among schools. Whatever the success of the market in meeting consumer preferences, it would be offset by the market's failure to satisfy the social goals of basic schooling.

Fortunately, we are not limited to choosing between the traditional educational bureaucracy on the one hand or an unmitigated free market for educational services on the other. There are several ways to create competition within a public school system. . . . The time is ripe to experiment with at least one of these plans for the children of the ghetto.

38

THE CASE FOR AN INCOME GUARANTEE

One possibly solution to hard core poverty cases is to provide a minimum level for all families by appropriate adjustments of the income tax. Arguing that present welfare programs provide incentives for poor people to remain poor, Professor Tobin proposes a "negative income tax" as a means of combatting poverty while retaining incentive.

James Tobin

James Tobin is Sterling Professor of Economics at Yale University and a former member of the Council of Economic Advisers.

From *The Public Interest* (Summer 1966), pp. 31–41. Reprinted by permission of National Affairs, Inc.

I

In the national campaign to conquer poverty there are two basic strategies, which may be labeled concisely, if somewhat inaccurately, "structural" and "distributive." The structural strategy is to build up the capacities of the poorest fifth of the population to earn decent incomes. The distributive strategy is to assure every family a decent standard of living regardless of its earning capacity. In my opinion both strategies are essential; correctly designed, they are more complementary than competitive. To date the main emphasis of the Federal "war on poverty" has been the structural approach. I shall argue that the war will not be won without a new and imaginative distributive strategy as well.

General economic progress raises the earning capacities of the populations at large—even of the less educated, less skilled, less experienced, less motivated, and less healthy. Even without Federal programs (other than overall fiscal and monetary policies to keep the labor force fully employed and the economy growing), the incidence of poverty gradually declines. Measuring poverty by the government's official income standard ($3130 a year for 4-person nonfarm families, and amounts estimated to yield comparable standards of living for households of other sizes and circumstances), its incidence has fallen from 22 percent to 17 percent since 1959.

The "war on poverty" testifies that the decline has not been fast enough for the American conscience. But accelerating it by structural measures is bound to be a slow and expensive process. Adults must be trained or retrained; they must acquire work experience, good work habits, self-confidence, and motivation; they must be made medically fit for regular employment; they must be placed in jobs and often moved to new locations. What is required is almost a case-by-case approach. Leaving the aged aside, there are about 8 million poor households including 9½ million persons of ages 22–54 and 3 million in ages 16–21. The task of upgrading the earning capacities of the present generation of adults is staggering, a fact which in no way diminishes the importance of the effort or the value of each individual success.

The earning capacities of the next generation may be successfully raised by general structural measures—radical improvements in the education, health, and residential environment of the 14 million children of the poor. Again, the urgent importance of these efforts is in no way dimmed by recognizing the great difficulties they confront.

But the structural strategy will take many years, probably more than a generation. Even then its success will be incomplete; there will remain a hard core of families with inadequate earning capacity because of ineradicable physical, psychological, or circumstantial disabilities. And in the interim many more families, with disabilities remediable but not remedied, will fail to earn a decent living.

Today's Symptoms, Tomorrow's Causes

A distributive strategy is necessary, too, and the sooner the better. Families must have a minimally decent standard of living, whether or not they now have the ability to earn it in the job market. This can be provided by public assistance, and to withhold it from poor families is neither just (since their disabilities are, if not irremediable, the consequences of past discriminations and deficiencies in public services) nor necessary (since the upper four-fifths of the nation can surely afford the 2 percent of Gross National Product which would bring the lowest fifth across the poverty line).

Sometimes income assistance is scorned as treating the symptoms of poverty, in contrast to the structural strategy, which treats the causes. This reproach is not justified. For one thing, there is nothing intrinsically wrong with treating symptoms, and sometimes it is the best the doctors can do. More seriously, the symptoms of today's poverty may be the causes of tomorrow's. The conditions of life in which many children now grow up may predestine them to low earning capacity as adults.

However, many of those who distrust the distributive strategy have a more sophisticated point in mind. They are afraid that more generous income assistance to the poor will actually retard improvements in their earning capacities. If a decent standard of living is guaranteed, why should anyone work to get it or to acquire the ability to earn it on his own? For centuries this cynicism about human nature has been the excuse by which the affluent have relieved their individual and collective consciences and pocketbooks of the burden of their less fortunate brethren.

We cannot dismiss the question just because it has a shabby history. "Human nature" is not a reason to withhold public subsidies from people with low-earning capacity. But it definitely is a reason to give the subsidies in a way that does not destroy but indeed reinforces the incentives of the recipients to work and to increase the economic value of their work. The war on poverty needs a distributive strategy, but one that is carefully designed to support and strengthen its structural strategy.

Unfortunately our present congeries of public assistance programs—Federal, state, and local—has just the opposite effect. The incentives built in to our present subsidy programs are perverse. Unless public assistance is reformed and rationalized, it will seriously handicap the structural weapons deployed in the campaign against poverty. An improved public assistance program will not be cheap. If it is designed to aid rather than retard the conquest of poverty, its cost will for some years be more than our present programs. But it offers the hope that the conditions giving rise to the need for public subsidies will gradually be remedied.

II

What are the defects of public assistance today? First is its inadequacy. Our governments administer a bewildering variety of welfare and social insurance programs, from Federal Old Age, Survivors, and Disability Insurance (OASDI) to township relief. *Yet half of the poor benefit from none of these; and most of the public money spent to supplement personal incomes goes to families above the poverty line.*

. . .

INCENTIVES IN REVERSE

Second, public assistance is geared to need in a manner that provides perverse incentives to those dependent upon it. One major destructive incentive is the one which AFDC gives for the break-up or nonformation of families. *Too often a father can provide for his children only by leaving both them and their mother.* It is hard to imagine a social contrivance more surely designed to perpetuate dependence on "welfare" in one generation after the other. We know that the major problems of poor people of all colors are related, as both cause and effect, to unstable and chaotic family structures. We know that, for historical reasons, Negro families tend to be matriarchal. We know the crucial importance of home environment in education, and we know the dangers of depriving boys of male adult models. To accentuate all these difficulties by deliberate public policy is a piece of collective insanity which it would be hard to match.

The "means test" provides other disincentives—disincentives to work, to save, to gain skills. The "means test" seems innocent enough in appearance and intent. It says that the welfare payments shall be made only if, and only to the extent that, the family cannot meet its needs (as officially calculated) from its own resources. Thus if, in a given locality, the effective standard of need (which may be only a fraction of an estimated minimal budget) for a mother and four children is $2500 a year, the family will receive $2500 from the state if its members earn nothing on their own, $1500

if they earn $1000, $500 if they earn $2000, and so on. This arrangement, under which your total take-home pay is the same no matter how much you earn, is obviously not designed to encourage work or training for future work. One way to describe it is to say that the marginal tax rate on earnings is (so long as earnings do not exceed $2500 in the example) 100 percent. The accuracy of this description, so far as incentive effects are concerned, is not impaired by the fact that the "tax" on additonal earnings is not a literal payment to the government but a reduction in the government payment to the family.

The means test also discourages thrift. Consider two self-supporting families, one of whom saves while the other incurs debts. When and if misfortunes occur, the welfare authorities will give full help to the second but will generally force the thrifty family to use up its savings. Similarly, a man who has over a lifetime of work acquired his own home may be required to surrender title to it if he can't get by without public assistance in his old age.

It is true that there remains the incentive to escape public assistance entirely, and, since the welfare standard of life is a meager one at best, this incentive may seem substantial. But to many welfare households, especially the broken homes, it is too big a jump to be a realistic aspiration. Unattainable goals may be demoralizing rather than motivating. Most welfare dependents cannot set their sights higher than part-time low-paid employment. Yet this may be extremely important, both to acquire work experience and rudimentary skill and to build up the family's morale and sense of achievement. The system is rigged against it; there is nothing in it for them.

The welfare system of the United States contains plenty of ironies. A nation which regards the integrity of the nuclear family as the very backbone of its social structure provides incentives for its dissolution. A society which views high marginal income tax rates as fatal to the incentives for effort and thrift essential to its economy imposes 100 percent rates on a large fraction of its population. The explanation of such bizarre behavior is probably that present welfare policies represent an uneasy compromise among several principles. Since the thirties our society has acknowledged its responsibility to assure through government a minimal standard of living for all citizens. But the corollary charge on the public purse has been accepted grudgingly, and the fear that the "privilege" of welfare might be abused has dominated policy.

A by-product of this dominant fear is that much of the considerable administrative effort in public welfare reduces to detective work, to make sure there are no "cheaters" on the rolls, and to close surveillance of the clients' sources and uses of funds, to make sure that tax money is not wasted in riotous living. Everything confirms welfare families in the demoralizing belief that they cannot manage their own affairs. This tendency is reenforced by the propensity of legislators to give assistance in kind—surplus foods, subsidized housing, medical care for the indigent or "medically indigent." Eligibility for these specific benefits is usually defined by a maximum income limit, awkward to administer and perverse in incentive effects.

III

An alternative approach, which commands the support of many economists of all political and ideological shades (Milton Friedman, Goldwater's chief economic advisor in 1964, was one of the first to suggest it) is a national system of income supplements graduated to income and to family size. For more fortunate citizens, personal income taxes likewise depend on income and family size; therefore the proposed income supplements can be called, not very felicitously, negative income taxes. They may also be regarded as Federally guaranteed incomes, since they involve, among other things, Federal payment of a specified amount to every family with zero income. . . .

The personal income tax would become a two-way street. At present, calculations of the tax form lead to two alternative outcomes: either the citizen owes something or he owes nothing. Under the proposal there would be a third possibility: the government owes him something. This would not carry the stigma of charity or relief; it would be a right of national citizenship symmetrical to the obligation to pay taxes. It would be uniform across the nation. A poor family would not suffer because of residence in a poor or unresponsive state or county, or because of migration. The government payment would not depend on the supposed causes of need (absence or disability of the husband, etc.) but simply on the fact of need as scaled to family income and size. Finally, the graduation of the "negative tax" to the family's income would, like that of the existing positive tax, give the family an incentive to earn more on its own.

For illustration, consider the following scheme: The Internal Revenue Service pays the "taxpayer" $400 per member of his family if the family has no income. This allowance is reduced by 33⅓ cents for every dollar the family earns; the incentive is that the family improves its situation by two-thirds of every dollar it earns. At an income of $1200 per person the allowance becomes zero. Above that income, the family pays taxes, still at the rate of ⅓ on each additional dollar. At some higher income its tax liability so computed becomes the same as it is now, and beyond that point the present tax schedule applies.

The impact of the proposal is exemplified for a married couple with three children in Table 1. The first two columns show how the present tax schedule treats the family. They assume that the family qualifies only for the standard deduction. The last two columns show how the proposed integrated schedule of allowances and taxes would treat the same family. The middle columns superimpose on the present tax law hypothetical public assistance, designed to see that the family has $2500 and administered by a strict means test. The proposed improvement in the incentive to the family to earn income on its own (to move down in the table) is clear from comparing columns (5) and (7).

Similar tables would apply to families of other sizes. It may not be desirable, however, to apply the basic formula of $400 per capita across the board. Instead, a financial incentive to limit family size could be built

in by diminishing and perhaps eliminating the extra amount allowed for an additional child when the size of the family is already large. This would make sense if, and only if, the government simultaneously were making sure that birth control information and technique are widely disseminated.

In the design of an integrated allowance and tax schedule a compromise must be struck among three objectives: (a) providing a high basic allowance for families with little or no earnings, (b) building in a strong incentive to earn more, and (c) limiting the budgetary cost of the scheme, and in particular minimizing the payment of benefits to those who do not need them. For example, in Table 1 the initial allowance might be raised to $3000. But if the 33⅓ percent "tax rate" were retained for incentive reasons, all the entries in columns (6) and (7) would be increased algebraically by $1000 (the last one only approximately so), and the table would have to be considerably lengthened to cover all the beneficiaries of the proposal. Obviously the

Table 1

ILLUSTRATION OF IMPACT OF PROPOSED INCOME ALLOWANCES:
MARRIED COUPLE WITH THREE CHILDREN

(1) Family Income before Federal Tax or Allowance	(2) Present Tax Schedule Tax (−)	(3) Present Tax Schedule Income after Tax	(4) Present Tax Schedule with Public Assistance Tax (−) or Assistance (+)	(5) Present Tax Schedule with Public Assistance Income after Tax or Assistance	(6) Proposed Schedule Tax (−) or Allowance (+)	(7) Proposed Schedule Income after Tax or Allowance
$ 0	$ 0	$ 0	$+2500	$2500	$+2000	$2000
1000	0	1000	+1500	2500	+1667	2667
2000	0	2000	+ 500	2500	+1333	3333
2500	0	2500	0	2500	+1167	3667
3000	0	3000	0	3000	+1000	4000
3700	0	3700	0	3700	+ 767	4467
4000	− 42	3958	− 42	3958	+ 667	4667
5000	−185	4815	− 185	4815	+ 333	5333
6000	−338	5662	− 338	5662	0	6000
7000	−501	6499	− 501	6499	− 333	6667
7963[1]	−654	7309	− 654	7309	− 654	7309
8000	−658	7342	− 658	7342	− 658	7342

1 Income level at which the present and proposed methods of calculating tax coincide; above this income the present tax schedule applies.

government would be paying sizable benefits to families who do not need them. This implication of a $3000 initial allowance could be escaped by raising the new "tax rate" to 50 percent; the break-even income level, at which there is no tax positive or negative, would remain $6000. But the right to retain half of one's own earnings is a less powerful incentive than retention of two-thirds.

I do not contend that the particular compromise struck in my illustrative proposal is optimal. But in discussing alternatives it is essential to keep in mind that some compromise is necessary, that there are inexorable conflicts among the three listed objectives.

. . .

39

Hard-core poverty is more than an economic problem. Poverty has social, political, and cultural roots as well as economic. Representative Curtis outlines some of the objections to the guaranteed income, or "negative income tax," as a solution to problems of poverty.

INCOME MAINTENANCE GUARANTEES

Thomas B. Curtis

Thomas B. Curtis is a member of the House of Representatives from Missouri.

From U.S. Congress, Joint Economic Committee, *Hearings before the Subcommittee on Fiscal Policy*, 90th Cong., 2nd sess., Vol. 1, Proceedings, pp. 414 ff.

The guaranteed annual income, like a guarantee of happiness, has a direct and simple appeal. The proponents imply that poverty can be wiped out in a single stroke by giving a subsidy to the poor. If poverty is a lack of income, then the solution is obvious; provide the income necessary to raise the poor family or individual above the poverty level. The beguiling simplicity of the idea is its most attractive—and dangerous feature. The writers of the United States Constitution resisted this simplicity and spoke of government providing for the pursuit of happiness, not happiness itself. So I think we must resist the present day simplicity and speak of providing for the opportunity to earn an income, not providing the income itself.

The trouble with this seemingly new theory is that the more we learn about poverty, particularly hard-core poverty, the more we realize that it is not just an economic problem. It is a problem with deep cultural, emotional, and political roots. In truth, hard-core poverty in the United States is as much a state of mind as a lack of money. Merely providing direct money payments to the poor will not solve the poverty problem. In fact, I believe that providing a guaranteed annual income would perpetuate poverty and might even make it worse.

. . .

Let us consider for a moment the major objections to the guaranteed income.

First, to what extent will common agreement be possible in the support and implementation of a guaranteed income? Assuming both the economic and political feasibility of some plan of guaranteed income, would this assure sufficient and broad enough support to avoid disruptive conflict and social disorganization?

The value system of Western Man has for centuries associated work with income. It is a Judeo-Christian ethic with special emphasis incorporated in the Protestant norm in American society.

Specifically, can a right to income without work be adopted without creating deep cleavages and conflicts in our society? Is it possible to have a dual set of values and norms; one predicated on income for work and one on income without work? Isn't it possible that the existing gulf between the middle-class culture and the subculture of poverty will be deepened and problems of national cohesiveness and accommodation be aggravated? In fact, another serious rift may develop within the lower economic class: between the approximately one-third of all American families that earn income above the poverty line but below the national median and those families receiving government subsidies. At a time when many analysts discern a growing alienation of the poor from the mainstream of American society, the divisive tendencies fostered by income guarantees are clearly anathema.

Any special system is composed of many interrelated units and functions. Any drastic change in one part of the social system will affect the total in many unforeseen and unpredictable ways. We have never been able to predict the total impact of change. Increasingly and frequently we have learned that the treatment of a social problem may produce additional problems and, in the final analysis, the treatment may be worse than the disease. The "side effects" may leave the patient worse off than before.

For example, the adoption of a form of income guarantee would have serious and disturbing effects on the future of private philanthropy, perhaps leading even to the virtual elimination of the private sector's role in solving social problems. A "side effect" such as this would be quite serious. In 1966, American private philanthropy totaled $13 billion, 8.6 times more than the expenditures for the OEO war on poverty that year. And as Richard Cornuelle points out in *Reclaiming the American Dream* (New York: Random House, 1963), private organizations excel in pinpointing and reacting to particular problems in specific areas. They have the adaptability and flexibility of response to these problems that government efforts have rarely shown and they are subject to the demanding discipline of the marketplace. If, however, the government guarantees sufficient income to meet basic needs, private charities would have a real task in convincing donors that any need for private efforts still exists and the valuable contributions of private charity could well be lost.

Second, the plan would help to perpetuate welfare as a way of life by sacrificing social services designed to eliminate the causes of need for an income guarantee. Proponents of guaranteed income plans fail to distinguish between those families and individuals who could and would make good use of an interim guaranteed income grant and those who would not. They also fail to distinguish between those in poverty and those who lead decent lives, although having no margin for waste or luxury. They would create a costly program—ranging from $5 to $24 billion a year—that would spread our resources . . . (cost estimates for programs from an article by Dr. Robert Lampman in *Social Action* [Nov. 1967]).

The provision of this "social conscience money" would lull us into a sense of complacency about the poverty problem and divert our attention from the critical need to provide remedial services to the hard-core poor.

In order to solve the problem of comparative poverty, we must be concerned with much more than providing income. For many of the comparative poor, providing income would not mean a better diet for the children, improved medical care, more adequate housing, or a move into self-sufficiency. There is evidence that prolonged chronic relief is a factor in the acceptance of a dependency state.

Any real remedy to this chronic poverty must be concerned with cultural change, with an alteration of attitudes toward life and work. This change is particularly required in the urban slums where apathy, social inadequacy, and an inability to cope with the environment are breeding-grounds for a form of self-perpetuating poverty that could infect the rest of the population with a host of social ills.

. . .

Third, the guaranteed annual income would slow down the rate of economic growth by reducing incentives to work and save. Automatically providing an adequate minimum standard of living to any citizen would be sufficient to eliminate incentives to work for most of those unemployed or those earning less than the minimum standard level. Those who earn only slightly more than the minimum might also decide not to work at all. Admittedly, the adverse incentive effect differs among plans, but in every instance there is at least some negative incentive effect. The result would be a lower gross national product and a lower rate of economic growth than would otherwise exist.

A recent empirical study by Professor Lowell E. Gallaway of the Wharton School of Finance and Commerce on the "Negative Income Tax Rates and the Elimination of Poverty" is helpful in this area. It throws some interesting light on the individual's labor market response to the receipt of transfer payment income. Professor Gallaway thinks the evidence of his study establishes a basis for a skeptical view of the contribution which the negative income tax can make to improving the income position of poverty groups with a relatively high degree of labor force participation. Certainly, further study is needed in this area. The Council of Economic Advisers comments: "There is an abundance of assertion and anecdote regarding the impact of work incentives on low-income Americans but very little real knowledge. 'Assertion' and 'anecdote' are hardly a solid foundation for the adoption of income guarantee proposals." (*Washington Post,* Sunday, June 23, 1968, p. B4.)

Economic growth also would suffer to the extent that a guaranteed annual income weakened incentives to save. With an annual income assured, the future for many individuals would become more certain. Families would be less likely on the whole to save for emergencies, retirement, death, and disability. The pressure on business to make substantial contributions to employee pension funds would also be less urgent, and this source of capital accumulation could decline sharply as well. The likely result would be a higher rate of current consumption, less saving, and a slowdown in the modernization and expansion of plant and equipment. . . .

Finally, discussions of some form of income guarantee have exhibited a marked indisposition to consider the administrative problems of such a program. Finding workable solutions would require an intensive research effort. Even at that, no income guarantee program, contrary to the hopes of some advocates, could be run without a large-scale administrative organization and an increased degree of social control of the individual.

The first problem is that of defining income. Certainly income as defined in the

Tax Code would be unacceptable. It is for this reason that any simple negative income tax is not feasible. Two computations of income would be required. First, a person would reckon income for regular income tax purposes. If this computation yielded a net income figure which was low enough to entitle the program to a tentative refund, he would then have to make another computation which in effect added back into his income items excluded in the regular tax computation. The one-half of capital gains excluded from taxable income is one example of income which would have to be added back before a person could claim a "refund." Tax exempt interest is another example.

The second problem is that of fluctuating income. Would we want to permit people to concentrate income in one year and claim a refund in the next year because their income in that year was low? Not everyone is in a position to reallocate income between years, but some people are able to do so. A person could, for example, realize capital gains in one year and capital losses in the next year, claiming a refund in the second year because net income is so low. Business profits and losses often can be shifted between years. Even for the poor and well-intentioned, underpayments and overpayments would be frequent because of unexpected work layoffs, sicknesses, accidents, etc.

The third problem is that of the weight to be given to wealth in determining entitlement to a payment from the Federal Government. Presently, under public assistance programs, savings as a source of funds for family support is taken into account. But the regular income tax computation takes no account of wealth. However rich a person may be, he might show a negative income in a year and pay no positive tax. The loss might make him eligible for a refund under a negative income tax unless wealth were taken into account in determining eligibility.

The fourth problem arises from the definition of the filing unit. Thus, under the regular income tax a husband and wife may elect to file joint or separate returns. Suppose the husband earns all of the family's income. Should the wife be permitted to file a separate return and claim a negative income tax refund?

. . .

PUBLIC SECTOR

PART FIVE

40

Writing as the Senator from Massachusetts, President Kennedy describes the variety of pressures under which decisions are made by the Congress and discusses the nature of the Congressman's responsibility to his constituents. This perceptive analysis of legislative behavior is a useful supplement to economic analysis in the examination of public policy issues.

COURAGE AND POLITICS

John F. Kennedy

The late President John F. Kennedy was United States Senator from Massachusetts when he wrote Profiles in Courage.

. . .

A nation which has forgotten the quality of courage which in the past has been brought to public life is not as likely to insist upon or reward that quality in its chosen leaders today—and in fact we have forgotten. We may remember how John Quincy Adams became President through the political schemes of Henry Clay, but we have forgotten how, as a young man, he gave up a promising Senatorial career to stand by the nation. We may remember Daniel Webster for his subservience to the National Bank throughout much of his career, but we have forgotten his sacrifice for the national good at the close of that career. We do not remember—and possibly we do not care.

"People don't give a damn," a syndicated columnist told millions of readers not so many years ago, "what the average Senator or Congressman says. The reason they don't care is that they know what you hear in Congress is 99 percent tripe, ignorance, and demagoguery and not to be relied upon. . . ."

Earlier a member of the Cabinet had recorded in his diary:

> While I am reluctant to believe in the total depravity of the Senate, I place but little dependence on the honesty and truthfulness of a large portion of the Senators. A majority of them are small lights, mentally weak, and wholly unfit to be Senators. Some are vulgar demagogues . . . some are men of wealth who have purchased their position . . . [some are] men of narrow intellect, limited comprehension, and low partisan prejudice. . . .

And still earlier a member of the Senate itself told his colleagues that "the confidence of the people is departing from us, owing to our unreasonable delays."

The Senate knows that many Americans today share these sentiments. Senators, we hear, must be politicians—and politicians must be concerned only with winning votes, not with statesmanship or courage. Mothers may still want their favorite sons to grow up to be President, but, according to a famous Gallup poll of some years ago, they do not want them to become politicians in the process.

Does this current rash of criticism and disrespect mean the quality of the Senate has declined? Certainly not. For of the three statements quoted above, the first was made in the twentieth century, the second in the nineteenth, and the third in the eighteenth (when the first Senate, barely underway, was debating where the Capitol should be located).

Does it mean, then, that the Senate can no longer boast of men of courage?

Walter Lippmann, after nearly half a century of careful observation, rendered in his recent book a harsh judgment both on the politician and the electorate:

> With exceptions so rare they are regarded as miracles of nature, successful democratic politicians are insecure and intimidated men. They advance politically only as they placate, appease, bribe, seduce, bamboozle, or otherwise manage to manipulate the demanding threatening elements in their constituencies. The decisive consideration is not whether the proposition is good but whether it is popular—not whether it will work well and prove itself, but whether the active-talking constituents like it immediately.

I am not so sure, after nearly ten years of living and working in the midst of "successful democratic politicans," that they are all "insecure and intimidated men." I am convinced that the complication of public business and the competition for the public's attention have obscured innumerable acts of political courage—large and small—performed almost daily in the Senate Chamber. I am convinced that the decline —if there has been a decline—has been less in the Senate than in the public's appreciation of the art of politics, of the nature and necessity for compromise and balance, and of the nature of the Senate as a legislative chamber. And, finally, I am convinced that we have criticized those who have followed the crowd—and at the same time criticized those who have defied it—because we have not fully understood the responsibility of a Senator to his constituents or recognized the difficulty facing a politician conscientiously desiring, in Webster's words, "to push [his] skiff from the shore alone" into a hostile and turbulent sea. Perhaps if the American people more fully comprehended the terrible pressures which discourage acts of political courage, which drive a Senator to abandon or subdue his conscience, then they might be less critical of those who take the easier road—and more appreciative of those still able to follow the path of courage.

The *first pressure* to be mentioned is a form of pressure rarely recognized by the general public. Americans want to be liked—and Senators are no exception. They are by nature—and of necessity—social animals. We enjoy the comradeship and approval of our friends and colleagues. We prefer praise to abuse, popularity to contempt. Realizing that the path of the conscientious insurgent must frequently be a lonely one, we are anxious to get along with our fellow legislators, our fellow members of the club, to abide by the clubhouse rules and patterns, not to pursue a unique and independent course which would embarrass or irritate the other members. We realize, moreover, that our influence in the club—and the extent to which we can accomplish our objectives and those of our constituents—are dependent in some measure on the esteem with which we are regarded by other Senators. "The way to get along," I was told when I entered Congress, "is to go along."

Going along means more than just good fellowship—it includes the use of compromise, the sense of things possible. We should not be too hasty in condemning all compromise as bad morals. For politics and legislation are not matters for inflexible principles or unattainable ideals. Politics, as John Morley has acutely observed, "is a field where action is one long second best, and where the choice constantly lies between two blunders"; and legislation, under the democratic way of life and the Federal system of Government, requires compromise between the desires of each individual and group and those around them. Henry Clay, who should have known, said compromise was the cement that held the Union together:

> All legislation . . . is founded upon the principle of mutual concession. . . . Let him who elevates himself above humanity, above its weaknesses, its infirmities, its wants, its necessities, say, if he pleases, "I never will compromise"; but let no one who is not above the frailties of our common nature disdain compromise.

It is compromise that prevents each set of reformers—the wets and the drys, the one-worlders and the isolationists, the vivisectionists and the anti-vivisectionists—from crushing the group on the extreme opposite end of the political spectrum. The fanatics and extremists and even those conscientiously devoted to hard and fast principles are always disappointed at the failure of their Government to rush to implement all of their principles and to denounce those of their opponents. But the legislator has some responsibility to conciliate those opposing forces within his state and party and to represent them in the larger clash of interests on the national level; and he alone knows that there are few if any issues where all the truth and all the right and all the angels are on one side.

Some of my colleagues who are criticized today for lack of forthright principles —or who are looked upon with scornful eyes as compromising "politicians"—are simply engaged in the fine art of conciliating, balancing, and interpreting the forces and factions of public opinion, an art essential to keeping our nation united and enabling our Government to function. Their consciences may direct them from time to time to take a more rigid stand for principle—but their intellects tell them that a fair or poor bill is better than no bill at all, and that only through the give-and-take of compromise will any bill receive the successive approval of the Senate, the House, the President, and the nation.

But the question is how we will compromise and with whom. For it is easy to seize upon unnecessary concessions, not as means of legitimately resolving conflicts but as methods of "going along."

There were further implications in the warning that I should "go along"—implications of the rewards that would follow fulfillment of my obligation to follow the party leadership whom I had helped select. All of us in the Congress are made fully aware of the importance of party unity (what sins have been committed in that name!) and the adverse effect upon our party's chances in the next election which any rebellious conduct might bring. Moreover, in these days of civil service, the loaves and fishes of patronage available to the legislator—for distribution to those earnest campaigners whose efforts were inspired by something more than mere conviction—are comparatively few; and he who breaks the party's ranks may find that there are suddenly none at all. Even the success of legislation in which he is interested depends in part on the extent to which his support of his party's programs has won him the assistance of his party's leaders. Finally, the Senator who follows the independent course of conscience is likely to discover that he has earned the disdain not only of his colleagues in the Senate and his associates in his party but also that of the all-important contributors to his campaign fund.

It is thinking of that next campaign—the desire to be reelected—that provides the *second* pressure on the conscientious Senator. It should not automatically be assumed that this is a wholly selfish motive—although it is not unnatural that those who have chosen politics as their profession should seek to continue their careers—for Senators who go down to defeat in a vain defense of a single principle will not be on hand to fight for that or any other principle in the future.

Defeat, moreover, is not only a setback for the Senator himself—he is also obligated to consider the effect upon the party he supports, upon the friends and supporters who have "gone out on a limb" for him or invested their savings in his career, and even upon the wife and children whose happiness and security—often depending at least in part upon his success in office—may mean more to him than anything else.

Where else, in a nontotalitarian country, but in the political profession is the indi-

vidual expected to sacrifice all—including his own career—for the national good? In private life, as in industry, we expect the individual to advance his own enlightened self-interest—within the limitations of the law—in order to achieve overall progress. But in public life we expect individuals to sacrifice their private interests to permit the national good to progress.

In no other occupation but politics is it expected that a man will sacrifice honors, prestige, and his chosen career on a single issue. Lawyers, businessmen, teachers, doctors, all face difficult personal decisions involving their integrity—but few, if any, face them in the glare of the spotlight as do those in public office. Few, if any, face the same dread finality of decision that confronts a Senator facing an important call of the roll. He may want more time for his decision—he may believe there is something to be said for both sides—he may feel that a slight amendment could remove all difficulties—but when that roll is called he cannot hide, he cannot equivocate, he cannot delay—and he senses that his constituency, like the Raven in Poe's poem, is perched there on his Senate desk, croaking "Nevermore" as he casts the vote that stakes his political future.

Few Senators "retire to Pocatello" by choice. The virus of Potomac Fever, which rages everywhere in Washington, breeds nowhere in more virulent form than on the Senate floor. The prospect of forced retirement from "the most exclusive club in the world," the possibilities of giving up the interesting work, the fascinating trappings and the impressive prerogatives of Congressional office, can cause even the most courageous politician serious loss of sleep. Thus, perhaps without realizing it, some Senators tend to take the easier, less troublesome path to harmonize or rationalize what at first appears to be a conflict between their conscience—or the result of their deliberations—and the majority opinion of their constituents. Such Senators are not political cowards—they have simply developed the habit of sincerely reaching conclusions inevitably in accordance with popular opinion.

Still other Senators have not developed that habit—they have neither conditioned nor subdued their consciences—but they feel, sincerely and without cynicism, that they must leave considerations of conscience aside if they are to be effective. The profession of politics, they would agree with political writer Frank Kent, is not immoral, simply nonmoral:

> Probably the most important single accomplishment for the politically ambitious is the fine art of seeming to say something without doing so. . . . The important thing is not to be on the right side of the current issue but on the popular side . . . regardless of your own convictions or of the facts. This business of getting the votes is a severely practical one into which matters of morality, of right and wrong, should not be allowed to intrude.

And Kent quotes the advice allegedly given during the 1920 campaign by former Senator Ashurst of Arizona to his colleague Mark Smith:

> Mark, the great trouble with you is that you refuse to be a demagogue. You will not submerge your principles in order to get yourself elected. *You must learn that there are times when a man in public life is compelled to rise above his principles.*

Not all Senators would agree—but few would deny that the desire to be reelected exercises a strong brake on independent courage.

The *third* and most significant source of pressures which discourage political courage in the conscientious Senator or Congressman—and practically all of the problems described in this chapter apply equally to members of both Houses—is the pressure of his constituency, the interest groups, the organized letter writers, the economic blocs, and even the average voter. To cope with such pressures, to defy them or even to satisfy them, is a formidable task. All of us occasionally have the urge to follow the example of Congressman John Steven McGroarty of California, who wrote a constituent in 1934:

> One of the countless drawbacks of being in Congress is that I am compelled to receive impertinent letters from a jackass like you in which you say I promised to have the Sierra Madre mountains reforested and I have been in Congress two months and haven't done it. Will you please take two running jumps and go to hell.

Fortunately or unfortunately, few follow that urge—but the provocation is there—not only from unreasonable letters and impossible requests, but also from hopelessly inconsistent demands and endlessly unsatisfied grievances.

In my office today, for example, was a delegation representing New England textile mills, an industry essential to our prosperity. They want the tariff lowered on the imported wool they buy from Australia, and they want the tariff raised on the finished woolen goods imported from England with which they must compete. One of my Southern colleagues told me that a similar group visited him not long ago with the same requests—but further urging that he take steps to (1) end the low-wage competition from Japan, and (2) prevent the Congress from ending—through a higher minimum wage—the low-wage advantage they themselves enjoy to the dismay of my constituents. Only yesterday two groups called me off the Senate floor—the first was a group of businessmen seeking to have a local Government activity closed as unfair competition for private enterprise; and the other was a group representing the men who work in the Government installation and who are worried about their jobs.

All of us in the Senate meet endless examples of such conflicting pressures, which only reflect the inconsistencies inevitable in our complex economy. If we tell our constituents frankly that we can do nothing, they feel we are unsympathetic or inadequate. If we try and fail—usually meeting a counteraction from other Senators representing other interests—they say we are like all the rest of the politicians. All we can do is retreat into the Cloakroom and weep on the shoulder of a sympathetic colleague—or go home and snarl at our wives.

We may tell ourselves that these pressure groups and letter writers represent only a small percentage of the voters—and this is true. But they are the articulate few whose views cannot be ignored and who constitute the greater part of our contacts with the public at large, whose opinions we cannot know, whose vote we must obtain, and yet who in all probability have a limited idea of what we are trying to do. (One Senator, since retired, said that he voted with the special interests on every issue, hoping that by election time all of them added together would constitute nearly a majority that would remember him favorably, while the other members of the public would never know about—much less remember—his vote against their welfare. It is reassuring to know that this seemingly unbeatable formula did not work in his case.)

These, then, are some of the pressures which confront a man of conscience. He cannot ignore the pressure groups, his constituents, his party, the comradeship of his colleagues, the needs of his family, his own pride in office, the necessity for compromise, and the importance of remaining in office. He must judge for himself which path to choose, which step will most help or hinder the ideals to which he is committed. He realizes that once he begins to weigh each issue in terms of his chances for re-election, once he begins to compromise away his principles on one issue after another for fear that to do otherwise would halt his career and prevent future fights for principle, then he has lost the very freedom of conscience which justifies his continuance in office. But to decide at which point and on which issue he will risk his career is a difficult and soul-searching decision.

But this is no real problem, some will say. Always do what is right, regardless of whether it is popular. Ignore the pressures, the temptations, the false compromises.

That is an easy answer—but it is easy only for those who do not bear the responsibilities of elected office. For more is involved than pressure, politics, and personal ambitions. Are we rightfully entitled to ignore the demands of our constituents even if we are able and willing to do so? We have noted the pressures that make political courage a difficult course—let us turn now to those Constitutional and more theoretical obligations which cast doubt upon the propriety of such a course—obligations to our state and section, to our party, and above all, to our constituents.

The primary responsibility of a Senator, most people assume, is to represent the views of his state. Ours is a Federal system—a Union of relatively sovereign states whose needs differ greatly—and my Constitutional obligations as Senator would thus appear to require me to represent the interests of my state. Who will speak for Massachusetts if her own Senators do not? Her rights and even her identity become submerged. Her equal representation in Congress is lost. Her aspirations, however much they may from time to time be in the minority, are denied that equal opportunity to be heard to which all minority views are entitled.

Any Senator need not look very long to realize that his colleagues are representing *their* local interests. And if such interests are ever to be abandoned in favor of the national good, let the constituents—not the Senator—decide when and to what extent. For he is their agent in Washington, the protector of their rights, recognized by the Vice-President in the Senate Chamber as "the Senator from Massachusetts" or "the Senator from Texas."

But when all of this is said and admitted, we have not yet told the full story. For in Washington we are "United States Senators" and members of the Senate of the United States as well as Senators from Massachusetts and Texas. Our oath of office is administered by the Vice-President, not by the Governors of our respective states; and we come to Washington, to paraphrase Edmund Burke, not as hostile ambassadors or special pleaders for our state or section, in opposition to advocates and agents of other areas, but as members of the deliberative assembly of one nation with one interest. Of course, we should not ignore the needs of our area—nor could we easily as products of that area—but none could be found to look out for the national interest if local interests wholly dominated the role of each of us.

There are other obligations in addition to those of state and region—the obligations of the party whose pressures have already been described. Even if I can disregard those pressures, do I not have an obligation to go along with the party that placed me in office? We believe in this country in the principle of party responsibility, and we recognize the necessity of adhering to party platforms—if the party label is to mean anything to the voters.

Only in this way can our basically two-party nation avoid the pitfalls of multiple splinter parties—whose purity and rigidity of principle, I might add—if I may suggest a sort of Gresham's Law of politics—increase inversely with the size of their membership.

And yet we cannot permit the pressures of party responsibility to submerge on every issue the call of personal responsibility. For the party which, in its drive for unity, discipline, and success, ever decides to exclude new ideas, independent conduct, or insurgent members, is in danger. In the words of Senator Albert Beveridge:

> A party can live only by growing, intolerance of ideas brings its death. . . . An organization that depends upon reproduction only for its vote, son taking the place of father, is not a political party, but a Chinese tong; not citizens brought together by thought and conscience, but an Indian tribe held together by blood and prejudice.

The two-party system remains not because both are rigid but because both are flexible. The Republican party when I entered Congress was big enough to hold, for example, both Robert Taft and Wayne Morse—and the Democratic side of the Senate in which I now serve can happily embrace, for example, both Harry Byrd and Wayne Morse.

Of course, both major parties today seek to serve the national interest. They would do so in order to obtain the broadest base of support, if for no nobler reason. But when party and officeholder differ as to how the national interest is to be served, we must place first the responsibility we owe not to our party or even to our constituents but to our individual consciences.

But it is a little easier to dismiss one's obligations to local interests and party ties than to face squarely the problem of one's responsibility to the will of his constituents. A Senator who avoids this responsibility would appear to be accountable to no one, and the basic safeguards of our democratic system would thus have vanished. He is no longer representative in the true sense, he has violated his public trust, he has betrayed the confidence demonstrated by those who voted for him to carry out their views. "Is the creature," as John Tyler asked the House of Representatives in his maiden speech, "to set himself in opposition to his Creator? Is the servant to disobey the wishes of his master?"

> How can he be regarded as representing the people when he speaks, not their language, but his own? He ceases to be their representative when he does so, and represents himself alone.

In short, according to this school of thought, if I am to be properly responsive to the will of my constituents, it is my duty to place their principles, not mine, above all else. This may not always be easy, but it nevertheless is the essence of democracy, faith in the wisdom of the people and their views. To be sure, the people will make mistakes—they will get no better government than they deserve—but that is far better than the representative of the people arrogating for himself the right to say he knows better than they what is good for them. Is he not chosen, the argument closes, to vote as they would vote were they in his place?

It is difficult to accept such a narrow view of the role of United States Senator— a view that assumes the people of Massachusetts sent me to Washington to serve merely as a seismograph to record shifts in popular opinion. I reject this view not because I lack faith in the "wisdom of the people," but because this concept of democracy actually puts too little faith in the people. Those who would deny the obliga-

tion of the representative to be bound by every impulse of the electorate—regardless of the conclusions his own deliberations direct—do trust in the wisdom of the people. They have faith in their ultimate sense of justice, faith in their ability to honor courage and respect judgment, and faith that in the long run they will act unselfishly for the good of the nation. It is that kind of faith on which democracy is based, not simply the often frustrated hope that public opinion will at all times under all circumstances promptly identify itself with the public interest.

The voters selected us, in short, because they had confidence in our judgment and our ability to exercise that judgment from a position where we could determine what were their own best interests, as a part of the nation's interests. This may mean that we must on occasion lead, inform, correct, and sometimes even ignore constituent opinion, if we are to exercise fully that judgment for which we were elected. But acting without selfish motive or private bias, those who follow the dictates of an intelligent conscience are not aristocrats, demagogues, eccentrics, or callous politicians insensitive to the feelings of the public. They expect—and not without considerable trepidation—their constituents to be the final judges of the wisdom of their course; but they have faith that those constituents—today, tomorrow, or even in another generation—will at least respect the principles that motivated their independent stand.

If their careers are temporarily or even permanently buried under an avalanche of abusive editorials, poison-pen letters, and opposition votes at the polls—as they sometimes are, for that is the risk they take— they await the future with hope and confidence, aware of the fact that the voting public frequently suffers from what ex-Congressman T. V. Smith called the lag "between our way of thought and our way of life." Smith compared it to the subject of the anonymous poem:

There was a dachshund, once so long
He hadn't any notion
How long it took to notify
His tail of his emotion;
And so it happened, while his eyes
Were filled with woe and sadness,
His little tail went wagging on
Because of previous gladness.

Moreover, I question whether any Senator, before we vote on a measure, can state with certainty exactly how the majority of his constituents feel on the issue as it is presented to the Senate. All of us in the Senate live in an iron lung—the iron lung of politics, and it is no easy task to emerge from that rarefied atmosphere in order to breathe the same fresh air our constituents breathe. It is difficult, too, to see in person an appreciable number of voters besides those professional hangers-on and vocal elements who gather about the politician on a trip home. In Washington I frequently find myself believing that forty or fifty letters, six visits from professional politicians and lobbyists, and three editorials in Massachusetts newspapers constitute public opinion on a given issue. Yet in truth I rarely know how the great majority of the voters feel, or even how much they know of the issues that seem so burning in Washington.

Today the challenge of political courage looms larger than ever before. For our everyday life is becoming so saturated with the tremendous power of mass communications that any unpopular or unorthodox course arouses a storm of protests such as John Quincy Adams—under attack in 1807 —could never have envisioned. Our political life is becoming so expensive, so mechanized, and so dominated by professional politicians and public relations men that the idealist who dreams of independent

statesmanship is rudely awakened by the necessities of election and accomplishment. And our public life is becoming so increasingly centered upon that seemingly unending war to which we have given the curious epithet "cold" that we tend to encourage rigid ideological unity and orthodox patterns of thought.

And thus, in the days ahead, only the very courageous will be able to take the hard and unpopular decisions necessary for our survival in the struggle with a powerful enemy—an enemy with leaders who need give little thought to the popularity of their course, who need pay little tribute to the public opinion they themselves manipulate, and who may force, without fear of retaliation at the polls, their citizens to sacrifice present laughter for future glory. And only the very courageous will be able to keep alive the spirit of individualism and dissent which gave birth to this nation, nourished it as an infant, and carried it through its severest tests upon the attainment of its maturity.

Of course, it would be much easier if we could all continue to think in traditional political patterns—of liberalism and conservatism, as Republicans and Democrats, from the viewpoint of North and South, management and labor, business and consumer, or some equally narrow framework. It would be more comfortable to continue to move and vote in platoons, joining whomever of our colleagues are equally enslaved by some current fashion, raging prejudice or popular movement. But today this nation cannot tolerate the luxury of such lazy political habits. Only the strength and progress and peaceful change that come from independent judgment and individual ideas—and even from the unorthodox and the eccentric—can enable us to surpass that foreign ideology that fears free thought more than it fears hydrogen bombs.

We shall need compromises in the days ahead, to be sure. But these will be, or should be, compromises of issues, not of principles. We can compromise our political positions, but not ourselves. We can resolve the clash of interests without conceding our ideals. And even the necessity for the right kind of compromise does not eliminate the need for those idealists and reformers who keep our compromises moving ahead, who prevent all political situations from meeting the description supplied by Shaw: "smirched with compromise, rotted with opportunism, mildewed by expedience, stretched out of shape with wire-pulling, and putrefied with permeation." Compromise need not mean cowardice. Indeed it is frequently the compromisers and conciliators who are faced with the severest tests of political courage as they oppose the extremist views of their constituents. It was because Daniel Webster conscientiously favored compromise in 1850 that he earned a condemnation unsurpassed in the annals of political history.

His is a story worth remembering today. So, I believe, are the stories of other Senators of courage—men whose abiding loyalty to their nation triumphed over all personal and political considerations, men who showed the real meaning of courage and a real faith in democracy, men who made the Senate of the United States something more than a mere collection of robots dutifully recording the views of their constituents, or a gathering of time-servers skilled only in predicting and following the tides of public sentiment.

. . .

41

THE THEORY OF SOCIAL BALANCE

John Kenneth Galbraith

Professor Galbraith argues that we allocate too many of our productive resources to unimportant private purposes and to creating artificial wants, and too few to such social purposes as slum clearance, education, and cultural activities. The result is a social imbalance which he argues should be remedied.

John Kenneth Galbraith is Professor of Economics at Harvard University.

This selection from John Kenneth Galbraith's The Affluent Society, 1969, pp. 251–69, is reprinted by permission of an arrangement with Houghton Mifflin Company, the authorized publishers.

It is not till it is discovered that high individual incomes will not purchase the mass of mankind immunity from cholera, typhus, and ignorance, still less secure them the positive advantages of educational opportunity and economic security, that slowly and reluctantly, amid prophesies of moral degeneration and economic disaster, society begins to make collective provision for needs which no ordinary individual, even if he works overtime all his life, can provide himself.

—R. H. Tawney[1]

The final problem of the productive society is what it produces. This manifests itself in an implacable tendency to provide an opulent supply of some things and a

[1] Equality (4th revised ed.), pp. 134–35.

niggardly yield of others. This disparity carries to the point where it is a cause of social discomfort and social unhealth. The line which divides our area of wealth from our area of poverty is roughly that which divides privately produced and marketed goods and services from publicly rendered services. Our wealth in the first is not only in startling contrast with the meagerness of the latter, but our wealth in privately produced goods is, to a marked degree, the cause of crisis in the supply of public services. For we have failed to see the importance, indeed the urgent need, of maintaining a balance between the two.

This disparity between our flow of private and public goods and services is no matter of subjective judgment. On the contrary, it is the source of the most extensive comment which only stops short of the direct contrast being made here. In the years following World War II, the papers of any major city—those of New York were an excellent example—told daily of the shortages and shortcomings in the elementary municipal and metropolitan services. The schools were old and overcrowded. The police force was understrength and underpaid. The parks and playgrounds were insufficient. Streets and empty lots were filthy, and the sanitation staff was underequipped and in need of men. Access to the city by those who work there was uncertain and painful and becoming more so. Internal transportation was overcrowded, unhealthful, and dirty. So was the air. Parking on the streets had to be prohibited, and there was no space elsewhere. These deficiencies were not in new and novel services but in old and established ones. Cities have long swept their streets, helped their people move around, educated them, kept order, and provided horse rails for vehicles which sought to pause. That their residents should have a nontoxic supply of air suggests no revolutionary dalliance with socialism.

The discussion of this public poverty competed, on the whole successfully, with the stories of ever-increasing opulence in privately produced goods. The Gross National Product was rising. So were retail sales. So was personal income. Labor productivity had also advanced. The automobiles that could not be parked were being produced at an expanded rate. The children, though without schools, subject in the playgrounds to the affectionate interest of adults with odd tastes, and disposed to increasingly imaginative forms of delinquency, were admirably equipped with television sets. We had difficulty finding storage space for the great surpluses of food despite a national disposition to obesity. Food was grown and packaged under private auspices. The care and refreshment of the mind, in contrast with the stomach, was principally in the public domain. Our colleges and universities were severely overcrowded and underprovided, and the same was true of the mental hospitals.

The contrast was and remains evident not alone to those who read. The family which takes its mauve and cerise, air-conditioned, power-steered, and power-braked automobile out for a tour passes through cities that are badly paved, made hideous by litter, blighted buildings, billboards, and posts for wires that should long since have been put underground. They pass on into a countryside that has been rendered largely invisible by commercial art. (The goods which the latter advertise have an absolute priority in our value system. Such aesthetic considerations as a view of the countryside accordingly come second. On such matters we are consistent.) They picnic on exquisitely packaged food from a portable icebox by a polluted stream and go on to spend the night at a park which is a menace to public health and morals. Just before dozing off on an air mattress, beneath a nylon tent, amid the stench of decaying refuse, they may reflect vaguely on the curious unevenness of their blessings. Is this, indeed, the American genius?

II

In the production of goods within the private economy it has long been recognized that a tolerably close relationship must be maintained between the production of various kinds of products. The output of steel and oil and machine tools is related to the production of automobiles. Investment in transportation must keep abreast of the output of goods to be transported. The supply of power must be abreast of the growth of industries requiring it. The existence of these relationships—coefficients to the economist—has made possible the construction of the input-output table which shows how changes in the production in one industry will increase or diminish the demands on other industries. To this table, and more especially to its ingenious author, Professor Wassily Leontief, the world is indebted for one of its most important of modern insights into economic relationships. If expansion in one part of the economy were not matched by the requisite expansion in other parts—were the need for balance not respected—then bottlenecks and shortages, speculative hoarding of scarce supplies, and sharply increasing costs would ensue. Fortunately in peacetime the market system operates easily and effectively to maintain this balance, and this together with the existence of stocks and some flexibility in the coefficients as a result of substitution, insures that no serious difficulties will arise. We are reminded of the existence of the problem only by noticing how serious it is for those countries—Poland or, in a somewhat different form, India—which seek to solve the problem by planned measures and with a much smaller supply of resources.

Just as there must be balance in what a community produces, so there must also be balance in what the community consumes. An increase in the use of one product creates, ineluctably, a requirement for others. If we are to consume more automobiles, we must have more gasoline. There must be more insurance as well as more space on which to operate them. Beyond a certain point more and better food appears to mean increased need for medical services. This is the certain result of the increased consumption of tobacco and alcohol. More vacations require more hotels and more fishing rods. And so forth. With rare exceptions—shortages of doctors are an exception which suggests the rule—this balance is also maintained quite effortlessly so far as goods for private sale and consumption are concerned. The price system plus a rounded condition of opulence is again the agency.

However, the relationships we are here discussing are not confined to the private economy. They operate comprehensively over the whole span of private and public services. As surely as an increase in the output of automobiles puts new demands on the steel industry so, also, it places new demands on public services. Similarly, every increase in the consumption of private goods will normally mean some facilitating or protective step by the state. In all cases if these services are not forthcoming, the consequences will be in some degree ill. It will be convenient to have a term which suggests a satisfactory relationship between the supply of privately produced goods and services and those of the state, and we may call it social balance.

The problem of social balance is ubiquitous, and frequently it is obtrusive. As noted, an increase in the consumption of automobiles requires a facilitating supply of streets, highways, traffic control, and parking space. The protective services of the police and the highway patrols must also be available, as must those of the hospitals. Although the need for balance here is extraordinarily clear, our use of privately produced vehicles has, on occasion, got far out of line with the supply of the related public services. The result has been hideous road congestion, an annual massacre of impressive proportions, and chronic colitis in the cities. As on the ground, so also in the air. Planes collide with disquieting consequences for those within when the public provision for air traffic control fails to keep pace with private use of the airways.

But the auto and the airplane, versus the space to use them, are merely an exceptionally visible example of a requirement that is pervasive. The more goods people procure, the more packages they discard and the more trash that must be carried away. If the appropriate sanitation services are not provided, the counterpart of increasing opulence will be deepening filth. The greater the wealth the thicker will be the dirt. This indubitably describes a tendency of our time. As more goods are produced and owned, the greater are the opportunities for fraud and the more property that must be protected. If the provision of public law enforcement services does not keep pace, the counterpart of increased well-being will, we may be certain, be increased crime.

The city of Los Angeles, in modern times, is a near-classic study in the problem of social balance. Magnificently efficient factories and oil refineries, a lavish supply of automobiles, a vast consumption of handsomely packaged products, coupled with the absence of a municipal trash collection service which forced the use of home incinerators, made the air nearly unbreathable for an appreciable part of each year. Air pollution could be controlled only by a complex and highly developed set of public services—by better knowledge stemming from more research, better policing, a municipal trash collection service, and possibly the assertion of the priority of clean air over the production of goods. These were long in coming. The agony of a city without usable air was the result.

The issue of social balance can be identified in many other current problems. Thus an aspect of increasing private production is the appearance of an extraordinary number of things which lay claim to the interest of the young. Motion pictures, television, automobiles, and the vast opportunities which go with the mobility, together with such less enchanting merchandise as narcotics, comic books, and pornographia, are all included in an advancing gross national product. The child of a less opulent as well as a technologically more primitive age had far fewer such diversions. The red schoolhouse is remembered mainly because it had a paramount position in the lives of those who attended it that no modern school can hope to attain.

In a well-run and well-regulated community, with a sound school system, good recreational opportunities, and a good police force—in short a community where public services have kept pace with private production—the diversionary forces operating on the modern juvenile may do no great damage. Television and the violent mores of Hollywood and Madison Avenue must contend with the intellectual discipline of the school. The social, athletic, dramatic, and like attractions of the school also claim the attention of the child. These, together with the other recreational opportunities of the community, minimize the tendency to delinquency. Experiments with violence and immorality are checked by an effective law enforcement system before they become epidemic.

In a community where public services have failed to keep abreast of private consumption things are very different. Here, in an atmosphere of private opulence and public squalor, the private goods have full sway. Schools do not compete with television and the movies. The dubious heroes of the latter, not Miss Jones, become the idols of the young. The hot rod and the wild ride take the place of more sedentary sports for which there are inadequate facilities or provision. Comic books, alcohol, narcotics, and switchblade knives are, as noted, part of the increased flow of goods, and there is nothing to dispute their enjoyment. There is an ample supply of private wealth to be appropriated and not much to be feared from the police. An austere community is free from temptation. It can be austere in its public services. Not so a rich one.

Moreover, in a society which sets large store by production, and which has highly effective machinery for synthesizing private wants, there are strong pressures to have as many wage earners in the family as possible. As always all social behavior is part of a piece. If both parents are engaged in private production, the burden on the public services is further increased. Children, in effect, become the charge of the community for an appreciable part of the time. If the services of the community do not keep pace, this will be another source of disorder.

Residential housing also illustrates the problem of the social balance, although in a somewhat complex form. Few would wish to contend that, in the lower or even the middle-income brackets, Americans are munificently supplied with housing. A great many families would like better located or merely more houseroom, and no advertising is necessary to persuade them of their wish. And the provision of housing is in the private domain. At first glance at least, the line we draw between private and public seems not to be preventing a satisfactory allocation of resources to housing.

On closer examination, however, the problem turns out to be not greatly different from that of education. It is improbable that the housing industry is greatly more incompetent or inefficient in the United States than in those countries—Scandinavia, Holland, or (for the most part) England—where slums have been largely eliminated and where *minimum* standards of cleanliness and comfort are well above our own. As the experience of these countries shows, and as we have also been learning, the housing industry functions well only in combination with a large, complex, and costly array of public services. These include land purchase and clearance for redevelopment; good neighborhood and city planning, and effective and well-enforced zoning; a variety of financing and other aids to the housebuilder and owner; publicly supported research and architectural services for an industry which, by its nature, is equipped to do little on its own; and a considerable amount of direct or assisted public construction for families in the lowest income brackets. The quality of the housing depends not on the industry, which is given, but on what is invested in these supplements and supports.

III

The case for social balance has, so far, been put negatively. Failure to keep public services in minimal relation to private production and use of goods is a cause of social disorder or impairs economic performance. The matter may now be put affirmatively. By failing to exploit the opportunity to expand public production we are missing opportunities for enjoyment which otherwise we might have had. Presumably a community can be as well rewarded by buying better schools or better parks as by buying bigger automobiles. By concentrating on the latter rather than the former it is failing to maximize its satisfactions. As with schools in the community, so with public services over the country at large. It is scarcely sensible that we should satisfy our wants in private goods with reckless abundance, while in the case of public goods, on the evidence of the eye, we practice extreme self-denial. So, far from systematically exploiting the opportunities to derive use and pleasure from these services, we do not supply what would keep us out of trouble.

The conventional wisdom holds that the community, large or small, makes a decision as to how much it will devote to its public services. This decision is arrived at by democratic process. Subject to the imperfections and uncertainties of democracy, people decide how much of their private income and goods they will surrender in order to have public services of which they are in greater need. Thus there is a balance, however rough, in the enjoyments to be had from private goods and services and those rendered by public authority.

It will be obvious, however, that this view depends on the notion of independently determined consumer wants. In such a world one could with some reason defend the doctrine that the consumer, as a voter, makes an independent choice between public and private goods. But given the dependence effect—given that consumer wants are created by the process by which they are satisfied—the consumer makes no such choice. He is subject to the forces of advertising and emulation by which production creates its own demand. Advertising operates exclusively, and emulation mainly, on behalf of privately produced goods and services.[2] Since management and emulative effects operate on

behalf of private production, public services will have an inherent tendency to lag behind. Automobile demand which is expensively synthesized will inevitably have a much larger claim on income than parks or public health or even roads where no such influence operates. The engines of mass communication, in their highest state of development, assail the eyes and ears of the community on behalf of more beer but not of more schools. Even in the conventional wisdom it will scarcely be contended that this leads to an equal choice between the two.

The competition is especially unequal for new products and services. Every corner of the public psyche is canvassed by some of the nation's most talented citizens to see if the desire for some merchantable product can be cultivated. No similar process operates on behalf of the nonmerchantable services of the state. Indeed, while we take the cultivation of new private wants for granted we would be measurably shocked to see it applied to public services. The scientist or engineer or advertising man who devotes himself to developing a new carburetor, cleanser, or depilatory for which the public recognizes no need and will feel none until an advertising campaign arouses it, is one of the valued members of our society. A politician or a public servant who dreams up a new public service is a wastrel. Few public offenses are more reprehensible.

So much for the influences which operate on the decision between public and private production. The calm decision between public and private consumption pictured by the conventional wisdom is, in fact, a remarkable example of the error which arises from viewing social behavior out of context. The inherent tendency will always be for public services to fall behind private production. We have here the first of the causes of social imbalance.

[2] Emulation does operate between communities. A new school or a new highway in one community does exert pressure on others to remain abreast. However, as compared with the pervasive effects of emulation in extending the demand for privately produced consumer's goods there will be agreement, I think, that this intercommunity effect is probably small.

IV

Social balance is also the victim of two further features of our society—the truce on inequality and the tendency to inflation. Since these are now part of our context, their effect comes quickly into view.

With rare exceptions such as the post office, public services do not carry a price ticket to be paid for by the individual user. By their nature they must, ordinarily, be available to all. As a result, when they are improved or new services are initiated, there is the ancient and troublesome question of who is to pay. This, in turn, provokes to life the collateral but irrelevant debate over inequality. As with the use of taxation as an instrument of fiscal policy, the truce on inequality is broken. Liberals are obliged to argue that the services be paid for by progressive taxation which will reduce inequality. Committed as they are to the urgency of goods (and also, as we shall see in a later chapter, to a somewhat mechanical view of the way in which the level of output can be kept most secure) they must oppose sales and excise taxes. Conservatives rally to the defense of inequality—although without ever quite committing themselves in such uncouth terms—and oppose the use of income taxes. They, in effect, oppose the expenditure not on the merits of the service but on the demerits of the tax system. Since the debate over inequality cannot be resolved, the money is frequently not appropriated and the service not performed. It is a casualty of the economic goals of both liberals and conservatives for both of whom the questions of social balance are subordinate to those of production and, when it is evoked, of inequality.

In practice matters are better as well as worse than this statement of the basic forces suggests. Given the tax structure, the revenues of all levels of government grow with the growth of the economy. Services can be maintained and sometimes even improved out of this automatic accretion.

However, this effect is highly unequal. The revenues of the federal government, because of its heavy reliance on income taxes, increase more than proportionately with private economic growth. In addition, although the conventional wisdom greatly deplores the fact, federal appropriations have only an indirect bearing on taxation. Public services are considered and voted on in accordance with their seeming urgency. Initiation or improvement of a particular service is rarely, except for purposes of oratory, set against the specific effect on taxes. Tax policy, in turn, is decided on the basis of the level of economic activity, the resulting revenues, expediency, and other considerations. Among these the total of the thousands of individually considered appropriations is but one factor. In this process the ultimate tax consequence of any individual appropriation is *de minimus*, and the tendency to ignore it reflects the simple mathematics of the situation. Thus it is possible for the Congress to make decisions affecting the social balance without invoking the question of inequality.

Things are made worse, however, by the fact that a large proportion of the federal revenues are preempted by defense. The increase in defense costs has also tended to absorb a large share of the normal increase in tax revenues. The position of the federal government for improving the social balance has also been weakened since World War II by the strong, although receding, conviction that its taxes were at artificial wartime levels and that a tacit commitment exists to reduce taxes at the earliest opportunity.

In the states and localities the problem of social balance is much more severe. Here tax revenues—this is especially true of the general property tax—increase less than proportionately with increased private production. Budgeting too is far more closely circumscribed than in the case of the federal government—only the monetary authority enjoys the pleasant privilege of underwriting its own loans. Because of this, increased services for states and localities regularly pose the question of more revenues and more taxes. And here, with great regularity, the question of social balance is lost in the debate over equality and social equity.

Thus we currently find by far the most serious social imbalance in the services performed by local governments. The F.B.I. comes much more easily by funds than the city police force. The Department of Agriculture can more easily keep its pest control abreast of expanding agricultural output than the average city health service can keep up with the needs of an expanding industrial population. One consequence is that the federal government remains under constant pressure to use its superior revenue position to help redress the balance at the lower levels of government.

V

Finally, social imbalance is the natural offspring of persistent inflation. Inflation by its nature strikes different individuals and groups with highly discriminatory effect. The most nearly unrelieved victims, apart from those living on pensions or other fixed provision for personal security, are those who work for the state. In the private economy the firm which sells goods has, in general, an immediate accommodation to the inflationary movement. Its price increases are the inflation. The incomes of its owners and proprietors are automatically accommodated to the upward movement. To the extent that wage increases are part of the inflationary process, this is also true of organized industrial workers. Even unorganized white collar workers are in a milieu where prices and incomes are mov-

ing up. The adaption of their incomes, if less rapid than that of the industrial workers, is still reasonably prompt.

The position of the public employee is at the other extreme. His pay scales are highly formalized, and traditionally they have been subject to revision only at lengthy interval. In states and localities inflation does not automatically bring added revenues to pay higher salaries and incomes. Pay revision for all public workers is subject to the temptation to wait and see if the inflation isn't coming to an end. There will be some fear—this seems to have been more of a factor in England than in the United States—that advances in public wages will set a bad example for private employers and unions.

Inflation means that employment is pressing on the labor supply and that private wage and salary incomes are rising. Thus the opportunities for moving from public to private employment are especially favorable. Public employment, moreover, once had as a principal attraction a high measure of social security. Industrial workers were subject to the formidable threat of unemployment during depression. Public employees were comparatively secure, and this security was worth an adverse salary differential. But with improving economic security in general, this advantage has diminished. Private employment thus has come to provide better protection against inflation and little worse protection against other hazards. Though the dedicated may stay in public posts, the alert go.

The deterioration of the public services in the years of inflation has not gone unremarked. However, there has been a strong tendency to regard it as an adventitious misfortune—something which, like a nasty shower at a picnic, happened to blight a generally good time. Salaries were allowed to lag, which was a pity. This is a very inadequate view. Discrimination against the public services is an organic feature of inflation. Nothing so weakens government as persistent inflation. The public administrations of France for many years, of Italy until recent times, and of other European and numerous South American countries have been deeply sapped and eroded by the effects of long-continued inflation. Social imbalance reflects itself in inability to enforce laws, including significantly those which protect and advance basic social justice, and in failure to maintain and improve essential services. One outgrowth of the resulting imbalance has been frustration and pervasive discontent. Over much of the world there is a rough and not entirely accidental correlation between the strength of indigenous communist parties or the frequency of revolutions and the persistence of inflation.

VI

A feature of the years immediately following World War II was a remarkable attack on the notion of expanding and improving public services. During the depression years such services had been elaborated and improved partly in order to fill some small part of the vacuum left by the shrinkage of private production. During the war years the role of government was vastly expanded. After that came the reaction. Much of it, unquestionably, was motivated by a desire to rehabilitate the prestige of private production and therewith of producers. No doubt some who joined the attack hoped, at least tacitly, that it might be possible to sidestep the truce on taxation vis-à-vis equality by having less taxation of all kinds. For a time the notion that our public services had somehow become inflated and excessive was all but axiomatic. Even liberal politicians did not seriously protest. They found it necessary to aver

that they were in favor of public economy too.

In this discussion a certain mystique was attributed to the satisfaction of privately supplied wants. A community decision to have a new school means that the individual surrenders the necessary amount, willy-nilly, in his taxes. But if he is left with that income, he is a free man. He can decide between a better car or a television set. This was advanced with some solemnity as an argument for the TV set. The difficulty is that this argument leaves the community with no way of preferring the school. All private wants, where the individual can choose, are inherently superior to all public desires which must be paid for by taxation and with an inevitable component of compulsion.

The cost of public services was also held to be a desolating burden on private production, although this was at a time when the private production was burgeoning. Urgent warnings were issued of the unfavorable effects of taxation on investment —"I don't know of a surer way of killing off the incentive to invest than by imposing taxes which are regarded by people as punitive."[3] This was at a time when the inflationary effect of a very high level of investment was causing concern. The same individuals who were warning about the inimical effects of taxes were strongly advocating a monetary policy designed to reduce investment. However, an understanding of our economic discourse requires an appreciation of one of its basic rules: men of high position are allowed, by a special act of grace, to accommodate their reasoning to the answer they need. Logic is only required in those of lesser rank.

Finally it was argued, with no little

[3] Arthur F. Burns, Chairman of the President's Council of Economic Advisers, *U.S. News & World Report*, May 6, 1955.

vigor, that expanding government posed a grave threat to individual liberties. "Where distinction and rank is achieved almost exclusively by becoming a civil servant of the state . . . it is too much to expect that many will long prefer freedom to security."[4]

With time this attack on public services has somewhat subsided. The disorder associated with social imbalance has become visible even if the need for balance between private and public services is still imperfectly appreciated.

Freedom also seemed to be surviving. Perhaps it was realized that all organized activity requires concessions by the individual to the group. This is true of the policeman who joins the police force, the teacher who gets a job at the high school, and the executive who makes his way up

the hierarchy of Du Pont. If there are differences between public and private organization, they are of kind rather than of degree. As this is written the pendulum has in fact swung back. Our liberties are now menaced by the conformity exacted by the large corporation and its impulse to create, for its own purposes, the organization man. This danger we may also survive.

Nonetheless, the postwar onslaught on the public services left a lasting imprint. To suggest that we canvass our public wants to see where happiness can be improved by more and better services has a sharply radical tone. Even public services to avoid disorder must be defended. By contrast the man who devises a nostrum for a nonexistent need and then successfully promotes both remains one of nature's noblemen.

42

PRIVATE VS. PUBLIC—COULD KENNETH GALBRAITH BE WRONG?

Is there a "social imbalance" as argued by Professor Galbraith? Are too few resources allocated to "public" goods in our affluent society? In this selection, Professor Wallich gives a thought-provoking response to Galbraith's charge, and to the problem of choosing between "public" and "private" goods.

Henry C. Wallich

Henry C. Wallich is Professor of Economics at Yale University and was a member of the Council of Economic Advisers during President Eisenhower's administration.

. . .

The critics are right in pointing out that new material needs also have been carried

to the fore by social and economic evolution—even though they mislabel them as public needs. In the good old days, when this was still a nation of farmers, most people had no serious retirement worries,

[4] F. A. Hayek, *The Road to Serfdom* (London: Routledge & Kegan Paul, Ltd., 1944), p. 98.

there was no industrial unemployment problem, good jobs could be had without a college degree, most diseases were still incurable—in short, social security, education, and health care found primitive and natural solutions within the family and among the resources of the neighborhood. Today, these solutions are neither adequate nor usually even possible.

Meanwhile mounting wealth and advancing technology have brought within reach the means of meeting these needs. We can afford to live better in every way —more creature comforts, more leisure, more attention to matters of the mind and the spirit. At the same time we can take better care of retirement, of unemployment, of illness, of education, of the possibilities opened by research, than ever before.

There are indeed new needs. The citizen-taxpayer has his choice of meeting them, as well as all his other needs, in one of two ways. He can buy the goods or services he wants privately, for cash or credit. Or he can buy them from the government, for taxes.

The nation as a whole pays taxes to buy public services as it pays grocery bills to buy groceries. The tax burden may be heavier for some individuals than for others. But the nation as a whole has no more reason to complain about the "burden" of taxes than about the "burden" of grocery bills—and no more reason to hope for relief.

Of the two stores, the private store today still is much the bigger. The public store is smaller, but it is growing faster.

Each store has some exclusive items. The private store sells most of the necessities and all of the luxuries of life, and in most of these has no competition from the government side. The public store has some specialties of its own: defense, public order and justice, and numerous local services that the private organization has not found profitable. But there is a wide range of items featured by both stores: provision for old age, health services, education, housing, development of natural resources.

THE NEW NEEDS

The bulk of the new needs are in this competitive area. The fashionable notion is to claim them all for the public store and to label them public needs. The statistics say otherwise. They say in fact two things:

First, the supply of this group of goods and services has expanded very rapidly in recent years; and second, they are being offered, in varying degrees, both by the private and the public suppliers. Let us run down the list.

Provision for old age is predominantly private. The average American family, realizing that while old age may be a burden, it is the only known way to achieve a long life, takes care of the matter in three ways: (1) by private individual savings— home ownership, savings deposits, securities; (2) by private collective savings— life insurance, corporate pension funds; and (3) by public collective savings through social security. Statisticians report that the two collective forms are advancing faster than the individual. The increases far exceed the rise in the Gross National Product of almost 80 percent (in current prices) over the past ten years; they do not indicate either that these needs are neglected or that they are necessarily public in character.

Education: the bulk of it is public; but a good part, particularly of higher education, is private. Total expenditures for all education have advanced in the last ten years from $9.3 billion to $24.6 billion ($19.3 billion of it public). Education's share in the national income has advanced from 3.8 percent to 5.8 percent. The silly story that we spend more on advertising than on education is a canard, though with its gross of over $10 billion, advertising does take a lot of money.

Health expenditures are still mainly private. At considerable expense, it is now possible to live longer and be sick less frequently or at least less dangerously. In the past, most people paid their own doctors' bills, although health care for the indigent has always been provided by public action or private philanthropy. Since the war, the proliferation of health insurance has given some form of collective but private insurance to three-quarters of our 182 million people. This has greatly reduced pressure for a national health service along British lines. For the aging, whose health-care needs stand in inverse proportion to their capacity to pay or insure, public insurance has finally been initiated and needs to be expanded. The total annual expenditure on health is estimated at over $25 billion, a little more than on education. Of this, about $6 billion is public.

So much for the allegation that the "new needs" are all public needs. Now for some further statistics on the public store, which is said to have been neglected. Some of them could make an investor in private growth stocks envious. Research expenditures (mainly for defense and atomic energy) have gone from about $1 billion to over $8 billion in the last ten years. Federal grants to the states have advanced from $2.2 billion to $7 billion during the same period. Social-security benefits rose from $1 billion to over $10 billion. All in all, public cash outlays (federal and state) advanced from $61 billion to $134 billion over ten years, 57 percent faster than the GNP.

For those who feel about public spending the way Mark Twain felt about whiskey, these figures may still look slim. (Mark Twain thought that while too much of anything was bad, too much whiskey was

barely enough.) To others, the data may suggest that the advocates of more public spending have already had their way. Could their present discontent be the result of not keeping their statistics up-to-date? In one of his recent pamphlets, Arthur M. Schlesinger, Jr., claims that the sum of the many neglects he observes (including defense) could be mended by raising public expenditures by $10 to $12 billion. That is well below the increase in public cash outlays that actually did take place in one single fiscal year, from $118.2 billion in 1958 to $132.7 billion in 1959. In the three fiscal years 1957–59, these outlays went up more than $31 billion, though the advance slowed down in 1960. More facts and less indignation might help to attain better perspective.

Some parts of federal, state, and local budgets have expanded less rapidly than those cited—in many cases fortunately. The massive buildup in defense expenditures from the late 'forties to the 'fifties has squeezed other programs. Unfortunately, on the other hand, some programs that both political parties have favored—including aid to education, to depressed areas, for urban renewal—have been delayed unduly by the vicissitudes of politics. But the figures as a whole lend little support to the thesis that politicians don't spend enough, and that the government store is not expanding fast enough.

THE CITIZEN IN THE STORES

The two stores—private and public—work very hard these days to capture the business of the citizen-taxpayer. Here is what he hears as he walks into the private store:

"The principal advantage of this store," the private businessman says, "is that you can shop around and buy exactly what you want. If I don't have it I'll order it. You, the consumer, are the boss here. To be sure, I'm not in business for charity but for profit. But my profit comes from giving you what you want. And with competition as fierce as it is, you can be sure the profit won't be excessive."

If the proprietor has been to Harvard Business School, he will perhaps remember to add something about the invisible hand which in a free economy causes the self-seeking of competitors to work for the common good. He will also, even without benefit of business school, remember to drop a word about the danger of letting the public store across the street get too big. It might endanger freedom.

As the citizen turns this sales talk over in his mind, several points occur to him. Without denying the broad validity of the argument, he will note that quite often he has been induced to buy things he did not really need, and possibly to neglect other, more serious needs. Snob appeal and built-in obsolescence promoted by expensive advertising don't seem to him to fit in with the notion that the consumer is king. Looking at the brand names and patents and trademarks, he wonders whether most products are produced and priced competitively instead of under monopoly conditions. The invisible hand at times seems to be invisible mainly because it is so deep in his pocket.

Bothered by these doubts, the citizen walks across the street and enters the public store.

"Let me explain to you," says the politician who runs it—with the aid of a horde of hard-working bureaucrats doing the chores. "The principles on which this store is run are known as the political process, and if you happen to be familiar with private merchandising they may seem unusual, but I assure you they work. First of all, almost everything in this store is free. We simply assess our customers a lump sum in the form of taxes. These, however, are based largely on each customer's ability to pay, rather than on what he gets from the store. We have a show of hands from the customers once a year, and the majority decides what merchandise the store is to have in stock. The majority, incidentally, also decides how much everybody, including particularly the minority, is to be assessed for taxes.

"You will observe," the politician continues, "that this store is not run for profit. It is like a cooperative, run for the welfare of the members. I myself, to be sure, am not in politics for charity, but for reelection. But that means that I must be interested in your needs, or you would not vote for me. Moreover, there are some useful things that only I can do, with the help of the political process, and in which you and every citizen have an interest. For instance, everybody ought to go to school. I can make them go. Everybody ought to have old-age insurance. I can make that compulsory too. And because I don't charge the full cost of the service, I can help even up a little the inequalities of life.

"By the way," the politician concludes, "if there is any special little thing you want, I may be able to get it for you, and of course it won't cost you a nickel."

The citizen has some fault to find with the political process too. He notes that there is not even a theoretical claim to the benefits of an invisible hand. Majority rule may produce benefits for the majority, but how about the other 49 percent? Nor is there the discipline of competition, or the need for profits, to test economy of operation. There is no way, in the public store, of adjusting individual costs and benefits. And the promise to get him some small favor, while tempting, worries him, because he wonders what the politician may have promised to others. The political process, he is led to suspect, may be a little haphazard.

He asks himself how political decisions get to be made. Sometimes, obviously, it is not the majority that really makes a decision, but a small pressure group that is getting away with something. He will remember that—after payments for major national security and public debt interest—the largest single expenditure in the federal budget is for agriculture, and the next for veterans. He may also recall that one of the first budgetary actions of the new Administration was to increase funds for agriculture by $3 billion.

THE EXPANDING BELT

Next, the citizen might consider the paralyzing "balance-of-forces" effect that often blocks a desirable reshuffling of expenditures. The allocation of public funds reflects the bargaining power of their sponsors, inside or outside the government. A classical example was the division of funds that prevailed in the Defense Department during the late 'forties. Army, Navy, and Air Force were to share in total resources in a way that would maximize military potential. By some strange coincidence, maximum potential was always achieved by giving each service the same amount of money. It took the Korean War to break this stalemate.

What is the consequence of the balance-of-forces effect? If the proponents of one kind of expenditure want to get more money for their projects, they must concede an increase also to the advocates of others. More education means more highways, instead of less; more air power means more ground forces. To increase a budget in one direction only is as difficult as letting out one's belt only on one side. The expansion tends to go all around. What this comes down to is that politicians are not very good at setting priorities. Increases in good expenditures are burdened with a political surcharge of less good ones.

The last-ditch survival power of federal programs is a specially illuminating instance of the balance of forces. If a monument were built in Washington in memory of each major federal program that has been discontinued, the appearance of the city would not be greatly altered. In contrast, when the Edsel doesn't sell, production stops. But the government is still reclaiming land to raise more farm surpluses and training fishermen to enter an occupation that needs subsidies to keep alive. Old federal programs never die, they don't even fade away—they just go on.

The citizen will remember also the ancient and honorable practice of logrolling. The unhappy fate of the Area Development bill illustrates it admirably. As originally proposed, the bill sought to aid a limited number of industrial areas where new jobs were badly needed. It got nowhere in the Congress. Only when it was extended to a large number of areas with less urgent or quite different problems, were enough legislators brought aboard to pass it. Because of the heavy political surcharge with which it had become loaded, President Eisenhower vetoed the bill. A bill was finally enacted early this year, long after aid should have been brought to the areas that needed it.

Finally, the citizen might discover in some dark corner of his mind a nagging thought: Any particular government program may be a blessing, but could their cumulative effect be a threat to freedom? He has heard businessmen say this so often that he has almost ceased to pay attention to it. He rather resents businessmen acting the dog in the manger, trying to stop useful things from being done unless they can do them. He is irritated when he hears a man talk about freedom who obviously is thinking about profit. And yet—is there any conclusive rebuttal?

THE CITIZEN'S FAILURES

The citizen would be quite wrong, however, if he blamed the politician for the defects of the political process. The fault lies with the process, or better with the way in which the process, the politician, and the citizen interact. The citizen therefore would do well to examine some of his own reactions and attitudes.

First, when he thinks about taxes, he tends to think of them as a burden instead of as a price he pays for a service. As a body, the nation's taxpayers are like a group of neighbors who decide to establish a fire department. Because none is quite sure how much good it will do him, and because each hopes to benefit from the contribution of the rest, all are prudent in their contributions. In the end they are likely to wind up with a bucket brigade.

But when it comes to accepting benefits, the citizen-taxpayers act like a group of men who sit down at a restaurant table knowing that they will split the check evenly. In this situation everybody orders generously; it adds little to one's own share of the bill, and for the extravagance of his friends he will have to pay anyhow. What happens at the restaurant table explains— though it does not excuse—what happens at the public trough.

Finally, in his reaction to public or free services, the citizen takes a great deal for granted, and seldom thinks of the cost. Public beaches mistreated, unmetered parking space permanently occupied, veterans' adjustment benefits continued without need —as well as abuses of unemployment compensation and public assistance—are some examples. This applies also, of course, to privately offered benefits, under health insurance, for instance. The kindly nurse in the hospital—"Why don't you stay another day, dearie, it won't cost you anything, it's all paid for by Blue Cross"—makes the point.

By removing the link between costs and benefits, the political process also reduces the citizen's interest in earning money. The citizen works to live. If some of his living comes to him without working, he would be less than rational if he did not respond with a demand for shorter hours. If these public benefits increase his tax burden so that his overall standard of living remains unchanged, the higher taxes will reduce his work incentive. Why work hard, if much of it is for the government?

THE POLITICAL DOLLAR AT A DISCOUNT

These various defects of the political process add up to an obvious conclusion: the dollar spent by even the most honest and scrupulous of politicians is not always a full-bodied dollar. It often is subject to a discount. It buys less than it should because of the attrition it suffers as it goes through the process, and so may be worth only 90 cents or 80 cents and sometimes perhaps less. The private dollar, in too many cases, may also be worth less than 100 percent. But here each man can form his own judgment, can pick and choose or refuse altogether. In the political process, all he can do is say Yes or No once a year in November.

The discount on the public dollar may be compensated by the other advantages of government—its ability to compel, to subsidize, to do things on a big scale and at a low interest cost. Whether that is the case needs to be studied in each instance. Where these advantages do not apply, the private market will give better service than the political process. For many services, there is at least some leeway for choice between the private and public store— health and retirement, housing, research, higher education, natural-resource development. Defense, on the other hand, as well as public administration, public works of all kinds, and the great bulk of education—while perhaps made rather expensive by the political process—leave no realistic alternative to public action.

The argument I have offered is no plea to spend more or less on any particular function. It is a plea for doing whatever we do in the most effective way.

43

PUBLIC SERVICE EMPLOYMENT

R. A. Gordon

One possible solution to the problem of high unemployment rates for certain groups is expanded public service employment. Professor Gordon examines the interactions between the short-range and long-range effects of public service employment and recommends enlarged programs to meet both sets of needs.

R. A. Gordon is Professor of Economics at the University of California, Berkeley.

From U.S. Congress, Senate, Committee on Labor and Public Welfare, *Hearings before the Subcommittee on Employment, Manpower, and Poverty, (Comprehensive Manpower Reform, 1972)*, 92nd Cong., 2nd sess., April 26, 1972, part 5, pp. 1540–1547.

. . .

First of all, we need to distinguish between the *short-run* and the *long-run* objectives of an enlarged public service employment program. The short-run objective is to reduce the present high rate of overall unemployment fairly quickly. This objective is short-run in nature and is tied to the stage of the business cycle in which we find ourselves. If this is the primary objective, the program is looked on as temporary, and an essential feature is a "trigger" that terminates the program when the unemployment rate falls to some predetermined figure, say, 4 or 4.5 per cent. And any effects of the program in reducing differentials in unemployment and wage rates are both incidental and temporary.

In contrast, a public service program with long-run objectives looks beyond the current phase of the business cycle. There are at least three sets of long-term objec-

tives that an expanded program of public service employment might seek to achieve. First, it might aim to bring about a *permanent* reduction in the differentially high unemployment rates of disadvantaged groups in the labor force and at the same time raise their relative wages. Second, it can hope to improve the unemployment-inflation trade-off so that we can maintain an unemployment rate of 4 per cent (or hopefully less) with a lower rate of inflation than in the last six years. And, finally, such an enlarged permanent program provides a means of financing a badly needed expanison of local public services without the increase in state and local tax rates that would otherwise be needed. These tax rates are already pressing against the ceiling.

These long-run objectives imply a *permanent* program of expanded public service employment, one that would not be suddenly discontinued when the national unemployment rate falls below some "trigger" figure. Further, these objectives imply a program that would be aimed not only at the unemployed as defined in the official statistics but also at those discouraged workers who, because they believe no jobs are available under what they consider to be acceptable conditions, have dropped out of the labor force, either temporarily or permanently. I should also include in the target population to be served those now employed in the so-called secondary labor market whose earnings, even on a full-time basis, fall below an acceptable level.

All of this suggests the need for an integrated two-tier system of public service employment. The foundation should be a large-scale, permanent program aimed at the long-run objectives that I have listed. Superimposed on this foundation should be a short-run, triggered program aimed at combating cyclical unemployment. . . .

Such an enlarged short-run cyclical program of public service employment should be superimposed on and integrated with a large-scale permanent program having the long-run objectives that I have described. . . .

I recommend a much enlarged program of public service employment that seeks to meet both the long-run and short-run objectives that I have described. Part of the program should aim at cyclical unemployment and would have a trigger. But there should also be a substantial nontriggered program aimed simultaneously at structural reform in the labor market and at increasing the level of public services available at the state and local levels.

. . .

I turn now to some of the particular advantages of an enlarged public service program, both in meeting our short-run need to reduce the overall unemployment rate as quickly as possible (without exacerbating inflationary pressures) and also in working toward the longer-run objectives of providing greater equality of employment opportunities as well as more liberal provision of needed public services.

Federal financing of local public service jobs works rapidly to increase employment. Many job slots have already been designed by local governments but have been left unfilled due to lack of revenue. As soon as Federal funds are allocated, local governments can immediately begin to hire individuals for these positions. This is what has in fact happened under the Emergency Employment Act of 1971, although here we are dealing with a relatively small program.

This direct and immediate hiring contrasts with the employment effects generated either by expanding Federal purchases of goods and services or by increased private spending resulting from a tax cut. Particularly during a recession, private employers do not necessarily and immediately respond to increased spending by increasing employment. To some extent, they can reduce inventories, increase hours for the existing work force, and even raise prices. Only gradually, as employers become confident that the increase in spending will be sustained and as they come more effectively to utilize those already employed, will they hire new workers. And the delays in hiring will be significant as the increase in demand works its way back from retailers and manufacturers of finished goods to the suppliers of parts and materials. In contrast, for the same amount of government expenditure, public service employment would put a larger number of people to work considerably more promptly.

All this suggests that the Federal government should have inaugurated a public service employment program earlier and on a considerably larger scale than that which was authorized by the Emergency Employment Act of 1971.

In the present inflationary context, it is important to remember that public service vacancies bid directly for the unemployed. A general increase in spending, in contrast, bids across the board for all kinds of labor and also for capital. Skilled labor is likely to become scarce while unskilled labor is still in surplus. If, as a long-term goal, we are to bring down the national unemployment rate to 4 per cent or less without incurring an unacceptable rate of inflation and without a permanent system of wage and price controls, we must expand the demand for those types of labor in excess supply. An across-the-board increase in demand large enough to absorb the unskilled and the underprivileged will eventually press on capacity, create new bottlenecks, and accelerate the rise in wages and prices. The creation of an adequate number of low-skilled public service jobs is an alternative to this inflationary expansion of aggregate demand across the board. It selectively bids for the labor still in surplus, without overbidding for labor in short supply. Particularly with the changes in the composition of labor *supply* that have been occurring, we should devise a corresponding pattern of expanding labor *demand*.

This is why public service jobs have an important role to play in a long-run program aimed at improving the inflation-unemployment trade-off and at permitting us to achieve and maintain a satisfactorily low national rate of unemployment. As the current economic recovery continues, unemployment will remain substantial for particular groups, as was the case during 1965–1969. If we try to reduce unemployment among ghetto residents or among youth to acceptable levels merely by expanding aggregate demand, we shall exacerbate the inflationary pressures that we are now striving to control. Certainly a better policy is to develop a long-range program for hiring the unemployed (and underemployed) in these groups directly without indiscriminate bidding for other labor in short supply. This can effectively be done through Federal financing of public service jobs.

One result of the large-scale absorption of the unskilled and the underprivileged into public service employment should be some upward pressure on the relatively low wages paid by private employers in the secondary labor market. To me, this is a result much to be desired. Such upward pressure on low wages in some sectors of the economy will undoubtedly create some difficult adjustment problems. Jobs will need to be redesigned; there will be a spur to investment in labor-saving equipment with some consequent loss of jobs; to some extent higher wages will be passed on in higher prices for particular commodities and services with a consequent change in the pattern of demand; and so on. These are adjustment problems that I think we can live with in order to achieve a greater equality of economic opportunity in this country.

I should like to mention another respect in which public service employment can "zero in" on the employment problems of certain underprivileged groups. Part of our unemployment problem, even in prosperity, has an important geographic dimension. Jobs are leaving the central city while the underprivileged remain. Similarly, rural Appalachia loses private employment, but many of the people remain. Unlike private industry, local government stays in the central city and in rural Appalachia. These government units are thus able to reach these pockets of unemployment. Indeed, the employment center can easily locate in the center of the high unemployment area. Jobs can be created within reasonable reach of the individual's residence.

I should like to conclude on a cautionary note that applies whether we view a program of public service employment as temporary or more or less permanent. It is important to recognize that more additional public service jobs will appear to be created by a given program than will in fact occur. This is because the local government will almost certainly *partly* substitute Federal for local revenues. The Federal funds will to some extent free local funds for other uses (purchase of other inputs, hiring of more skilled employees at higher salaries, etc.), including possibly some reduc-

tion in the size of the tax increase that would have occurred without the Federal program. Existing and proposed legislation carries provisions to prevent this, but it is almost certain to happen to some extent. I do not believe that this leakage is to be regretted, since it substitutes financing by progressive Federal income taxes for regressive local property taxes. But this leakage does mean that this must be allowed for in setting targets and providing funds for any particular program.

. . .

44

The "energy crisis" has forced us to look deeply into public policy related to all sources of energy. Professor Adelman examines policies and controls with respect to natural gas resources, and recommends movement toward a freer market as a partial solution to persistent shortages.

THE PROBLEM OF NATURAL GAS SUPPLY

M. A. Adelman

M. A. Adelman is Professor of Economics at MIT.

From U.S. Congress, Senate, *Hearings before the Committee on Interior and Insular Affairs, (Natural Gas Policy Issues)*, 92nd Cong., 2nd sess., February 25, 1972, part 1, p. 54 ff.

. . .

THE PROBLEM AND ITS HISTORY

There is now a severe shortage of natural gas, which means that at current prices much more is demanded than is available. To help extricate ourselves we might look first at how we became entangled. The original fault, if you will excuse me for saying so, was in the Congress. The Natural Gas Act was ambiguous on whether the price at the wellhead was or was not subject to regulation. The controversy was

carried up to the Supreme Court, which in 1954 decided that it was. . . .

The Federal Power Commission might set as its goal the closest possible simulation of competition in markets that were not competitive, and the acceptance of prices in markets that were competitive. Indeed, this is the normal practice in public utility regulation. The purchase price of supplies, and the hire of labor and of contractors by—say—an electric power company are accepted as being necessary to obtain those goods and services. But a commission is expected to be diligent in seeing that no above-market prices are paid—say—by collusion between the purchasing company and its suppliers. The possibility of such collusion is, of course, the reason why many of the largest service companies were divested years ago by the Securities and Exchange Commission under the Public Utility Holding Company Act.

Indeed, of all the various goods and services that enter into the provision of electric power, telephones, gas pipelines and distribution, and so on, it is only the price of capital funds, the rate of return, that is closely regulated. Even there the rate of return is drawn from the competitive capital market. The rate of return is supposed to be just sufficient to ensure an adequate flow of capital, which means the regulated company must pay the market price for debt and equity funds.

I believe the FPC could have followed this approach and limited their role to certifying when a gas price was generated in an effectively competitive market and could then be accepted like any price for labor or supplies. Where the Commission was not satisfied that the price was competitive, it would need to fix one that came as close as possible to a competitive result. But since natural gas was in general a competitive industry, these exceptional cases would have been relatively few and could easily be fitted into a general competitive framework.

Perhaps that option has been foreclosed by the decisions of the courts since the 1954 Phillips decision. In any case, the Federal Power Commission took an altogether different road in the late 1950s. Perhaps the Commission felt that some action was needed to hold back or roll back field prices of natural gas, which rose very rapidly after World War II until they leveled off around 1958.

These price increases were the direct result of the rapid building of new long-distance pipelines, which transformed the natural gas market from regional to nearly national. For the first time the need of far-off consumers became effective demand in the marketplace. At any given price, the amount consumers demanded became much greater. Prices rose, greatly increasing the supply of new gas, until supply and demand were equated. But the price increase naturally upset some people and caused them to think of lower prices as a good thing in themselves.

There is no use quarreling about tastes or why one man's good is another man's bad. But to call a market competitive is not to praise but only to predict. If a market is competitive, then fixing the price below the market level will inevitably create a large excess demand, just as fixing the price above the competitive level induces a large excess supply. If you wish to fix the price below the competitive level, for whatever good reason, it is wiser to face the consequences. The harder you shove away a fact, the harder it hits you on the rebound.

For a time, an attempt was made to regulate prices by a rate base and rate of return thereon. This finally collapsed in sheer confusion. The next stage was to set area price ceilings. In effect, prices were frozen at 1960 levels.

. . .

In the early and middle 1960s, price ceilings may have happened to coincide with prices that would have been generated in the market place. This is because the demand for gas in the field is essentially a demand for blocks of reserves to be used in the future. Hence the demand for reserves is two-fold—replacing gas as it is used up, and providing a stock to take care of increased consumption. The demand for reserves is much like the demand for producers' plant and equipment.

It is sensitive to expected increases in

sales to the final consumer, and can rise or fall disproportionately to changes in current sales.

For example, suppose I sell 100 cubic feet per year, and expect to sell an additional five cubic feet next year. I am in the market to sign up a twenty-year supply, or 100 cubic feet of reserves this year. But suppose the growth in demand is leveling off, and I expect it to increase by only two cubic feet next year. Then I try to sign up only forty cubic feet of reserves. The sales of gas to consumers are still expanding, yet my demand for reserves has dropped 60 per cent.

It is very likely that some such recession took place in the late 50s and early 60s. In my book I said one was to be expected though I could not say when.

But as of the mid-1960s, for the longer run, the prospect was of smaller supplies per unit of labor and capital expended, that is, higher unit cost. The statistics of the AAPG (American Association of Petroleum Geologists) on discovery of new fields, with a six-year lag to allow for the development—which gives us a fairly good picture—show an irregular but strong downturn after the early or mid-1950s in the ultimate reserves found in any one year.

But the amounts discovered during 1947–1954 exceeded the amounts developed. In other words, during that time, although the rate of increase was declining, the stock was being replenished faster than it was being impounded into reserves and committed to pipelines. During 1954–1960, this turned around and the subtractions were greater than the additions. For the whole period 1945–1960, the process was in approximate balance. But after 1960, the stock of new fields was not being replenished at more than a fraction of the amount put into reserves.

. . .

This promised future trouble, but as usual the exact time when the scarcity would begin to pinch was unpredictable. The gas shortage might have developed slowly and given us more time to react to it. Unfortunately, in the late 1960s a number of unforeseen developments intervened to increase demand and restrict supply.

The concern with air pollution in the great urban centers led industrial consumers, especially electric powerplants, to substitute gas for coal and oil.

The second important disturbance was, the strong inflation we have suffered since 1964, originally due perhaps to the mishandling of the economics of the Vietnam War, but obviously later taking on a life of its own. The inflation was especially strong in construction costs, making gas development much more expensive. Rising costs pushed against the price ceilings and discouraged normal expenditures.

Pollution regulation and inflation were not predictable. Even had the regulators been much better informed than I think it possible for any regulators to be, and even had they chanced to hit on just that set of prices that cleared the market, or that anybody would regard as about right in the early 1960s, the shortage would have come about anyway because regulation could not adapt in time. As a result, there is an unfavorable effect on risk. Added to the normal risks of gas development and exploration, which risks are compensated in a competitive market by the price, came an additional risk, . . . that of unfavorable or simply slow regulatory action.

HIGHER RISK MEANS HIGHER COST

The result has been a matter of common notoriety since 1968. Far more is demanded than can be supplied. Reserves have not only failed to expand but have actually decreased in the past few years. Arrangements are being made to bring in foreign supplies at prices that are a multiple of what is now being paid.

These are the classic symptoms of price being fixed below the market-clearing level in a competitive market. Were the market monopolized, as was claimed and as some no doubt honestly believe, fixing the price below the market level, that is, the monopoly level, would actually bring out more supply. For fixing the price would remove the inducement to restrict supply. Sellers would then find it in their interest to produce and sell everything so long as the price returned at least their cost of capital. Hence the shortage now observed is the normal reaction of a competitive gas market.

INCREASED GAS PRICES BY REGULATION NOT A SOLUTION

The problem now is: what can be done to relieve the shortage, in such a way as to minimize undesired side effects in other domains of energy?

One suggestion is for the Federal Power Commission to increase the price sufficiently to evoke "enough" additional supply. I do not think such a policy can succeed, for two reasons.

First, we do not know how much new supply will be evoked at any given higher price. True there is an unmistakable association between higher gas prices and higher gas supply, all else being equal. But the relation is not precise at all. Furthermore, even if there were a reasonably close past relation between an additional cent per mcf and a given addition to reserves developed, it would not necessarily hold for the future.

. . .

The second reason why price cannot be manipulated to bring in the right amount of desired new supply is that the amount of gas worth bringing in depends on the price of the gas, for the price will determine to what extent buyers of gas will want it in preference to the other fuel. Here too our knowledge is no basis for any fine tuning.

. . .

For all we know, a relatively small increase in gas price would do the trick. Nearly two-thirds of the natural gas is today consumed by industrial users, including electricity generation. Nearly all of this amount, and also much of the commercial use—office buildings, stores, apartment houses and the like—is used as a cheaper substitute for oil and coal. As the price of gas moves, and is expected to stay, above the price of coal or oil, the customer will give it up in favor of liquid or solid fuel. A relatively small decrease in the amount demanded by industrial users would accommodate a considerable growth in consumption by household users, to whom the gas is much more valuable, as evidenced by the fact that they are willing to pay a considerably higher premium.

. . .

CONCLUSION

Let me try to sum up the problem as I see it. There are a number of energy sources that are in large measure substitutes for one another. We ought to work toward that position where our total fuel bill is minimized, including in the bill the cost of security.

We cannot know what the cost is of more oil versus less gas or vice versa, until we have a set of prices that gives us this information. Gas prices have been held down during a time of rising real costs and also a rising price level, thereby promoting excess demand and restricting supply. At this point we are acting in the dark. We need a free market in gas to encourage supply, restrict demand, and tell us what steps are advisable: What commitments to make now, publicly and privately, to ex-

pand supply, and provide a basis on which we can estimate how much is likely to be imported.

. . .

45

TOWARD A RATIONAL POLICY FOR OIL AND GAS IMPORTS

The United States is heavily dependent on foreign sources of petroleum and petroleum products. This paper, prepared as a policy statement for a committee of the United States Senate, proposes some interesting alternatives to continued dependence on foreign gas and oil.

A. R. Tussing

A. R. Tussing is Professor of Economics at the Institute of Social Economics and Government Research, University of Alaska.

From U.S. Congress, Senate, Committee on Interior and Insular Affairs, *Toward a Rational Policy for Oil and Gas Imports*, 1973, pp. 18–22.

. . .

ALTERNATIVES TO IMPORTS

Dependence of the United States upon imported energy is not inevitable and is not dictated by an absolute deficiency in the resource base of primary fuels. The nation has enough oil and gas in the ground to meet current levels of demand for one or two decades at least, and enough coal, oil shale, and uranium for hundreds of years. This resource base could in principle sustain many decades of increased growth in energy consumption, and at any chosen degree of national self-sufficiency in energy supply.

The growing reliance of the United States upon imported energy—primarily oil, but increasingly in increments of natural

gas—has three major causes. *First,* domestic energy consumption is growing at exponential rates and faster than was anticipated. *Second,* available low-cost resources of domestic oil and gas, with the exception of offshore deposits and in Alaska, have been seriously depleted. *Third,* environmental stresses and a new emphasis upon environmental protection are making an increasing proportion of potentially available domestic energy resources inaccessible or unusable at current prices and with current technology.

The present situation is a logical outcome of past policy decisions. There appear to be four major options by which increased self-sufficiency in energy supply could be attained and the major increases in energy imports could be slowed or even reversed.

The options available all involve controversy; they might have major impacts on life styles; they have varying degrees of political acceptability; and they all involve trade-offs with other important public values. The options are: (1) general or selective relaxation of standards for air and water quality and land use; (2) substantially higher costs for energy, in the form of higher consumer prices or in the form of direct and indirect subsidies; (3) new government programs to stimulate technological development; and (4) new regulatory programs to conserve energy.

A retreat in public policy regarding any major area of environmental concern is neither likely nor desirable. Forecasts of future energy balances, and national energy policy, must assume that standards for use of land, waters, and the atmosphere, and for health and safety will become more and not less stringent. However, there are important areas of public policy where the trade-offs among environmental values are still poorly understood or poorly reflected in decision-making. Important examples include comparison of the environmental impact of offshore petroleum development with its alternatives, including massive imports by supertanker; the optimum locations for deep-water ports, refineries, and power plants; and the total impact of auto emission control systems, stack gas cleaners, and other devices for environmental protection that also increase total energy consumption by reducing thermal efficiency. Improved knowledge and improved decision-making machinery with respect to such issues can enhance domestic energy supplies without increasing environmental damage.

Resolution of the serious environmental issues regarding Outer Continental Shelf (OCS) leasing and pipelines from Alaska are logical and prominent elements in any program to control energy imports. Oil and gas from the OCS and oil from Northern Alaska offer the opportunity to make very large additions to domestic energy supplies at economic costs considerably less than the current prices of either domestic or imported fuels. In both of these cases the early limits to low-cost supplies are not geological nor technological, but result from administrative delays and legal disputes over their environmental implications. The most effective potential actions by the Federal government to increase the supplies of domestic energy within the next five to ten years, even without increases in real (constant dollar) prices, clearly include the acceleration of OCS oil and gas leasing and the assurance of a transportation outlet for North Slope oil.

The Outer Continental Shelf and Alaska may be the only exceptions to the rule that increased domestic supplies of primary energy can not be made available except at increased costs. This generalization applies both to conventional resources of oil and gas, and to energy in gaseous, liquid, or electrical form produced from more abundant resources such as coal, oil shale, and uranium.

There is some debate among geologists, petroleum engineers, and economists regarding the size of the resource base of ultimately recoverable oil and gas, and the degree of responsiveness of exploration, discovery, and development of reserves to the prices of oil and gas, respectively. Nevertheless, there is no question that prices do have an impact upon exploration and development activity, and upon recovery rates. Moreover, it is significant that the oil and gas industry *believes* that supplies of conventional hydrocarbons are highly price-elastic, even onshore and in the Lower 48.

Almost unlimited quantities of environmentally acceptable liquids, pipeline quality gas, or electricity could be made available from resources like oil shale and coal, which are far more abundant than crude oil and natural gas. The costs of these fuels are expected to be somewhat greater than could be supported by present prices; estimates for different fuels range from (sixty-seven cents to $1.50 per million BTU) (four to nine dollars per barrel) in 1972 prices. The technology for conversion of coal and oil shale at these levels is moreover not yet wholly proved and lead times for these technologies are believed to be on the five-to-ten year range, compared with one or two years for conventional onshore oil and gas exploration.

It follows that one means of limiting the rapid growth of oil and gas imports is a federal policy favoring higher domestic energy prices. The availability of increasing supplies of domestic fuels, both conventional and unconventional, but only at increasing prices, has created a direct trade-off between the nation's interest in low-cost energy and its interest in relative self-sufficiency of energy supplies. As long as the landed price of imported oil remains cheaper than its domestic equivalents, the greater security of domestic supplies is available only at higher costs, and constant or lower real prices are possible only at a sacrifice in self-sufficiency and security of supply.

There is no alternative to higher consumer prices for gas, and a more rational system of natural gas pricing can be shown to be in the direct interest of consumers. There is no policy option that could continue the availability of any fuel in large amounts, at costs as low as the present prices of natural gas. Higher prices today for natural gas in the field may actually result in *lower* consumer prices for gas in the foreseeable future than would otherwise be the case. Current prices, which average about twenty cents per mcf at the well and forty-five cents at the city gate, have created a shortage of gas both by en-

couraging its consumption as industrial boiler fuel and by depressing incentives to develop new reserves. To fill this growing shortage, gas distributors are contracting for imported or manufactured supplements at eighty cents to two dollars per mcf, several times the regulated prices of conventional gas supplies. The current gas shortage might be resolved at a considerably smaller cost to consumers than these supplements by allowing an appropriate increase in the prices of new supplies of domestic natural gas.

The prominence of the Federal government's influence over the price of oil, plus the availability of cheaper imports, place practical limits upon the deliberate use of oil prices as a tool to increase domestic energy supplies. As long as the Federal government effectively controls crude oil prices by discretionary control over oil imports, any national energy policy that requires oil prices to rise much more rapidly than the general rate of inflation is not likely to be publicly acceptable. A conscious policy encouraging higher prices will require an exceptionally compelling case that its benefits in greater security exceed its consumer costs, and that these benefits could not be obtained by some other policy at lower costs.

No matter how effective tax "incentives" might be in stimulating increases in domestic output, they are more likely to be eroded than increased in the foreseeable future.

Enhanced tax preferences for domestic production of primary energy would in some respects be equivalent to price increases as incentives for developing new supplies. However, the existing collection of percentage depletion allowances, the expensing of drilling costs and dry holes, and credits for foreign taxes, are regarded with deep suspicion by many Americans. Compared to price increases, their cost-effectiveness as incentives is doubtful, and by passing some of the tax benefit on to consumers in the form of lower prices, they tend to discourage energy conservation. It is even possible that repeal or reduction of the tax preferences might indirectly improve the prospects for increasing domestic supplies, if it were accompanied by compensating price increases, because it would reduce the biggest single handicap to the oil and gas industry's public credibility and to public acceptance of other energy policies that would seemingly benefit that industry.

Research and development efforts in near and mid-term energy technology can have a powerful impact upon future import requirements. An effective and economical technique for removing sulfur from Appalachian coals or from their stack gases would allow coal to displace both imported fuel oil and domestic natural gas as fuel for electric power generation in many places where they must now be used as boiler fuel because of air quality problems. This development would have a powerful and almost immediate influence upon U.S. energy balances. Research in the environmentally acceptable conversion of oil shale and coal to liquid fuels, pipeline-quality gas or electricity could have a major payoff in five to ten years. Although future conversion costs for the various techniques are currently uncertain, there is an excellent likelihood that at least one of them will be capable of large increments of energy within a commercially acceptable range of costs. Federal support of additional research and development in conversion of coal and oil shale is justified even if they do not now appear competitive with other fuels, because the availability of such options can help establish a ceiling over the future prices of imported fuels.

Research and development efforts on fuel cells and magnetohydrodynamics, which would greatly increase the efficiency of electric power generation, or on geothermal power are likely to have their major impact on the energy economy and upon import requirements in the 1980s. The commercial application of exotic energy sources such as breeder, fusion, or solar power is not likely within the time horizon considered here.

Finally, deliberate measures to encourage energy conservation are an obvious part of the strategy to limit imports. Assessments of the practical opportunities for reducing the growth of energy demand differ widely. The potential means toward energy conservation (and the policy issues involved) parallel those for increasing energy supplies: direct controls, higher energy prices, taxes and subsidies, and outlays for research and development; they involve comparable policy trade-offs and political problems.

46

Income maintenance programs, family assistance plans, and similar proposals to provide minimum family incomes have been criticized because they might reduce work incentives. This HEW report gives the results of controlled experiments designed to determine if incentives to work are indeed reduced as a result of income maintenance programs.

INCOME MAINTENANCE EXPERIMENTS

Department of Health, Education, and Welfare

Taken from *Income Maintenance Experiments,* material submitted by
the Department of Health, Education, and Welfare to the Committee
on Finance, U.S. Senate, February 18, 1972, pp. 4–11.

. . . .

DESCRIPTION OF THE EXPERIMENTS

There are four income maintenance experiments currently funded by HEW and OEO. The New Jersey and rural experiments are sponsored by OEO and the Seattle/Denver and Gary experiments are sponsored by HEW. All of these experiments focus on the controversial problem of work incentive in an income maintenance system. The first two OEO experiments deal almost exclusively with this crucial question and are designed to determine the effects of financial treatments on the work response of male-headed families in both rural and urban areas. Male-headed families are of particular interest since they constitute a large portion of the working poor population that was not covered under previous welfare programs. Thus, if there is indeed any disincentive to work in an income maintenance system, it will be most discernible in the work effort of those working already (that is, primarily male-headed low-income families) who may choose to reduce their work effort if offered a minimum annual income support that may approach their previous net income.

. . .

To date only one of the experiments has been in operation long enough to report

any preliminary results, the New Jersey project. This is because the experiments must operate for at least a two- or three-year period before one can say with a high degree of certainty that the results observed were not simply distortions in the behavior of the experimental population that resulted from the newness of the project. Since the objective of the experiments is to measure the long-run response of families to an income maintenance program, the families must be able to regard the experimental payment as being secure for a reasonable length of time. Because these projects are intended to be carefully controlled experiments, it is important to limit as much as possible the perception in the minds of the experimental population that they are a special group, since this could very well bias the results. Therefore, it is not in the best interests of the overall experimental effort to make any partial findings generally available before the end of the project.

FINDINGS FROM THE NEW JERSEY EXPERIMENT

OEO issued a brief initial report of findings from the New Jersey experiment in February, 1970, and subsequently a more extensive report of those findings was issued by the Institute for Research on Poverty of the University of Wisconsin in June. Further preliminary results concerning the work effort of participants in the experiment were released by OEO in May, 1971. However, even the latest findings must be qualified as preliminary in the sense that they are based on only the first year's experience of the total population and eighteen months for one-half of the sample. Thus some allowances must be made for the possibility of distortions in behavior of the experiment population produced during the start-up phase. A brief summary of the New Jersey findings are:

(a) There is no evidence indicating a significant decline in weekly family earnings as a result of the income assistance program.

(b) Low-income families receiving supplementary benefits tend to reduce borrowing, buy fewer items on credit, and purchase more of such consumer goods as furniture and appliances.

(c) The Family Assistance Program, excluding the Day Care Program and Work Training provisions, can be administered at an annual cost per family of between $72 and $96. Similar costs for the current welfare system run between $200 and $300 annually per family.

The more extensive analysis of work effort response released in May, 1971, supports the earlier preliminary findings and further refines the data.

The only statistically significant difference in earning that was found between the experimental and control groups was a reduction in the earnings of wives in the yearly sample. However, this difference does seem to disappear at the end of the eighteen-month period. As a result of the average number of workers per family declining, the total number of hours worked per experimental family is slightly less than for the control group.

However, since there are no significant earnings differences between these two groups, the results imply that the experimental families have significantly increased their average hourly earnings compared with the control group. Indeed, the average family hourly earnings appear to have increased by 20 per cent for experimental subjects as compared to only 8 per cent for the controls.

It is important to note also, that there was no significant differential in the number of hours worked per family among the various income maintenance plans, indicating that the various combinations of tax rates and guarantee levels have not yet affected the number of hours a family works.

There are several plausible explanations for these observations. The availability of a "cushion" in the form of experimental benefits may allow the prime worker the freedom not to accept the first job he can find, but rather to seek one that is more appropriate to his skills and interests and pays a higher wage.

Another view suggests that when a family initially experiences an abrupt increase in income, there will be a tendency to "invest," rather than consume a substantial portion of the increase. Thus we may see an increase in the purchase of durable goods and/or an increase in "human capital" investment in the form of training and/or increased time spent searching for better jobs. Such behavior may account for part of the reduction in hours observed, as well as increased hourly earnings. This approach suggests that labor force participation and hours of work would return toward normal, and hourly earnings would stabilize at a new (higher) level. The hypothesis can only be tested as data covering a longer time span becomes available.

FINDINGS FROM THE OTHER INCOME MAINTENANCE EXPERIMENTS

In addition to the New Jersey experiment, there are three other income maintenance experiments, the rural experiment funded by OEO and the Seattle-Denver and Gary experiments, which are funded by DHEW. Since these experiments have been in operation for either just one year or are just beginning, research findings on individual behavioral response will not be available for at least two years. However, several important lessons have been learned in developing designs and administrative structure for these experiments.

The first and most important lesson arises from the fact that HEW experiments explicitly cover the current welfare population and, in so doing, attempt to replace the current layering of welfare and other in-kind benefits by a single integrated income maintenance program that preserves work incentives and eliminates horizontal inequities and vertical "notches." One lesson of this attempt is that it is impossible to achieve such integration without making some current recipients worse off unless fairly high guarantee levels are established for experimental purposes. For example, in Seattle it was necessary to modify the design structure by allowing rather generous day care allowances for all single-parent families since these are currently available to such families from the welfare department. In Gary, despite the existence of a maximum AFDC payment of $2,100 for a family of four, it was necessary to raise the minimum experimental guarantee to $3,300, and even at that level it will not provide superior benefits to some 30 per cent of current welfare families. The anomaly occurs because Indiana welfare payments are at a minimum, not reduced at all for earnings below $2,560. Furthermore, given virtually un-limited work expense allowances, payments are in practice not reduced for some considerable distance beyond that earning level.

Another equally important finding is that certain administrative details can be among the most important determinants of the character and impact of an income maintenance program. Chief among these is the definition of an accounting period for determining eligibility for benefits. For example, the use of an annual accounting period will result in an income maintenance system far different from that which employs a monthly accounting period (which is similar to that being employed in the current welfare system), both in terms of cost, equity and work incentives. A brief analysis of the data obtained from the Seattle Income Maintenance Experiment showed that caseloads may be doubled when one uses a monthly accounting period rather than an annual accounting period.[1] Of a random sample of 100 male-headed families in Seattle with incomes below $15,000 annually, only 19 per cent were eligible for payments on the basis of an annual accounting period, whereas with a monthly accounting period another 23 per cent became eligible.

Furthermore, families that are similarly situated in terms of income over a short period (such as a month) may have quite disparate incomes over a long period (such as a year) and vice versa. Take for example two four-person families with total annual earned income of $4,320 (the FAP breakeven point), but one family earns it over an entire twelve-month period while the other earns all of it during a six-month period. Under an annual accounting period

---

[1] The accounting period systems noted here are but two of a number of differing accounting period systems which can be varied to achieve different program objectives.

neither family would receive any benefit payments since both are over the FAP beakeven point. However, under a monthly accounting system the former family would still receive no payments but the latter family would receive $800 worth of benefits as a result of the way in which its earned income was distributed. Thus the monthly accounting system will not treat families who earned the same annual income in an equitable manner, if their incomes are unevenly distributed.

The significance of the choice of an accounting period on cost, caseload, and equity, as illustrated above, was brought out during the technical development of the income maintenance projects. This preliminary information has already been useful to the Ways and Means Committee in their selection of an accounting period system for the welfare reform bill reported out by the Committee.

Another almost as important lesson learned both in New Jersey and from analysis of the three-year baseline data collected in Seattle is that given the variability of income flows among the poor, regular reporting of income and prompt adjustment of payments is essential to keep program costs within tolerable bounds.

·   ·   ·

INTERNATIONAL ECONOMY

PART SIX

47

"Petition from the Manufacturers of Candles, Wax-Lights, Lamps, Chandeliers, Reflectors, Snuffers, Extinguishers; and from the Producers of Tallow, Oil, Resin, Alcohol, and Generally of Every Thing Used for Lights."

Do we need a tariff to shut out the sunlight so as to create jobs for candlemakers? In a classic satire, Frederic Bastiat exposes the fallacies underlying the argument that we need tariffs to protect workers against "unfair" foreign competition.

PETITION FROM THE MANUFACTURERS OF CANDLES

Frederic Bastiat

Frederic Bastiat was a noted French economist of the nineteenth century.

From *Sophisms of Protection* (New York: G. P. Putnam's Sons, 1874), pp. 73–80.

To the Honorable Members of the Chamber of Deputies:

"Gentlemen,—You are in the right way: you reject abstract theories; abundance, cheapness, concerns you little. You are entirely occupied with the interest of the producer, whom you are anxious to free from foreign competition. In a word, you wish to secure the *national market* to *national labor*.

"We come now to offer you an admirable opportunity for the application of your ——what shall we say? your theory? no, nothing is more deceiving than theory;— your doctrine? your system? your principle? But you do not like doctrines; you hold systems in horror; and, as for principles, you declare that there are no such things in political economy. We will say then, your practice; your practice without theory, and without principle.

243

"We are subjected to the intolerable competition of a foreign rival, who enjoys, it would seem, such superior facilities for the production of light, that he is enabled to *inundate* our *national market* at so exceedingly reduced a price, that, the moment he makes his appearance, he draws off all custom from us; and thus an important branch of French industry, with all its innumerable ramifications, is suddenly reduced to a state of complete stagnation. This rival, who is no other than the sun, carries on so bitter a war against us, that we have every reason to believe that he has been excited to this course by our perfidious neighbor England. (Good diplomacy this, for the present time!) In this belief we are confirmed by the fact that in all his transactions with this proud island, he is much more moderate and careful than with us.

"'Our petition is, that it would please your honorable body to pass a law whereby shall be directed the shutting up of all windows, dormers, sky-lights, shutters, curtains, vasistas, œil-de-bœufs, in a word, all openings, holes, chinks, and fissures through which the light of the sun is used to penetrate into our dwellings, to the prejudice of the profitable manufactures which we flatter ourselves we have been enabled to bestow upon the country; which country cannot, therefore, without ingratitude, leave us now to struggle unprotected through so unequal a contest.

"We pray your honorable body not to mistake our petition for a satire, nor to repulse us without at least hearing the reasons which we have to advance in its favor.

"And first, if, by shutting out as much as possible all access to natural light, you thus create the necessity for artificial light, is there in France an industrial pursuit which will not, through some connection with this important object, be benefited by it?

"If more tallow be consumed, there will arise a necessity for an increase of cattle and sheep. Thus artificial meadows must be in greater demand; and meat, wool, leather, and above all, manure, this basis of agricultural riches, must become more abundant.

"If more oil be consumed, it will cause an increase in the cultivation of the olive-tree. This plant, luxuriant and exhausting to the soil, will come in good time to profit by the increased fertility which the raising of cattle will have communicated to our fields.

"Our heaths will become covered with resinous trees. Numerous swarms of bees will gather upon our mountains the perfumed treasures, which are now cast upon the winds, useless as the blossoms from which they emanate. There is, in short, no branch of agriculture which would not be greatly developed by the granting of our petition.

"Navigation would equally profit. Thousands of vessels would soon be employed in the whale fisheries, and thence would arise a navy capable of sustaining the honor of France, and of responding to the patriotic sentiments of the undersigned petitioners, candle merchants, etc.

"But what words can express the magnificence which *Paris* will then exhibit! Cast an eye upon the future and behold the gildings, the bronzes, the magnificent crystal chandeliers, lamps, reflectors, and candelabras, which will glitter in the spacious stores, compared with which the splendor of the present day will appear trifling and insignificant.

"There is none, not even the poor manufacturer of resin in the midst of his pine forests, nor the miserable miner in his dark dwelling, but who would enjoy an increase of salary and of comforts.

"Gentlemen, if you will be pleased to reflect, you cannot fail to be convinced that there is perhaps not one Frenchman, fro the opulent stock holder of Anzin down to the poorest vender of matches, who is not interested in the success of our petition.

"We foresee your objections, gentlemen; but there is not one that you can oppose to us which you will not be obliged to gather from the works of the partisans of free trade. We dare challenge you to pronounce one word against our petition, which is not equally opposed to your own practice and the principle which guides your policy.

"Do you tell us, that if we gain by this protection, France will not gain, the consumer must pay the price of it?

"We answer you:

"You have no longer any right to cite the interest of the consumer. For whenever this has been found to compete with that of the producer, you have invariably sacrificed the first. You have done this to *encourage labor,* to *increase the demand for labor.* The same reason should now induce you to act in the same manner.

"You have yourselves already answered the objection. When you were told: The consumer is interested in the free introduction of iron, coal, corn, wheat, cloth, etc., your answer was: Yes, but the producer is interested in their exclusion. Thus, also, if the consumer is interested in the admission of light, we, the producers, pray for its interdiction.

"You have also said, the producer and the consumer are one. If the manufacturer gains by protection, he will cause the agriculturist to gain also; if agriculture prospers, it opens a market for manufactured goods. Thus we, if you confer upon us the monopoly of furnishing light during the day, will as a first consequence buy large quantities of tallow, coals, oil, resin, wax, alcohol, silver, iron, bronze, crystal, for the supply of our business; and then we and our numerous contractors having become rich, our consumption will be great, and will become a means of contributing to

the comfort and competency of the workers in every branch of national labor.

"Will you say that the light of the sun is a gratuitous gift, and that to repulse gratuitous gifts, is to repulse riches under pretence of encouraging the means of obtaining them?

"Take care,—you carry the deathblow to your own policy. Remember that hitherto you have always repulsed foreign produce, *because* it was an approach to a gratuitous gift, and *the more in proportion* as this approach was more close. You have, in obeying the wishes of other monopolists, acted only from a *half-motive;* to grant our petition there is a much *fuller inducement.* To repulse us, precisely for the reason that our case is a more complete one than any which have preceded it, would be to lay down the following equation: $+ \times + = -$; in other words, it would be to accumulate absurdity upon absurdity.

"Labor and Nature concur in different proportions, according to country and climate, in every article of production. The portion of Nature is always gratuitous; that of labor alone regulates the price.

"If a Lisbon orange can be sold at half the price of a Parisian one, it is because a natural and gratuitous heat does for the one, what the other only obtains from an artificial and consequently expensive one.

"When, therefore, we purchase a Portuguese orange, we may say that we obtain it half gratuitously and half by the right of labor; in other words, at *half price* compared to those of Paris.

"Now it is precisely on account of this *demi-gratuity* (excuse the word) that you argue in favor of exclusion. How, you say, could national labor sustain the competition of foreign labor, when the first has everything to do, and the last is rid of half the trouble, the sun taking the rest of the business upon himself? If then the *demi-gratuity* can determine you to check competition, on what principle can the *entire gratuity* be alleged as a reason for admitting it? You are no logicians if, refusing the demi-gratuity as hurtful to human labor, you do not *à fortiori*, and with double zeal, reject the full gratuity.

"Again, when any article, as coal, iron, cheese, or cloth, comes to us from foreign countries with less labor than if we produced it ourselves, the difference in price is a *gratuitous gift* conferred upon us; and the gift is more or less considerable, according as the difference is greater or less. It is the quarter, the half, or the three-quarters of the value of the produce, in proportion as the foreign merchant requires the three-quarters, the half, or the quarter of the price. It is as complete as possible when the producer offers, as the sun does with light, the whole in free gift. The question is, and we put it formally, whether you wish for France the benefit of gratuitous consumption, or the supposed advantages of laborious production. Choose, but be consistent. And does it not argue the greatest inconsistency to check as you do the importation of coal, iron, cheese, and goods of foreign manufacture, merely because and even in proportion as their price approaches *zero*, while at the same time you freely admit, and without limitation, the light of the sun, whose price is during the whole day at *zero?*"

48

A PLEA FOR PROTECTION

Here the head of a trade association presents in vivid form the traditional arguments of domestic industries for protection against foreign competition that promises to win away American markets—in a statement intended to win congressional votes for continuation of the tariff.

B. C. Deuschle

When this was written, B. C. Deuschle was President of the Shears, Scissors, and Manicure Implement Manufacturers Association.

From U.S. Congress, House of Representatives, *Hearings Before the Committee on Ways and Means*, 87th Cong., 2nd sess., on H.R. 9900, 1962, pp. 1656–59.

The association respectfully wishes to record with this committee its strong opposition to H.R. 9900 in its present form. This bill could destroy industries such as ours and add to the unemployment problem.

During the past 15 years representatives of our association have appeared before this committee and other congressional committees, the Committee for Reciprocity Information and the Tariff Commission, to present our views on the impact of imported scissors and shears on our domestic industry.

We have never requested or suggested that a complete embargo be placed on the import of scissors and shears. All that we have asked for and desire is a fair competitive opportunity, not an advantage.

To date we have not obtained relief in any form.

We believe that H.R. 9900 would make matters worse. H.R. 9900 provides for new

Presidential authority to reduce or eliminate duties. We realize that Title III of H.R. 9900 provides for adjustment assistance, but the criteria are general and too much is left to the discretion of the President in granting assistance.

Injury or threat of injury as it is written into our present escape clause cannot be properly defined. When 42 manufacturers out of 50 cease manufacturing and go out of business within 12 years as a direct or indirect result of excessive imports, and the Tariff Commission as well as the President decide that there is no injury or threat of injury, something should be done.

Imports of shears and scissors valued over $1.75 per dozen import value have reached the proportion that they represent 95 percent of domestic production of scissors and shears in this category.

We realize that the domestic scissor and shear industry with its 1,000-plus employees accounts for only a fraction of 1 percent of the gross national product, but we see this as no justification for letting the industry be completely destroyed by imports produced with low-cost labor.

The workers in the domestic scissor and shear industry do not want to become wards of the State; they want to use their skills, which have taken years to develop. These workers are not interested in retraining; over many years they have developed a skill they are proud of and want to continue the work they are happy doing.

If the scissors and shears imported during 1961 had been manufactured in the United States, it would have provided over two million man-hours of factory work, or full-time employment for over 1,000 American employees.

Domestic manufacturers of scissors and shears have modernized and automated their operations in an effort to meet foreign competition. But foreign manufacturers also have modern equipment and with their lower wage rates are underselling domestic

firms in the U.S. market at today's rate of duty.

H.R. 9900 would give the President unrestricted authority to reduce duties and thereby further reduce the cost of imported scissors and shears in our market. Under the provisions of this bill, scissors and shears would be buried in a category with many other items and the duty cut 50 percent.

This would mean a reduction of at least 20 cents per pair at the retail level for scissors and shears now being retailed at $1 to $1.29 per pair.

If this is permitted, we do not need a crystal ball to see the results. There are only eight domestic firms now remaining of the 50 operating in the United States prior to the 50 percent reduction in import duty during 1950–51.

These few remaining manufacturers would be forced to close their doors and discharge their employees. The United States would then become wholly dependent on imported scissors and shears.

We cannot understand how it could be in the national interest to permit such a loss. We would lose the skills of the employees and management of the industry as well as the capital investment in production equipment. In the event of a national emergency and imports cutoff, the United States would be without a source of scissors and shears, basic tools for many industries and trades essential to our defense.

The scissor and shear industry is one of the oldest in the world. The skill was brought to the United States from Germany at a time when the United States needed new industry and a scissor and shear industry in particular.

Scissors and shears of all sizes and types are used in every school, retail establishment, office, factory, hospital, and home in the United States. Scissors cannot be classified as a luxury, gimmick, or novelty.

Scissors are used to separate us from our

mothers at birth; to cut our toenails; to trim the leather in our shoes; to cut and trim the materials used in every piece of clothing that we wear.

They are used to cut our fingernails, to trim our mustaches, the hair in our ears and nose, and to cut the hair on our heads —even down to the end of the road when our best suit or dress is cut down the back so that the undertaker can dress us for the last ride. Scissors are truly used from birth to death. They are essential to our health, education, and general welfare.

I ask you, gentlemen, is this an industry that should be permitted to become extinct in this country?

49

THE ADVANTAGES OF FLEXIBLE EXCHANGE RATES

Of all the economists arguing that foreign exchange rates should be determined by free market forces, Professor Friedman is the most outspoken. In this selection, he describes the basis for his position and the effects of freely fluctuating exchange rates on the balance of payments.

Milton Friedman

Milton Friedman is Professor of Economics at the University of Chicago.

From U.S. Congress, Joint Economic Committee, *Hearings: The United States Balance of Payments (Part 3—The International Monetary System: Functioning and Possible Reform)*, 88th Cong., 1st sess., 1963, pp. 451–59.

Discussions of U.S. policy with respect to international payments tend to be dominated by our immediate balance-of-payments difficulties. I should like today to approach the question from a different, and I hope more constructive, direction. Let us begin by asking ourselves not merely how we can get out of our present difficulties but instead how we can fashion our international payments system so that it will best serve our needs for the long pull; how we can solve not merely this balance-of-payments problem but the balance-of-payments problem.

A shocking, and indeed, disgraceful feature of the present situation is the extent to which our frantic search for expedients to stave off balance-of-payments pressures has led us, on the one hand, to sacrifice major national objectives; and, on the other, to give enormous power to officials of foreign governments to affect what should be purely domestic matters.

Foreign payments amount to only some 5 percent of our total national income. Yet they have become a major factor in nearly every national policy.

I believe that a system of floating exchange rates would solve the balance-of-payments problem for the United States far more effectively than our present arrangements. Such a system would use the flexibility and efficiency of the free market to harmonize our small foreign trade sector with both the rest of our massive economy and the rest of the world; it would reduce problems of foreign payments to their proper dimensions and remove them as a major consideration in governmental policy about domestic matters and as a major preoccupation in international political negotiations; it would foster our national objectives rather than be an obstacle to their attainment.

To indicate the basis for this conclusion, let us consider the national objective with which our payments system is most directly connected: the promotion of a healthy and balanced growth of world trade, carried on, so far as possible, by private individuals and private enterprises with minimum intervention by governments. This has been a major objective of our whole postwar international economic policy, most recently expressed in the Trade Expansion Act of 1962. Success would knit the free world more closely together, and, by fostering the international division of labor, raise standards of living throughout the world, including the United States.

Suppose that we succeed in negotiating far-reaching reciprocal reductions in tariffs and other trade barriers with the Common Market and other countries. To simplify exposition I shall hereafter refer only to tariffs, letting these stand for the whole range of barriers to trade, including even the so-called voluntary limitation of exports. Such reductions will expand trade in general but clearly will have different effects on different industries. The demand for the products of some will expand, for others contract. This is a phenomenon we are familiar with from our internal development. The capacity of our free enterprise system to adapt quickly and efficiently to such shifts, whether produced by changes in technology or tastes, has been a major source of our economic growth. The only additional element introduced by international trade is the fact that different currencies are involved, and this is where the

payment mechanism comes in; its function is to keep this fact from being an additional source of disturbance.

Suppose then that the initial effect is to increase our expenditures on imports more than our receipts from exports. How could we adjust to this outcome?

One method of adjustment is to draw on reserves or borrow from abroad to finance the excess increase in imports. The obvious objection to this method is that it is only a temporary device, and hence can be relied on only when the disturbance is temporary. But that is not the major objection. Even if we had very large reserves or could borrow large amounts from abroad, so that we could continue this expedient for many years, it is a most undesirable one. We can see why if we look at physical rather than financial magnitudes.

The physical counterpart to the financial deficit is a reduction of employment in industries competing with imports that is larger than the concurrent expansion of employment in export industries. So long as the financial deficit continues, the assumed tariff reductions create employment problems. But it is no part of the aim of tariff reductions to create unemployment at home or to promote employment abroad. The aim is a balanced expansion of trade, with exports rising along with imports and thereby providing employment opportunities to offset any reduction in employment resulting from increased imports.

Hence, simply drawing on reserves or borrowing abroad is a most unsatisfactory method of adjustment.

Another method of adjustment is to lower U.S. prices relative to foreign prices, since this would stimulate exports and discourage imports. If foreign countries are accommodating enough to engage in inflation, such a change in relative prices might require merely that the United States keep prices stable or even that it simply keep them from rising as fast as foreign prices.

But there is no necessity for foreign countries to be so accommodating, and we could hardly count on their being so accommodating. The use of this technique therefore involves a willingness to produce a decline in U.S. prices by tight monetary policy or tight fiscal policy or both. Given time, this method of adjustment would work. But in the interim, it would exact a heavy toll. It would be difficult or impossible to force down prices appreciably without producing a recession and considerable unemployment. To eliminate in the long run the unemployment resulting from the tariff changes, we should in the short run be creating cyclical unemployment. The cure might for a time be far worse than the disease.

This second method is therefore also most unsatisfactory. Yet these two methods —drawing on reserves and forcing down prices—are the only two methods available to us under our present international payment arrangements, which involve fixed exchange rates between the U.S. dollar and other currencies. Little wonder that we have so far made such disappointing progress toward the reduction of trade barriers, that our practice has differed so much from our preaching.

There is one other way and only one other way to adjust and that is by allowing (or forcing) the price of the U.S. dollar to fall in terms of other currencies. To a foreigner, U. S. goods can become cheaper in either of two ways—either because their prices in the United States fall in terms of dollars or because the foreigner has to give up fewer units of his own currency to acquire a dollar, which is to say, the price of the dollar falls. For example, suppose a particular U.S. car sells for $2,800 when a dollar costs 7 shillings, tuppence in British money (i.e., roughly £1 = $2.80). The price of the car is then £1,000 in British money. It is all the same to an Englishman —or even a Scotsman—whether the price of

the car falls to $2,500 while the price of a dollar remains 7 shillings, tuppence, or, alternatively, the price of the car remains $2,800, while the price of a dollar falls to 6 shillings, 6 pence (i.e., roughly £1 = $3.11). In either case, the car costs the Englishman £900 rather than £1,000, which is what matters to him. Similarly, foreign goods can become more expensive to an American in either of two ways—either because the price in terms of foreign currency rises or because he has to give up more dollars to acquire a given amount of foreign currency.

Changes in exchange rates can therefore alter the relative price of U.S. and foreign goods in precisely the same way as can changes in internal prices in the United States and in foreign countries. And they can do so without requiring anything like the same internal adjustments. If the initial effect of the tariff reductions would be to create a deficit at the former exchange rate (or enlarge an existing deficit or reduce an existing surplus) and thereby increase unemployment, this effect can be entirely avoided by a change in exchange rates which will produce a balanced expansion in imports and exports without interfering with domestic employment, domestic prices, or domestic monetary and fiscal policy. The pig can be roasted without burning down the house.

The situation is, of course, entirely symmetrical if the tariff changes should initially happen to expand our exports more than our imports. Under present circumstances, we would welcome such a result, and conceivably, if the matching deficit were experienced by countries currently running a surplus, they might permit it to occur without seeking to offset it. In that case, they and we would be using the first method of adjustment—changes in reserves or borrowing. But again, if we had started off from an even keel, this would be an undesirable method of adjustment. On our side, we should be sending out useful goods and receiving only foreign currencies in return. On the side of our partners, they would be using up reserves and tolerating the creation of unemployment.

The second method of adjusting to a surplus is to permit or force domestic prices to rise—which is of course what we did in part in the early postwar years when we were running large surpluses. Again, we should be forcing maladjustments on the whole economy to solve a problem arising from a small part of it—the 5 percent accounted for by foreign trade.

Again, these two methods are the only ones available under our present international payments arrangements, and neither is satisfactory.

The final method is to permit or force exchange rates to change—in this case, a rise in the price of the dollar in terms of foreign currencies. This solution is again specifically adapted to the specific problem of the balance of payments.

Changes in exchange rates can be produced in either of two general ways. One way is by a change in an official exchange rate; an official devaluation or appreciation from one fixed level which the government is committed to support to another fixed level. This is the method used by Britain in its postwar devaluation and by Germany in 1961 when the mark was appreciated. This is also the main method contemplated by the IMF which permits member nations to change their exchange rates by 10 percent without approval by the Fund and by a larger amount after approval by the Fund. But this method has serious disadvantages. It makes a change in rates a matter of major moment, and hence there is a tendency to postpone any change as long as possible. Difficulties cumulate and a larger change is finally needed than would have been required if it could have been made promptly. By the time the change is made, everyone is aware that a change is pending

and is certain about the direction of change. The result is to encourage flight from a currency, if it is going to be devalued, or to a currency, if it is going to be appreciated.

There is in any event little basis for determining precisely what the new rate should be. Speculative movements increase the difficulty of judging what the new rate should be and introduce a systematic bias, making the change needed appear larger than it actually is. The result, particularly when devaluation occurs, is generally to lead officials to "play safe" by making an even larger change than the large change needed. The country is then left after the devaluation with a maladjustment precisely the opposite of that with which it started, and is thereby encouraged to follow policies it cannot sustain in the long run.

Even if all these difficulties could be avoided, this method of changing from one fixed rate to another has the disadvantage that it is necessarily discontinuous. Even if the new exchange rates are precisely correct when first established, they will not long remain correct.

A second and much better way in which changes in exchange rates can be produced is by permitting exchange rates to float, by allowing them to be determined from day to day in the market. This is the method which the United States used from 1862 to 1879, and again, in effect, from 1917 or so to about 1925, and again from 1933 to 1934. It is the method which Britain used from 1918 to 1925 and again from 1931 to 1939, and which Canada used for most of the interwar period and again from 1950 to May 1962. Under this method, exchange rates adjust themselves continuously, and market forces determine the magnitude of each change. There is no need for any official to decide by how much the rate should rise or fall. This is the method of the free market, the method that we adopt unquestioningly in a private enterprise economy for the bulk of goods and services. It is no less available for the price of one money in terms of another.

With a floating exchange rate, it is possible for governments to intervene and try to affect the rate by buying or selling, as the British exchange equalization fund did rather successfully in the 1930s, or by combining buying and selling with public announcements of intentions, as Canada did so disastrously in early 1962. On the whole, it seems to me undesirable to have government intervene, because there is a strong tendency for government agencies to try to peg the rate rather than to stabilize it, because they have no special advantage over private speculators in stabilizing it, because they can make far bigger mistakes than private speculators risking their own money, and because there is a tendency for them to cover up their mistakes by changing the rules—as the Canadian case so strikingly illustrates—rather than by reversing course. But this is an issue on which there is much difference of opinion among economists who agree in favoring floating rates. Clearly, it is possible to have a successful floating rate along with governmental speculation.

The great objective of tearing down trade barriers, of promoting a worldwide expansion of trade, of giving citizens of all countries, and especially the underdeveloped countries, every opportunity to sell their products in open markets under equal terms and thereby every incentive to use their resources efficiently, of giving countries an alternative through free world trade to autarchy and central planning—this great objective can, I believe, be achieved best under a regime of floating rates. All countries, and not just the United States, can proceed to liberalize boldly and confidently only if they can have reasonable assurance that the resulting trade expansion will be balanced and will not interfere with major domestic objectives. Float-

ing exchange rates, and so far as I can see, only floating exchange rates, provide this assurance. They do so because they are an automatic mechanism for protecting the domestic economy from the possibility that liberalization will produce a serious imbalance in international payments.

Despite their advantages, floating exchange rates have a bad press. Why is this so?

One reason is because a consequence of our present system that I have been citing as a serious disadvantage is often regarded as an advantage, namely, the extent to which the small foreign trade sector dominates national policy. Those who regard this as an advantage refer to it as the discipline of the gold standard. I would have much sympathy for this view if we had a real gold standard, so the discipline was imposed by impersonal forces which in turn reflected the realities of resources, tastes, and technology. But in fact we have today only a pseudo gold standard and the so-called discipline is imposed by governmental officials of other countries who are determining their own internal monetary policies and are either being forced to dance to our tune or calling the tune for us, depending primarily on accidental political developments. This is a discipline we can well do without.

A possibly more important reason why floating exchange rates have a bad press, I believe, is a mistaken interpretation of experience with floating rates, arising out of a statistical fallacy that can be seen easily in a standard example. Arizona is clearly the worst place in the United States for a person with tuberculosis to go because the death rate from tuberculosis is higher in Arizona than in any other State. The fallacy in this case is obvious. It is less obvious in connection with exchange rates. Countries that have gotten into severe financial difficulties, for whatever reason, have had ultimately to change their exchange rates or let them change. No amount of exchange control and other restrictions on trade have enabled them to peg an exchange rate that was far out of line with economic realities. In consequence, floating rates have frequently been associated with financial and economic instability. It is easy to conclude, as many have, that floating exchange rates produce such instability.

This misreading of experience is reinforced by the general prejudice against speculation; which has led to the frequent assertion, typically on the basis of no evidence whatsoever, that speculation in exchange can be expected to be destabilizing and thereby to increase the instability in rates. Few who make this assertion even recognize that it is equivalent to asserting that speculators generally lose money.

Floating exchange rates need not be unstable exchange rates—any more than the prices of automobiles or of government bonds, of coffee or of meals need gyrate wildly just because they are free to change from day to day. The Canadian exchange rate was free to change during more than a decade, yet it varied within narrow limits. The ultimate objective is a world in which exchange rates, while free to vary, are in fact highly stable because basic economic policies and conditions are stable. Instability of exchange rates is a symptom of instability in the underlying economic structure. Elimination of this symptom by administrative pegging of exchange rates cures none of the underlying difficulties and only makes adjustment to them more painful.

The confusion between stable exchange rates and pegged exchange rates helps to explain the frequent comment that floating exchange rates would introduce an additional element of uncertainty into foreign trade and thereby discourage its expansion. They introduce no additional element of uncertainty. If a floating rate would, for example, decline, then a pegged rate would

be subject to pressure that the authorities would have to meet by internal deflation or exchange control in some form. The uncertainty about the rate would simply be replaced by uncertainty about internal prices or about the availability of exchange; and the latter uncertainties, being subject to administrative rather than market control, are likely to be the more erratic and unpredictable. Moreover, the trader can far more readily and cheaply protect himself against the danger of changes in exchange rates, through hedging operations in a forward market, than he can against the danger of changes in internal prices or exchange availability. Floating rates are therefore more favorable to private international trade than pegged rates.

It is not the least of the virtues of floating exchange rates that we would again become masters in our own house. We could decide important issues on the proper ground. The military could concentrate on military effectiveness and not on saving foreign exchange; recipients of foreign aid could concentrate on how to get the most out of what we give them and not on how to spend it all in the United States; Congress could decide how much to spend on foreign aid on the basis of what we get for our money and what else we could use it for and not how it will affect the gold stock; the monetary authorities could concentrate on domestic prices and employment, not on how to induce foreigners to hold dollar balances in this country; the Treasury and the tax committees of Congress could devote their attention to the equity of the tax system and its effects on our efficiency, rather than on how to use tax gimmicks to discourage imports, subsidize exports, and discriminate against outflows of capital.

A system of floating exchange rates would render the problem of making outflows equal inflows unto the market where it belongs and not leave it to the clumsy and heavy hand of government. It would leave government free to concentrate on its proper functions.

In conclusion, a word about gold. Our commitment to buy and sell gold for monetary use at the fixed price of $35 an ounce is, in practice, the mechanism whereby we maintain fixed rates of exchange between the dollar and other currencies—or, more precisely, whereby we leave all initiative for changes in such rates to other countries. This commitment should be terminated. The price of gold should be determined in the free market, with the U.S. Government committed neither to buying gold nor to selling gold at any fixed price. This is the appropriate counterpart of a policy of floating exchange rates. With respect to our existing stock of gold, we could simply keep it fixed, neither adding to it nor reducing it; alternatively, we could sell it off gradually at the market price or add to it gradually, thereby reducing or increasing our governmental stockpiles of this particular metal. In any event, we should simultaneously remove all present limitations on the ownership of gold and the trading in gold by American citizens. There is no reason why gold, like other commodities, should not be freely traded on a free market.

50

Many economists, as well as most businessmen and bankers, favor maintaining fixed rates of exchange between currencies. Professor Wallich describes the reasons for retaining fixed exchange rates and argues that some of the advantages suggested for flexible exchange rates may not be valid.

A DEFENSE OF FIXED EXCHANGE RATES
Henry C. Wallich

Henry C. Wallich is Professor of Economics at Yale University, and he was a member of the Council of Economic Advisers during President Eisenhower's administration.

From United States Balance of Payments: Hearings Before the Joint Economic Committee, 88th Congress, 1st Session (1963), p. 495.

. . . Let me say at the outset that I conceive of my paper as a defense of fixed rates. The title indicates that I would like to see the pros and cons weighed because there are pros and cons, of course.

Flexible rates have achieved a high measure of acceptance in academic circles, but very little among public officials. This raises the question whether we have a parallel to the famous case of free trade: almost all economists favor it in principle, but no major country ever has adopted it. Does the logic of economics point equally irrefutably to flexible rates, while the logic of politics points in another direction?

The nature of the case, I believe, is fundamentally different. Most countries do practice free trade within their borders, although they reject it outside. But economists do not propose flexible rates for the States of the Union, among which men, money, and goods can move freely, and which are governed by uniform monetary, fiscal, and other policies. Flexible rates are to apply only to relations among countries that do not permit free factor movements across their borders and that follow, or may follow, substantially different monetary and fiscal policies. It is the imperfections of the world that seem to suggest that flexible rates, which would be harmful if applied to different parts of a single country, would do more good than harm internationally.

It is quite arguable that the Appalachian area would benefit if it could issue a dollar of its own, an Appalachian dollar which in that case would sell, probably, at 60 or 90 cents. Exports from that region would increase, and unemployment would diminish. A great many good things would happen, but we are also aware of what it would do to the economy of the United States—and, therefore, we do not propose that solution. The question is, Do we want to look upon the world as quite different from the United States, as hopelessly divided into self-contained units where cooperation and efforts to coordinate policies are doomed to frustration? In that case, flexible rates may be the best way to avoid a very bad situation. But should we not try to establish within the world something that begins to approximate the conditions that prevail within a country, in the way of coordination of policies, freer flow of capital and of goods and so try to achieve the benefits of one large economic area within the world? That is what we should try for.

Now to resume: The proponents of flexible rates argue, in effect, that flexible rates can help a country get out of almost any of the typical difficulties that economies experience. This is perfectly true. If the United States has a balance-of-payments deficit, a flexible exchange rate allows the dollar to decline until receipts have risen and payments fallen enough to restore balance. If the United States has unemployment, flexible rates can protect it against the balance-of-payments consequences of a policy of expansion. We would then have less unemployment. If the United States has suffered inflation and fears that it will be undersold internationally, flexible rates can remove the danger.

All of these advantages are quite clear.

Other countries have analogous advantages. If Chile experiences a decline in copper prices, flexible rates can ease the inevitable adjustment. If Germany finds that other countries have inflated while German prices have remained more nearly stable, flexible rates could help to avoid importing inflation. If Canada has a large capital inflow, a flexible rate will remove the need for price and income increases that would otherwise be needed to facilitate the transfer of real resources.

There are other adjustments, however, that must be made in all of these cases. If a country allows its exchange rate to go down, some price adjustments still remain to be made. Furthermore, each time a country makes this kind of adjustment, allowing its exchange rate to decline, other countries suffer. If the U.S. dollar depreciates, we undersell the Europeans. It could be argued that if the U.S. price levels go down instead of the exchange rate, we also undersell the Europeans, and if because of a declining price level we have unemployment we would be buying still less from them. Nevertheless, there is a difference. A price adjustment tends to be slow and is likely to be no greater than it need be and tends to be selective for particular commodities. In contrast, an exchange rate movement is unpredictable. It can be large—we could easily have a drop of 10 or 20 percent in an exchange rate. It comes suddenly. And it compels other countries to be on their guard.

Why, given the attractions of flexible rates, should one advise policy-makers to stay away from them? Since the dollar problem is the concrete situation in which flexible rates are being urged today, it is in terms of the dollar that they must be discussed. In broadest terms, the reason why flexible rates are inadvisable is that their

SPOT EXCHANGE RATES FOR U.S. DOLLAR IN CANADA AS OF THE END OF THE MONTH (AUGUST 1950–JUNE 1962)

	January	February	March	April	May	June	July	August	September	October	November	December
Canada:												
1950								1.105	1.105	1.053	1.040	1.053
1951	1.055	1.046	1.051	1.068	1.068	1.067	1.056	1.058	1.055	1.048	1.036	1.017
1952	1.003	1.000	.987	.980	.983	.974	.964	.961	.960	.967	.973	.971
1953	.970	.983	.982	.986	.991	.994	.994	.992	.981	.980	.975	.974
1954	.971	.965	.980	.986	.981	.979	.973	.970	.970	.970	.969	.966
1955	.972	.988	.983	.989	.984	.986	.984	.985	.990	.998	1.000	.999
1956	.999	.999	.999	.997	.989	.981	.981	.980	.977	.968	.959	.960
1957	.958	.958	.956	.958	.956	.953	.948	.948	.965	.959	.968	.985
1958	.982	.979	.975	.970	.964	.959	.962	.973	.948	.969	.966	.964
1959	.969	.973	.968	.962	.962	.955	.959	.952		.947	.949	.953
1960	.953	.951	.957	.966	.988	.980	.976	.970	.978	.976	.978	.996
1961	.991	.988	.989	.988	.988	1.036	1.031	1.031	1.030	1.033	1.042	1.043
1962	1.046	1.050	1.050	1.050	1.090	1.086						

SPOT EXCHANGE RATES FOR U.S. DOLLAR IN MEXICO AS OF THE END OF THE MONTH (JANUARY 1948–OCTOBER 1949)

	January	February	March	April	May	June	July	August	September	October	November	December
1948	4.86	4.86	4.86	4.86	4.86	4.86	4.86[1]	6.83	6.89	6.91	6.89	6.88
1949	6.88	6.97	6.97	7.00	8.06	8.22[2]	8.65	8.65	8.65	8.65		

SOURCE: International Financial Statistics.

[1] Through July 21. Average for July 22–Dec. 31 was 6.81.
[2] June 1–17. On June 17 rate fixed at 8.65 pesos per U.S. dollar.

successful functioning would require more self-discipline and mutual forbearance than countries today are likely to muster. Exchange rates are two sided—depreciation for the dollar means appreciation for the European currencies. To work successfully, a flexible dollar, for instance, must not depreciate to the point where the Europeans would feel compelled to take counteraction. I believe that the limits of tolerance, before counteraction begins today are narrow and that a flexible dollar would invite retaliation almost immediately.

In the abstract, the European countries perhaps ought to consider that if the United States allows the dollar to go down, it is doing so in the interests of all-round equilibrium. They ought perhaps to consider that with a stable dollar rate the same adjustment might have to take place through a decline in prices here and a rise in prices there. In practice, they are likely to be alive principally to the danger of being undersold by American producers if the dollar goes down, in their own and third markets. The changing competitive pressure would fall unevenly upon particular industries, and those who are hurt would demand protection.

The most likely counteraction might take one of two forms. The Europeans could impose countervailing duties, such as the United States also has employed at times. They could alternately also depreciate European currencies along with the dollar or, what would amount to almost the same thing, prevent the dollar from depreciating. This might involve the European countries in the purchase of large amounts of dollars. If they are to peg the dollar, they could minimize their commitment by imposing a simple form of exchange control that the Swiss practiced during the last war. The Swiss purchased dollars only from their exporters, also requiring their importers to buy these dollars thereby stabilizing the trade dollar, while allowing dollars from capital movements—finance dollars—to find their own level in the market.

The large volume of not very predictable short-term capital movements in the world today makes such reactions under flexible rates particularly likely.

Chairman Douglas: Is that not what has been done for the last 2 years or so by Great Britain and the Netherlands?

Mr. Wallich: Yes, in mild form for securities; that is correct, sir.

A sudden outflow of funds from the United States, for instance (because of the fear of budget deficits or many other things that could happen), would tend to drive the dollar down. As a result, American exporters could undersell producers everywhere else in the world. It seems unlikely that foreign countries would allow a fortuitous short-term capital movement to have such far-reaching consequences. It would not even be economically appropriate to allow a transitory fluctuation in the capital account of the balance of payments to have a major influence on the current account. Such a fluctuation should not alter the pattern of trade, because the situation is likely to be reversed. Other countries therefore would probably take defensive action to make sure that no industry is destroyed and after several years may have to be rebuilt because of the ups and downs of short-term capital movements.

It can be argued that under flexible rates the effects of such a movement would be forestalled by stabilizing speculation on a future recovery of the dollar. This is possible. It is possible also, however, that speculation would seek a quick profit from the initial drop in the dollar, instead of a longer run one from its eventual recovery. Then short-run speculation would drive the dollar down farther at first. In any case there is not enough assurance that speculators will not make mistakes to permit basing the world's monetary system upon the stabilizing effects of speculation.

In the case of countries which import much of what they consume, such as England, a temporary decline in the local currency may even be self-validating. If the cost of living rises as the currency declines, wages will rise. Thereafter, the currency may never recover to its original level.

This points up one probable consequence of flexible exchange rates: A worldwide acceleration of inflation. In some countries the indicated ratchet effect of wages will be at work. If exchange rates go down, wages will rise, and exchange rates cannot recover. In the United States the rise in the cost of imports would not be very important. But the removal of balance-of-payments restraints may well lead to policies that could lead to price increases. The American inflation of the 1950s was never defeated until the payments deficit became serious. Elsewhere, the removal of balance-of-payments disciplines might have the same effect. Rapid inflation in turn would probably compel governments to intervene drastically in foreign trade and finance.

Chairman Douglas: The payment deficit as a means of checking price advances—are you welcoming that?

Mr. Wallich: No, I do not, but I am aware, Mr. Chairman, that there is a choice to be made here—more employment or more stable prices. If we pursued more sensible policies and exerted a little more self-restraint, this choice would not be upon us. But if we insist on raising costs and raising prices in the presence of unemployment then this unpleasant choice must be made. As Mr. Friedman has said, it is quite clear that the discipline of the balance of payments has made for a more restrictive policy in this country than would have been followed in the absence of this discipline. It is quite conceivable that the absence of balance-of-payments disciplines would have strong inflationary effects in some countries. In that case governments would be compelled immediately to intervene drastically in foreign trade and finance; in other words, flexible exchange rates would contribute to their own extinction or to exchange control.

The prospect that flexible rates would greatly increase uncertainty for foreign traders and investors has been cited many times. It should be noted that this uncertainty extends also to domestic investment decisions that might be affected by changing import competition or changing export prospects. It has been argued that uncertainties about future exchange rates can be removed by hedging in the future market. This, however, involves a cost even where cover is readily available. The history of futures markets does not suggest that it will be possible to get cover for long-term positions. To hedge domestic investment decisions that might be affected by flexible rates is in the nature of things impracticable.

The picture that emerges of the international economy under flexible rates is one of increasing disintegration. Independent national policies and unpredictable changes in each country's competitive position will compel governments to shield their producers and markets. The argument that such shielding would also automatically be accomplished by movements in the affected country's exchange rate underrates the impact of fluctuations upon particular industries, if not upon the entire economy. That international integration and flexible rates are incompatible seems to be the view also of the European Common Market countries, who have left no doubt that they want stable rates within the EEC. The same applies if we visualize the "Kennedy round" under the Trade Expansion Act. I think if we told the Europeans that, after lowering our tariffs, we were going to cast the dollar loose and let it fluctuate, we would get very little tariff reduction. They would want to keep up their guard.

If the disintegrating effects of flexible rates are to be overcome, a great deal of policy coordination, combined with self-discipline and mutual forbearance, would be required. The desired independence of national economic policy would in fact have to be foregone—interest rates, budgets, wage and prices policies would have to be harmonized. If the world were ready for such cooperation, it would be capable also of making a fixed exchange rate system work. In that case, flexible rates would accomplish nothing that could not more cheaply and simply be done with fixed rates. It seems to follow that flexible rates have no unique capacity for good, whereas they possess great capacity to do damage.

. . .

51

Traditionally, economists have advocated fluctuating international exchange rates, while bankers and businessmen have favored exchange-rate stability. An American businessman whose firm does much business abroad believes that his company can not only accommodate the floating rates but that it can do so more effectively than when the foreign exchanges are subject to government control.

WHY A BUSINESSMAN WANTS FLOATING EXCHANGE RATES

J. W. Van Gorkom

J. W. Van Gorkom is President of Trans Union Corporation, and a member of the Committee for Economic Development, an organization of Business Executives concerned about research on public policy issues.

From *Business Week*, March 24, 1972, pp. 32, 34.

In recent months I have read countless analyses of the international monetary problem, but all of the suggestions for improving the system seem inadequate through the eyes of a businessman. They simply fail to recognize how fundamentally the situation and needs have changed. The proposals represent only patches when what is needed is a complete restructuring of the system, as the crises of recent weeks have forcefully demonstrated. Fortunately, recent events have also pointed the way to a permanent solution.

The design of a satisfactory system should depend on the answers to two questions: What must the system do? Under what circumstances must it operate?

I have shaped my answer to these questions into four basic "requirements."

REQUIREMENT I

International trade in the future will have to be balanced. This means that each country will have to attain equilibrium in its "basic balance," which includes its trading account plus long-term investments and returns thereon.

The present system has not produced

balanced trade, and the large surpluses of some countries have been made possible only by the outflow of huge amounts of dollars from the United States. Now the other countries say they want no more dollars, and gold has been effectively demonetized, meaning that countries will not use their gold to settle trade deficits because of the wide disparity between the official price of gold and the free market price. In such circumstances, there is no alternative to balanced trade. Without dollars or gold to finance the trade surpluses, they must cease, and the corresponding deficits will likewise cease.

REQUIREMENT II

The plan must permit each country to adopt such domestic monetary and fiscal policies as it sees fit. All countries want the monetary system to work, but our experience in recent years demonstrates conclusively that no country will accept low growth rates, high unemployment, or any other material domestic economic detriment out of loyalty to the international monetary system. We must accept the cold fact that each country will follow its own domestic game plan, and this will cause disequilibriums between the economies of the various countries. Such disequilibriums will demand changes in exchange rates if trade is to be balanced.

REQUIREMENT III

Operation of the adjustment mechanism must not depend upon a determination of who is to "blame" for the disequilibrium. This requirement follows logically from Requirement II. In the past, the question of "blame" has been debated for months on end while serious trade imbalances went uncorrected. World trade today is too complex to fix blame clearly, and such a determination is of no real value anyway. If we are to have balanced trade, the adjustment in rates must be made regardless of who caused the disequilibrium.

REQUIREMENT IV

The system should not encourage restrictions on capital investment. Restrictions on capital movements are very much an obstacle to the growth of international trade. They may be a greater detriment than the uncertainty of exchange rates.

The present monetary system encourages capital restrictions by overemphasizing the fixed nature of the rates. This leads countries to impose restrictions on capital movements to protect exchange rates that no longer reflect the economic reality.

The present system, therefore, fails on all four counts. There is really no such thing as a fixed rate. In any sound system, the exchange rates must change as the underlying economies of the countries change. Today the amount of such changes and their timing represent the arbitrary decisions of governments, usually arrived at by a form of high-level haggling. Because they seldom reflect market forces, such rates do not lead to balanced trade. Furthermore, as we have recently seen, the market is now capable of bringing enormous pressure against such arbitrary rates and forcing a correction. If the free market must eventually ratify or reject any rates set by governments, why not let it set the rates in the first place?

Almost all the proposals for reforming the monetary system are advanced, in the name of protecting and encouraging foreign trade, by economists and bankers whose experience in foreign trade is either very limited or highly specialized.

As a businessman, I am convinced that the system that will best meet these four requirements is one based on flexible exchange rates that are determined day by day in the free marketplace. Under such a system, nations would be prohibited from intervening in any currency or from otherwise interfering with market forces, except in special circumstances and with advance approval of a body such as the International Monetary Fund. Each currency, including the dollar, would be free to find its own rate of exchange with every other currency. The adjustment mechanism would work constantly, reflecting continual inputs from every country concerning growth in the money supply, government budget deficits, trade balances, and similar data. The basic law of supply and demand would then control exchange rates. Instead of the large, infrequent, arbitrary lurches in rates that characterize today's system, there would be tiny daily changes based on the underlying economic facts.

Such a system would facilitate balanced trade, because if Japan, for example, began to run trade surpluses, the yen would rise in value, thereby increasing the competitiveness of other countries that are in deficit. Furthermore, each nation would be free to adopt its own domestic policies and still obtain its fair share of world trade. If France begins increasing its money supply by 20 per cent in order to "get its economy moving," and Germany is increasing its money supply by only 4 per cent, the franc would cheapen in relation to the mark. Germans will then be able to pay the higher prices prevailing in France's inflated domestic market, but there need be no change in the price structure of Germany. This is an important collateral benefit, because, under the present system, countries frequently are charged with "exporting" their inflation to other countries.

The proposal system should eliminate all restrictions on capital movements that have been designed to maintain a fixed rate of exchange, and these constitute a large percentage of such restrictions. The system will likewise discourage "hot money" flows by exposing the owners of such funds to an exchange risk that the present system virtually eliminates.

What is the source of opposition to flexible rates?

The central banks of other countries oppose them because the banks want to maintain their own rates even if that frustrates market forces. They do this either to obtain a trading advantage or out of fear that our economic power will overwhelm them if the dollar exchange rate is not maintained at a certain level. The first reason is contrary to the whole idea of balanced trade, and however valid the latter fear may have been in the past, it is certainly invalid today. Flexible rates would make it just as difficult for the United States to run continual surpluses as it would for all other countries.

Other authorities agree that a flexible system technically does have many advantages, but they still oppose its adoption on three grounds:

Competitive Devaluations

It is argued that under a flexible system, nations will rig their exchange rates to produce "dirty floats" for their own competitive advantage. Why are they so concerned about a dirty float when the real problem is the dirty fixed rates that the present system fosters? For years, Japan and Germany, for example, have maintained their currencies at dirty fixed levels—"dirty" in the sense that they have been undervalued in relation to other currencies and have been maintained at those artificial levels to provide a competitive advantage over the United States and other countries. Such tactics are perfectly legal under today's system, whereas under the proposed system a dirty float would be prohibited and subject to appropriate penalties. Incidentally, to maintain their dirty fixed rates, other countries have had to absorb huge quantities of dollars ($2.6 billion by Germany in one day), and it is ironic that they now complain about these "unwanted" dollars after they have enjoyed the high employment and growth rates that such tactics gained for them.

Speculative Pressures

There is concern that under a flexible rate system, speculators will be able to exert undue influence on exchange rates for their own benefit. Here again, it is hard to understand this fear, because speculators have a much greater advantage under a fixed-rate system than under a flexible rate system. Today a rate can be so far out of line with economic reality that the opportunity is obvious to all speculators. This permits them to act in concert to exploit such a situation with little or no risk to themselves. Under the proposed system, such a situation could not occur, and efforts to disrupt the market would carry the risk of substantial loss to the speculators.

Speculators will exist, of course, under any system. Under a flexible rate system they will perform the same useful service that speculators in any commodity perform by maintaining a continuous, orderly market for that commodity. With the threat of arbitrary government action removed, they should be willing to accept the risks necessary to establish an effective futures market in currencies.

Too Complex

It is charged that a system of flexible rates is too complex, that the task of maintaining so many rates is beyond our ability.

I thoroughly disagree. The marketplace has repeatedly demonstrated its ability to set the prices of hundreds of commodities, and it can certainly meet this challenge. I am certain that the sophisticated financial institutions of the world, assisted by computers and the worldwide information and communications network, can do the job well.

I have a very clear preference for rates set by the flexible system. As a businessman, I have confidence in the ability of my organization to understand and successfully operate under rates set by market forces. I have very limited confidence in our ability to predict what a government will do and when it will act. Flexible rates determined by the free market may not be perfect, but they would be better for business than those set by government action.

Events of the past sixty days have provided unexpectedly strong support for a system of flexible rates. First, they have gone far to dispel the myth that wide-scale floating would bring chaos. Second, they have raised serious doubts that governments can any longer maintain rates that the market does not believe are correct. In this sense, recent events may be saying that floating rates are the only sustainable system for the future.

52

SOME ESSENTIALS OF INTERNATIONAL MONETARY REFORM

The Chairman of the Federal Reserve Board gives his views on the state of international monetary arrangements, and describes how the present system should be reformed in several important ways if viable and practical relationships between the currencies of the nations of the world are to be preserved.

Arthur Burns

Arthur Burns is Chairman of the Board of Governors of the Federal Reserve System, and formerly Chairman of President Eisenhower's Council of Economic Advisers.

From the *Federal Reserve Bulletin*, June, 1972, pp. 546–549.

We all have to ponder this basic question: Given the constraints of past history, what evolution of the monetary system is desirable and at the same time practically attainable? For my part, I should like to take advantage of this gathering to consider some of the elements that one might reasonably expect to find in a reformed monetary system.

First of all, a reformed system will need to be characterized by a further strengthening of international consultation and cooperation among governments. Our national economies are linked by a complex web of international transactions. Problems and policies in one country inevitably affect other countries. This simple fact of interdependence gives rise to constraints on national policies. In a smoothly functioning system, no country can ignore the implications of its own actions for other countries or fail to cooperate in discussing and resolving problems of mutual concern. The task of statesmanship is to tap the great reservoir of international good will that now exists and to make sure that it remains undiminished in the future.

Sound domestic policies are a second requirement of a better world economic order. A well-constructed international mon-etary system should, it is true, be capable of absorbing the strains caused by occasional financial mismanagement in this or that country—such as are likely to follow from chronic budget deficits or from abnormally large and persistent additions to the money supply. But I doubt if any international monetary system can long survive if the major industrial countries fail to follow sound financial practices. In view of the huge size of the American economy, I recognize that the economic policies of the United States will remain an especially important influence on the operation of any international monetary system.

Third, in the calculable future any international monetary system will have to respect the need for substantial autonomy of domestic economic policies. A reformed monetary system cannot be one that encourages national authorities to sacrifice either the objective of high employment or the objective of price stability in order to achieve balance of payments equilibrium. More specifically, no country experiencing an external deficit should have to accept sizable increases in unemployment in order to reduce its deficit. Nor should a surplus country have to moderate its surplus by accepting high rates of inflation. Domestic policies of this type are poorly suited to the political mood of our times, and it would serve no good purpose to assume otherwise.

I come now to a fourth element that should characterize a reformed monetary system. If I am right in thinking that the world needs realistic and reasonably stable exchange rates, rather than rigid exchange rates, ways must be found to ensure that payments imbalances will be adjusted more smoothly and promptly than under the old Bretton Woods arrangements.

The issues here are many and complex. There was a consensus at the Smithsonian meeting that wider margins around parities can help to correct payments imbalances, and should prove especially helpful in moderating short-term capital movements—thereby giving monetary authorities somewhat more scope to pursue different interest rate policies. Our experience has not yet been extensive enough to permit a confident appraisal of this innovation. It is clear, however, that no matter how much the present wider margins may contribute to facilitating the adjustment of exchange rates to changing conditions, the wider margins by themselves will prove inadequate for that purpose.

We may all hope that at least the major countries will pursue sound, noninflationary policies in the future. We should nevertheless recognize that national lapses from economic virtue will continue to occur. In such circumstances, changes in parities—however regrettable—may well become a practical necessity. Moreover, even if every nation succeeds in achieving noninflationary growth, structural changes in consumption or production will often lead to shifts in national competitive positions over time. Such shifts will also modify the pattern of exchange rates that is appropriate for maintaining balance of payments equilibrium.

In my judgment, therefore, more prompt adjustments of parities will be needed in a reformed monetary system. Rules of international conduct will have to be devised that, while recognizing rights of sovereignty, establish definite guidelines and consultative machinery for determining when parities need to be changed. This subject is likely to become one of the central issues, and also one of the most difficult, in the forthcoming negotiations.

Let me turn to a fifth element that should characterize a reformed monetary system. A major weakness of the old system was its failure to treat in a symmetrical manner the responsibilities of surplus and deficit countries for balance of payments adjustment. With deficits equated to sin and surpluses to virtue, moral as well as financial pressures were very much greater on deficit countries to reduce their deficits than on surplus countries to reduce surpluses. In actual practice, however, responsibility for payments imbalances can seldom be assigned unambiguously to individual countries. And in any event, the adjustment process will work more efficiently if surplus countries participate actively in it. In my view, all countries have an obligation to eliminate payments imbalances, and the rules of international conduct to which I referred earlier will therefore need to define acceptable behavior and provide for international monitoring of both surplus and deficit countries.

Sixth, granted improvements in the promptness with which payments imbalances are adjusted, reserve assets and official borrowing will still be needed to finance in an orderly manner the imbalances that continue to arise. Looking to the long future, it will therefore be important to develop plans so that world reserves and official credit arrangements exist in an appropriate form and can be adjusted to appropriate levels.

This brings me to the seventh feature of a reformed international monetary system. It is sometimes argued that, as a part of reform, gold should be demonetized. As a practical matter, it seems doubtful to me that there is any broad support for eliminating the monetary role of gold in the near future. To many people, gold remains a great symbol of safety and security, and these attitudes about gold are not likely to change quickly. Nevertheless, I would expect the monetary role of gold to continue to diminish in the years ahead, while the role of Special Drawing Rights increases.

The considerations that motivated the International Monetary Fund to establish the SDR facility in 1969 should remain valid in a reformed system. However, revisions in the detailed arrangements governing the creation, allocation, and use of SDRs will probably be needed. In the future, as the SDRs assume increasing importance, they may ultimately become the major international reserve asset.

Next, as my eighth point, let me comment briefly on the future role of the dollar as a reserve currency. It has often been said that the United States had a privileged position in the old monetary system because it could settle payments deficits by adding to its liabilities instead of drawing down its reserve assets. Many also argue that this asymmetry should be excluded in a reformed system. There thus seems to be significant sentiment in favor of diminishing, or even phasing out, the role of the dollar as a reserve currency. One conceivable way of accomplishing this objective would be to place restraints on the further accumulation of dollars in official reserves. If no further accumulation at all were allowed, the United States would be required to finance any deficit in its balance of payments entirely with reserve assets.

I am not persuaded by this line of reasoning, for I see advantages both to the United States and to other countries from the use of the dollar as a reserve currency. But I recognize that there are some burdens or disadvantages as well. And, in any event, this is an important issue on which national views may well diverge in the early stages of the forthcoming negotiations.

I come now to a ninth point concerning a new monetary system, namely, the issue of convertibility of the dollar. It seems unlikely to me that the nations of the world, taken as a whole and over the long run, will accept a system in which convertibility of the dollar into international reserve assets—SDRs and gold—is entirely absent. If we want to build a strengthened monetary system along one-world lines, as I certainly do, this issue will have to be resolved. I therefore anticipate, as part of a total package of long-term reforms, that some form of dollar convertibility can be reestablished in the future.

I must note, however, that this issue of convertibility has received excessive emphasis in recent discussions. Convertibility is important, but no more so than the other issues on which I have touched. It is misleading, and may even prove mischievous, to stress one particular aspect of reform to the exclusion of others. Constructive negotiations will be possible only if there is a general disposition to treat the whole range of issues in balanced fashion.

We need to guard against compartmentalizing concern with any one of the issues, if only because the various elements of a new monetary system are bound to be interrelated. There is a particularly important interdependence, for example, between improvements in the exchange-rate regime and restoration of some form of convertibility of the dollar into gold or other reserve assets. Without some assurance that exchange rates of both deficit and surplus countries will be altered over time so as to prevent international transactions from moving into serious imbalance, I would deem it impractical to attempt to restore convertibility of the dollar.

My tenth and last point involves the linkage between monetary and trading arrangements. We cannot afford to overlook the fact that trade practices are a major factor in determining the balance of payments position of individual nations. There is now a strong feeling in the United States that restrictive commercial policies of some countries have affected adversely the markets of American business firms. In my judgment, therefore, the chances of success of the forthcoming monetary conversations will be greatly enhanced if parallel conversations get under way on trade problems, and if those conversations take realistic account of the current and prospective foreign trade position of the United States.

In the course of my remarks this morning I have touched on some of the more essential conditions and problems of international monetary reform. Let me conclude by restating the elements I would expect to find in a new monetary system that meet the test of both practicality and viability:

First, a significant further strengthening of the processes of international consultation and cooperation;

Second, responsible domestic policies in all the major industrial countries;

Third, a substantial degree of autonomy for domestic policies, so that no country would feel compelled to sacrifice high employment or price stability in order to achieve balance of payments equilibrium;

Fourth, more prompt adjustments of payments imbalances, to be facilitated by definite guidelines and consultative machinery for determining when parities need to be changed;

Fifth, a symmetrical division of responsibilities among surplus and deficit countries for initiating and implementing adjustments of payments imbalances;

Sixth, systematic long-range plans for the evolution of world reserves and official credit arrangements;

Seventh, a continued but diminishing role for gold as a reserve asset, with a corresponding increase in the importance of SDRs;

Eighth, a better international consensus than exists at present about the proper role of reserve currencies in the new system;

Ninth, reestablishment of some form of dollar convertibility in the future;

And finally, tenth, a significant lessening of restrictive trading practices as the result of negotiations complementing the negotiations on monetary reform.

I firmly believe that a new and stronger international monetary system can and must be built. Indeed, I feel it is an urgent necessity to start the rebuilding process quite promptly. It is not pleasant to contemplate the kind of world that may evolve if cooperative efforts to rebuild the monetary system are long postponed. We might then find the world economy divided into restrictive and inward-looking blocs, with rules of international conduct concerning exchange rates and monetary reserves altogether absent.

As we learned last fall, a world of financial manipulations, economic restrictions, and political frictions bears no promise for the future. It is the responsibility of financial leaders to make sure that such a world will never come to pass.

ECONOMIC GROWTH

PART SEVEN

53

Should the nation have an "economic growth" goal, along with its other big economic objectives? Professor Tobin says yes and supports his answer with several arguments. Dr. Stein has serious doubts and sharpens some of the issues we face on this score.

ECONOMIC GROWTH AS AN OBJECTIVE OF GOVERNMENT POLICY

James Tobin and Herbert Stein

James Tobin is Sterling Professor of Economics at Yale University and a former member of the Council of Economic Advisers. Herbert Stein is a member of President Nixon's Council of Economic Advisers.

From "Economic Growth as an Objective of Government Policy," by James Tobin and "Comment," by Herbert Stein, *American Economic Review* (May 1964), pp. 4–8, 10–15. Reprinted by permission.

In recent years economic growth has come to occupy an exalted position in the hierarchy of goals of government policy, both in the United States and abroad, both in advanced and in less developed countries, both in centrally controlled and decentralized economies. National governments proclaim target growth rates for such diverse economies as the Soviet Union, Yugoslavia, India, Sweden, France, Japan—and even for the United Kingdom and the United States, where the targets indicate dissatisfaction with past performance. Growth is an international goal, too. The Organization for Economic Cooperation and Development aims at a 50 per cent increase in the collective gross output of the Atlantic Community over the current decade.

Growth has become a good word. And the better a word becomes, the more it is invoked to bless a variety of causes and the more it loses specific meaning. At least in professional economic discussion, we need to give a definite and distinctive meaning to growth as a policy objective. Let it be neither a new synonym for good things in general nor a fashionable way to describe other economic objectives. Let growth be something it is possible to oppose as well as to favor, depending on judgments of social priorities and opportunities.

I

In essence the question of growth is nothing new, but a new disguise for an age-old issue, one which has always intrigued and preoccupied economists: the present versus the future. How should society divide its resources between current needs and pleasures and those of next year, next decade, next generation?

The choice can be formalized in a way that makes clear what is essentially at stake. A consumption path or program for an economy describes its rate of consumption at every time point beginning now and extending indefinitely into the future. Not all imaginable consumption paths are feasible. At any moment future possibilities are limited by our inherited stocks of productive resources and technological knowledge and by our prospects for autonomous future increase in these stocks. Of feasible paths, some dominate others; i.e., path A dominates B if consumption along path A exceeds consumption along path B at every point of time. I hope I will incur no one's wrath by asserting that in almost everyone's value scheme more is better than less (or certainly not worse), at least if we are careful to specify more or less of what. If this assertion is accepted, the interesting

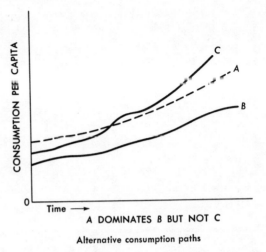

A DOMINATES B BUT NOT C

Alternative consumption paths

choices are between undominated or efficient feasible paths; e.g., between a pair A and C where A promises more consumption at some points in time but less at others. See the figure. In particular, I take growthmanship to be advocacy of paths that promise more consumption later in return for less earlier.

. . .

1. Growth Versus Full Employment

To accelerate growth is not the same thing as to increase the utilization of existing resources, manpower, and capital capacity. In the formulation sketched above, a consumption path with underutilization is dominated or inefficient. By putting the idle resources to work, consumption can be increased both now and in the future. The same is true of other measures to improve the efficiency of allocation of resources. We can all agree, I presume, on the desirability of growth measures free of any cost. If that is the meaning of growth policy, there is no issue.

For short periods of time, stepping up the utilization of capacity can increase the recorded rate of growth of output and consumption. But over the decades fluctuations in the utilization of capacity will have a minor influence compared to the growth of capacity itself. To express the same point somewhat differently, the subject of economic growth refers mainly to supply, or capacity to produce, rather than to demand. In the short run, accelerating the growth of demand for goods and services can, by increasing the rate of utilization of capacity, speed the growth of output. But in the long run, output and real demand cannot grow faster than capacity. If monetary demand is made to set a faster pace, it will be frustrated by a rate of inflation that cuts real demand down to size.

Public policy affecting aggregate demand should be aimed at maintaining a desired rate of utilization and capacity. Economists and other citizens will differ on how high this rate should be, because they differ in the weights they attach to additional employment and output, on the one hand, and to the risks of faster price inflation, on the other. But however this balance is struck, monetary and fiscal policies can in principle hit the target utilization rate just as well whether the economy's capacity is growing at five per cent or three per cent or zero per cent.

Full employment is, therefore, not a reason for faster economic growth; each is an objective in its own right. In an economy suffering from low rates of utilization of manpower and capital resources, accelerating the growth of aggregate demand may well be the need of the hour. But this ought not be considered growth policy in the more fundamental sense. Tax reduction today has sufficient justification as a means of expanding demand and raising the rate of utilization. It is probably an unfortunate confusion to bill it as a growth measure, too.

I do not mean, of course, that the rate of growth of the economy's capacity is in practice wholly independent of its rate of utilization. In principle they may be independent. Demand can be expanded in ways that do not accelerate, indeed may even retard, the growth in capacity itself. But as a rule some of the output resulting from an increase in utilization will be used in ways that expand future capacity. Thus the Great Depression deprived the nation and the world of investment as well as consumption; we, as well as our fathers, bear the cost. The proposed tax reduction, even though its major impact is to stimulate consumption, will nonetheless increase the share of national capacity devoted to capital accumulation. It is in this sense that it can be called a growth measure. But there may be ways to expand demand and utilization to the same degree while at the same time providing both more stimulus for and more economic room for capacity-building uses of resources now idle.

2. Noneconomic Reasons for Growth

Economic growth may be a national objective for noneconomic reasons, for national prestige or national strength or national purpose.

No doubt much of the recent dissatisfaction with U.S. growth is motivated by unfavorable comparisons with other countries, especially the Soviet Union. If current rates are mechanically extrapolated, it is easy to calculate that the U.S. will not be first in the international statistical comparisons in our great-grandchildren's textbooks. Presumably the American nation could somehow stand and even rationalize this blow to our national pride, even as we survive quadrennial defeats by Russian hordes in the Olympics. At any rate, it is not for professional economists to advise the country to act differently just to win a race in statistical yearbooks. The cold war will not be so easily won, or lost, or ended.

International competition in growth may, however, be of importance in the battle for prestige and allegiance among the "uncommitted" and less developed countries. These nations place a high premium on rapid economic progress. They will not—so the argument runs—choose the democratic way in preference to communism, or market economies in preference to centrally directed economies, unless our institutions show by example that they can outperform rival systems. A political psychologist rather than an economist should evaluate this claim. But it has several apparent weaknesses: (a) Rate of growth is not the only dimension of economic performance by which our society will be judged by outside observers. Equality of opportunity and of condition, humanity, understanding, and generosity in relation to less privileged people in our own society and abroad—these are perhaps more important dimensions. (b) The U.S. is not the only noncommunist economy. The examples of Western Europe (in particular the contrast of Western to Eastern Germany) and Japan are more relevant to the rest of the world, and they give convincing evidence of the economic vitality of free societies. (c) What is much more important is a demonstration that an underdeveloped country can progress rapidly under democratic auspices. Without this kind of demonstration, faster growth of affluence in already affluent societies may cause more disaffection than admiration.

On the score of national strength, there is a case for growth. But it is more subtle than the facile association of military power with generalized civilian economic capacity. Nuclear technology has made this connection looser than ever. A country is not necessarily stronger than another just because it has a higher GNP. Great productive capacity may have been the decisive reserve of military strength in the last two World Wars, but nowadays it is useless if it remains unmobilized until the cataclysmic buttons are pushed. A country with smaller GNP can be as strong or even stronger if it persistently allocates enough of its GNP to military purposes. And in the age of over-kill, apparently there can be a point of saturation.

Should we grow faster to be better prepared to meet possible future needs for output for military purposes—or for other uses connected with national foreign policy? If we do not, we will have to meet such needs when they arise by depriving other claimants on national production, principally consumption, at the time. But in order to grow faster, we have to deprive these claimants now. Hence the national power argument seems to boil down to the economist's calculation after all; i.e., to the terms of trade between current and future consumption.

But there is an important exception. Some hazards are great enough to bias our choice to favor the future over the present, to accept less favorable payoffs than we otherwise would. We might conceivably be challenged one day to a duel of overriding priority, involving all-out commitment of resources to military uses, foreign aid, space adventures, or all of these together. A high GNP might be the difference between victory and defeat rather than the difference between more or less consumption. In other words, this contingency is one that could be met only by sacrifices of consumption in advance, not by sacrifices at the time.

As for national purpose, it is surely conceivable that a growth target could inspire, galvanize, and unite the nation. But is not the only objective that could serve this purpose, nor is it necessarily the best candidate.

3. Growth in What?

The formulation of the growth issue sketched above presents it as a choice among available consumption paths. The concentration on consumption deserves some elaboration and explanation—especially because growth performance and aspiration are popularly expressed in terms of gross or net national product.

Some of the noneconomic reasons for favoring faster growth also suggest that GNP is the relevant measure, especially if it is the most usual and visible measure. But as economists we would make welfare or utility depend on consumption. We would require the investment part of GNP to derive its value from the future consumption it supports. After all, a future in which the rate of growth of GNP reaches fantastic heights has no appeal if the fruits of the achievement are never consumed. We must heed the "golden rule" of capital accumulation: there is a saving ratio and a corresponding capital intensity that maximize consumption. Persistent saving in excess of the rule makes GNP higher but consumption lower.

Neither GNP nor consumption, as ordinarily measured, counts leisure. Yet I do not understand advocates of faster growth to be taking a stand in favor of goods and services priced in the market and against leisure. Should the trend toward shorter hours, longer vacations, and earlier retirements accelerate, the rate of growth of consumption as measured in the national accounts might decline. But a decline for this reason should not bother a growth-oriented economist. The *Affluent Society* to the contrary notwithstanding, the conventional wisdom of economics was long since liberated from the fallacy that only produced goods and services yield utility and welfare. Economists do have prejudices against biasing the price system in favor of leisure and against forcing the leisure of involuntary unemployment on anyone. But those are other matters. The consumption whose growth path concerns us should include leisure valued at the real wage. Needless to say, it should also allow for consumption goods and services provided by government.

Finally, is the relevant measure aggregate consumption or consumption per capita? Later in the lecture I shall be concerned with social indifference curves between consumption at one date and at a later date. . . . What measure of consumption should the axes of such a diagram represent? The answer depends on questions like the following: Do we discharge our obligation to the next generation if we enable them to enjoy the same aggregate consumption even though there will be more of them to share it? Should we, on the other hand, sacrifice today in order to raise per capita consumption half a century from now just because there will then be more consumers? Or should generations count in some sense equally regardless of size?

These are not easy questions for the social philosopher, but revealed social preferences lean towards per capita consumption. Presumably we do not value increase in population for its own sake. We might if sheer numbers were important for national power. But in general we are content to leave population trends to free choice; indeed, we seek to enlarge parents' ability to limit births at their discretion. Neither immigration nor subsidies for child-bearing are advanced as growth proposals. In the world at large, certainly, the commonly accepted aim is to retard the growth of population, not to accelerate it.

. . .

II

In this section I propose to argue: (1) that government might legitimately have a growth policy, and indeed could scarcely avoid having one, even if private capital markets were perfect; (2) that capital markets are far from perfect and that private saving decisions are therefore based on an overconservative estimate of the social return to saving; and (3) that the terms on which even so advanced an economy as our own can trade present for future consumption seem to be very attractive.

1. Government Neutrality In Intertemporal Choice

Many economists and many other citizens will argue that the government should be neutral as between present and future. In their view the capital markets produce an optimal result, balancing the time preferences of individuals, freely expressed through their consumption and saving behavior, against the technological opportunities for substituting consumption tomorrow for consumption today. Let us assume for the moment that government can be neutral in some meaningful sense and that the capital markets perform their assigned function. Even so, I believe government should have a growth policy, and only by accident a neutral one.

I fail to see why economists should advise the public that it is wrong for them collectively to supplement (or diminish) the provisions for the future they are making individually. I agree to the desirability of satisfying human preferences—that is what our kind of society and economy is all about. But I have never been able to understand why the preferences of individuals are worthy of respect only when they are expressed in the market, why the preferences of the very same individuals expressed politically should be regarded as distortions. Sometimes economists come close to rationalizing all market results and private institutions by the argument that they would not occur and survive if they were not optimally satisfying individuals' preferences. But political results and public institutions are not granted the benefit of presumptive justification-through-existence.

In both arenas preferences certainly need to be guided by full and accurate information. In the arena of government policy, it is the business of economists to help the society know what it is doing, to understand the choices, benefits, costs, and risks it confronts, not simply to repeat *ad nauseam* that the best thing to do is nothing.

The case for explicit government policy in intertemporal social choice is especially strong. More than any other social institution, government represents the permanence and continuity of the society. And in a democracy one way in which each generation uses government is to protect the interests of unborn generations against its own shortsighted and selfish instincts.

We cannot be sure that lineal family ties will give individuals sufficient motivation to provide for society's future. Suppose the individuals of a whole generation, deciding that their children and grandchildren might better start from scratch, were to proceed to consume their capital. Good capital markets might reflect this epidemic of acute time preference in a perfectly Pareto-optimal way. But would we as a nation feel that we were collectively discharging our obligations to our successors?

Through many activities of government, including conservation and public education, we have recognized a generalized obligation to equip the next generation—an obligation wholly distinct from our individual provisions for our own children. This generalized obligation acquires special force if we take seriously our ideals of equality of opportunity. We like to think that our society gives the members of each generation an equal chance in the race, or at least that their chances are not predetermined by family backgrounds. Besides requiring investment in human beings on a basis other than ability to pay, this ideal suggests redistributive taxation of estates. And if estate taxation dulls incentives to save for specific heirs, the government needs to replenish saving collectively.

But what is growth-neutral government finance anyway? I have already dismissed as farfetched one answer; namely, that any government finance is growth neutral when it is fully and accurately foreseen, and accordingly offset, by taxpayers and by the beneficiaries of government services. Often a balanced budget is considered a growth-neutral fiscal policy. The budget in this rule is not, of course, the conventional U.S. administrative budget. Rather the rule suggests that (a) net government investment should be covered by borrowing, with the Treasury competing in the capital markets with private investors for private saving, and that (b) other government expenditure, including allowance for consumption of public capital, should be covered by current taxes or fees.

The rule is clear cut and has intuitive appeal. But it seems to bias social choice against the future when there is simply a shift in public preference from private consumption, present and future, to collective consumption, present and future. The rule would levy only enough new taxes to cover the additional collective consumption. But the evidence is that taxpayers would pay some of these new taxes from saving (especially if the collective consumption the taxes finance were of regrettable necessities like national defense rather than of services that clearly yield utility now and in the future). Interest rates would rise and investment would be curtailed, even though no shift in social time preference has occurred. Clearly the 10 per cent of GNP which the cold war has forced us to devote persistently to national defense has not come wholly from private or public consumption. True neutrality evidently would require a tighter fiscal policy the bigger the government's budget for current consumption.

But in any case, the quest for neutrality is probably a search for a will-of-the-wisp.

For it is not only the overall budget position of government but also the specifics of taxation and expenditure which affect intertemporal choices. We have not yet learned how to implement the welfare economist's lump-sum taxes. I have already given one example of a tax which is desirable in view of other social objectives but is bound to affect incentives for private accumulation of wealth. It will suffice to remind you also that our methods of taxation necessarily favor one kind of current consumption, leisure, both as against other current consumption and as against future consumption of products and leisure.

The major policy proposals of growthmen boil down to the suggestion that government should save—or save more—by making investments on its own account, subsidizing the investments of others, or by channeling tax money through the capital markets into private investment. This last item is the major purpose of the full employment budget surplus for which Councils of Economic Advisers longed under both Presidents Eisenhower and Kennedy.

It is now widely recognized that in principle the government can match aggregate demand to the economy's capacity in a variety of ways. Its various instruments for regulating or stabilizing demand affect consumption and investment differently. A strong pro-growth policy would restrict consumption by taxation or by economy in government's current expenditure while stepping up public investment and encouraging private investment through tax incentives or low interest rates and high liquidity. The government cannot avoid choosing some combination of its demand-regulating instruments. Therefore government is bound to affect the composition of current output and society's provision for the future. Let us debate this choice of policy mixtures on its merits, weighing growth against its costs and against other objectives of policy, without encumbering the debate with a search for that combination which meets some elusive criterion of neutrality.

2. Imperfections in Private Capital Markets

I turn now to the second subject: the efficiency of the capital markets. Do private saving decisions reflect the real payoffs which nature and technology offer the economy? There are several reasons to believe that the answer is negative.

Monopoly and Restrictions of Entry. The evidence is that the rates of return required of real investment projects by U.S. business corporations are very high—typically more than 10 per cent after allowance for depreciation, obsolescence, and taxes. Rates of this magnitude are not only required *ex ante* but realized *ex post*. Why do these rates so greatly exceed the cost of borrowed funds, the earnings-to-price ratio of equity issues, and in general the rates of return available to savers?

One reason clearly is that the relevant markets are not purely competitive. A monopolistic or oligopolistic firm limits its expansion in product markets, its purchases in factor markets, and its calls on capital markets, because the firm takes into account that prices and rates in these markets will turn against it. The managers seek to maintain a market valuation of the firm in excess of the replacement cost of its assets, the difference representing the capitalized value of its monopoly power, often euphemistically called good will. Restrictions and costs of entry prevent other firms from competing this difference away. Foresighted and lucky investors receive the increases in the firm's market value in the form of capital gains. But the willingness of savers to value the assets of the firm above their cost, i.e., to supply capital at a lower rate of return than the firm earns internally, is not

translated into investment either by this firm or by others. One effect is to depress rates of return in more competitive sectors of the economy. But another result is to restrict total saving and investment.

Risks, Private and Social. Risks provide a second reason for the observed divergence between the rates of return satisfactory to savers and those typically required of real investment projects. Some of these are risks to the economy as well as to the owners of the business: technological hazards, uncertainties about consumer acceptance of new products, or uncertainties about the future availability and social opportunity cost of needed factors of production. Even though these are social as well as private risks, it is not clear that society should take a risk-averse position towards them and charge a risk premium against those projects entailing more uncertainties than others. Presumably society can pool such risks and realize with a very small margin of uncertainty the actuarial return on investments.

Moreover, some of the private risks are not social risks at all. Consider, for example, uncertainties about competition and market shares; if several rivals are introducing a new process or new product, the main uncertainties in the investment calculation of each are the future actions of the others. Consider, further, the high and sometimes prohibitive cost which many firms impute to external funds—apparently as insurance against loss of control to new shareowners, or, with extremely bad luck, to bondholders. If savers were offered the rates of return asked of and earned by business investments, in the form of assets that impose no more risk on the holder than is commensurate to the social risks involved, presumably they would choose to save more.

It is true, on the other hand, that some net saving is now motivated by personal contingencies that are likewise social risks of a much smaller order. But our society has created insuring institutions, both private and public, to reduce the need for oversaving to meet such contingencies. Except in the field of residential construction, it has created few similar institutions to prevent private risk-aversion from leading to underinvestment.

External Returns to Investment. Some investments yield benefits which cannot be captured by the individual or firm making the initial outlay. Research and development expenditures and outlays for training of personnel are obvious cases in point. Government policy has already recognized this fact both in tax law and in government expenditures, and it is difficult to judge whether this recognition is sufficient. Kenneth Arrow has pointed out that not only R and D but all forms of investment activity share in some degree the property that B may learn from A's doing. The support which this observation gives to a general policy of encouraging investment is somewhat tempered by reflecting that the same social process of "learning by doing" can occur in production of goods and services for current consumption. However, experience is most important as a teacher in new situations, and innovations are likely to require investment.

In regard to investment in human capacities and talents, it is by no means clear that public outlays are yet sufficient to reap the external benefits involved, or even that the relevant capital markets are sufficiently developed to permit individuals to earn the private benefits. I recognize that calculations of the rate of return to educational outlays depend critically on how much of these outlays are charged to current consumption. As an educator and ex-student I am inclined to rate high the immediate utility-producing powers of education.

3. The Payoff to Social Saving

The burden of my remarks so far is that we cannote escape considering growth or, more precisely, intertemporal choice as an issue of public economic policy. We cannot assume, either, that the market settles the issue optimally or that government can be guided by some simple rules of neutrality. We—and there I mean the economics profession and the country and not the three of us speaking tonight—must confront head-on the question whether the social payoff of faster growth in higher future consumption validates its cost in consumption foregone today. The issue that needs to be joined is typified by the contrast between Denison, who estimates a very high investment requirement for a one point increase in the medium-term growth rate (a ten point increase in the ratio of current gross investment to GNP) and Solow, who calculates a marginal investment requirement only about one-fifth as high.

Fortunately the profession has now begun the task of computing rates of return on various kinds of investment, tangible and intangible. Thanks to theoretical advances in growth models and in handling the knotty problems of technological progress, vintage capital, and obsolescence, we have a better conceptual foundation for these tasks than we did only a few years ago. Phelps, using the same conceptual approach as Solow, has estimated the overall rate of return on tangible investment in the U.S. to be about 14 per cent in 1954. And even this figure seems conservative in relation to some target rates of return of large industrial corporations reported by Lanzillotti.

. . .

COMMENT—BY HERBERT STEIN

First, we are not impartial between generations. The next generation is our children and we are a child-oriented society. There is an old story about the immigrant who never in his life got to eat the white meat of chicken. When he was a child in the old country the parents got the white meat and when he became a parent in America the children got the white meat. We may all value white meat tomorrow less than white meat today, but some us value white meat for our children more than white meat for ourselves.

Second, I suspect, though I have taken no census, that people in general tend to underestimate the rate at which incomes will rise through time and therefore overestimate the need for saving.

Third, people save for protection against private risks which would not require saving by the society as a whole.

Fourth, apparently a large sector of the population is driven by what a colleague of Professor Tobin has called "the Puritan ethic," which embodies a strong compulsion to save.

However, let us assume that we have discovered that we are saving too little. Let us assume further that we have persuaded everyone to accept the moral imperative: take what thou hast and give to the rich, that is to the future, so that they may be richer still. I shall not stop to ask what arguments could be used to persuade someone who did not find this idea spontaneously appealing. I would like to ask how the government gets into this picture, since Professor Tobin's paper is about growth as an objective of government policy.

Why should individuals require the help of government in order to carry out temporally impartial savings decisions if that is what individuals want to do? Ample savings media exist without further action by government. The effectiveness of one individual's saving does not depend on whether other people are also saving. There is no critical mass that the savings must reach. It is not necessary that everyone should save in some particular way, which has to be specified by a central authority.

I suppose that government enters the picture if an effective majority of the population desires to save at the socially appropriate rate but some significant minority does not. Then government becomes the instrument by which the majority forces the minority to save more than it wishes. I do not think we can brand this as illegitimate a priori. Government is an instrument of force, and we use it properly for many important purposes. But the use of force deprives some people of some part of their freedom. This is a cost and it should be minimized, or not incurred except for highly important gains. If we take the position that every departure from any optimum calls for government action, that not a sparrow falleth without becoming a concern of government, I fear we shall have more government than we can manage and less freedom than we would like.

In a special way, Professor Tobin's paper recognizes this. I refer to his few comments on population policy. If we are concerned, as Professor Tobin suggests we should be, with the growth of per capita incomes, it would seem natural that we should be concerned with the growth of population. But he accepts the fact that we do not have, and should not have, a government population policy. I think this is because he recognizes that the private freedom involved here is too important to be impaired for the sake of optimizing the rate of growth of per capita consumption.

Does not the same kind of question arise, even though on a different emotional scale, with respect to individuals' freedom to use their own incomes? Don't we have to ask not only whether saving and investment are below the social optimum but also whether the deficiency is so great and the consequence so serious as to justify government action?

This leads me to Professor Tobin's discussion of government neutrality towards growth. He demonstrates convincingly that government cannot be neutral with respect to growth, but inevitably affects growth in a variety of ways. If I have used the word "neutral" in this connection in the past, I recant. I would offer as a substitute for the word "neutral" the word "indifferent." Surely the government can be indifferent about economic growth. We would not expect the government to have a policy about every consequence of its actions. The pattern of government expenditures affects the distribution of the population among states and localities. But this does not require the government to have a policy about the regional distribution of the population, and we do not, except in extreme cases where there is distress. Something does not become an objective of government policy simply by being a consequence of government policy.

I do not want to run the notion of indifference into the ground. I only offer it as a feasible alternative to growth policy—more feasible than neutrality. There may be cases in which government action impairs growth and serves no other useful purpose. Such cases would call for correction. But we would expect these cases to be few and quantitatively unimportant. The big government actions that affect growth also have other objectives and effects. The import of a policy of indifference is that these actions should be determined by consideration of objectives other than speeding up growth—primarily and in general.

In the end, as Professor Tobin said at the beginning, the question is whether more growth is worth its cost. He has computed the cost in terms of present consumption foregone, compared it with the discounted value of the future consumption gained, and concluded that there would be a net gain. Whether such a computation can be done with any objectivity, especially in view of the difference in income levels between present and future generations is doubtful. Whether, however it is done, the result would come out in the direction indicated, is at least uncertain. But if I remain skeptical, it is not primarily for these reasons. It is primarily because of the costs not included in this calculation. These are the costs of the measures that government may have to take in order to make us save substantially more. Among these possible costs are reduction in our freedom to dispose of our own incomes, growth in the role of government as investor, impairment of the equity of the tax system, reduction of important government expenditures that do not qualify as investment, and diversion of the limited problem-solving capacities of government from other critical issues. These are the risks that make me hesitate to raise the further enrichment of our grandchildren into the top ranks of government policy objectives.

If any grandchildren of mine should ever read these words, I hope they will not think that I disregard their interests. I expect that they will be richer than we are, and hope that they will be even richer than I expect them to be. But to make them richer still is not, in my opinion, among the most valuable things we can do for them. It is much more important to pass on to them a world of reasonable security, in which they have substantial freedom to manage their own affairs and dispose of their own incomes, in which the relatively poor among them are relatively less poor, and in which the Indians and Guatemalans and Ghanaians are much less poor relative to the Americans. If we can do this, our grandchildren will have no cause to think bad of us. Perhaps we can achieve this and still accelerate future growth. But our energies and intelligence, our capacities for leadership and followership, our ability to govern ourselves, our stock of objectivity and altruism are all limited—more limited than our national income. I fear that if we set ourselves too many high-priority goals we shall achieve none of them. The best is the enemy of the good. May we not have to forego the effort to achieve the best of all possible worlds in order to increase the chance of achieving the merely good?

54

FISCAL AND FINANCIAL POLICIES FOR GROWTH

Paul A. Samuelson

This presentation of monetary and fiscal policies that could be used to promote faster growth, without regard to political feasibility or the impact of these policies on other aspects of the economy, should help you evaluate the wide range of growth policy alternatives in terms of your own objectives.

Paul A. Samuelson is Professor of Economics at Massachusetts Institute of Technology.

From the *Proceedings of a Symposium on Economic Growth,* sponsored by the American Bankers Association (February 25, 1963), pp. 89–100. Reprinted by permission.

. . .

Before presenting the following list, I want to make clear its essential nature. It is a list of programs that can have important bearings on economic growth. It is a fairly comprehensive list. But it most definitely is not the list of measures that I personally would favor for the United States. It is not even a list of measures that I personally would favor if there were no political feasibility constraints upon American policy.

An example may make this clear. In the following list, I mention the possibility of replacing graduated income taxes by indirect taxes, such as federal excises or value-added taxes. This is not politically feasible, in my amateur's view. But even if it were politically feasible, I personally would be opposed to such a move: it would offend against my sense of "equity"; its desired effects could be achieved by other programs that are less objectionable and even if this were not so, I might as a personal value judgment feel that this deliberate fostering of inequality represented too stiff a price to pay for some extra growth. Nevertheless, I have put this item on the agenda for discussion because it is a policy with a bearing on growth. Similarly, I mention in the list the problem of a changed external value of the dollar. I do not do this because I favor such a move or consider it at all politically feasible; I include this subject on the agenda because it is a topic that some economists think is relevant to the problem of growth.

I do not know how to make clear enough that this is in the real sense of the term an "academic" roundup of all the topics related to our subject here today.

GOVERNMENT EXPENDITURE POLICY FOR GROWTH

1. Expenditure on useful public assets that are *durable* is more conducive to growth than expenditure on current public items.

2. Government expenditure, directly or by subsidy, to basic and applied *science* and to *research and development* is an important growth policy. (Why shouldn't private enterprise carry this ball? It does in part; but since no private firm can hope to keep to itself the social fruits of its innovational work, there is a prima-facie case for public expenditure and subsidy. While improvements in knowledge are an unmixed blessing, the effect of rapid innovation *can* be to lower profits and to intensify the problem of sluggish investment; or it *can* stimulate profits and investment, depending upon its qualitative character.)

3. Public expenditure on *education* and *training* programs can contribute much to growth. Human capital has a profit yield like that of material capital, but our market system does not carry human investment to an optimal point. (I personally believe that much of education ought to be defended on other grounds than growth, and suspect that many current economists have gone overboard in reckoning the social yield on educational investment in humans. But, like all professors, I am for more and better education on its own current merits.)

4. Public expenditure on *health research and care,* by the Federal Government or by its subsidies to states and localities, can contribute to growth. (I personally think this effect may be overrated and that these should stand and fall largely on their great human welfare merits in the here and now.)

5. Public expenditure on various forms of *social overhead capital,* including conservation and perhaps some cautious experiments with "indicative planning" of the French type, are policies conducive to growth.

6. Public expenditure to *reduce risk of private investments,* by insurance, subsidy or bail-out devices, or by joint participation or direct Government ownership and operation represents contributions to growth that are not quite the same thing as the ordinary notion of Government capital formation. Provided the good effects are not offset by harmful effects (psychological and/or real), these could be further devices for accelerating growth. Also, many public expenditure programs have directly favorable effects on private production and should be expanded in a balanced program for growth.

All the above public expenditure programs were designed to increase the rate at which America's full-employment potential national product can be made to grow. The next point has relevance to the problem of helping achieve growth by contriving to reduce underemployment and cut into the gap between actual and potential production.

7. *Any public expenditure on goods and services,* if not offset by more-than-equivalent new taxes and if it impinges on an underemployed economy which, for balance-of-payments or other reasons, cannot be brought to full employment by expansionary monetary policy, will cause real GNP to grow; aside from the first-round creation of useful public product, there will be the induced further rounds of private product (consumption and investment). In all candor, if one takes very seriously the international constraint and the ideological constraint against large deficits, then the Administration's avoidance of expanding civilian Government expenditures cannot be defended as economically mandatory.

8. Expansion of *welfare transfer expenditure,* not offset by taxation, would also have the above effects. But there is no presumption that this can be done with less need to create a sizable deficit.

TAX POLICIES FOR GROWTH

9. Obviously, tax policies designed to spur *research* are desirable. We have al-

ready legislated loopholes in our tax law to encourage patents, and the 1963 tax bill will further liberalize the right to expand research expenditures. There is really not much more that taxation can do in this important field.

10. Allowing *faster depreciation* for tax purposes can stimulate capital formation and growth. The 1954 legislative change and the 1963 guidelines are important here. Policies, like those in Germany, Sweden and other nations, in which a large fraction of the value of an asset can be written off in the first and second year, *cannot* be justified as a return to fair recognition of true economic depreciation (inclusive of obsolescence) needed to measure true *money income;* let us face it, they are deliberate bribes to coax out faster growth. (Note that faster depreciation of an item merely puts off the day of taxes: it is an interest-free, equity type loan from government to business, and if business is already liquid, its effect can be weak.)

11. *The tax investment credit,* proposed by Kennedy and Dillon and so spurned by business, is a genuine give-away designed to coax out investment. The ante on this could be raised.

12. *Permitting assets to be depreciated on a base that is inflated along with the price level* would represent a change from the present system that taxes money income toward a new system that taxes *real* income. This ought to shift the balance away from hoarding money toward investing in things—just as our present LIFO methods for treatment of inventory represent a give-away from the standpoint of correct taxation of *money* income.

13. *Lenient treatment and definition of what is called "capital gain"* rather than ordinary income ought to encourage "venturesome" investment. Indeed, raising ordinary tax rates and lowering "capital-gains rates" should be very stimulating to invest-

ment and capital formation as well as to wheeler-dealer speculation. Loopholes can be bribes to coax out investment, albeit they can also distort resource use.

14. Improving devices for "tax averaging," through generous carrybacks and carryforwards and other income-spreading devices, should remove the most important penalties against risk taking in our tax system. This gets the least attention in popular discussions of the present day, but it is economically about the most important policy for growth and equity. If the 1963 Kennedy-Dillon spreading reforms are enacted, our tax structure will be fairly optimal in this vital respect.

15. Changing from a graduated system of income taxation to a *graduated system of consumption and wealth taxation,* if it were politically and administratively feasible, would perhaps be the single most important policy to achieve growth without sacrifice of "equity." The penalty on investing for the future would then be removed, and the fruits of windfall gains would get taxed when spent or held.

16. It is popularly believed that our *high marginal rates of taxation on upper incomes* are the most important obstacle to dynamic investment and growth and reducing them is crucial. Careful study of the effects upon personal effort and on risk taking show this popular notion to be much exaggerated, and even to be possibly the reverse of the truth. The present system practically drives a rich man into venturesome investment, so as to convert ordinary income into what are treated as capital gains. I favor the Kennedy-Dillon 1963 tax package in which high marginal rates are brought down from a 91 to a 65 per cent top. But I do so primarily because the present system, in which people are subject to high rates which they can avoid by taking advantage of loopholes, is both unaesthetic and distorting. It is not because I

expect it immediately to give our system a strong fillip toward growth and capital formation.

17. *A reduction in the corporate tax rate* might be stimulating to investment and growth.[1] Corporations early in 1963 look to be rather unusually liquid, so the actual increase in the funds left with them perhaps cannot be expected to be as stimulating to investment as in more normal times. There are some economists who think that excess capacity implies a marginal profitability to further investment of practically zero, so that it would be much more potent to engineer an increase in output toward capacity than to try to induce an increase in the ratio of capital to existing output. I am not of this school, but I must admit that events of the last few years have not strengthened my case. This group believes that stimulating current investment, so that you engineer a spurt like that of 1956–57, will merely mean excess capacity in subsequent years and you will pay in sluggishness then for anything you contrive now. (A shrewd Wall Street analyst told me he disliked the fast depreciation of the 1954 tax code because he thought it had led to the 1956–57 overinvestment which was eroding profits; he favored a cut in corporate taxes instead, precisely because he thought it would accrue to the stockholders and not be used to stimulate capital formation and undermine profits.)

Whether a cut in the corporate tax rate will stimulate investment much depends on the perplexing problem of the incidence of that tax. Gaylord Freeman, Vice-Chairman of The First National Bank of Chicago, told a recent *Life* forum on tax cutting that such

a tax may well get passed on to consumers; so removing it would not swell profits and thereby coax out investment. Professor Richard Musgrave, at the same conference, reported on a statistical investigation in which he found that the corporate tax was shifted on to consumers. Even if it were true that the tax was shifted completely on to consumers but that the mechanism by which this came about was through the creation of less capital formation, this Musgrave-Freeman point would not invalidate the hope that cutting rates from 52 per cent to 47 per cent or lower would stimulate investment and growth. (This has been pointed out by the C.E.D. report, "Reducing Tax Rates for Production and Growth," December 1962, pp. 15–26.) Musgrave, however, suspects that the incidence takes place primarily through the fact that businessmen will administer their prices at lower levels if they have to pay less corporate tax: I must confess that this notion that businessmen are successful in pricing to a certain after-tax profit and no more seems unlikely to me. And I must report that Professor Arnold Harberger of Chicago has done research that casts doubt on the shifting of the corporate tax away from capital.

It would seem plausible that certain modernization and other investment projects that yield only a 16 per cent before-tax profit and a bare 8 per cent after-tax profit might be refused by business this year; however, a sizable reduction in the corporate or individual tax rate could convert the after-tax yield into a return high enough to motivate this investment. To be sure, lowering the cost of debt and equity capital by massive Federal Reserve expansionary credit policies could achieve this same result and more; but a country—like Canada —with an overvalued currency might not be able to afford such policies, whereas the tax-cut route could extend to domestic in-

---

[1] Wiping out the corporate layer of taxation is an extreme case of this. Back in 1945 when many economists favored such a move, I regarded the corporate tax as a lesser evil than any feasible alternatives, precisely because corporations are good poolers of risks.

vestors, a privilege not bestowed on investment abroad. If this be discrimination, lay the blame on the overvaluation of the currency.

Fifteen years ago Musgrave, together with Professor Evsey Domar (now of M.I.T.), made an important point that is overlooked in most modern discussions. When the Government taxes so as to become your senior partner, it shares in your losses as well as gains; so *reducing* the tax rate does to some degree have the offsetting result of *increasing* the riskiness of private investment. It is not necessary that businessmen master this argument for it to be valid; it is enough that their profits be subject to the effect, and that habits and decisions adjust to the facts of the situation. This is not the place for me to become technical; but you can see that depressing points like this are what undermine to some extent the rosy hopes for strong results from business tax reduction. Later a similar point will come out.

18. *Shifting from a system that depends heavily on graduated income taxes to one that depends on ungraduated consumption taxation would be conducive to thriftiness out of a full-employment income.* If such thriftiness tended to become abortive and led to unemployment, growth would be hurt not helped. The result could be a mix of demand at full employment more conducive to capital formation rather than current consumption. Historically, capitalism has, teleologically speaking, used income inequality as a source of growth. If profits are the reward to people with a knack for picking good investment and if such people are thrifty, then leaving profits in their hands ought to lead to a good qualitative mix of venturesome investment as well as to a good overall total of investment. Whether modern democracies wish to purchase growth of this type at this cost is not a matter that I pronounce on here.

It is important to note that the mere fact that a man is in a high tax bracket does not discourage his investment. If I can expense my investment by ultrafast depreciation or by any means, or if my 90 per cent tax is one based upon my consumption, then wiping out all taxation would seem to convert a project with a before-tax return of 20 per cent and an after-tax return of 2 per cent into a project with after- and before-tax return of 20 per cent. What could be more stimulating to investment than that after-tax rise from 2 to 20 per cent, a tenfold change? Alas, the calculation is wrong and misleading. While subject to a 90 per cent tax, a dollar of investment does not cost me $1 but rather only 10¢ since the Government pays the other 90 per cent. If I relate my 2¢ gain to *my* 10¢ investment, I come out with the same 20 per cent after-tax return that 20¢ on a dollar gives me when there is no tax at all.[2] New businesses, it is true, do not have this advantage.

While countries like Germany and Sweden and Britain tax relatively more than we do, they get a smaller fraction of their revenues from graduated income taxes. In the case of Sweden and Britain, this is not because our marginal rates are so much higher than theirs: at comparable levels of income they are not even so high. But it is because we are more prosperous, so that many more of our people are in high enough income brackets to pay appreciable direct taxes. Fostering inequality to stimulate capital formation, as we have seen, does have cause-and-effect validity. There is an alternative way of producing the same increase in capital formation but leaving its fruits more evenly divided among the populace; but this will appear later in the "expansionary credit policy *cum* fiscal austerity package" discussion.

If I were hired as an economist for the

[2] The day after writing these lines I met the head of a large corporation who mentioned that they were test marketing a profitable new product "half at government expense."

whole group of people who have incomes above $15,000 per year and asked to develop a program best designed in terms of their self-interest, I could not come up with any proposal better than that our present reliance on graduated income taxes be altered by drastically reducing the degree of graduation, exchanging for much of the revenue lost a sales or value-added tax at the Federal level. Professional ethics would require me to state to my clients that the evidence does not suggest to me that, in the present decade, such a change would contribute much to economic growth or to overall efficiency; but it would have significant effects (what we economists call "income" rather than "substitution" effects) in moving us back toward the greater inequality of incomes that prevailed in 1929. If hired by the rest of the community, it would of course be my duty to make this last point clear to the public.

19. *Using ad hoc tax baits to promote worthy causes could be part of a growth program.* I may illustrate this point by quoting a German economist who appeared as a guest at a C.E.D. meeting:

> I realize that the American and German practices are quite different. We in Germany are supposed to be a free enterprise economy, but we freely use the tax system to accomplish what we think needs to be accomplished. Thus, if we want more construction, Dr. Erhard shapes tax programs that subsidize building. If we wish to push exports, we use the tax system to do so. Then, when times change and we don't want these activities emphasized, we remove the tax bait and push something else. On the other hand, you economists in America seem to try to set up fairly what is to be defined as true income and then you try to tax the different kinds of incomes at uniform rates: while there is much to be said for this as a matter of equity, it ties your hand as far as achieving special purposes.

I think this quotation speaks for itself and needs no comment from me.

MONETARY POLICY AND FISCAL POLICY

Here at the end I come to the most important part of my subject. While it is right that fiscal policy should receive much emphasis these days, it is in the realm of monetary policy that a mixed enterprise system like ours can do the most to slow down or step up its rate of growth. Classical economists have always emphasized that channeling resources away from current consumption and toward capital formation is an important way of increasing the ability of an economic system to produce more in the future. Indeed the classical economists were hipped on this subject and tended to place all their emphasis on capital formation as the sole source of progress. Today we have redressed the balance: we also emphasize the crucial role of the technical innovations that can take place even when a nation is doing no net saving according to the usual way of measuring saving and capital formation. Perhaps we have gone too far in redressing the balance: numerous studies by Solow, Fabricant, Kendrick, and others abroad have led to the tentative conclusion that the largest fraction of progress comes from changes in the production function rather than from increases in the stock of capital. Nonetheless, for each extra dollar of resources that the nation can channel into capital formation, there is made possible more than a dollar of additional future consumption: depending upon whether you believe the estimates of Denison or other writers, you will find that society earns 10 to 20 per cent per annum on its effective investments. These rates are not riskless, to be sure; but they are far greater than the four per cent gilt-edge rates which prevail for long-term bonds of the highest quality.

20. *Central bank credit policies that reduce the cost of borrowing and increase the availability of credit to formers of real capital are the single most important programs*

for causing the "deepening of capital" which steps up the growth potential of a nation. It is odd that the expressions "easy money" or "cheap money" have such a risqué connotation to them: actually they are the puritanical way of shifting a well-run nation away from consumption and toward more rapid growth. If Max Weber, Tawney, and Sombart wanted to preach the Protestant Ethic for a twentieth-century economy, their emphasis would have to shift away from the Calvinist emphasis upon nonconsumption toward programs which ensure the channeling of resources into capital formation. For me to give up wanting to buy today's bread is not enough to guarantee that bridges and plants will get built: only if the interest rate and capital market mechanisms which create an effective demand for capital are brought into play does my Calvinistic abstention result in anything but unemployment and unused capacity. How wrong, therefore, on cause-and-effect grounds are arguments like the following, which I collect in my files from utterances by distinguished men of affairs: "Higher interest rates will encourage more saving and less consumption; since we need more investment, the best thing the Federal Reserve can do to promote capital formation is make money tight enough to cause interest rates to firm up." Economists regard this as a fine example of incorrect reasoning; and if this day's sun sets after having had someone here make sense of it, I shall consider today's visit the most valuable one of the year, for it will have taught me something very important.

I realize, of course, that our present international balance of payments makes it difficult to use this most important growth policy and will comment on that matter in a moment. I realize, too, that when easy money brings a nation too much demand-pull, this can contribute to inflation and have bad social effects and bad repercus-

sions for growth; my next point will deal with that matter. But right here I ought to comment on whether an easy money policy which is good for the country is also good for the banking industry and for property owners generally. On the whole, since there is considerable evidence that the relative shares of property and of labor do not change much, one would expect that the owners of property as a whole are benefited by an easy money growth policy. I do not see that banks are any exception to this rule, and indeed policies which expand their reserves and earning assets might be expected to help them even when other property owners are being hurt by a decline in yields. The whole point of such a growth policy is to cause investment to take place that will bring down yields; so particular *rentiers*, particularly retired persons, might find themselves worse off even when the total return to property has gone up. And I must admit that there is the possibility that inducing a "deepening" of capital could cause its yield to decline at such a rate as to reduce the total return to property. Even a euthanasia of the *rentier* class is an eventual possibility, though unlikely: this points up the fact that there need not always be a harmony of interest between the part and the whole; what is good for the United States need not be good for some special part of it.

A number of recent econometric studies suggest that lower interest rates do have a stimulating effect on capital formation spending, which is in contrast to the more pessimistic findings of economists one or two decades ago. I do not wish to make too much of such fragmentary studies. And one has to admit that much of capital formation is financed by large corporations out of internal funds generated from undistributed profits and from depreciation accruals. Short-run variations in Federal Reserve policy are not likely to affect much the decision of the Aluminum Company or of du Pont to build a factory that is clearly needed. Yet even their decisions can, in the longer run, be influenced by the general environment of credit tightness or ease. This general environment can influence stock prices and corporate payout ratios. It can encourage or discourage firms from using their internal funds to buy up other firms or to go into new lines. While internal funds can be thought of as a separate pool from external funds, these two are loosely interconnected. Just as the Pacific and Atlantic oceans do not have the same level, as the locks in the Panama Canal show, so the effective yields externally may differ from those internally. But there is enough indirect connection between the two oceans to keep their levels from deviating by too much; and in the same way, lowering the levels of yields in the external market can help bring down gradually the yields within even the largest firms.

21. *A strong growth-inducing policy of monetary ease, if it succeeds in producing overall employment, can be combined with an austere fiscal policy, in which tax rates are kept high enough and/or expenditure rates low enough, so as to remove inflationary pressures of the demand-pull type and succeed in increasing the net capital formation share of our full-employment income at the expense of the current consumption share.* Such a package has been advocated for many years by such liberal economists as James Tobin, E. C. Brown, R. A. Musgrave, and me; and it has been greeted with some skepticism by the labor movement and by such economists as Alvin Hansen, Gerhard Colm, Robert Eisner, and Leon Keyserling. The Kennedy Administration, because of the international deficit problem, has not been able to make progress with such a program. So long as monetary policy is limited by international constraints, this "new look" program cannot

get off the ground. If such a program cannot be tried, or if it actually lacks technical potency because of the impossibility of engineering an increase in the capital-output ratio by increasing the availability of capital, then a nontotalitarian economy like ours cannot do a great deal to speed up its growth.

22. *To the extent that a currency is temporarily or permanently overvalued, the case is strengthened for various unorthodox monetary policies designed to reduce long-term interest rates and increase the availability of risk-capital to domestic users, while not at the same time letting short-term interest rates fall to levels that will cause cool money to migrate to foreign markets and thereby worsen our international balance of payments.* Thus, the costs in terms of growth of an adherence to a "bills only" (or "—preferably") doctrine would be intensified in an era of international deficits. Conventional monetary policy has not usually been interpreted to include policies designed to bring the rates of risky investment down toward the gilt-edge rates; if such measures could be devised, they would do much to energize private capital and promote growth.

The wage inflation that is now going on in Europe is doing as much to correct our international balance of payments as anything we have yet contrived. Still there are some academic economists who claim that this is too slow a process and that the American dollar may be overvalued. If that should some day prove to be so, some of them would favor direct import and capital controls. Some would favor suspending gold payments and letting the dollar be a floating currency. To the criticism that other countries can be expected to devalue as much as the United States, this reply is given: "If other countries are willing to hold our obligations at the same value in terms of their own currencies, well and good; the important thing is not to hamstring employment and growth domestically." Because some members of the press construed my remarks as favoring or contemplating a change in the external value of the dollar, I want to repeat that the above remarks report on academic attitudes and refer to vague future contingencies rather than to present actualities. What I do personally want to stress is this: When a currency is overvalued, adjusting to that situation by running a sluggish slow-growth economy is a remedy worse than the disease. The correct things should be done, and if that should reveal the untenability of existing parities, it will have been time to learn about the hard facts of life.

One final apology: I wish I could have come here and promised that balancing the budget, preserving monetary discipline, reducing Government expenditures, and busting the monopoly powers of labor unions would usher in an era of prosperity and growth without inflation or tears. It was not my heart that kept me from doing so; it was my head, and my fear of being in violation of the laws of fraud, that compelled me to say less agreeable words.

55

GROWTH AND ANTIGROWTH: WHAT ARE THE ISSUES?

According to some people, growth is neither necessary nor desirable for most advanced nations. The author gives the basis for the "antigrowth" view, which rests largely on the negative impact of growth on the quality of life in general and the environment in particular.

E. J. Mishan

E. J. Mishan is Professor of Economics at the London School of Economics and Political Science.

From *Challenge* (May–June 1973) 16, no. 2, p. 26 ff.

. . .

THE PHYSICAL POSSIBILITY OF SUSTAINED GROWTH

Let us first consider the physical possibility of growth. To ask whether the world *can* continue to maintain a 2 to 3 per cent growth rate is to pose a question about technological possibilities. It might well be that GNP, as conventionally measured, could grow at this rate *provided* all resources were properly allocated. This means that all productive services would have to be correctly priced. *Uneconomic* pollution of air, water, and so forth would have to be prevented. Indeed, an ideal allocation might require that all, or nearly all, productivity gains be utilized to increase leisure, which would imply that "real" goods per capita would not grow, or would grow very little. This "constant-physical product" economic growth obviously would be very much easier to maintain over time than the conventional "increasing-physical product" growth.

But is it realistic to expect such allocative wisdom to prevail under existing economic and political institutions? To ask about the actual prospects of growth, we must also speculate about the changes, if any, in political and economic institutions that are likely to be brought about by changes in public attitudes. At the same time, we must abstract from certain present dangers that threaten human survival itself—the danger of ecological catastrophe from ruthless interference in the biosphere, the danger of genetic calamity from increased radiation or new chemicals, the danger of nuclear Armageddon. Each of these threats has arisen from economic and technological growth, and each will be further aggravated by such growth in the future.

. . .

We may reasonably conclude, therefore, that *were there to be no technological innovation in the future*, we simply would not be able to continue to grow indefinitely. The earth and its resources are all too finite, and our continued absorption of them on an ever larger scale must eventually exhaust them. The only question would be when.

The crucial variable in all optimistic forecasts, and in all declarations of faith, is technological innovation. Living in a world that is today being transformed before our eyes by new applications of science, we have an almost irresistible presumption in favor of scientific capability. If it merely sounds possible, the layman is ready to believe it will happen.

Thus we are ready to accept the idea of a vast proliferation of nuclear power plants over the earth, with problems of space solved and with radiation and heat hazards all kept well under control. And we are ready to imagine also that technology will discover increasingly more efficient and inexpensive ways of recycling materials. As for food supplies, the optimistic view is that the problem can be solved by intensive monoculture that utilizes large tracts of land and large amounts of chemical fertilizers and pesticides—the methods of the so-called green revolution. We are to ignore the social consequences of such agrotechnology on the economy of the hundreds of thousands of Asian villages, and the urban problems that follow the disruption of traditional ways of life.

I do not want to sound too cynical. It may all be wonderfully possible—or we may all be wonderfully lucky. I would simply affirm that there is room for legitimate doubt. The advance of technology in the West over the past 200 years might well be attributable to especially favorable circumstances. Up to the present there was no problem of limits to the assimilative capacity of the biosphere, or of the availability of cheap fossil fuels. As for scientific progress, we may be running into diminishing returns to the scale of research—partly because of an incipient breakdown in communications among an expanding array of narrowly focused specialists.

Perhaps there are no solutions to a number of problems that scientists are working on. It may be that what we want to do just cannot, in the nature of things, ever be done—though it may take us decades to realize this. Finally, it is possible—alas, more than possible—that should we succeed in wrestling some of nature's closest secrets from her breast, we shall live to wish we had not.

A sustained per capita growth rate of 3 per cent per annum implies that the average income in 150 years will be about 100 times as large as the average income today, and 10,000 times as large in another 150 years. Just contemplate the amounts of energy and materials required to meet such fantastic standards. Just what shape will expenditures of this magnitude take? And how on earth (literally) will a person manage to absorb them?

THE DESIRABILITY OF SUSTAINED ECONOMIC GROWTH

Assuming that per capita growth could be maintained indefinitely at current rates, we must still ask whether such growth is desirable. Has economic growth promoted social welfare in the recent past, and is it likely to do so in the future? An odd assortment of arguments come up in this debate, a number of which are definitely "nonstarters." We can save time and heat by recognizing some of them before going any farther.

First, there is the frequent statement that technology—the main force behind current economic growth—is itself neutral. One cannot associate it with good or evil attributes and "it all depends on how man uses it." But the *potential* of science and technology is not the issue. Their *actual* effects are. Intelligent conjecture about the future presupposes some knowledge of the reach of modern science and also some idea of the probable scientific developments over the foreseeable future. From this we can speculate about some of the more likely consequences on our lives, bearing in mind the limitations of men and the driving forces of modern institutions, economic and political.

. . .

Nor is it, for similar reasons, legitimate to argue that we should seek the "optimal," or just right, rate of growth. One can imagine some distillation of economic growth, som essence purified of all harmful external effects, that cannot fail to result in ideal human progress. But such flights of inspiration offer no plausible picture of the future and no guide to action. Economists all know that a narrow range of adverse spillovers— such as air and water pollution, noise, congestion, and tourist blight—can be reduced given some political effort. Yet in judging the quality of life over the last two decades, we obviously cannot abstract from the brute facts of expanding pollution. So, also, in debating the foreseeable future, it is not the potential ideal that is at issue, but the political likelihood of realizing significant reductions in each of the familiar forms of pollution.

The "need" to maintain the momentum of economic growth in order to enable us to do good deeds like helping the poor, promoting high culture, or expanding higher education is also not on the agenda. This argument might win ethical support even if it were agreed that economic growth actually entailed a decline in social welfare for the majority of people. But the fact is that such worthy objectives can all be realized *without* sustained economic growth. In the United States, so much is produced that is trivial and inane, if not inimical, that we already have more than enough to transfer resources for these more meritorious purposes.

. . .

Having, hopefully, cleared away some of the verbal undergrowth that tends to impede the progress of this debate, we are better able to perceive the issues that can be decisive. The issues can be divided, arbitrarily perhaps, into two categories:

1. In the first are the conventional array of adverse spillovers—air pollution, water pollution, solid waste pollution, noise, uglification of town and country—all of which have increased alarmingly since the war. The question is whether they have more than offset the "normal" expectations of welfare gains from economic growth.

2. In the second category are the remaining consequences of economic growth. How much weight is to be given to those pervasive repercussions that are less tangible and more complex than the familiar external diseconomies? Unwittingly, through

the process of continually and unquestioningly adapting our style and pace of life to technological and commercial possibilities, we may be losing irrevocably traditional sources of comfort and gratification.

It is difficult to draw a balance sheet summarizing the net welfare effects of the increased output of goods and the concomitant spillovers in the last few years. Even if we had all the physical data—from the hazards of chemical pesticides to rising levels of noise, from oil fouled beaches the world over, to forest cropping and earth stripping—we should, in a closely interdependent economic system, be faced with the almost impossible task of evaluation. My inclination is to describe what has been happening on the advancing pollution front in impressionistic terms, taking it for granted that the balance of the argument will be restored by the unremitting efforts of commercial advertising, establishment politicians, company chairmen, and the spate of articles in our newspapers and magazines that speak loudly of the goodies we have and of goodies yet to come.

The incidence of a single spillover alone—be it foul air, endless traffic bedlam, noise, or fear of criminal violence—can be enough to counter all of the alleged gains of economic prosperity. Let a family have five television sets, four refrigerators, three cars, two yachts, a private plane, a swimming pool, and half a million dollars' worth of securities. What enjoyment is left if it fears to stroll out of an evening, if it must take elaborate precautions against burglary, if it lives in continuous anxiety lest one or another, parent or child, be kidnapped, mutilated, or murdered? A fat bag of consumer goods, an impressive list of technical achievements, can hardly compensate for any one of such perils that have come to blight the lives of millions of Americans.

. . .

If it is conceded that, once subsistence levels have been passed, the sources of man's most enduring satisfactions spring from mutual trust and affection, from sharing joy and sorrow, from giving and accepting love, from openhearted companionship and laughter; if it is further conceded that in a civilized society the joy of living comes from the sense of wonder inspired by the unfolding of nature, from the perception of beauty inspired by great art, from the renewal of faith and hope inspired by the heroic and the good—if this much is conceded, then is it possible to believe that unremitting attempts to harness the greater part of man's energies and ingenuity to the task of amassing an ever greater assortment of material possessions can add much to people's happiness? Can it add more than it subtracts? Can it add anything?

Recognizing the darker side of economic growth, we must conclude that the game is not worth the candle. And the answer to the question of whether continued economic growth in the West brings us any closer to the good life cannot be other than a resounding No.

56

Some writers have forecast the collapse of the world economy under the strains of continued growth and its impact on living standards and the resource base. In response, Professor Solow points out some conceptual flaws in the "Doomsday" models that underlie the "overshoot, collapse, and doom" predictions. In addition, Solow believes the very forces contributing to collapse will lead to pressures for altered resource use patterns and to technological changes that may offset the predicted "collapse."

IS THE END OF THE WORLD AT HAND?

Robert M. Solow

Robert Solow is Professor of Economics at MIT.

From *Challenge* (March–April 1973) 16, no. 1, p. 39 ff.

* * *

OVERSHOOT, COLLAPSE, DOOM

There is, as you know, a school of thought that claims that continued economic growth is in fact not possible anymore, or at least not for very long. This judgment has been expressed more or less casually by several observers in recent years. What distinguishes the "Doomsday Models" from their predecessors is that they claim to much more than a casual judgment: they deduce their beliefs about future prospects from mathematical models or systems analysis. They don't merely say that the end of the world is at hand—they can show you computer output that says the same thing.

Characteristically, the Doomsday Models do more than just say that continued economic growth is impossible. They tell us why: in brief, because (*a*) the earth's natural resources will soon be used up; (*b*) increased industrial production will soon strangle us in pollution; and (*c*) increasing population will eventually outrun the world's capacity to grow food, so that famine must eventually result. And, finally, the models tell us one more thing: the world will end with a bang, not a whimper. The natural evolution of the world econ-omy is not at all toward some kind of smooth approach to its natural limits, wherever they are. Instead, it is inevitable—unless we make drastic changes in the way we live and organize ourselves—that the world will overshoot any level of population and production it can possibly sustain and will then collapse, probably by the middle of the next century.

I would like to say why I think that the Doomsday Models are bad science and therefore bad guides to public policy. I hope nobody will conclude that I believe the problems of population control, environmental degradation, and resource exhaustion to be unimportant, or that I am one of those people who believe that an adequate response to such problems is a vague confidence that some technological solution will turn up. On the contrary, it is precisely because these are important problems that public policy had better be based on sound and careful analysis. I want to explain some of my reasons for believing that the global models don't provide even the beginnings of a foundation of that kind.

The first thing to realize is that the characteristic conclusion of the Doomsday Models is very near the surface. It is, in fact, more nearly an assumption than a conclusion, in the sense that the chain of logic from the assumptions to the conclusion is very short and rather obvious.

The basic assumption is that stocks of things like the world's natural resources and the waste disposal capacity of the environment arc finite, that the world economy tends to consume the stock at an increasing rate (through the mining of minerals and the production of goods), and that there are no built-in mechanisms by which approaching exhaustion tends to turn off consumption gradually and in advance. You hardly need a giant computer to tell you that a system with those behavior rules is going to bounce off its ceiling and collapse to a low level. Then, in case anyone is inclined to relax into the optimistic belief that maybe things aren't that bad, we are told: Imagine that the stock of natural resources were actually twice as big as the best current evidence suggests, or imagine that the annual amount of pollution could be halved all at once and then set to growing again. All that would happen is that the date of collapse would be postponed by T years, where T is not a large number. But once you grasp the quite simple essence of the models, this should come as no surprise. It is important to realize where these powerful conclusions come from, because if you ask yourself, "Why didn't I realize earlier that the end of the world was at hand?", the answer is not that you weren't clever enough to figure it out for yourself. The answer is that the imminent end of the world is an immediate deduction from certain assumptions, and one must really ask if the assumptions are any good.

It is a commonplace that if you calculate the annual output of any production process, large or small, and divide it by the annual employment of labor, you get a ratio that is called the productivity of labor. At the most aggregative level, for example, we can say that the GNP in 1971 was $1,050 billion and that about 82 million people were employed in producing it, so that GNP per worker or the productivity of a year of labor was about $12,800. Symmetrically, though the usage is less common, one could just as well calculate the GNP per unit of some particular natural resource and call that the productivity of coal, or GNP per pound of vanadium. We usually think of the productivity of labor as rising more or less exponentially, say at 2 or 3 per cent a year, because that is the way it has in fact behaved over the past century or so since the statistics began to be collected. The rate of increase in the productivity of labor is not a constant of nature. Sometimes it is faster, sometimes slower. For example, we know that labor productivity must have increased more slowly a long time ago, because if we extrapolate backward at 2 per cent a year, we come to a much lower labor productivity in 1492 than can possibly have been the case. And the productivity of labor has risen faster in the past twenty-five years than in the fifty years before that. It also varies from place to place, being faster in Japan and Germany and slower in Great Britain, for reasons that are not at all certain. But it rises, and we expect it to keep rising.

Now, how about the productivity of natural resources? All the Doomsday Models will allow is a one-time hypothetical increase in the world supply of natural resources, which is the equivalent of a one-time increase in the productivity of natural resources. Why shouldn't the productivity of most natural resources rise more or less steadily through time, like the productivity of labor?

Of course it does for some resources, but not for others. Real GNP roughly doubled between 1950 and 1970. But the consumption of primary and scrap iron increased by about 20 per cent, so the productivity of iron, GNP per ton of iron, increased by about 2.5 per cent a year on the average during those twenty years. The U.S. consumption of manganese rose by 30 per cent in the same period, so the productivity of manganese went up by some 70 per cent in 20 years, a bit under 2.25 per cent a year. Aggregate consumption of nickel just about doubled, like GNP, so the productivity of nickel didn't change. U.S. consumption of copper, both primary and secondary, went up by a third between 1951 and 1970, so GNP per pound of copper rose at 2 per cent a year on the average. The story on lead and zinc is very similar, so their productivity increased at some 2 per cent a year. The productivity of bituminous coal rose at 3 per cent a year.

Naturally, there are important exceptions, and unimportant exceptions. GNP per barrel of oil was about the same in 1970 as in 1951: no productivity increase there. The consumption of natural gas tripled in the same period, so GNP per cubic foot of natural gas fell at about 2.5 per cent a year. Our industrial demand for aluminum quadrupled in two decades, so the productivity of aluminum fell at a good 3.5 per cent a year. And industrial demand for columbium was multiplied by a factor of twenty-five: in 1951 we managed $2.25 million of GNP (in 1967 prices) per pound of columbium, whereas in 1970 we were down to $170 thousand of GNP per pound of columbium. On the other hand, it is a little hard to imagine civilization toppling because of a shortage of columbium.

Obviously many factors combine to govern the course of the productivity of any given mineral over time. When a rare natural resource is first available, it acquires new uses with a rush; and consumption goes up much faster than GNP. That's the columbium story, no doubt, and, to a lesser extent, the vanadium story. But once the novelty has worn off, the productivity of a resource tends to rise as better or worse substitutes for it appear, as new commodities replace old ones, and as manufacturing processes improve. One of the reasons the productivity of copper rises is because that of aluminum falls, as aluminum replaces copper in many uses. The same is true of coal and oil. A resource, like petroleum, that is versatile because of its role as a source of energy, is an interesting special case. It is hardly any wonder that the productivity of petroleum has stagnated, because the consumption of energy—both as electricity for domestic and industrial use and in the automobile—has recently increased even faster than GNP. But no one can doubt that we will run out of oil, the coal and nuclear fission will replace oil as the major sources of energy. It is already becoming probable that the high-value use of oil will soon be as feed stock for the petrochemical industries, rather than as a source of energy. Sooner or later, the productivity of oil will rise out of sight, because the production and consumption of oil will eventually dwindle toward zero, but real GNP will not.

So there really is no reason why we should not think of the productivity of natural resources as increasing more or less exponentially over time. But then overshoot and collapse are no longer the inevitable trajectory of the world system, and the typical assumption-conclusion of the Doomsday Models falls by the wayside. We are in a different sort of ball game. The system might still burn itself out and collapse in finite time, but one cannot say with any honesty that it must. It all depends on the particular, detailed facts of modern economic life as well as on the economic policies we and the rest of the world pursue. I don't want to argue for any particular counterstory; all I want to say now is that the overshoot-collapse pattern is built into the models very near the surface, by assumption, and by implausible assumption at that.

SCARCITY—AND HIGH PRICES

There is at least one reason for believing that the Doomsday story is almost certainly wrong. The most glaring defect of the Forrester-Meadows models is the absence of any sort of functioning price system. I am no believer that the market is always right, and I am certainly no advocate of laissez faire where the environment is concerned. But the price system is, after all, the main social institution evolved by capitalist economies (and, to an increasing extent, socialist economies too) for registering and reacting to relative scarcity. There are several ways that the working of the price system will push our society into faster and more systematic increases in the productivity of natural resources.

First of all, let me go back to the analogy between natural resources and labor. We are not surprised to learn that industry quite consciously tries to make inventions that save labor, that is, permit the same product to be made with fewer man-hours of work. After all, on the average, labor costs amount to almost three-fourths of all costs in our economy. An invention that reduces labor requirement per unit of GNP by 1 per cent reduces all costs by about 0.75 per cent. Natural resource costs are a much smaller proportion of total GNP, something nearer 5 per cent. So industry and engineering have a much stronger motive to reduce labor requirements by 1 per cent than to reduce resource requirements by 1 per cent, assuming—which may or not be true—that it is about as hard to do one as to do the other. But then, as the earth's supply of particular natural resources nears exhaustion, and as natural resources become more and more valuable, the motive to economize those natural resources should become as strong as the motive to economize labor. The productivity of resources should rise faster than now—it is hard to imagine otherwise.

There are other ways in which the market mechanism can be expected to push us all to economize on natural resources as they become scarcer. Higher and rising prices of exhaustible resources lead competing producers to substitute other materials that are more plentiful and therefore cheaper. To the extent that it is impossible to design around or find substitutes for expensive natural resources, the prices of commodities that contain a lot of them will rise relative to the prices of other goods and services that don't use up a lot of resources. Consumers will be driven to buy fewer resource-intensive goods and more of other things. All these effects work automatically to increase the productivity of natural resources, that is, to reduce resource requirements per unit of GNP.

. . .

Every analysis of resource scarcity has to come to terms with the fact that the prices of natural resources and resource products have not shown any tendency to rise over the past half-century, relative to the prices of other things. This must mean that there have so far been adequate offsets to any progressive impoverishment of deposits—like improvements in the technology of extraction, savings in end uses, or the availability of cheaper substitutes. The situation could, of course, change; and very likely some day it will. If the experienced and expert participants in the market now believed that resource prices would be sharply higher at some foreseeable time, prices would *already* be rising, as I will try to explain in a moment. The historical steadiness of resource prices suggests that buyers and sellers in the market have not been acting as if they foresaw exhaustion in the absence of substitutes, and therefore sharply higher future prices. They may turn out to be wrong; but the Doomsday Models give us absolutely no reason to expect that —in fact, they claim to get whatever meager empirical basis they have from such experts.

. . .

CROWDING ON PLANET EARTH

I have less to say about the question of population growth, because it doesn't seem to involve any difficult conceptual problems. At any time, in any place, there is presumably an optimal size of population —with the property that the average person would be somewhat worse off if the population were a bit larger, and also worse off if the population were a bit smaller. In any real case it must be very difficult to know what the optimum population is, especially because it will change over time as technology changes, and also because it is probably more like a band or zone than a sharply defined number. I mean if you could somehow plot a graph of economic welfare per person against population size, there would be a very gentle dome or plateau at the top, rather than a sharp peak.

. . .

As it happens, recent figures seem to show that the United States is heading for a stationary population: that is to say, the current generation of parents seems to be establishing fertility patterns that will, if continued, cause the population to stabilize some time during the next century. Even so, the absolute size of the population will increase for a while, and level off higher than it is now, because decades of population growth have left us with a bulge of population in the childbearing ages. But I have already argued that a few million more or less hardly make a difference; and a population that has once stabilized might actually decrease, if that came to seem desirable.

At the present moment, at least for the United States, the danger of rapid population growth seems to be the wrong thing to worry about. The main object of public policy in this field ought to be to ensure that the choice of family size is truly a voluntary choice, that access to the best birth-control methods be made universal. That seems to be all that is needed. Of course, we know very little about what governs voluntary fertility, about why the typical notion of a good family size changes from generation to generation. So it is certainly possible that these recent developments will reverse themselves and that population control will again appear on the agenda of public policy. This remains to be seen.

In all this I have said nothing about the Doomsday Models because there is practically nothing that needs to be said. So far as we can tell, they make one very bad mistake: in the face of reason, common sense, and systematic evidence, they seem to assume that at high standards of living, people want more children as they become more affluent (though over most of the observed range, a higher standard of living goes along with smaller families). That error is certainly a serious one in terms of the recent American data—but perhaps it explains why some friends of mine were able to report that they had run a version of the Forrester World Dynamics Model starting with a population of two people and discovered that it blew up in 500 years.

Apart from placing the date of the Garden of Eden in the fifteenth century, what else is new?

. . .

PAYING FOR POLLUTION

Resource exhaustion and overpopulation: that leaves pollution as the last of the Doomsday Devils. The subject is worth a whole lecture in itself, because it is one of those problems about which economists actually have something important to say to the world, not just to each other. But I must be brief. Fine print aside, I think that what one gets from the Doomsday literature is the notion that air and water and noise pollution are an inescapable accompaniment of economic growth, especially industrial growth. If that is true, then to be against pollution is to be against growth. I realize that in putting the matter so crudely I have been unjust; nevertheless, that is the message that comes across. I think that way of looking at the pollution problem is wrong.

A correct analysis goes something like this. Excessive pollution and degradation of the environment certainly accompany industrial growth and the increasing population density that goes with it. But they are by no means an inescapable by-product. Excessive pollution happens because of an important flaw in the price system. Factories, power plants, municipal sewers, drivers of cars, strip-miners of coal and deep-miners of coal, and all sorts of generators of waste are allowed to dump that waste into the environment, into the atmosphere and into running water and the oceans, without paying the full cost of what they do. No wonder they do too much. So would you, and so would I. In fact, we actually do—directly as drivers of cars, indirectly as we buy some products at a

price that is lower than it ought to be because the producer is not required to pay for using the environment to carry away his wastes, and even more indirectly as we buy things that are made with things that pollute the environment.

This flaw in the price system exists because a scarce resource (the waste disposal capacity of the environment) goes unpriced; and that happens because it is owned by all of us, as it should be. The flaw can be corrected, either by the simple expedient of regulating the discharge of wastes to the environment by direct control or by the slightly more complicated device of charging special prices—user taxes—to those who dispose of wastes in air or water. These effluent charges do three things: they make pollution-intensive goods expensive, and so reduce the consumption of them; they make pollution-intensive methods of production costly, and so promote abatement of pollution by producers; they generate revenue that can, if desired, be used for the further purification of air or water or for other environmental impovements. Most economists prefer this device of effluent charges to regulation by direct order. This is more than an occupational peculiarity. Use of the price system has certain advantages in efficiency and decentralization. Imposing a physical limit on, say, sulfur dioxide emission is, after all, a little peculiar. It says that you may do so much of a bad thing and pay nothing for the privilege, but after that, the price is infinite. Not surprisingly, one can find a more efficient schedule of pollution abatement through a more sensitive tax schedule.

But this difference of opinion is minor compared with the larger point that needs to be made. The annual cost that would be necessary to meet decent pollution abatement standards by the end of the century is large, but not staggering. One estimate says that in 1970 we spent about $8.5 billion (in 1967 prices), or 1 per cent of GNP, for pollution abatement. An active pollution abatement policy would cost perhaps $50 billion a year by 200, which would be about 2 per cent of GNP by then. That is a small investment of resources: you can see how small it is when you consider that GNP grows by 4 per cent or so every year, on the average. Cleaning up air and water would entail a cost that would be a bit like losing one-half of one year's growth, between now and the year 2000. What stands between us and a decent environment is not the curse of industrialization, not an unbearable burden of cost, but just the need to organize ourselves consciously to do some simple and knowable things. Compared with the possibility of an active abatement policy, the policy of stopping economic growth in order to stop pollution would be incredibly inefficient. It would not actually accomplish much, because one really wants to reduce the amount of, say, hydrocarbon emission to a third or a half of *what it is now*. And what no-growth would accomplish, it would do by cutting off your face to spite your nose.

THE END OF THE WORLD— A MATTER OF TIMING

In the end, that is really my complaint about the Doomsday school. It diverts attention from the really important things that can actually be done, step by step, to make things better. The end of the world *is* at hand—the earth, if you take the long view, will fall into the sun in a few billion years anyway, unless some other disaster happens first. In the meantime, I think we'd be better off passing a strong sulfur emissions tax, or getting some Highway Trust Fund money allocated to mass transit, or building a humane and decent floor under family incomes, or overriding President Nixon's veto of a strong Water Quality Act, or reforming the tax system, or fending off starvation in Bengal—instead of worrying about the generalized "predicament of mankind."

57

In the eyes of many of the world's poorer peoples America is rich beyond comprehension. Two reporters who have seen much of the world's misery ponder America's abundance and ask what can be done, beyond cold-war measures, to help the poor nations.

WHY ARE WE BLESSED?

Peggy and Pierre Streit

Peggy and Pierre Streit are writers on economic affairs.

From *The New York Times Magazine*, January 8, 1961; copyright © 1961/1969 by The New York Times Company. Reprinted by permission.

Shiraz, Iran

"Eighty-eight per cent of the people in America own television sets." There it is, the shortest of items in today's local English-language newspaper—there, amid the news about Iran, the cold war, and world crisis. "Eighty-eight per cent of the people in America own television sets"—the mere tick of a statistic, addressed, as it were, to whom it may concern. And our thoughts turn back to seven years of travel in the Middle East and Asia.

We think of India and the daily drive we made to New Delhi from our home on the outskirts of the city. On the way there was a small refugee village and in it a dump heap. Each day, as we passed, we watched the village dogs and the village women, side by side, clawing through the refuse with unnerving intensity for scraps of food.

And we remember Kabul, Afghanistan, its newly paved streets dusted with a thin coat of sand blown in from the plains. Roaming those streets was a band of dirty, barefoot scavenger boys—all seven or eight years old, each with a square metal can strapped to his back. They followed the carriages, searching for horse droppings, and when they found some they scooped up the manure with their small hands and, with a deft practiced motion, tossed it over their shoulders into the cans, to be sold later to Afghan farmers.

We remember, a few winters ago, a little girl on the sleet-covered streets of South Teheran. Her head was bent into a wind that blew her cotton dress against her legs. She was barefoot. As she walked the flesh of her heels, cracked by the cold, left little arcs of blood in the snow.

And so, this morning, as we read that 88 per cent of all Americans own television sets, we ask ourselves, as we have so often before, what we and what our countrymen have done to merit the bounty and the comfort with which we live, and what so much of the world has done to warrant its destitution.

Why is it that we can look forward this evening to the quiet comfort of an ample meal while, not two miles away, thousands of drought-driven Iranian nomads are on their weary way south in search of food for themselves and their gaunt animals? Why is it that we can buy clothes—clothes we don't really need—while in Calcutta thousands of men, women, and children who sleep under bridges and in doorways lack even a piece of cloth to put between themselves and the pavement?

Why are we permitted to look to tomorrow without fear of want, when for so many in this world, tomorrow may well bring flood, famine, or disease to destroy all that they cherish? Why are we permitted to enjoy the blessings of freedom and security, knowing that well-established democratic institutions in the United States have peacefully elected a new President, while in most of the underdeveloped world there is no freedom, there are no democratic institutions—or even much understanding of them or hope that they may soon provide the blessings enjoyed in the West?

Why have we been so fortunate? It would be pleasant to believe we have earned our good fortune because we have worked harder than the millions of people we see toiling on barren land. But we know better.

We have seen too many Indian farmers trudging behind primitive, wooden plows under a searing sun; we have seen too many Nepalese women bent double in their rice fields, their legs covered with leeches; we have seen too many Iranian children hunched over their ill-lit carpet looms, to have any such illusions. We know that never in our lives have we worked, one day, as hard as most of the people in the world work each day. We cannot lay claim to our comfortable lives because of diligence.

Perhaps we have been luckier than most because we are wiser, and wisdom brings its just rewards. But we are mindful of the many thoughtful, stimulating evenings spent under thatched roofs discussing the problems of the world with illiterate Indian or Afghan or Iranian farmers. It has been made abundantly clear to us that a man may be uneducated, but he may also be wise; he may be poor, but he may also have dignity; he may be hard-pressed, but he may also maintain his pride. Thus, we cannot believe that we or our countrymen are more fortunate than others because we have a monopoly on intelligence.

Perhaps we are blessed above others because we are more generous, more honest, or more dedicated. But this is not a point we would care to have to defend against the hungry peasants who have insisted on sharing their meals with us; against impoverished farmers who have gone to great lengths to return to us things we left in their villages; against the hundreds of young people we have met whose work for their young, struggling countries demands a kind of personal sacrifice we have never known.

We ask ourselves, then, if perhaps our good fortune is not due to our system of government, to our freedom and democracy, and if these are not our just inheritance from the men who won them in the United States—from George Washington, Thomas Jefferson, and Abraham Lincoln. But this, too, we must reject. For, we ask, what have *we personally* ever done, more than most of the other people of the world, to earn or merit these blessings?

We can find no satisfactory reason, in short, to explain why, in a world that now has the capability of caring for *all* its people, there are so many poor and so few rich. And we feel very strongly that in this fact—in the very magnitude of the disparity of living standards, in the very number of people involved, in the very enormity of the injustice—a self-evident truth emerges: that apart from preserving the peace, the first, overriding, frighteningly pressing task of this year and this century is to feed, clothe, and unleash from fear the millions who, through no fault of their own, live in such desolation.

This is a massive and urgent undertaking. It is no longer one for a few missionaries or teachers but one requiring the marshaling of the intellectual, material, and spiritual resources of nations—nations rich enough to provide 88 per cent of their people with television sets. Whatever contributes to this mobilization, whatever speeds this process must be welcomed.

What *could* speed this process? To date,

the greatest—one might almost say the only —impetus to this mobilization has been the cold war.

In the past fifteen years the tremendous job of bridging the gap between the affluence of the West and the poverty of the East has begun. In the seven years we have been travelling in this part of the world we have seen enormous accomplishment. Much of it has been due to Western aid. But a big part has also been played by the Russians.

Honesty compels us to admit, however, that the principal reason the United States has undertaken to help raise the world's standard of living is not that there are poor people who rightfully should be sharing more equally the good things of the earth, but that Americans are afraid that if they do not do something about their misery, the miserable will turn to the Communists in desperation. And undoubtedly the forces that motivate the Communists are very similar. The Soviets have undertaken a share of the burden, not because the welfare of the people is a primary concern, but because they want their ideology to prevail and aid is one means to that end.

It would be pleasant to believe that were East and West not embroiled in a cold war both the United States and the Soviet Union would continue their help to the underdeveloped world. But, regretfully, we haven't that much faith. If the cold war ended tomorrow, so, we fear, would the bulk of the efforts being made to help the earth's unfortunates.

We wonder, actually, whether when the history of these days is written a century from now, the cold war may not emerge as one of the greatest boons that mankind has ever known. Certainly, it seems to have been the one force powerful enough to marshal the intellectual and material resources of the United States on a national scale in behalf of the underprivileged, and to cause other countries to follow the American lead with aid programs of their own.

But we wonder if the cold war may not also emerge as a boon to the overprivileged —the 88 per centers. One can hope that it may prove to be a force that, carrying Americans to the far corners of the earth and opening their front pages, their eyes, and their hearts to the needs around them, will finally transform a response based on fear and self-preservation into a true concern for justice and the welfare of all men.

COMPARATIVE SYSTEMS

PART EIGHT

58

THE SOVIET SYSTEM IN TRANSITION

The Soviet Union apparently has been moving slowly in the direction of an economy more responsive to market forces, at least for some sectors. Some of the factors influencing this movement and some of the consequences for economic organization are explored in this selection.

Rush V. Greenslade

Rush V. Greenslade is an economist with the U.S. Central Intelligence Agency. (Caveat: It should be noted that the views presented in this article are those of the author and are not necessarily those of the Central Intelligence Agency or the U.S. government).

From *New Directions in the Soviet Economy,* studies prepared for the Subcommittee on Foreign Economic Policy of the Joint Economic Committee. Part I, 89th Congress, 2nd Session, 1966, p. 3.

Let us admit the case of the conservative: If we once start thinking, no one can guarantee where we shall come out, except that many objects, ends, and institutions are doomed.

— John Dewey

In October 1961 Communists from all over the globe gathered in Moscow for the 22d Party Congress. This ceremonial assembly was the crowning achievement of Khrushchev's party career. At the previous Party Congress in 1959 he had announced the final victory of socialism and the advent of a new historical stage of development, the all-out building of communism. At the 22d Congress he completed the process of ousting Stalin from his place in the pantheon of party greats, and even from his resting place in the mausoleum. He staked his own claim to a seat on the right hand of Lenin by promulgating the party's 20-year program, upon the completion of which the U.S.S.R. would have arrived at or near the stage of full communism.

Economic growth at a tumultuous pace was so well established under socialism (after Stalin's errors had been corrected by Khrushchev) that a time table for the advent of communism could be set by economic milestones. The first and most breathtaking, catching up with the United States in industrial production, was promised for 1970. After that, the satisfaction of all economic needs and desires, "all that a man could reasonably want," would be within the grasp of the bountifully productive socialist economy. According to the party program, food supply would double, there would be an apartment for each family, and services would be increasingly provided free of charge.

The contrast between the old man's illusions and the present economic conditions and prospects could hardly be more obvious. Since the 22d Party Congress, agriculture has progressed so little that wheat, which was formerly exported, has been imported for the last 3 years. Soviet GNP has not gained on U.S. GNP and may even have lost a little. Industrial production has gained very little on U.S. production. Urban housing has barely kept up with urban population. Throughout the land the great slogan of catching up with the United States in 1970 is heard no longer.

More chilling to party hopes than these economic developments is an apparent loss of faith in the economic system itself. In 1961 the system of central administrative direction of the economy under the tight rein and driving whip of the Communist Party was unquestioned—at least publicly. Since then, first academicians, then economic administrators and now the highest party leaders have openly acknowledged the grave deficiencies of the command economy.

Was the premise of the 21st and 22d Party Congresses correct; that the construction of socialism was finally completed and the material base for communism laid? Subsequent experience suggests that the premise was not quite true. State ownership is accomplished; industrial capacity has been built; but this capacity still provides little for Soviet consumers, and more important, the economic organization, whatever its past triumphs, is now found wanting.

Premier Kosygin's speech to the Party Plenum in September 1965 proposed a series of reforms in economic organization, the inspiration for which was not Karl Marx or Lenin and certainly not Stalin. Its intellectual sources were the late Oscar Lange, the experience of Yugoslavia, and the writings of the liberal faction of the Soviet economic profession. The proposals include the first timid steps away from tight central direction of the economy and toward a market socialism. Many westerners anticipated much bolder steps and were disappointed at the vague and partial program outlined by Kosygin. The boldness of the step, however, is much less significant than the direction. It is a step that will be very difficult to stop or reverse. The future course and ultimate destination of the reform, however, is far from clear.

Kosygin's proposals follow from a complex of developments—economic, intellectual, and ideological—which, starting slowly after the death of Stalin, have unfolded with astonishing speed in the last few years. Although the depth and the diversity of this evolution argue for its irreversibility, they do not provide a chart of its future directions. The survey that follows will review the highlights of the economic changes of the last 10 years as they bear on future possibilities. These are:

1. The slowdown in economic growth;
2. The revolution in economic thought;
3. The developments in economic organization.

I. THE SLOWDOWN IN ECONOMIC GROWTH

The slowdown of economic growth in the U.S.S.R. is now a well-known story. The recent State Department press release, *U.S.S.R. Falters in Economic Growth Race with the United States,* sets forth the main measures of Soviet growth. These measures show that in 1961–65 as compared with 1956–60, the average annual rate of growth of GNP fell from 6 percent to 4 percent; the growth of industrial production dropped from 8 percent to 6 percent, and that of agricultural production from 3½ percent to 2 percent. An even more dramatic change would appear, both for industry and agriculture, if growth were measured from 1950 instead of 1955. Other measures confirm and extend the story. According to Soviet statistics, the average annual growth of state fixed investment dropped from 12 percent in 1950–59 to 8 percent in 1960–64; the growth of overall investment (that is, including private and kolkhoz investment) declined from 13 percent to 6 percent. The average annual rate of increase in consumption was 6.8 percent in 1950–59, but 3.9 percent in 1960–64.

Soviet announced statistics of national income and industrial production show much the same slowdown in growth as the Western calculations, and Soviet press comment has explicitly admitted the retardation. Premier Kosygin described it in these words in his speech at the Party Plenum in September 1965:

It should be noted that in the past few years there has been a certain decline in national income and industrial output per ruble of fixed production assets. The rate of growth of labor productivity in industry, which is also an important index of the effectiveness of social production, has slowed down somewhat in recent years.

. . .

Most observers would have agreed that the rate of growth of the Soviet economy must eventually slow. But the suddenness of the change, like a horse going lame, surprised many, including this writer. Two important developments in the late 1950s, the surge of defense expenditures and the shortening of the work week from 46 to 41 hours, surely contributed to the timing and magnitude of the slowdown in growth and in productivity. The direct effect was a loss of labor and capital inputs into the civilian economy. Indirectly, by preempting for the advanced weapons programs the most efficient research and development resources —men, materials, and equipment—the defense effort must also have contributed to the drop in the effectiveness of new investment. However, this still leaves unanswered the questions of why the system was unable to adjust to these developments and why the growth of factor productivity continued to be slow through 1965.

A critical factor seems to lie in the ability of the system to cope with technological complexity and change. In *The Economics of Soviet Planning,* Professor Bergson[1] presents a comparison of Soviet and United States net national product in 1960 in both dollar prices and ruble prices and of the respective capital and labor inputs. Soviet net national product per unit of input ranges from two-fifths to two-thirds of that of the United States according to various alternative calculations. This large difference suggests a still massive technological lag in the U.S.S.R., a suggestion that is confirmed by Western observations and by

[1] Abram Bergson, "The Economics of Soviet Planning" (New Haven: Yale University Press, 1964), p. 342.

Soviet reporting on the technological backwardness of the chemical industry (e.g., synthetic fibers), petroleum refining, highway transportation, consumer durables, animal husbandry, and many other activities. Investment opportunities with high net yields, of the kind that Western Europe and Japan have been reaping lately, are still available in profusion to the U.S.S.R. But the growth of output has slowed to rates now less than in the United States. The difficulties in the current period thus apparently stem from an inability to take advantage of new technology. This situation contrasts sharply with the impressive results of the wholesale adoption of new techniques in the thirties. But whether the nature or the complexity of new technology has changed, or whether the poor recent performance was inherent in the system is still arguable. . . .

In discussing the recent economic developments, Soviet economists accept without question the past development strategy and use it to justify the economic system that went with it. They have adopted the argument that centralized planning and control were necessary and desirable at the earlier stage of rapid industrialization, but that the economy has now become too large and complex to be planned in detail at the center. Present conditions call for some decentralization, as in the current reforms. By implication, the complexity of the economy accounts for the slowdown. This argument is only half right at best. The Russian economy was too complex for central planning right from the start of the 5-year plans. These plans were fulfilled, if at all, only by the high priority sectors, mainly heavy industry. But, by Stalin's simple scale of priorities, this was success enough.

The priorities and wants of the present leaders have multiplied prodigally. Agriculture of necessity has become high priority and a large claimant on investment resources. The seriousness of the housing shortage is recognized. With respect to clothing and shoes, the leaders are striving not only for greater quantities, but also for acceptable quality. Finally, consumer durables, even automobiles, are being promised and scheduled for large increases in the new 5-year plan.

These expanded wants create a much more difficult managerial problem than Stalin's single-minded approach. There are no entrepreneurs in the U.S.S.R., none working for the state at any rate. Or rather, there is only one, the leadership. When the leadership initiates more activities than it can control and manage, management and control drift inexorably into the hands of an amorphous bureaucracy. To say that the economy has become more diverse, complicated, and specialized is only to say that the leaders now want more activities than they can manage. In particular they now want a variety of finished goods as well as intermediate goods.

The expansion of the Soviet regime's wants and priorities is a development that was inherent in its strategy from the beginning. The rationale of the industrialization drive of the thirties and again in the early postwar period was that the building of heavy industry was a precondition for and the quickest way to obtain a profusion of consumer goods. The desirability of this strategy of development and of the organization that implemented it must be judged not by its success in achieving its immediate objective of building a heavy industry capacity but by the success in reaching its ultimate objective of producing consumer goods.

The Soviet economy's poor performance in the production of consumer goods is well known. It is also clear that the Soviet notion that a massive intermediate and capital goods capacity will automatically produce a finished consumer goods capacity still remains to be vindicated. To be sure, the right kind of intermediate and capital goods capacity could produce plant and equipment for consumer goods, but the present leaders are finding that the capacity they inherited from yesterday's planners is not the right kind. The machine-building industry has still not been able to produce a respectable line of agricultural machines. When the time came to build plants for plastics and synthetic fibers, Soviet industry had neither the know-how, designs, equipment, or materials for the job. The Soviet-built plants have experienced inordinate delays in construction and in achieving capacity output after completion. The growth of these modern chemicals has depended in large part on imported plants. The machine tool industry, which has outproduced all others in the world in number of machine tools, is not able to equip a modern automobile plant. In order to meet the new 5-year plan for automobiles, the Soviet leaders have turned to Fiat in Italy to provide an automobile design and a complete manufacturing plant. Other consumer durables reflect the same problem—the lack of versatility and flexibility of Soviet heavy industry, which was primarily designed to reproduce itself.

The ability of Soviet industry to produce a variety of apparently effective advanced weapons and space equipment is an exception which proves a more general rule: that what success Soviet industrial management has had has been due to concentration on a few high priority fields.

. . .

How serious is it for the CPSU to accept the slower growth and give up the hope of catching the United States or even Western Europe in per capita production? The party's platform for the people has always been the future; indeed, the party justified the sacrifice of well being, freedom, and even life in the present as the necessary price of Utopia in the future. It is hard to

see how the party could give up its central ambitions of success for its system, welfare for the people, and world power for itself. Reconciliation with a moderate growth and a pale and lagging imitation of Western life could be bought by a forgetting and forgiving by both the party and the people that is hard to conceive. What role the party's economic program plays Khrushchev explicitly revealed at the 22d Party Congress:

> The party's third program heralds the coming of a period in which all the difficulties and privations which the Soviet people have endured for the sake of their great cause will be made good a hundredfold.

The party surely will not accept economic stagnation without a fierce struggle or without attempting to substitute some other emotive goal for that of catching up with the West. Any alternative goal—such as rapid growth in standard of living—is likely to be no easier to attain than the restoration of rapid overall growth. The dilemma for the party is that the causes of the slowdown and the party's tangible raison d'être are rooted equally deep in the system.

II. THE REVOLUTION IN ECONOMIC THOUGHT

Stalin, living, lay like a dense smog over Russia, smothering the people, their minds, and any words other than his own imbecilic slogans. His death was a release from suffocation for the party, and the clearing wind of his passing let a few rays of hope gleam even for ordinary people. Gradually men began to do what men do naturally, to think, to ask what they are after, to use their brains to tackle problems. The party leaders themselves were no less eager to make fresh beginnings, to forge new tools and new ideas, although the ideological goals remained the same. In due time economists were cautiously invited into the problem-solving process. The assignments were narrowly prescribed—the effectiveness of investment and the basis for pricing —but the process of thought, once started, leads from one thing to another. Under a disguise of mathematics those interested in economic problems soon were exploring far beyond the boundaries that the party had marked for their inquiry.

The image adopted by the Russians for Stalinism and its aftermath was the "freeze" and the "thaw." But the upwelling of economic thought over the last 10 years testifies that minds were not frozen, even if tongues were. As one Western writer has shown, Soviet economists in only a few years have recreated all of the essential features of Western economic theory.[2] With the Marxist labor theory of value as the point of departure, this is an impressive leap forward.

The labor theory of value states that the price of a product (in the long run) should be equal to the labor costs of producing it including, of course, the labor costs of the material input and of the capital consumed. This begs the questions of how wages are set. The Soviets, however, have long since recognized the usefulness of supply and demand for wage setting. The elements missing from the labor theory of value that are crippling to analysis of the Soviet economy are:

1. Charges on capital and land—i.e., interest and rent.
2. The role of demand in pricing and hence in the guidance of production.
3. The pivotal function of profits in transforming the price signals into compelling incentives for producers.

All three of the elements are now openly recognized and discussed in Soviet economic literature. Furthermore, they are now also explicitly guiding organizational proposals. All three elements were highlighted in Kosygin's speech last September on improving the economic system.[3]

The stage of development of economic thought that lay behind Kosygin's speech was arrived at by way of many bitter intellectual and ideological battles. When Kantorovich's path-breaking presentation of linear programing, *The Best Use of Economic Resources,* was published in 1959, it was very unfavorably reviewed by two leading conservative economists, Boyarskiy and Katz. Kantorovich recommended the use of a set of "shadow prices" that would reflect the scarcity of products relative to demand. Reviewers correctly pointed out that this approach directly contradicted the labor theory of value. The argument sputtered on for years until the piling up of unsalable inventories of consumer goods made the discussion silly. Now, Soviet writers talk freely about demand. Even the notions of utility and marginal utility are mentioned[4] though certainly not widely accepted.

The ideas of interest and rent have slowly but persistently crept into the discussions of effectiveness of investment. The impetus for this was simply the obvious waste of capital goods going on all around. Liberman's proposal to use the ratio of profit to capital stock as an indicator of enterprise performance was intended to promote economy in the use of capital. Other economists simply advocated an interest charge, a point of view that met determined resistance. Speaking in 1964 to the conference on the use of mathematics in economics, the dean of Soviet economists, Strumilin, still held out against the use of such a capitalistic device.

[2] Robert W. Campbell, in *Slavic Review,* October 1961, pp. 402–18.

[3] *Pravda,* Sept. 28, 1965.

[4] For example, A. L. Vaynshteyn at the conference on the use of mathematics in economics, *Voprosy Ekonomiki,* No. 9, 1964, p. 75.

Profit was dramatically thrust into public discussion by Liberman in 1962. By then the advantages of profit incentives were so generally accepted that the conservative school confined its objections to the use of profit as the only success indicator. The conservatives argued that it should be only one of many, and they said in particular that fulfillment of the output plans must still be required; otherwise, there would be no plan. This is certainly true. If profit and prices alone guide production, then planning as the Soviets know it is out of business.

Although the advocates of reform devote endless pages to proving that profit, demand and a charge on capital are not inconsistent with Marxist theory or with Lenin's views, it is plain to see that the inspiration for all the new ideas is Western economic theory and practice. The objections of the conservatives center on this point. No Soviet writer, up to now, has dared to assemble the separate elements into a unified theory, for such a theory would simply be the marginal economic analysis that is familiar in the West. By talking of each element separately in the context of the present system of planning, the reformers disguise the fatal similarity to capitalist thought.

A nearly disastrous split between two schools of reform delayed the influence of the reformers for several years. The two schools were (1) the advocates of improving central planning through mathematical methods implemented by computers, and (2) the decentralizers, who wished to reduce the scope and detail of planning and to rely more on profit incentives and initiative at the enterprise level. Older economists, like Nemchinov, wrote as if both approaches were necessary, but the issue grew sharper as the younger cyberneticists, e.g., Glushkov, seemed to argue that decentralization was unnecessary since in a few years computers would be able to solve economic problems much more efficiently than enterprise managers.

. . .

The ranks of reform economists were finally closed in 1964 at the conference on mathematical economics in Moscow. The issue was decided in favor of merging the use of mathematics with decentralization. Although a few conservatives fought a half-hearted rear-guard action, Kantorovich—the inventor of linear programing and the most famous of the Soviet mathematical economists—made the key speech, in which he endorsed economic levers, reduced planning, and decentralization. He called for a greater degree of ". . . the replacement of imperative indications with the utilization of more flexible and sometimes more effective economic levers of regulation." And he said:

> At the same time the economic evaluations obtained in the compilation of the general centralized plan with the aid of mathematical optimization make it possible for *efficient decentralized* decisions to be made along with an achievement of coordination between the profitableness of enterprises and national economic profitableness.
>
> The principle of unified centralized planning of the main directions of economic development that has fully proven itself will be preserved in effective combination with *considerable freedom and initiative at the local level.*[5]

. . .

As things stand now, Marxist economic theory is being increasingly bypassed, and all new initiatives derive from Western theory and practice. The only question is how far and how fast market processes will be adopted. The current debate is between the use of markets to make the plan work better and the use of markets to replace the

[5] Reported in *Voprosy Ekonomiki*, No. 9, 1964, pp. 81–82; italics by the writer.

plan. Although Sukharevsky[6] stated the official position to be the former, his emphatic defense of the plan bespoke a bitter and unresolved conflict raging behind the scenes, and his conclusion was belied by his own arguments that the scope and detail of the plan could and should be reduced.[7]

The comprehensive central plan is the last defense of the party's economic ideology. The skeptics will ask: If the plan can be replaced, what was the use of adopting it in the first place? Nevertheless, if the current partial reforms do not work, the only advice that will be advanced will be to move further in the direction of market socialism. No other body of reform thought has any standing in the Soviet economic profession.

III. THE DEVELOPMENTS IN ECONOMIC ORGANIZATION

On September 27, 1965, Premier Kosygin delivered his remarkable speech to the Central Committee on reorganizing the economy. A large part of the speech dealt with a change from the sovnarkhoz, or territorial organization, to a ministerial form. The interesting proposals, however, dealt with incentives and increased freedom for enterprises. As such, they constituted, along with the experiments of 1964–65, the first official move away from the principle of centralized state planning.

All of Khrushchev's many reorganizations were simply a shuffling of boxes, the replacement of one organ of command with another. A particular case in point was the substitution of regional sovnarkhozes for the industrial ministries in 1957. The reversal of Khrushchev's reform by Kosygin testifies to its insignificance. Merely changing the line of command did not change the

[6] Deputy chairman of the state committee on labor and wages.

[7] Voprosy Ekonomiki, No. 10, 1965, pp. 14–31.

basic nature of the command economy, nor correct its deficiencies. Kosygin's other proposals, in contrast, call upon an entirely different principle, the principle of voluntary choice and market trading, to govern activities that were formerly planned.

As a liberal, decentralizing proposal, the newest Soviet scheme is neither the first nor the most radical in the European Communist countries. It is less liberal than the Czech proposals of 1964 and pales in significance when compared with the conscious and comprehensive attempt of the Yugoslavs to use market trading and decentralized controls. Indeed, the timidity of the latest Soviet reform surprised many Western observers, who had been led to believe by the fairly radical Soviet academic discussion that a dramatic step toward market socialism would be taken. The step that actually was taken is an attempt to have both systems, to season central planning with pinches of marketing and profiteering. The direction of the reform is significant, but its scope is not as yet.

Specifically, Kosygin proposed:

1. A percentage charge on invested capital to be paid by enterprises; that is, an interest rate.
2. A reduction in the number of obligatory targets for the enterprises; the 3 dozen or so old targets are to be replaced by eight or nine. Of these, the controlling ones seem to be the plan for output of the main commodities, the overall wage fund, total value of sales, and profit. The latter two replace the targets for cost reduction and for the ill-famed gross value of output as determinants of the bonuses for managers. The incentives and freedom of action of enterprises are to be reinforced by leaving more of the profit in specially created enterprise funds for bonuses, cultural expenditures, and investment.

. . .

The theme of these reforms, faint but consistent, is market socialism. But along with the new, Kosygin valiantly affirmed the old. He defended the planning of production and denounced "the uncontrolled mechanism of the market." Although profits, interest, and a bit of marketing are included in the reforms, the output of principal products of the enterprise will still be planned. This unequivocal ambivalence probably wipes out any hope of success for this round of reforms.

. . .

IV. PROSPECTS: EVOLUTION OR REVOLUTION?

The history of the Soviet economy since the death of Stalin has been one of recurring reforms and reorganizations. Kosygin's reform is not likely to be the last one. The basic deficiencies of central planning have not been touched, and the dissatisfaction of the intellectuals is deep rooted. One prognosis put forward by a number of Western observers is an evolutionary development toward market socialism. This view argues that the current cautious reforms will be followed by others going farther in the same direction. Thus, as tensions arise between the new system and the old, the leadership will progressively increase the flexibility of the plan, of prices, and of the freedom of the enterprise until at last the plan disappears and markets take over.

There is much to be said against this view. It is difficult to picture the party and the planners presiding over the dissolution of planning. Second, a market system is a tricky thing to manage, even when the leadership believes in it. Such a leadership necessarily would have to put up with a great deal of messiness. The difficulties that the Russians observe in Yugoslavia must give them pause—price instability, inflation followed by spasms of price reform and devaluation, monopoly profits in some areas and heavy subsidies in others, and investments wasted on ice cream parlors and football fields. The so-called "chaos of the market," which Soviet writers all seem to fear, is well exemplified there. And finally, neither the economic bureaucracy nor the local party apparatus is likely to accede gracefully to its own withering away.

. . .

Despite these doubts about gradual evolution, I am inclined to believe that liberal reform in the U.S.S.R. (and in the Eastern European Communist countries as well) is past the point of no return. The economic performance of the present system presents the leaders with a choice of some kind of drastic reform of the system or of falling farther and farther behind Western Europe in productivity and standard of living.

. . .

59

A former Soviet plant manager describes the way in which Soviet managers are motivated and how economic decisions are influenced by political considerations. (It should be noted that Mr. Ryapolov was a Soviet manager prior to recent changes in the direction of greater reliance on market forces).

I WAS A SOVIET MANAGER

Gregory Ryapolov

Gregory Ryapolov, who now lives in the U.S., was formerly a Soviet factory manager.

From *Harvard Business Review* (January–February, 1966). © 1966 by the President and Fellows of Harvard College; all rights reserved.

. . .

STATUS AND TRAINING

The salary and benefits of a Soviet plant director are very low when compared to those of an American. However, if one compares the status of a Soviet director with that of an ordinary Soviet citizen, then it has considerable advantages. For example, the plant director and the chief engineer (second in command in a Soviet factory) are afforded comfortable apartments or houses at company expense. They are given automobiles for official and personal use. They are also given preference in obtaining vacations in rest homes and sanatoriums at the expense of their enterprise. They get 24 days' leave a year, as against the regular two-week vacations for other employees. Directors of large and important plants are entitled to even longer personal leave.

Directors of factories have other special privileges. Many plants, particularly the large ones, have special executive dining rooms. The director of the Elektrosila plant in Leningrad, for instance, has a private dining room, bedroom, and reception room. Some managers have personal rest rooms and let their secretaries keep the keys.

Management personnel in the U.S.S.R. see themselves as belonging to a special economic category, almost resembling a military rank in the army. As is known, a very sharp division of society into classes exists in the Soviet Union. Class affiliation is determined by the material, administrative, and Party position of the people concerned. It is characteristic of the upper classes to be contemptuous of the lower. The greater the class difference between two individuals, the greater the gulf between them in mutual relationships. For example, when a director's wife has a new baby, he invites only the people of his own rank to the celebration, and never an ordinary worker or an engineer.

. . .

Promotion and Advancement

Under the present system, before a person becomes a director, he undergoes a long period of technical training at a factory; he starts as a line engineer and ends as chief plant engineer. Unfortunately, there are no special schools for the training of management personnel in the U.S.S.R. There are no business schools such as those in the United States. A plant manager thus spends the major part of his life working in factories. As a result, he is dedicated to production and loves it. He loves it for its own sake, not for the material rewards.

Prior to World War II, only loyal members of the Communist Party, devoid of any technical training, were appointed plant directors. This situation was radically altered in 1950, and the changes then made have continued in effect to the present. Currently, only an engineer with a great deal of practical experience can become a plant manager.

A similar change took place in the management of Party organizations in factories; only engineers can now become secretaries of plant Party committees and of district Party committees in industrial districts. Similarly, in agricultural districts, only trained agronomists can be Party secretaries in *kolkhozi* (collective farms) or *sovkhozi* (state farms), or be district Party secretaries. The same practice prevails in *oblast* (comparable to a county) and republic Party organizations. Engineers, agronomists, and other specialists with higher education have even made their appearance in the Central Committee of the Communist Party of the Soviet Union and its Presidium.

. . .

Caught in the Middle

The plant director is not his own boss. He is caught in a vise between the Party and the state organs and bureaucrats, on the one hand, and the plant workers and employees, on the other. The former pressure, threaten, and punish, while the latter are sullen and passive. A "good" director is not the one who concerns himself with the needs of his workers; he is the one who faithfully serves the Party. The Party bureaucrats cannot harm the director if he dutifully and carefully implements the tasks set forth by the Party and the state organs. But a catastrophe ensues for the director when he fails to carry out the Party's directives. Then the Party tries to set the workers and employees against him, and, under the guise of worker criticism, it will ruin him completely.

This almost happened to me once; I was saved by sheer luck. Here is what happened:

Before I was named director of the AEG Union plant (producing generators, switchgear, and electrical components) in Vienna, the Party had decided to make a Communist showplace of the factory. The previous director had been forced to hire as many Austrian Party members as possible for the factory. When I took over, almost 90 percent of the workers and employees were Communists. (The other 10 percent were primarily engineers and other technical and highly skilled workers. Communists could be found to fill only a few of these positions.) Although some of the Party members were good workers, many were lazy and incompetent. Some, in fact, were just bums. Consequently the factory operated very badly. Plans were not fulfilled—not even on paper; the reject rate was very high; labor discipline was terrible; and productivity was low.

The situation got steadily worse, and I decided on desperate measures. One morning—it was in early March 1953— I dismissed the head of the cadre section, and with him some 200 of his workers, almost all of whom were Communists. The Party secretary immediately got on the phone to the ministry in Moscow. That afternoon he called a meeting of all workers in the plant. I half expected to be dismissed on the spot, or worse. But just as the meeting was about to get underway, we received word from Moscow of the death of Comrade Stalin. In the resulting confusion, my firing of this group was overlooked, and apparently forgotten.

Defensive Tactics

A great deal of responsibility is imposed on the Soviet director. He must continually defend his actions before the Party management and government officials. The scope of his responsibility is so great that he is constantly subject to political or criminal action. In order to be always prepared to defend himself, he issues a tremendous number of written orders and directives. It is completely immaterial that no one carries them out. What is important is that they can be used for defense in case of a plant investigation. The director carries out directives from above only if they are received in a written form. He does not acknowledge any oral or telephone instructions from his superiors. To give an example:

> An official in the ministry called me up one day and told me to invest over a million rubles in the purchase of some new machine tools, which we badly needed for the plant I was managing. I told him no, not unless I got a written order. He ranted and raved, said there was not time, was no need for it in this case, and so on, but I refused to give in. I told him: "An order may not be armor, but it can protect me just the same." I never received the order, and I still do not know why he refused to write it out.

MANAGERS VS. PLANNERS

The greatest evil lies in the system of planning, accounting, and control. Approximately 2,000 different planning and accounting forms, containing more than 3,000 indicators, are used in large electrical engineering plants such as the Elektrosila plant in Leningrad. It is not hard to imagine the size of the work force required to carry out this nonproductive task. I have heard from directors of large machine-building plants that about 2,500 different plan-reporting forms are in use in that industry. The forms cover 3,000 indexes, and each form is filled out from 2,000 to 3,000 times a year. Up to a billion numerical entries have to be made annually. . . .

Production plans are issued to the plants without due consideration of real capabilities. Plan fulfillment of the preceding year serves as the chief criterion. If the plant has overfulfilled the plan by 10 percent, the next year's plan will be increased by 5 percent to 8 percent. If the plan has been underfulfilled by 10 percent, the next year's plan will be reduced by 5 percent to 8 percent. This is what is called "scientific" socialist planning.

In most cases, production plans are drawn up on the basis of national requirements, without serious reference to a particular plant's capabilities. In the course of the year, the previously approved plans are changed and supplemented hundreds of times. These directives are issued by various planning authorities and very often contradict one another.

As a rule, there is a complete lack of coordination between the plans for output and those for raw material and technical supply. The plants continually experience a shortage of materials. Material quotas for plants are planned on a quarterly basis but are issued monthly (I am writing about the electrical engineering industry). A particularly difficult situation exists in the case of very critical items, such as copper insulating materials, rolled and calibrated steel products, ball and roller bearings, and insulating varnishes and paints. It is impossible to secure delivery of these materials on time.

The Invaluable Tolkhachi

In order to obtain hard-to-get materials, the plants hire representatives who live permanently near the supply bases. By the end of each month these representatives, through superhuman efforts, scrape up the necessary materials. These are shipped by plane, train, trucks, and sometimes even in briefcases. These plant representatives are known as *tolkhachi* (expediters). They are officially carried on the plant's rolls as engineers and economists, but they do not work in the factory. They belong to an illegal class, a special category of swindlers engendered by the Soviet economic system. Their job is to deliver the raw materials to the plant on schedule. To achieve this, they resort to all kinds of illegal machinations. I think that in America they would all end up in jail.

It seems to me that many in the West have an erroneous conception of the role of *tolkhachi*. They perform an absolutely vital function, even if it is illegal. The fact is that material supply is extremely poorly organized. The plants are given monthly allocations of certain materials with a list of bases where they may be obtained. In reality, however, there will be no materials or very few materials at the bases listed—except for those who arrive first or who bribe the base chief. Consequently, in order to push their orders through ahead of turn and get the needed materials, plants must have their *tolkhachi* permanently stationed near the bases.

It is impossible for a factory to obtain any material or equipment on time without these representatives. Sometimes the materials are available at the base, but there are no transportation facilities. The *tolkhach* on the scene must then find transport vehicles, such as trucks or railroad cars, and load and ship the materials to his plant. To do this, he must again bribe the officials in charge of the vehicles. The following experience is illustrative:

> When I was working as chief engineer in the Svobodinskaya Electrical Machine Building Plant, located in Kursk, we ordered five trucks from the Stalin Works in Moscow. This plant replied that it could deliver the trucks, but since the plan for production of truck bodies had not been fulfilled, it would

have to ship the trucks without them. What were we to do? We could not use the trucks without bodies, but if we did not accept the order, we would receive no more trucks that year.

> We called in the plant *tolkhach* and asked him what to do. He said to just leave it to him; he'd find a way. He went out and bought two tons of apples and some geese from the *kolkhozniki* (members of farm collectives), loaded them on a factory truck, and brought them to the Stalin plant in Moscow. The following week we received the five trucks—complete with bodies.

Master of Deception

This distressing situation is permanent, and because the plants cannot operate on schedule, the plans are either underfulfilled or falsified. The principal cause lies in the fact that *Gosplan* (State Planning Commission) generally plans for more materials and equipment than are actually available. As a result, everyone is engaged in tearing the others apart, outbidding each other, and reselling materials as one would a ticket to a concert by the pianist Horowitz.

. . .

POLITICS BEFORE ECONOMICS

Bureaucrats from the higher administrative organizations and the Party always seek to convert the director and the chief engineer into mechanical robots for carrying out their unrealistic plans by crudely threatening them with a stick. The administrative bureaucrats rarely visit the plants. When they do, it is not for the purpose of obtaining information or rendering assistance but, rather, for enforcing authority, preparing charges, or imposing penalties.

The Party and its various control organs place politics before economics. Managers hold to the opposite view, that economics and technology are more important and that politics must serve to advance them. They see what economic setbacks are caused by Communist dogma. Consequently, they try to soften and reduce the damage by doing everything they can think of to thwart the politicians, but it is not easy to do.

Credit and Blame

During my years in Soviet industry, the majority of us in management tried to show concern for our workers and employees. We requested overtime pay, increased wages, and improvement of the workers' living conditions. We also opposed the use of economic pressure on the workers, such as raising piecework norms. But the ever-watchful eye of the Party very carefully scrutinized all such actions that we directors took. The Party could not permit one of us to become popular with our employees. And when it did permit small material gains, then it announced that it was the Party—not the director—who was showing concern for his people.

All that was good was attributed to the Party, and all that was bad, to the director. For example, if the workers' wages were low and they were not provided with living quarters, if the dining rooms were dirty and the food was bad, if the rest rooms and shower rooms were filthy—all that was the fault of the director. I remember experiences like the following:

> One director for whom I worked became concerned about the excessive number of accidents on two of his production lines— a common situation in Soviet industry, where safety measures are all but overlooked. On his own initiative he installed new lights and provided guard rails and other protective equipment. The Party secretary promptly gave orders to the members of the Party committee to spread the word among the workers that the Party had thought of this and, in its

> concern for the welfare of the workers, had demanded that the director take measures to protect them. Naturally the director did not dare deny this.

As long as a plant's operations are progressing well, the Party supports the director. It praises and rewards him. But it always stresses that he is the Party's pupil and its loyal son. However, as soon as the plans cease to be fulfilled and there is no hope of immediate fulfillment, the Party shoves the entire blame onto the director. It asserts that all this happened because he lost touch with the Party and became a poor Communist.

. . .

PROGRESS AHEAD?

What about "Libermanism" and the new economic reforms announced late in 1965 by Premier Alexei N. Kosygin?

Many people in the West interpret Libermanism incorrectly. It is true that in the beginning—in September 1962—Ye. Liberman proposed to upgrade considerably the role of profit in the Soviet economy. Profit was to become the prime mover of the economy and a major stimulus in the growth of labor productivity. Economic process was to develop from the bottom, not from the top. These proposals were evaluated in the West as "creeping toward capitalism," which in fact they were. However, because these proposals affected the basic principles of the Communist doctrine and thus threatened the role and rule of the Party, Liberman was censured.

When Liberman spoke again, it was in terms more acceptable to the Party. This time he proposed the upgrading of the role of profit, not for the purpose of promoting capitalism, but merely as an aid in evaluating and encouraging performance and only for the purpose of achieving profitable operations. "Profit in our country is not a social goal and the prime mover of the economy," he said; or again, "Although profit is not the purpose of production, it can be used as a guide in evaluating the efficiency of enterprise operations." Recently he has been trying to reduce the role of profit in the Soviet economy to a purely functional status, as one of the numerous indicators of enterprise performance. In fact, this is what the role of profit currently amounts to.

Under the present socialist system, net profit alone cannot become the main indicator of enterprise efficiency. In the first place, the amount of profit in a Soviet enterprise does not depend directly on the organization, since industry must be guided by the so-called wholesale prices, which are administered and bear no relation to enterprise efficiency. Besides, with the use of profit as the main indicator, other planning gradients, such as product assortment and quality, would get out of control, and there would be many problems with the turnover tax (a sales tax at the wholesale level).

. . .

60

CHINA: ECONOMIC POLICY AND ECONOMIC RESULTS, 1949–1971

Mainland Chinese economic policies and consequent economic growth have undergone several distinct phases since 1949, including the "Great Leap Forward" and the "Cultural Revolution." These and other eras of recent Chinese economic policy are carefully analyzed, and the author concludes that economic prospects for China in the near future are good.

Arthur G. Ashbrook, Jr.

Arthur G. Ashbrook, Jr., is an economist with the U.S. Central Intelligence Agency (Caveat: It should be noted that the views presented in this article are those of the author and are not necessarily those of the Central Intelligence Agency or the U.S. Government.)

From "China: Economic Policy and Economic Results, 1949–1971," a study prepared for *People's Republic of China, An Economic Assessment,* a compendium of papers submitted to the Joint Economic Committee, 92nd Cong., 2nd sess., May 18, 1972, p. 3 ff.

"China has stood up." These words of Chairman Mao Tse-tung summarize China's emergence as a strong nation-state after a century of humiliation at the hands of foreign powers. Since 1949, the Communist leadership has been directing China's enormous human assets and rich natural resources toward the building of a modern industrial nation self-sufficient in technology and capable of supporting large armies equipped with nuclear weapons.

In pursuit of this overriding goal, the People's Republic of China (PRC), under Chairman Mao, has vigorously pursued an economic policy of military-industrial expansion, agricultural collectivization, national self-sufficiency, and consumer egalitarianism. Priorities in the allocation of economic resources accordingly have called for:

(*a*) rapid growth in military-industrial capacity and output;

(*b*) provision of the minimum amount of consumption goods consistent with productive efficiency and popular morale; and

(*c*) mastery of modern technology through large-scale absorption of foreign technology and a massive program for scientific-technical education.

The results of these policies and priorities, applied over two decades of Communist rule of China, have been mixed—striking economic successes, partial failures, and unfinished tasks. For the period as a whole, China's economic growth has been strong but erratic. Two periods of social and political upheaval—the Great Leap Forward of the late 1950s and the Cultural Revolution of the late 1960s—have temporarily thrown economic policy into disarray and have interrupted the momentum of growth. Any economic survey of China must take account of the effects of these swings from settled political conditions to political turbulence and back again. . . .

NO ORDINARY LDC

The image of China as a desperately poor nation with most of its people living in misery and degradation is an image of the past. At the start of 1972, the People's Republic of China is by no means an ordinary less-developed country. No run-of-the-mill LDC could boast of the following achievements:

The feeding and clothing of an estimated 865 million people.

The detonation of thirteen nuclear devices.

The launching of two space satellites.

The production of sizable numbers of jet aircraft, submarines, tanks, missiles, and other engines of war.

The achievement of self-sufficiency in petroleum.

The construction of huge industrial complexes in remote areas.

The building of bridges across the Yangtze.

The extension of the rail network through some of the world's most difficult terrain.

The training and seasoning of a first-class industrial labor force.

The conducting of extensive scientific research in various fields of knowledge.

The maintenance of a sizable and growing economic aid program.

NOR A MODERN INDUSTRIAL NATION

While no ordinary LDC, China is not a modern industrial nation either. Eighty-five per cent of its people live in rural areas and are engaged in most cases in backbreaking tasks in agriculture, construction, and transport. Even in urban areas only a fraction of the labor force works in modern factories, the great majority being hewers and drawers like their rural countrymen. Moreover, those fortunate enough to be in desk jobs are often sent into the fields and workshops for a month or two in line with Chairman Mao's determination to erase the distinction between manual and mental work.

Not only primitive working conditions but also spartan living conditions distinguish China from the modern industrial nations. In order to support a powerful military establishment and a massive investment program, Peking must treat the population as an input into the production process—to be fueled, maintained, and repaired, not catered to. Several factors have enabled the Communist leadership to successfully carry out this policy of spartan living conditions. Number one, the Chinese people have taken tremendous pride in China's national resurgence and have been receptive to explanations of the necessity for self-sacrifice, even though the explanations seem to be wearing a little thin by now. Number two, the policy of egalitarianism, especially the restrained living standards of the bigwigs, make low living standards easier to accept. (Chairman Mao launched the Cultural Revolution in part because the bureaucrats were losing the spirit of egalitarianism.) Number three, except for the near-starvation years of 1960–61, living standards have been stabilized under Communist rule, and the mass of people are palpably better off than in the pre-Communist era. Number four, there have been gradual improvements in recent years in the quality and variety of food and clothing, the conditions of housing, the availability of consumer durables, and the level of social services. Number five, the strong net of Communist controls makes grumbling dangerous.

THREE PARTIAL FAILURES

The drive for the collectivization of agriculture must be included among the partial failures of the regime. In the beginning there was the "land reform" of the early 1950s when the landlords were shot or dispossessed and the land distributed to individual peasants. This was quickly followed by a succession of campaigns for collectivization—leading to mutual-aid teams, next to small agricultural producer cooperatives, then to large cooperatives (akin to the Soviet collective farm), and finally to the notorious commune, the unwieldy supercollective of the Great Leap Forward era (1958–60). After the collapse of the Leap Forward, a three-tier system of agricultural control was established, consisting of a paler version of the commune with constituent "production brigades" and "production teams." The small production team was given responsibility for day-to-day agricultural decisions, and the regime was forced to permit a large amount of private farming, trade, and handicrafts. Agricultural policy today is a compromise between doctrinaire ideas about collectivization and practical measures necessary to stimulate output.

The policy of attaining economic self-sufficiency also must be reckoned a partial failure. In the 1950s the fledgling regime entered into agreements with the Soviet Union to supply 300 modern industrial plants that would have given the Chinese a tremendous shove toward self-sufficiency by the end of three five-year plans (1953–67). The orderly buildup of industrial capacity, however, was interrupted by the Leap Forward attempt at instant industrialization. The abrupt withdrawal of the Soviet technicians in mid-1960 when only half of the 300 plants were completed crushed any hopes for self-sufficiency over the near term. In the 1960s Peking turned to Japan and Western Europe for material and technical support, but political turmoil of the Cultural Revolution (1966–69) again postponed prospects for self-sufficiency by reducing the flow of outside support and shutting down the system of technical education for four years. In short, much of China's military-industrial success to date has rested on foreign assistance—on plants erected from Soviet blueprints, on production of Soviet-model weapons, and on machinery imported from the West or copied from Western prototypes.

The policy of economic self-sufficiency

is an unqualified success in one important dimension. The Chinese have no long-term foreign debt in contrast to other developing countries such as India, Pakistan, Indonesia, and Egypt which are staggering under a heavy burden of external debt.

A third partial failure involves the system of economic motivation and incentives. In the 1960s the Communist government had built up a reservoir of good will among much of the populace—based on the pride and excitement of China's new independence and power. This reservoir was improvidently drained during the Leap Forward and the Cultural Revolution when political excesses interrupted the drive toward military-industrial power. Thereafter, people seemed to respond less rapidly to spiritual incentives. The persistent warnings of the propagandists against falling victim to the sugar-coated bullets of material incentives began to fall on deaf ears. The young people—two-thirds of the population have no personal memory of China's humiliation—have had to be indoctrinated in order to understand the "past bitterness" of life under capitalism. They are not enthusiastic about settling down for a lifetime of hard work in the countryside even for Chairman Mao and the revolution. Finally, Peking ruefully admits that a majority of the scientists and educators do not really support the official ideology.

The major economic problems posed by the uncertain state of motivation are the extent to which spartan living conditions will have to be relaxed at the expense of military-industrial development and the extent to which material incentives and wider income differentials will have to be accepted by the Government. Dealing with these problems poses increasing difficulties to Peking. The economy is steadily growing more complex, witness the wider range and more advanced technology of military-industrial goods and the higher and more diverse skills required in the labor force. As people acquire more education and work at more technical jobs, they presumably will expect commensurate increases in living standards. And they will respond increasingly to technocratic, rather than ideological imperatives.

RATES OF GROWTH

In the 1950s the Chinese began the development of an elaborate economic statistical system, faithfully copying the Soviet statistical organization and procedures. This embryonic system was a victim of the excesses of the Leap Forward. Since that time, Peking has enforced a statistical blackout so complete that only a handful of national economic figures have been released since 1960. Outside observers, however, have been able to piece together a good general appraisal of trends in the economy through use of foreign trade data, the accounts of travelers and refugees, and the cryptic discussions of economic issues in the Chinese press. Rough-hewn estimates of average annual rates of growth since 1952 thus may be derived, as follows:

LONG-TERM ANNUAL RATE OF GROWTH

Item:	Percentage
Gross national product (GNP)	4
Population	2
GNP per capita	2
Agricultural production	2
Industrial production (1952 base)	8
Industrial production (1957 base)	6
Foreign trade	5

These numerical estimates show that economic results have paralleled economic policy in the PRC. Investment has been concentrated in the industrial sector, and industrial growth accordingly has outstripped agricultural growth. Agricultural growth, in turn, has been just sufficient to support the growing population at minimum standards. The growth of foreign trade was greatest in the 1950s when broad-scale Soviet support was forthcoming: in the 1960s, the total volume of trade never exceeded the level of 1959, with selective imports of key plants and equipment from non-Communist countries taking over the leading role.

Whereas the preceding tabulation showed the strength of China's economic growth, the following tabulation shows its erratic nature:

GNP INDEX, 1957 = 100

Event:	
Start of First Five-Year Plan (1952)	72
End of First Five-Year Plan (1957)	100
Top of Leap Forward (1958)	116
Fallback from Leap Forward (1961)	88
Post-Leap recovery (1966)	128
Cultural Revolution dip (1968)	122
Current level (1971)	157

COMPLEXITIES IN POLICY AND POLICYMAKING

The Communist leadership under Chairman Mao does not have a single clear-cut set of economic marching orders which are uniformly put into action at the lower party and economic administrative levels. In the first place, radical swings in economic policy occur at the top because of realignments of political power, changes in the underlying economic situation, and a cyclical pattern of advance and retreat in ideological matters. Moreover, there are inevitable delays in the implementation of new policies as well as varying interpretations and degrees of resistance at lower levels. Indeed, economic administration is marked by a bargaining process in which the needs of various interest groups must to a certain extent be negotiated and compromised. Furthermore, economic results often are not reported accurately to the center, especially when the reporting units are small and scattered. The central authorities may have only an imperfect notion of the economic situation in much of their vast territory. Peking's writ thus may have surprisingly little force in the outlook of the economy, especially when there is conflict or uncertainty at the top. One important consequence of these institutional forces is that the amplitude of swings in economic policy is much greater than the amplitude of changes in actual economic events.

Contributing to the complexity in policymaking is the constant change in economic needs. The economy in two short decades has moved from the tasks of restoring operations in basic production facilities to the tasks of manufacturing and deploying complex weapons systems. Chairman Mao himself is aging and does not bring the same perspective to the economy and society as when he was a young guerrilla chieftain in beleaguered revolutionary areas. Mao can hardly welcome what he perceives as China's drift toward Galbraith's "new industrial state" with its hierarchy of technocrats. The Chinese Communist propagandists use the concept "red versus expert" to distinguish those persons with proper ideological credentials from those with mere technical expertise.

SCOREBOARD IN EARLY 1972

In early 1972, the second year of the Fourth Five-Year Plan, the PRC is pursuing a moderate economic policy with impressive economic results. GNP is running at an annual rate of roughly U.S. $130 billion or $150 per capita. In the various sectors of the economy:

Industrial capacity and production are expanding steadily with emphasis being put on the construction of large new industrial complexes in the interior and hundreds of medium and small plants in local areas;

Armaments output is increasing across the board, and a variety of new weapons are coming into production;

Agricultural production continues to need and get increased supplies of chemical fertilizers, pesticides, irrigation equipment, and improved seeds, although adverse weather in 1971 held production to the level of 1970;

Transportation and communication facilities are being expanded in capacity and extended to remote areas;

Foreign trade continues to serve as an indispensable conduit for modern equipment and technology from Japan and Western Europe; and

The lot of the rank-and-file worker and peasant is gradually improving.

PROSPECTS

Economic prospects for the remainder of the Fourth Five-Year Plan (1971–75) are good, barring a new outburst of radical economic policies or a succession of two or three bad harvests. Output from the industrial sector should grow at 5 per cent to 10 per cent per year based on new capacity now under construction or planned. Agriculture should continue to keep abreast of population. Foreign trade probably will increase in the 3 per cent to 5 per cent range annually with Japan continuing to be China's largest trading partner. China will still have to grapple with its unfinished economic tasks in this period—the feeding, training, useful employment, and proper motivation of its huge and rapidly growing population; the continued modernizing of its industry, armed forces, and educational system; and the establishing of an economic planning and control mechanism flexible enough to cope with the complexities of twentieth century economic life. In the early 1970s China almost certainly will be widening its lead over the ordinary LDCs and yet at the same time it may be falling farther behind the dynamic industrial nations of Europe and, of course, Japan.

. . .